The Chaldean Catholic Church

This book provides a modern historical study of the Chaldean Catholic Church in Iraq from 2003 to 2013, against a background analysis of the origins and ecclesiological development of the Chaldean community from the sixteenth century onward.

The book offers an insight into the formation of Chaldean ecclesiological identity and organisation in the context of the Chaldeans as a community originating from the ecclesial traditions of the Church of the East and as an Eastern Catholic Church in union with the Holy See. The book argues for the gradual and consistent development of a Chaldean identity grounded and incarnated in the Mesopotamian-Iraqi environment, yet open to engaging with cultures throughout the Middle East and West Asia and, especially since 2003, to Europe, North America and Australasia. It also examines the effects of religious and administrative policies of the governors of Mesopotamia-Iraq on the Chaldeans, from their formation in the sixteenth century until the installation of the new Chaldean patriarch, Louis Raphael I Sako, in March 2013. Furthermore, the book provides a unique analysis of the history of Iraq, by placing the Chaldeans fully into that narrative for the first time.

Providing a thorough overview of the history of the Chaldeans and an in-depth assessment of how the 2003 invasion has affected them, this book will be a key resource for students and scholars of Middle East Studies, Modern History and History of Christianity as well as for anyone seeking to understand the modern status of Christians in Iraq and the wider Middle East.

Kristian Girling is currently a freelance researcher and writer. He was a Visiting Fellow at Boston College's School of Theology and Ministry from 2016–2017. He completed his PhD at the Centre for Eastern Christianity, Heythrop College in 2016. Kristian's research focuses on the modern history of Eastern Christianity particularly in the Middle East.

Culture and Civilization in the Middle East
General Editor: Ian Richard Netton
Professor of Islamic Studies, University of Exeter

For a full list of books in the series, please go to: www.routledge.com/middleeast
studies/series/SE0363

This series studies the Middle East through the twin foci of its diverse cultures
and civilisations. Comprising original monographs as well as scholarly surveys, it
covers topics in the fields of Middle Eastern literature, archaeology, law, history,
philosophy, science, folklore, art, architecture and language. While there is a plurality of views, the series presents serious scholarship in a lucid and stimulating
fashion.

53 **Women and Leadership in Islamic Law**
A Critical Analysis of Classical Legal Texts
David Jalajel

54 **Orthodoxy and Islam**
Theology and Muslim-Christian Relations in Modern Greece and Turkey
Archimandrite Nikodemos Anagnostopoulos

55 **Ibn al-Haytham's Geometrical Methods and the Philosophy
of Mathematics**
A History of Arabic Sciences and Mathematics Volume 5
Roshdi Rashed

56 **New Horizons in Qur'anic Linguistics**
A grammatical, semantic, and stylistic analysis
Hussein Abdul-Raof

57 **Arabs and Iranians in the Islamic Conquest Narrative**
Memory and Identity Construction in Islamic Historiography, 750–1050
Scott Savran

58 **The Chaldean Catholic Church**
Modern History, Ecclesiology and Church-State Relations
Kristian Girling

The Chaldean Catholic Church
Modern History, Ecclesiology and Church-State Relations

Kristian Girling

LONDON AND NEW YORK

First published 2018 by Routledge

2 Park Square, Milton Park, Abingdon, Oxfordshire OX14 4RN
52 Vanderbilt Avenue, New York, NY 10017

Routledge is an imprint of the Taylor & Francis Group, an informa business

First issued in paperback 2019

Copyright © 2018 Kristian Girling

The right of Kristian Girling to be identified as author of this work
has been asserted by him in accordance with sections 77 and 78 of the
Copyright, Designs and Patents Act 1988.

All rights reserved. No part of this book may be reprinted or reproduced
or utilised in any form or by any electronic, mechanical, or other means,
now known or hereafter invented, including photocopying and recording,
or in any information storage or retrieval system, without permission in
writing from the publishers.

Notice:
Product or corporate names may be trademarks or registered trademarks,
and are used only for identification and explanation without intent to
infringe.

British Library Cataloguing-in-Publication Data
A catalogue record for this book is available from the British Library

Library of Congress Cataloging-in-Publication Data
A catalog record for this book has been requested

ISBN: 978-1-138-04005-2 (hbk)
ISBN: 978-0-367-88866-4 (pbk)

Typeset in Times New Roman
by Apex CoVantage, LLC

Contents

List of graphs	x
List of maps	xi
List of tables	xii
Acknowledgements	xiii

Introduction   1

Nomenclature 2
  Nestorian 2
  East Syriac 3
The significance of church-state relations in East Syriac
  history 3
Note on approach 4
The origins and status of the Church of the East to
  the late Medieval Period 6
Bibliography 7

1   The origins and early development of the Chaldean
    Catholic community (fifteenth to eighteenth centuries)   10

Chaldean origins 10
First union 11
The status of the Church of the East in 1450 and the
  development of hereditary succession to the patriarchate 12
First Chaldean hierarchy in union with the Holy See 14
  East Syriac and Latin ecclesiological perspectives on the
    proto-Chaldean community 15
  Historical context of Sulaqa's engagement with the Holy
    See 17
  East Syriac perspectives on the Petrine See 19
The early Chaldean Catholic community and Sulaqa's
  legacy 22

vi *Contents*

Chaldean Catholic identity development in the sixteenth
  century 24
Sulaqa's successors 24
Latin presence in Mesopotamia (I) 27
Legitimist line of patriarchs (1591–1700) 28
Ottoman administrative influence 29
The establishment of the Josephite patriarchal line in Amid 30
Why be a Chaldean? 34
Latin presence in Mesopotamia (II) and the unification of the
  Chaldean communities 36
Dembo and Yohannan as opposition figures 38
Bibliography 41

2 Political change in Mesopotamia and the origins of
  the modern Chaldean Church (1830–1918)   **46**
Ecclesiological discourse and developments 46
  The heritage of the undivided Church of the East 48
Nicholas I Zaya 49
Changes among the Ottomans 49
Eastern Catholic consolidation, the Chaldeans and the First
  Vatican Council 51
  Consolidation prior to the First World War 53
Chaldean missions to the Church of the East 55
Massacre without remorse: 1915–1918 56
  First World War and start of massacres 57
    East Syriac-Russian relations 57
    Start of the Massacres 58
    Impact on the Chaldeans 60
Bibliography 62

3 Re-discovering the Chaldean narrative in modern
  Iraq (1918–2003)   **66**
Building on current scholarship 67
A new political order: 1918–1947 69
Chaldean state and inter-communal relations 70
The military élite and the Assyrians 71
Emmanuel II Thomas (1900–1947) 73
Iraq as a nation and Chaldean involvement in political
  activity 75
Joseph VII Ghanima (1947–1958) and the end of the
  monarchy 77
1958 rebellion against the Iraqi monarchy 78
Paul II Cheikho, the Iraqi state and the new Catholic
  ecclesiology of the Second Vatican Council 80

Contents vii

Christian involvement with revolutionary movements 81
Republican governments and the rise of the IBP 83
Political change impacts on the Chaldeans 84
  Mesopotamian identity 86
Cheikho, the Baath and Saddam Hussein 86
The Iran-Iraq War 1980–1988 88
Tariq Aziz 89
The Kurdish rebellions and Christian
  involvement 90
  Nature of combat and effects on Chaldeans 91
Raphael I Bidawid (1989–2003) 94
Second Gulf War 1990–1991 and migration 95
Post-war Iraq 95
Chaldean migration 1991–2003 97
Meeting the varied needs of the Chaldeans 99
Final years of Hussein and Bidawid 100
Modern ecumenism and Chaldean involvement 101
Prelude to the invasion of 2003 102
Bibliography 104

4   The Chaldean Church in the new Iraq (2003–2013)   112

Chaldean identity post-invasion 112
Historical Overview (2003–2008) 113
  Radical alteration of life expectations 113
  The effects of the invasion by Coalition forces in 2003
    on the Chaldean community and initial attempts to
    reconstruct civil society 114
  Christians speaking with one voice? 115
  The rise of violence against Christians 116
  Social and psychological affects after the end of
    Baath party rule 117
A new constitutional order and Chaldean involvement? 119
The Iraqi civil war (2006–2007) and effects on the
  Chaldeans 121
Regional effects of the war and the Chaldean response 125
Historical overview (2008–2013) 127
  Chaldean responses to a new Iraqi society 128
  Iraqi electoral process and government formation
    (2003–2013) 128
  Christian political representation 129
  Chaldean identity in post-war Iraq 130
  Situating the Chaldean narrative in Iraq and within the wider
    Catholic community (2010–2013) 131
Bibliography 133

viii *Contents*

5 Chaldean ecclesiology and ecclesial organisation in Mesopotamia-Iraq

What is ecclesiology and how has it been altered? 136
Chaldean status quo *in northern Iraq (2003–2013) 137*
Diocesan study overview 138
Archdiocese of Erbil 141
  Chaldean ecclesiastical life in Ankawa 142
  Parishes outside of Erbil 147
  Conclusion: Archdiocese of Erbil 150
Archdiocese of Kirkuk-Sulaymaniya 150
  Ecclesial organisation in Sulaymaniya 152
Archdiocese of Kirkuk 154
  Kirkuki Chaldean population 154
  Conclusion: Archdiocese of Kirkuk-Sulaymaniya 157
Dioceses of Zakho-Amadiya and Akra 157
  Diocese of Akra 157
  Zakho-Amadiya ecclesial history 159
  Zakho-Amadiya ecclesial organisation 163
  Chaldean villages and towns in the Diocese of
    Zakho-Amadiya 165
  Note on Amadiyan diocesan records 170
  Conclusion: Dioceses of Zakho-Amadiya and Akra 170
Diocese of Alqosh 171
  Ecclesial Organisation 174
  Teleskef 175
  Conclusion: Diocese of Alqosh 178
Archdiocese of Basra 178
  Ecclesial organisation – churches in Basra city 183
  Conclusion: Archdiocese of Basra 184
Archdiocese of Baghdad 184
  Ecclesial organisation in Baghdad 191
  Baghdad and East Syriac ecclesiology 191
  Conclusion: Archdiocese of Baghdad 193
Archdiocese of Mosul 194
  Ecclesial organisation in Mosul Archdiocese 197
  Mosul (city) 198
  Holy Ghost parish 200
  Conclusion: Mosul (city) 202
  Telkef 202
  Karamles 203
  Conclusion: Archdiocese of Mosul 205
Bibliography 209

136

Contents ix

6 The Chaldean community in Jordan   213

Chaldean origins to Jordan 214
The status of the Chaldean community in the Jordanian
    Christian context 215
Conclusion: Chaldean presence to Jordan 218
Bibliography 219

Conclusion   221

Mesopotamia-Iraq and the patriarchal office's influence on
    Chaldean identity formation 221
Zones of Chaldean ecclesial influence in Iraq 223
The Holy See, the Chaldeans and the Church of the East 225
The Chaldean presence to Iraq in the context of the rise of
    Da'esh 230
Bibliography 231

Appendix A: overview of the Iraqi political
    system post-2003   233
Appendix B: Chaldean population estimate
    in northern Iraq, 2013   235
Appendix C: the Church of the East in the twentieth
    century: a brief overview   236
Index   239

Graphs

5.1	Number of Chaldean baptisms and weddings in Ankawa 1885–2012	144
5.2	Ankawa Chaldean population growth 2000–2013	145
5.3	Number of baptisms in Armota, Shaqlawa and Qusenjaq 1950–2012	148
5.4	Baptisms at Mar Gewargis parish, Zakho 1989–2013	168
5.5	Number of baptisms and weddings in Amadiya Diocese 1950–2013	170
5.6	Number of baptisms and weddings in Teleskef 1950–October 2013	176
5.7	Baptisms in the Archdiocese of Basra 1867–2012	181
5.8	Baptisms Baghdad parish group A 1958–2012	189
5.9	Baptisms Baghdad parish group B 1958–2012	190
5.10	Baptisms – Archdiocese of Mosul, 1870–October 2013	199

Maps

1.1	Northern Iraq, eastern Turkey, northern Iran and principal sites of East Syriac-Chaldean activity from the sixteenth century	15
5.1	Erbil and surrounding region	142
5.2	Zakho, Duhok and surrounding region	164
5.3	Mosul and surrounding region	173
5.4	Central and southern Iraq	179

I developed Maps 1.1, 5.1, 5.2, 5.3 and 5.4 from data available at *Open Street Map* <www.openstreetmap.org>, which is available under the Open Database License (ODbL). For further details of this license and use of map data please refer to: <www.openstreetmap.org/copyright> and <http://opendatacommons.org/licenses/odbl/1.0/>. The original map data is © OpenStreetMap contributors and available under the Open Database License and the cartography is licensed under the Creative Commons Attribution-ShareAlike 2.0 license (CC BY-SA). <https://creativecommons.org/licenses/by-sa/2.0/>

Tables

4.1	Baptismal records from selected Baghdadi parishes, 2005–2008	121
4.2	Number of Chaldean families in Ankawa 2000–2007	123
5.1	Principal villages/towns (by diocese) visited during research in October 2013 in which a Chaldean presence was found	140
5.2	Chaldean population in the Archdiocese of Erbil 1969–2012	145
5.3	Total number of Chaldean families in Ankawa by year 2008–2013	146
5.4	Chaldean population in the dioceses of Kirkuk and Sulaymaniya 1949–2013	146
5.5	Chaldean population in the Diocese of Akra 1958–2012	158
5.6	Chaldean population in the dioceses of Zakho and Amadiya 1949–2010	162
5.7	Chaldean population of the Diocese of Zakho by settlement (Group A)	163
5.8	Chaldean population of the Diocese of Zakho by settlement (Group B)	164
5.9	Total Chaldean population in the Diocese of Alqosh, 1970–2012	174
5.10	Chaldean population in the Diocese of Alqosh, October 2013 by settlement	175
5.11	Chaldean population in the Archdiocese of Basra 1959–2012	183
5.12	Baptisms in Chaldean parishes in use prior to 1958 – Archdiocese of Baghdad	191
5.13	Chaldean population, Archdiocese of Baghdad, 1980–2012	192
5.14	Chaldean population, Diocese of Mosul, 1969–2013	197
BM1.1	Number of Chaldeans in northern Iraqi dioceses 1990–2013	235

Acknowledgements

This book was the fruit of work undertaken over a five-year period from 2012–2017. I have been greatly fortunate to have received support from an array of individuals and institutions to ensure its completion.

In the first instance, I am particularly grateful to His Grace Bashar Warda CSsR, Chaldean Archbishop of Erbil who provided me with a grant which permitted me to complete this research project. The Living Stones of the Holy Land Trust, the Jerusalem and the Middle East Church Association and the St Jude's Trust all also kindly supported me through grant funding.

I am also very thankful for the kindness, hospitality, time and resources which Archbishop Warda and all the members of the Chaldean Church in northern Iraq offered me during fieldwork in the region in October 2013. Likewise, the Chaldean communities in the UK and Jordan were strong supporters of my research during visits in 2012–2014 and May–June 2013, respectively. Rev. Frs Imad Twal and Khalil Jaar of the Latin Patriarchate of Jerusalem and Rev. Fr Raymond Moussali of the Chaldean Catholic Church very generously acted as my hosts during research in the Hashemite Kingdom of Jordan.

My colleague at Heythrop College, Anthony O'Mahony, Director of the Centre for Eastern Christianity, throughout the research and writing process offered exacting but essential vital critique of my work along with substantial academic advice for which I am very grateful. My research assistant at Boston College, Jack Nuelle, very kindly advanced the editing of the text in its final stages.

I am very grateful to my parents for their care and support during the initial research and writing of the book, their advice during times of reflection on research and the opportunity they have offered to permit me to complete the book in a quiet and peaceful environment. Likewise, my fiancée, Caitlin, has been a strong source of support, encouragement and advice during the editing and writing up process.

Finally, I must recognise the continued direction and sustained substantial support which Dr Suha Rassam has granted during the research and writing of the book. Without her interest in and commitment to raising awareness of Iraqi Christians in Iraq, the wider Middle East and internationally, research would never have begun, and it is to her that this book is principally dedicated.

xiv *Acknowledgements*

In honour of the Blessed Virgin Mary and in remembrance and recognition of all the suffering Christians of Iraq:

> For whatsoever is born of God, overcometh the world: and this is the victory which overcometh the world, our faith. Who is he that overcometh the world, but he that believeth that Jesus is the Son of God?
>
> 1 John 5: 4–5

Introduction

This book provides a modern historical study of the Chaldean Catholic Church in Iraq from 2003 to 2013, against a background analysis of the origins and ecclesiological development of the Chaldean community from the sixteenth century onward.

I attempt to bring the Chaldeans into the full light of Iraqi history. I am aiming to move away from a scholarly focus on the Shia-Sunni, Arab-Kurd dichotomies which dominate contemporary Iraqi Studies, and also am hoping to avoid considering the East Syriac tradition in isolation and merely as another aspect of ecclesiastical history. Instead, I will consider the tradition and its communities as integral to the pluralistic societies of Mesopotamia-Iraq.

Chaldean identity is expressed partly in accordance with the distinctive East Syriac ecclesial traditions which developed from at least the second century as the 'church across the border' and outside of the limits of the Roman Empire in Persia (Healey 2010; Brock 1982). The other major aspect of Chaldean identity is the community's close relationship with the Holy See since the sixteenth century and other Eastern Catholic churches especially those of the Syriac traditions. The growth of a large international Chaldean Catholic diaspora makes it difficult to bring together the strands of historical memory and to clarify the earliest origins of the Chaldean identity. In addition, the origins of this identity, as well as what it actually means to have entered into union with the Holy See and to become a Chaldean, have not been greatly considered in scholarship nor within the Church.

The most recent authors to consider the historical development of the East Syriac churches in detail have been Wilmshurst (2011, 2000), Rassam (2010), Murre-van den Berg (2009), Teule (2008), Baumer (2006) and Baum and Winkler (2003). All of these authors have greatly contributed to the increasing academic and popular awareness of Christianity in Mesopotamia-Iraq and the East Syriac communities especially since the invasion of Iraq in 2003. However, no study has brought together an overview of Chaldean historical development with discussion of the community's status as an Eastern Catholic Church in union with the Holy See. The following work is distinct as an ecclesiastical history due to its consideration of the Chaldean Church's ecclesiological ethos, and by maintaining awareness of the Chaldean status as an Eastern Catholic Church in union with the Holy See and as one of the descendant communities of the undivided Church of the East. This study focuses on this issue due to the increased loss of knowledge and

2 *Introduction*

awareness among the contemporary community of Chaldean history as a result of enforced migration following the 2003 Iraq War.

Overall, then, the work has a threefold approach. First, it will function as an ecclesiological study of the development of the Chaldean Church. Second, it will explore the status of the ecclesial community in Iraq as of 2013. Third, it will examine the effects of religious and administrative policies of the governors of Mesopotamia-Iraq on the Chaldeans, from their formation in the sixteenth century until the installation of the new Chaldean patriarch, Louis Raphael I Sako, in March 2013.

Nomenclature

The nomenclature used to describe the Church of the East and the Chaldeans does give rise to some confusion, particularly in non-specialist literature.

Nestorian

The chief query nearly universally raised when first encountering the East Syriac communities relates to the title *Nestorian* as applied to the Church of the East. This relates to the view that the Church throughout its history has consistently pursued an extreme dyophysite Christology and denied that the Blessed Virgin could be described as the 'Mother of God'. Both issues aligned with the perceived heresy which the Patriarch of Constantinople, Nestorius, pursued in the early fifth century until the Council of Ephesus in 431 where he was deposed and subsequently entered exile (Baum and Winkler 2003, 22–5). As will be seen, the East Syriac tradition has been perceived to be linked with a Christology associated with Nestorius into the contemporary era. This situation continues despite direct rejections from church leaders and researchers, and Christological treatises refuting the claims or, at the very least, attempting to give context to the situation and a comprehensive explanation of the Christology which the churches currently and historically have ascribed to themselves (Brock 2004; Soro 1996; Chediath 1982). Moreover, some scholarship from the mid-twentieth century to the present argues that neither the Church of the East was Nestorian nor that Nestorius actually professed any un-orthodox notions (Seleznyov 2008; Brock 1996; Halleux 1993; Braaten 1963; Anastos 1962).

The Christological controversy is not the direct concern of this study, but it is vital to be cognisant of the dispute and aware that it has coloured views of the Church of the East by nearly all who have interacted with or studied the community into the present. It has also been an inhibiting factor against the Church of the East – and the Chaldeans by extension – from gaining greater credence and indeed respect in the contemporary international Christian community (cf. Thompson 2013). The effects of the association have been unfortunate and, in some respects, have de-legitimised the achievements of the Church of the East in its missionary work and its maintenance of distinctive ecclesial traditions in the eyes of external observers. Moreover, it has led to the Church being under-reported in academic and popular histories of the international Christian community. Indeed, the East Syriac churches not fitting into a Latin, Byzantine or reformed church paradigm provokes a challenge for researchers. However, it is one which must be met head on, and with the intention of bringing the East Syriac tradition into mainstream ecclesiastical history. Further, it must proceed with the view that research on the Church is integral to a full account of global missionary activity.

East Syriac

As a collective term for members of the Church of the East and Chaldeans, East Syriac or East Syrian is *du jour*, and fits most appropriately with the non-Christologically focused identity which Chaldeans and members of the Church of the East pursue. During the Medieval Period, the East Syriacs referred to themselves as *Maddenhaye* or Easterners (Murre-van den Berg 2005). This was a means to consolidate their identity by way of comparison with those Christians of the West: Miaphysites, Byzantines and Latins, and related to their use of the Syriac dialect which developed among the Christian communities who resided east of Nisibis, the great centre of the East Syriac intellectual tradition. Self-association and identification with Nestorius did take place – he was venerated as a saint – but was far removed from forming the core of their identity (Seleznyov 2010). During the missionary efforts of the Late Antique and Medieval periods, the focus was to gain converts through annunciating the Gospel and the distinctiveness of Christian revelation and not by diverting accusations of a perceived heresy among those who had never before encountered Christianity.

The significance of church-state relations in East Syriac history

Relations with the contemporary temporal power were and are a strong theme throughout East Syriac history. The leadership of the temporal powers under whose administration East Syriac communities have resided never converted to their form of Christianity. Therefore, it was perceived as necessary to engender an amicable working relationship with lay élites. Such engagements were vital to the effective operation of the East Syriac churches, and an opportunity to engage in aggregating a system of client-patron relationships. This allowed the East Syriac community to gain permission to build churches and monasteries or agreement for the appointment of senior clergy. The head of the Church of the East in the Sasanian period was ratified on a *de facto* basis by the Shah, whilst in the Ottoman era the heads of Chaldean and traditionalist East Syriac factions competed for recognition by the local governor as *the* legitimate successor to the patriarchs of the undivided Church of the East.

From the fifth century the Church of the East engaged closely with socio-economic and political structures of the Sasanian Empire whilst simultaneously disengaging from contemporary Christological debates of the Roman world (Brock 1982). The East Syriac presence, in time, became a defining aspect of

4 *Introduction*

Mesopotamian and Persian society and challenged the dominance of Zoroastrianism as the state religion. With the Muslim invasions of West Asia and the disintegration of the Zoroastrian religion, East Syriac élites were key to the sustaining of the Ummayad dynasty's rule in Mesopotamia and the running of the administrative processes left by the Sasanians (Morony 2009). East Syriac Christians made themselves indispensable to the Muslim leadership, and they gained high status during the Abbasid dynasty. Dickens notes of Patriarch Timothy I:

> Although he lived his whole life in the heartland of the Arab Caliphate and thus never visited most of the extensive territory under his patriarchal authority, Timothy was very conscious of ruling over a jurisdiction much larger than any other on earth, whether civil or ecclesiastical. Not only was he a trusted figure at the caliphal court, the head of the largest *dhimmi* under Muslim rule (those living in 'Babel', Persia and Assyria); there were also far-off and exotic territories beyond the pale of Islam that were 'under this patriarchal throne', including the lands of the Indians *(Beth Hinduwāyē)*, Chinese *(Beth Ṣināyē)*, Tibetans *(Beth Tuptāyē)* and Turks *(Beth Ṭurkāyē)*. This undoubtedly gave him considerable prestige and influence in the eyes of the Abbasid caliphs.
>
> (Dickens 2010, 120)

The attainment of such a position was maintained under other patriarchs into the Mongol era, until the rise of Tamerlane saw a definitive shift away from a normative co-operative working relationship with the state due to the extensive anti-Christian persecution which the Timurids enacted. With the emergence of Ottoman hegemony in the Middle East, a new system of church-state relations developed along the more bureaucratic lines of the *millet*. This administration of religious communities in effect returned to the same *status quo* as encouraged under the Sasanians, whereby the temporal élite engaged with the leader of each group. This relationship was the chief means for the community to interact with the state. Following Iraq's establishment in 1921, such a relationship was retained, with the Chaldean patriarch becoming a member of the Iraqi Senate until 1958. Furthermore, and until 2003, the state deferred to the patriarch during interactions with the community. The sustained position of power which such an arrangement granted to the patriarch added substantially to the influence of his ecclesiastical authority. Only he was capable of interceding on behalf of the community on issues of universal concern and of distributing resources which he derived from the state.

Note on approach

My approach to researching and writing about the East Syriac churches is to maintain awareness of them as derived from an international Christian tradition, or as Murre-van den Berg describes them, as a 'world church' (2005). I suggest the communities largely lacked such an awareness from the early modern era

Introduction 5

until 2003. The Chaldean hierarchy was able to engage well with the cultural and societal *milieu* of Iraq, but was more challenged to engage with Western societies, where large proportions of the Chaldean population came to reside. This is unfortunate, when we consider that the precedent for the East Syriac community, throughout its history, was to engage with local culture and permit the acculturation of local traditions to the Church. As a result, the East Syriac tradition gradually lost that capability – which it once held – of appealing to a wide audience and potential converts.

Attempting to approach modern East Syriac ecclesiastical history in a comprehensive manner and place it in the broader context of the full scope of the international and Mesopotamian history of the Church of the East is a comparatively 'young' area of study. This field was largely instigated from the 1960s by the substantial work of Jean Maurice Fiey OP. Fiey attempted to bring together the known threads of East Syriac history into a contiguous narrative and to detail the development of the Church of the East from its earliest origins to his era (Fiey OP 1980, 1965, 1959).

In attempting to build on Fiey's work, I aim to further understand the pragmatic issues with which East Syriac Christians were faced in their day-to-day lives, and what was understood to be their ecclesiological identity: what did East Syriac bishops in sixteenth century Mesopotamia perceive as their ecclesial relationship with the papacy? How did the Chaldean communities of northern and southern Iraq relate one to another under the Baath state, and how did the No-Fly-Zone in northern Iraq affect their governance? How did the Chaldean community relate to the patriarch during the Iran-Iraq War? What was the strength of East Syriac cultural and social contributions to wider Iraqi society under the rule of the monarchy? These are but a few suggested areas of scholarship which could be pursued but have yet to be fully explored, if at all, in research on the East Syriac tradition.

By way of comparison, the study of the modern history of the Church of the East and Chaldean Church is often just as opaque as the study of the East Syriac communities during their 'golden' era in West and Central Asia (c. sixth–eleventh centuries). Tang and Winkler, for example, particularly pick up on the significant question of how the Christians in Transoxiana related to the patriarch of Baghdad and as to the degree of devolved ecclesial authority the local bishops held (Tang and Winkler 2013). The opacity they face in answering this question is related to limits on source material (whether written records or archaeological remains), and is paralleled in the opacity scholars face studying the contemporary East Syriac communities. Principal challenges are the inability to access much of Iraq due to ongoing major conflicts since 1980, the lack of available or extant written records, and the recent physical destruction of Christian communities in Iraq due to attacks by Da'esh. Perhaps the most pressing issues remain, however, the lack of interest or willingness from native and non-native researchers to engage in historical reflection, to persevere in studies of the modern history of the Chaldean Church, and to provide a greater academic context in which to fit this study.

The origins and status of the Church of the East to the late Medieval Period

The Church of the East is that Christian community which developed in Mesopotamia and Persia from at least the second century and gradually gained a sense of ecclesial distinctiveness apart from the church in the Roman Empire. This distinctiveness was shaped by political expediency – being under Sasanian Persian rule from 224; a perception that ecclesiastical organisation should follow a principle of subsidiarity with the local bishops not necessarily reliant on deference to the five patriarchates of the west (Alexandria, Antioch, Constantinople, Jerusalem and Rome); and a different emphasis in their Christology, with the Church of the East favouring the theological oeuvre of Theodore of Mopsuestia and the Antiochene school, which promoted dyophysite Christology and the significance of Christ's humanity (McLeod 2000, 451–4; cf. Wigram 1910, 155–9).

From the early fifth century, the hierarchy of the church consolidated its ecclesiastical organisation (and a commitment to self-governance and ecclesial independence) at the local Mesopotamian synods of Isaac (410) and Dadisho (424) (Fiey OP 1970, 113; cf. Brock 1985, 125–6). The East Syriac bishops perceived their existing Christology as in accord with the deposit of Faith of the Apostles and saw less need to engage with disputes conducted in arenas theologically, geographically and politically removed from their community.

There has existed a general perception that the defining cut-off point of the Church of the East's relationship with the Roman church took place at the Council of Ephesus in 431 over disputes regarding the human and divine natures of Christ. This perception led to its *de facto* separation from the rest of the Christian oikumene through an unwillingness to condemn Nestorius and ratify the canons of the Council. However, as the Council of Ephesus was an event in the Roman – not Sasanian – world, the Church of the East likely did not regard it as obligatory to engage with the Council's proceedings (Baum and Winkler 2003, 30). As the East Syriac community's focus shifted towards the east, we should perhaps regard its ecclesiological development as a gradual, if definitive, process of incarnating Christianity in the Mesopotamian-Persian environment and becoming *the* church of the Sasanian world.

Nonetheless, Ephesus, and its shift away from a sufficiently nuanced Christological paradigm – as perceived by members of the Church of the East – expedited a reformulation of where the future of the East Syriac tradition lay. The ecclesiastical schools of Edessa and Nisibis reinforced East Syriac identity and culture, and by the late fifth century, missionary clergy were active in pursuing a policy of expansion into Central Asia. Missionary expansion from the fifth to eleventh centuries saw ecclesial structures established throughout Asia to China. During the early to high Medieval periods, the Church of the East had the widest geographical jurisdiction of any Christian community in the world and held substantial influence among the Abbasid and Mongol empires. However, the Church entered into a period of gradual decline from the fourteenth century onward.

From a position of at least 100 dioceses in the late thirteenth century, the Church was reduced to three occupied sees by the mid-sixteenth century (Wilmshurst

Introduction 7

2011, 259–60, 302–3). Such a relatively rapid change of the status quo was caused through the highly destructive invasion of Tamerlane. Further, the Church of the East had also been weakened through competing pressure from Islam, Taoism, Buddhism and the West Syriac church.

Those who were to emerge as the Chaldeans were remnants of the East Syriac community residing in northern Mesopotamia, eastern Asia Minor and north-west Persia. The patriarchs of the late fourteenth and early fifteenth centuries attempted to consolidate what remained of the Church. I suggest that there were strong communal memories of the Church's missionary activities. However, it was recognised how difficult it would be to complete missions in the same way, as the socio-religious nature of West and Central Asia was irreversibly changed from the consolidation of Islam to these regions.

A memory of former links with churches internationally was perhaps why engaging with Latin envoys proved attractive to East Syriac leaders. The Church of the East retained an awareness of the See of Peter's rôle and status in the Christian world of Late Antiquity. Rebuilding a relationship with the Holy See offered a possible opening to also reclaim communion with the wider Christian oikumeme. From the thirteenth century onward, engagements with the Latin church increased in number. It is here the following historical narrative begins.

Bibliography

Anastos, Milton V. 1962. 'Nestorius Was Orthodox'. *Dumbarton Oaks Papers* 16: 117–40.
Baum, Wilhelm, and Dietmar W. Winkler. 2003. *The Church of the East: A Concise History*. Translated by Miranda G. Henry. London: RoutledgeCurzon.
Baumer, Christoph. 2006. *The Church of the East: An Illustrated History of Assyrian Christianity*. London: Tauris.
Braaten, Carl E. 1963. 'Modern Interpretations of Nestorius'. *Church History* 32 (September): 251–67. doi:10.2307/3162772.
Brock, Sebastian. 1982. 'Christians in the Sasanian Empire: A Case of Divided Loyalties'. In *Religion and National Identity*, edited by Stuart Mews, 1–19. Studies in Church History 18. Oxford: Blackwell for the Ecclesiastical History Society.
———. 1985. 'The Christology of the Church of the East in the Synods of the Fifth to Early Seventh Centuries: Preliminary Considerations and Materials'. In *Aksum, Thyateira: A Festschrift for Archbishop Methodios of Thyateira and Great Britain*, edited by George Dion Dragas, 125–42. London, Athens: Thyateira House. www.worldcat.org/oclc/12890593.
———. 1996. 'The "Nestorian" Church: A Lamentable Misnomer'. *Bulletin of the John Rylands Library* 78: 23–35.
———. 2004. 'The Syriac Churches in Ecumenical Dialogue on Christology'. In *Eastern Christianity: Studies in Modern History, Religion and Politics*, edited by Anthony O'Mahony, 44–65. London: Melisende.
Chediath, Geevarghese. 1982. *The Christology of Mar Babai the Great*. Kottoyam: Oriental Institute of Religious Studies.
Dickens, Mark. 2010. 'Patriarch Timothy I and the Metropolitan of the Turks'. *Journal of the Royal Asiatic Society*, Third Series, 20 (2): 117–39. doi:10.1017/S1356186309990460.
Fiey OP, Jean Maurice. 1959. *Mossoul Chrétienne: Essai Sur l'histoire, l'archéologie et l'état Actuel Des Monuments Chrétiens de La Ville de Mossoul*. Recherches Publiées

8 Introduction

Sous La Direction de l'Institut de Lettres Orientales de Beyrouth 12. Beirut: Imprimerie Catholique.

———. 1965. *Assyrie Chrétienne – Contribution a l'Étude de l'Histoire et de la Géographie Ecclésiastiques et Monastiques du Nord de l'Iraq.* Vol. I. 3 vols. Recherches publiées sous la direction de l'Institut de Lettres Orientales de Beyrouth, XXII. Beirut: Imprimerie Catholique.

———. 1970. *Jalons pour une histoire de l'Église en Iraq.* Corpus Scriptorum Christianorum Orientalium, v. 310. Louvain: Secrétariat du Corpus SCO.

———. 1980. *Chrétiens syriaques sous les Abbassides, surtout à Bagdad (749–1258).* Corpus Scriptorum Christianorum Orientalium, 420; Subsidia t. 59. Louvain: Secrétariat du CorpusSCO.

Halleux, André de. 1993. 'Nestorius: Histoire et Doctrine'. *Irénikon* 66: 38–51, 163–78.

Healey, John. 2010. ' "The Church Across the Border" the Church of the East and Its Chaldaean Branch'. In *Eastern Christianity in the Modern Middle East*, edited by Anthony O'Mahony and Emma Loosley, 41–55. Culture and Civilization of the Modern Middle East 20. Abingdon: Routledge.

McLeod, Frederick G. 2000. 'Theodore of Mopsuestia Revisited'. *Theological Studies* 61 (3): 447–80. doi:10.1177/004056390006100303.

Morony, Michael G. 2009. *Christians in Iraq After the Muslim Conquest.* Analecta Gorgiana 111. Piscataway, NJ: Gorgias Press.

Murre-van den Berg, Heleen L. 2005. 'The Church of the East in the Sixteenth to the Eighteenth Century: World Church or Ethnic Community?'. In *Redefining Christian Identity: Cultural Interaction in the Middle East Since the Rise of Islam*, 301–20. Orientalia Lovaniensia Analecta 134. Louvain: Peeters.

———. 2009. 'Chaldeans and Assyrians: The Church of the East in the Ottoman Period'. In *The Christian Heritage of Iraq: Collected Papers from the Christianity of Iraq I-V Seminar Days*, edited by Erica C. D. Hunter, 146–64. Piscataway, NJ: Gorgias Press.

Rassam, Suha. 2010. *Christianity in Iraq: Its Origins and Development to the Present Day.* New Edition. Leominster: Gracewing Publishing.

Seleznyov, Nikolai N. 2008. 'The Church of the East & Its Theology: History of Studies'. *Orientalia Christiana Periodica* 74: 115–31.

———. 2010. 'Nestorius of Constantinople: Condemnation, Suppression, Veneration With Special Reference to His Name in East-Syriac Christianity'. *Journal of Eastern Christian Studies* 62 (3–4): 165–90. doi:10.2143/JECS.62.3.2061116.

Soro, Bawai. 1996. 'Reception of the "Common Christological Declaration" in the Assyrian Church of the East – an Occasion for Christian Joy and for Cultural Vitality'. In *Second Non-Official Consultation on Dialogue Within the Syriac Tradition*, edited by Alfred Stirnemann and Gerhard Wilflinger, 63–70. Syriac Dialogue 2. Vienna: Pro Oriente.

Tang, Li, and Dietmar Winkler. 2013. 'Introduction'. In *From the Oxus River to the Chinese Shores: Studies on East Syriac Christianity in China and Central Asia*, edited by Li Tang and Dietmar Winkler, 5–9. Orientalia – Patristica – Oecumenica 5. Zürich: Lit Verlag.

Teule, Herman. 2008. *Les Assyro-Chaldéens: Chrétiens d'Irak, d'Iran et de Turquie.* Fils d'Abraham. Turnhout: Brepols.

Thompson, Glen L. 2013. 'How the Jingjiao Became Nestorian: Western Perceptions and Eastern Realities'. In *From the Oxus River to the Chinese Shores: Studies on East Syriac Christianity in China and Central Asia*, edited by Li Tang and Dietmar W. Winkler, 417–39. Orientalia – Patristica – Oecumenica 5. Vienna: Lit Verlag.

Wigram, William Ainger 1910. *An Introduction to the History of the Assyrian Church or the Church of the Sassanid Persian Empire 100–640 A.D.* London: SPCK. https://books.google.com/books?id=hrlgAAAAMAAJ&dq=inauthor%3A%22William%20Ainger%20Wigram%22&pg=PP1#v=onepage&q&f=false.

Wilmshurst, David. 2000. *The Ecclesiastical Organisation of the Church of the East 1318–1913*. Corpus Scriptorum Christianorum Orientalium ; Subsidia, vol. 582. tomus 104. Lovanii: Peeters.

———. 2011. *The Martyred Church: A History of the Church of the East.* Sawbridgeworth, Hertfordshire: East and West.

1 The origins and early development of the Chaldean Catholic community (fifteenth to eighteenth centuries)

Chaldean origins

The first establishment of an East Syriac community in union with the Holy See and use of the term *Chaldean* came in the mid-fifteenth century. However, in the two centuries prior to this event, encounters with Latin representatives brought members of the Church of the East into short periods of communion or near communion with the Holy See.

The overarching trend in the period c. 1230–1445 was for East Syriac bishops, patriarchs, priests or laymen to enter into union with the Holy See on an individual or small group basis – there was no movement to bring the whole East Syriac community into union and to form a new ecclesial rite or church. The inability to expand or sustain contacts happened in light of changing political circumstances and the prevailing Muslim cultural environment in West Asia. In such a context, and without a very clearly defined vision and support for an East Syriac community in union with the Roman See, returning to the Christian community of one's origins is not surprising.

Latin missionary activities in West Asia derived from an interest in engaging with the Mongol political élites who increasingly dominated the area from the 1240s and appeared open to conversion to Christianity. There also existed a desire to bring local churches into union with the pope and to consolidate the Christian presence in the Holy Land and wider Middle East in the context of the Sixth and Seventh Crusades (1228–1229 and 1248–1254) (cf. Gillman and Klimkeit 1999, 243).

The first attempt at major Latin engagement came in 1246. Pope Innocent IV (1243–1254) sent Dominican missionaries to meet with the East Syriac patriarch, Sabrisho V ibn al-Masihi (1226–1256).[1] In response, Sabrisho provided a statement of belief in 1247 as evidence of the compatibility of his theology with that of the Latin church and hence the suitability of communion with the Church of the East, but nothing further resulted at that time (Labourt 1908a, 559; Wilmshurst 2011, 238–9).

Perhaps the most well known of these temporary reunions came in 1304, when the East Syriac patriarch Yahballaha III (1281–1317) met with Dominican representatives in the then Il-Khanate capital of Maragha, north-west Persia. The

Origins and early development   11

patriarch completed a Latin confession of faith addressed to Pope Benedict XI (Goormachtigh OP 1896, 274–5; Bruns 2013, passim). Nonetheless, the reunion proved only fleeting, with the synod of the Church of the East condemning Yahballaha's act and disavowing the link with the Holy See. Yahballaha held an interest in the Latin world throughout his ecclesial career which perhaps stemmed from his own cosmopolitan background. Of Turkic Uyghur origins and one of the few non-Mesopotamian or Persian patriarchs of the Church of the East, he was responsible for sending the monk Rabban Sawma on a diplomatic mission to meet with the principal religious and political leaders of Europe in the late thirteenth century. It is possible that the bishops viewed him as someone acting outside of established conventions and advancing to open an attitude towards engagement with other Christian communities.

Aside from direct engagements with the East Syriac patriarch, other encounters with Latin ecclesiastics and crusader élites from the eleventh century were concentrated in Damascus, Jerusalem, Tripoli, Edessa, Cyprus and Antioch (Teule 2003b, 108–12; Langdale and Walsh 2007, 108). On a popular basis, it seems likely individual members of the East Syriac community were sufficiently interested in the Latin church to consider transferring their allegiance to it, or took part in Latin religious life – whether through mere curiosity or with a view to gaining influence within the Crusader States (Weltecke 2011, 108; Dauvillier 1979, 642–3). The novelty of living under Christian jurisdiction when for so long they had been governed by largely Muslim élites may have been highly attractive.

First union

The Church of the East sustained its presence across the Mediterranean and Middle East into the fifteenth century even if in many instances its extant diocesan structures were small. This continued geographical spread was a testament to the resilience of the faith of its members despite challenges, and indicative of a capability to comfortably develop in a variety of cultural contexts.

The community remained especially strong on Cyprus. Members of the Church of the East enjoyed extended interactions with the Latin and other Eastern Christian traditions present to the island.[2] It was in this context that *Chaldean* was first used to describe a bishop in union with the Holy See. The East Syriac Metropolitan of Cyprus, Timothy, in concord with the Council of Florence on 7 July 1445, entered into union with the Roman Pontiff following the encouragement of the Latin archbishop on Rhodes, Andreas of Colassae OP (Labourt 1908a, 559; Finnerty 1907, 474). Andreas pursued a papal directed policy which sought to bring into union a full sweep of those local churches who, it was perceived, remained apart from the pope's oversight and which required necessary readjustment of ecclesiastical organisation. A chief purpose of Florence was to secure the reconciliation of Byzantium and all the Christian communities of the East with the Latin West in spiritual as well as temporal affairs (Gill SJ 1959, 321–7, 335–7).

12 *Origins and early development*

The choice of the term *Chaldean* to describe the East Syriac faction was approved by Pope Eugene IV and was derived from an awareness of the community's use of the Syriac language – referred to as Chaldean in Europe (Yacoub 2004, 387–8; cf. Galleti 2003, 45–8). This Chaldean province was not maintained, as conflict occurred over the extent of Latinisation which was acceptable to the new converts when changes in East Syriac liturgical practices were requested (cf. Le Coz 1995, 327; Wilmshurst 2000, 64; Labourt 1908a, 559).

As of 1445, it would seem unlikely that a Chaldean ecclesial identity to which other East Syriacs could adhere had time to develop distinct from the Church of the East. The group existed in isolation and by the mid-sixteenth century had merged into the Cypriot Maronite or Latin communities or returned to their previous religious affiliation (Wilmshurst 2011, 304; Tfinkdji 1913, 7). The Holy See was not intending to seek and create a Chaldean ecclesial community with which it was to be in union at this juncture, rather the opportunity arose for bringing East Syriac Cypriots into the Latin ordinary's jurisdiction (Yacoub 2004, 386).

The emergence of Chaldean communities from the Church of the East should be seen in the context of broader trends in the Latin church and successive popes' interests in the Christians of the eastern Mediterranean. Furthermore, the 108-year period between the first named Chaldean group's establishment in 1445 on Cyprus to that established in 1553 in Mesopotamia was framed by the Councils of Florence and Trent (1431–1449 and 1545–1563). Florence largely focused on defining the status of papal jurisdiction and the relationship between the Latin and Byzantine worlds as well as with Ethiopian, Syriac, Coptic and Armenian churches. Trent affected virtually the entire ecclesiological understanding of the Latin church and caused the reawakening of an uncompromising missionary zeal for bringing all men into union with the Holy See and ensuring they conformed to what was perceived as orthodox belief. From Trent, there was a definitive shift away from encouraging a plurality of local churches in communion with one another to a church of a plurality of ecclesial rites under the pope's leadership and direction.

Following the Council of Trent, to enter into union with the Holy See entailed a definitive juridical separation from one's previous religious allegiance. For East Syriac communities entering into union with the Holy See, this required their submission to the pope's jurisdiction and recognition of his authority over all their ecclesiastical affairs. However, we should note that Latin engagements with the East Syriacs were on a path which took several turns prior to settling on a confirmed outlook for gaining them as adherents. For the Holy See, there was a qualitative difference in seeking a bishop's allegiance to entering into union with the patriarch of an entire church. The former is the leader of a diocese, whereas the latter is heir to an institution which oversaw the East Syriac Christian tradition throughout Asia.

The status of the Church of the East in 1450 and the development of hereditary succession to the patriarchate

During the period 1450–1550, the Church of the East was still in an era of recovery from the decline it experienced during and after the Islamisation of the

Origins and early development 13

Mongol empires from the mid-thirteenth century and Tamerlane's (b. c. 1330 d. 1405) invasions during the fourteenth century (cf. Gillman and Klimkeit 1999, 151, 234–7; Wilmshurst 2000, 19). The paths of Mongol and Timurid expansion mirrored in reverse the East Syriac missionary work of Late Antique and Medieval eras.

Following the Council of Ephesus in 431, East Syriac ecclesial life was oriented away from engagement with the Latin church and the patriarchates of Jerusalem, Antioch, Alexandria and Constantinople through sustained missionary activity throughout Central and East Asia for much of the next 900 years. The extent of this activity is something which the aforementioned churches would likely not have been fully aware. The patriarch's overall direction of affairs from the early Medieval period emanated from his residence in the Abbasid capital Baghdad and later the Mongol Il-Khanate capital of Maragha and was mediated via a network of dioceses extending throughout Asia.

The status of East Syriac Christianity in Asia changed from accepted to persecuted with the Mongol élites' conversion to Islam, the withdrawal of toleration for non-native religious traditions in China, and the subsequent brutality of Tamerlane. Those communities, far from the patriarchal leadership, struggled to contend with the aggressive stance of the temporal powers and slowly acquiesced to Islam or moved to the traditional East Syriac heartlands of northern Mesopotamia where the patriarch had retreated.

When we consider the decline of the Church of the East in the full light of historical reflection it was perhaps an unsurprising turn of events. The missionary fervour which had characterised ecclesial life from the 430s to c. 1300 could not be sustained indefinitely. By the fourteenth century expansion had reached its zenith and, I suggest, an institutional exhaustion prevailed. In secular affairs, this was paralleled in the expansion and decline of the Mongol empire. The devolution of Ghengis Khan's conquests into successor states from 1260 was a natural process given the difficulties of ruling such vast territories.

Perhaps most detrimental to the possibility of future missionary expansion was a gradual reduction in intellectual and ecclesial resources with the monastic candidates upon which the Church had relied for leadership beginning to disappear – a personnel crisis which could not be easily overcome. Further, where in other contexts the Church had previously been able to rely on the state's patronage of its institutions at times of weakness, during later Mongol rule this was also lost.

A final factor from that era, which was likely crucial in the Church's status in Central Asia, were ongoing outbreaks of plague from the thirteenth century which would have had substantial implications for the community at all levels. Tombstones with Syriac inscriptions found at Semirache, Kirghizstan, provide indication of the extent of the disease among the faithful (Missick 1999, 99–100; cf. Dickens 2009, 14–15ff.).

In considering these factors, we ought also to note a potential indicator of a severe East Syriac decline: the very limited extant written records from the fourteenth to mid-sixteenth centuries. Nonetheless, given the physically destructive nature of military campaigns and anti-Christian persecutions of that period,

14 *Origins and early development*

material may have been lost rather than not produced. The period 1000–1300 had seen a renaissance in Syriac literary production among monastics in West Asia, and in the context of often supportive patronage of the Abbasid caliphs in Baghdad from the eighth century (see Teule 2002, 2003a). Furthermore, at least up until the second decade of the fourteenth century, advanced theological material was produced such as Abdisho of Nisibis' *Book of the Pearl*. This text provides a concise outline of East Syriac Christological thought at a time when the community was at a crossroads in its historical trajectory and re-engaging with other Christian traditions (Wilmshurst 2011, 274). It is suggestive that this was a community looking for means to re-establish its identity and organisation.

First Chaldean hierarchy in union with the Holy See

The Church of the East's shrinking geographical remit and decline in the number of qualified candidates for leadership positions afforded the family of Patriarch Shemon IV Basidi (1450–1497) an opportunity to consolidate control over the remaining dioceses (cf. Wilmshurst 2000, 193). One method to ensure control was considered to be via the establishment of hereditary succession to the patriarchal office, and, from 1450, it became normative for the patriarch to name a nephew as his successor with the title 'guardian of the throne' – *Natar Kursya* (Valognes 1994, 415; Murre-van den Berg 1999, 237). A chief benefit of this procedure was for clear continuity in church leadership and governance following the patriarch's death. We cannot be certain that Shemon IV was desirous of maintaining such a system indefinitely. The position of decline which the Church was in, however, suggests the measure was considered acceptable and it was only once increasing nepotism became a sustained procedure that it was viewed as necessary to actively oppose it as detrimental to East Syriac ecclesial organisation.

By the time of Patriarch Shemon VII (1539–1558), opposition to hereditary succession began to be openly expressed. Shemon VII originally consecrated his nephew, Hnanisho, as bishop when age twelve in 1539 and later appointed him as a metropolitan. However, Hnanisho died in 1545, and his brother, Eliya, also a minor, became *Natar Kursya* by 1550 (Wilmshurst 2011, 297–8). Shemon VII's preference for his family and their influence in East Syriac affairs was so sufficiently opposed by 1552 that Yohannan Sulaqa, superior of the monastery of Rabban Hormizd in Alqosh, was elected as a new patriarch in resistance with the support of bishops from Erbil, Salmas and Adarbaigan (Wilmshurst 2011, 302–3).

Initially, Sulaqa held the patriarchal office only as an administrator. For the Sulaqite faction to conduct their ecclesiastical administration in a canonical manner and according to East Syriac tradition, Sulaqa required consecration as patriarch from at least one bishop of metropolitan rank. A bishop of metropolitan rank had greater seniority in church affairs and often had responsibility for a geographically larger or more densely populated see than a bishop of ordinary rank (cf. Messmer 1907). As the bishops who supported Sulaqa had not attained this rank, an alternative cleric of sufficient seniority was sought in the person of the pope. An advantage of seeking support from the Roman See was the distance geographically and politically from the ongoing disputes in Mesopotamia.

Origins and early development 15

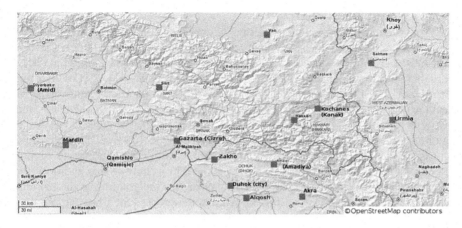

Map 1.1 Northern Iraq, eastern Turkey, northern Iran and principal sites of East Syriac-Chaldean activity from the sixteenth century

East Syriac and Latin ecclesiological perspectives on the proto-Chaldean community

The Sulaqite faction's interest in the papacy was consolidated following meetings with Franciscan missionaries present in the town of Amid (Diyarbakir), in southeast Asia Minor. Subsequently, Sulaqa and his supporters met with representatives of the Custodian of the Holy Land in Jerusalem to determine if they should travel onward to Rome.[3] The Church of the East had a long-standing tradition of pilgrimage to Jerusalem with, it appears, community members also resident there into the early modern era (Brock 2006, 194–6; Meinardus 1967, 123–9; cf. Fiey OP 1969, passim). Such a tradition of connection to the spiritual centre of the Christian world perhaps echoed in the minds of Sulaqa and his coterie. A fruitful meeting we can assume took place in Jerusalem, as Sulaqa received advice to meet directly with Pope Julius III (1550–1555) and was consecrated patriarch in April 1553 (Baumer 2006, 248; Wilmshurst 2000, 22).

It seems unlikely the contemporary actors would have conceived of the significance with which this event would come to be held, or as to whether they shared the same view as to the future development of an East Syriac patriarchate in union with the Holy See.[4] Establishing an East Syriac patriarchate which derived its legitimacy from the Holy See was remarkable given the geographical and practical, if not formal, ecclesiastical separation of over a thousand years between the *de facto* patriarch of the west and the patriarch with jurisdiction for much of Asia. Moreover, Sulaqa's investiture marked the start of Latin attempts to reconcile the entire membership of the Church of the East to union with the Holy See as a key focus of missionary activity. These efforts continued consistently despite the difficult political and religious situation which Latin missionaries encountered, and in the face of tribal and familial divisions among the East Syriac communities.

16 *Origins and early development*

It was nearly 300 years later (1838) before a stable and unified Chaldean community was consolidated.

From Sulaqa's perspective, it appears he approached the pope with an awareness that the occupant of the Roman See was known to be the apostolic descendant of St Peter and a validly ordained prelate who could convey legitimate holy orders (Murre-van den Berg 2005, 315 n. 42; Wilmshurst 2011, 298). However, it is unclear if there was especial awareness of the Tridentine nature of papal authority by the proto-Chaldeans. From the Council of Trent's conclusion, the Holy See professed its teaching and leadership role to be the supreme ecclesial authority which all other Christians should acknowledge. In approaching the pope for ecclesiastical faculties, a patriarchal candidate would be expected to submit to papal jurisdiction. A formal acknowledgement procedure of this authority for Eastern Christian leaders in union with the pope was the granting of the pallium (an ecclesiastical vestment). A further layer to the process for Christians associated with East Syriac Christology was a confirmation of post-Ephesian orthodoxy and acceptance of the decisions of subsequent ecumenical councils. This extra step was required to formally dissociate themselves from association with Nestorius' suspected opinions on Christ's humanity and divinity, whether or not they actually held to his Christology.

In the broader context, Sulaqa and his supporters were one of several Eastern Christian groups brought into union with the Holy See which gradually emerged as an Eastern Catholic rite from the mid-sixteenth century. As each instance was varied by geography and chronology, it could not be said to be a standardised procedure but one in which the Holy See and Latin representatives pursued a model which was thought best for each situation with overarching shared themes. The case of the East Syriac tradition was particular because it seemed paradoxical (to Latin eyes) that a once so successful and large institution as the Church of the East should for so long have been associated with the thought of Nestorius *and* not in active communion with the Holy See. The scale of the Church of the East's missionary achievements suggested it was necessary for the Holy See to approach this community in a manner different to that of encounters with other Eastern Christians.

The Church of the East was the first church to have brought Christianity to Central and East Asia, and the encounter between Sulaqa and the Holy See was, in effect, a process which would join two global churches in communion. Although much reduced compared with its breadth in the Medieval period, in Sulaqa's time, East Syriac Christians were still present to Mesopotamia, north-west Persia, eastern Asia Minor and South Asia. There were also likely descendant members of the Church still living in the Holy Land and Cyprus (cf. Meinardus 1967, 120–1). Whether they sustained an active practice of the East Syriac tradition is less clear. However, that the community still existed in a variety of geographical environments was of significance to how Sulaqa positioned his approach to the Holy See and Latin representatives. If not in a strong contemporary position as compared with the East Syriac patriarchs of the Medieval era, he at least could underline how he was the heir to these traditions and institutions.

Origins and early development   17

Sulaqa appears to have been aware of the regional spread of the East Syriac tradition spending some time with the Portuguese ambassador to the Holy See to discuss the situation of Christians in South Asia. If Sulaqa had survived longer than his untimely death in 1555, this meeting could have been the best means to secure the independence of the East Syriac community from Portuguese-dominated Latin jurisdiction and, in principle, a more cordial relationship in the long term in South Asia. Sulaqa's death was a substantial barrier to the effective continuation of the Chaldean project given such amount of time had been invested in him and his training for the development of the community with the support of Latin missionaries.

Historical context of Sulaqa's engagement with the Holy See

The Chaldean patriarchate which was to develop as a result of Sulaqa's meetings emerged between two institutions: the Latin church and the Church of the East. Each held to a distinctive understanding of their duties and responsibilities in sustaining the Christian tradition and, as of the mid-sixteenth century, greatly differed in their capability to act in defence of that tradition and to extend it.

As the Church of the East was in a weakened state, Sulaqa's engagement with the Holy See and Latin representatives could not be said to have taken place at an equitable level and Sulaqa's group was not representative of the *entire* East Syriac ecclesial community. Therefore, and as the relationship with the Holy See developed, differing visions for long-term outcomes were also envisioned: Sulaqa seeking a means to revivify the Church of the East but the Holy See seeking to bring into union, on a large scale, members of the East Syriac tradition.

This was a series of events taking place concurrent with the Council of Trent (1545–1563) that was fortuitous from the perspective of the Holy See. The events offered an opportunity to comprehend how Eastern Christians might be absorbed into the Latin milieu not as churches in communion with the Holy See but as subordinate to the jurisdiction of the papacy and part of *one Catholic Church*. Given the context of Sulaqa asking for consecration, this was a situation which implied he was also to defer to the Holy See, whereas Sulaqa regarded this as a senior bishop granting him necessary ecclesiastical status to govern his own church. Whether the full context of this was understood by Sulaqa is not clear; that is, he was to be not just in union with, but also under, the Holy See's jurisdiction.

For Sulaqa, in choosing to engage with the Holy See, his immediate and overriding concern was to secure the East Syriac community under his leadership. Until introduced by Latin representatives, concerns regarding the compatibility of East Syriac and Latin Christology and ecclesiology were not raised. Sulaqa was entering a world in which concepts of the juridical boundaries of the Church, and the status of the Roman See, were paramount to Latin self-understanding and identity and were being reinforced by the Council of Trent. Such a milieu, and the themes which it emphasised, would have largely been outside of his day-to-day frame of reference. In seeking the aid of the Holy See, Sulaqa was not denying his own heritage or no longer acting in the East Syriac tradition, but was seeking

18 Origins and early development

a readjustment of his ecclesial position which permitted him to act as head of the Church of the East as 'patriarch in resistance'. This is important to note, for as the Chaldean community developed between Latin and East Syriac traditions, it had to come to some understanding of its place in the Christian world overall and how it related to its particular ecclesial heritage.

What principally complicated the relationship between the Holy See and the proto-Chaldeans was the question of whether this was a return of part of the East Syriac church to communion with the Roman Patriarch, union between two churches or a reunion of churches? The twentieth century Chaldean scholar-priest Yusif Habbi concluded that for the Holy See, it was a return to communion, and conducted in such a manner to emphasise that a reunion of ecclesiastical offices and organisation was necessary (Habbi 1966, 99).

When we consider the independence of East Syriac ecclesial life from the Synod of Dadisho in 424, the notion of the need to fulfil Latin procedures to confirm Sulaqa's position as patriarch may have seemed doubly remarkable when the Church of the East had for so long survived and acted independently of the papacy (cf. Habbi 1966, 200). Moreover, we might consider the East Syriac circumstances as quite particular when compared with other Eastern Christian communities who were geographically closer and more readily accessible to members of the Latin world. This isolation of an apostolic church apart from widespread engagement with the Latin church demonstrated an alternative type of ecclesial organisation which survived without the oversight of the Holy See.

For the proto-Chaldean community in approaching the Holy See, this was not a context of seeking reunion or abjuration of erroneous belief, but of re-engaging with the Holy See after a long absence and gaining support to rectify a difficulty in ecclesiastical organisation. However, for the Holy See, there was no doubt of the need for rectifying an issue – this in terms of returning from error and reuniting to the fullness of the Faith as held by the Latin church (Habbi 1966, 212). This distinction is important, as it clarifies the position of the East Syriac tradition and its understanding of self into the sixteenth century: its Christology and orthodoxy remained consistent from the fifth century and did not require any adjustment.

With Sulaqa emerging out of an East Syriac community with relatively limited geographic and ecclesial horizons as of the sixteenth century, it is unclear as to his level of awareness of the intricacies of the positions which his community held to during earlier eras where greater ecclesiological reflection was possible. Moreover, it seems unlikely Sulaqa would necessarily accept the jurisdiction of the pope over his patriarchal leadership as anything more than a legitimate if convenient method to grant him sufficient ecclesiastical rank to return to Mesopotamia as head of the non-hereditary East Syriac faction. Sulaqa perhaps regarded his engagement with the pope as akin to the rôle which the Roman patriarch had in patristic times as an arbiter in matters of ecclesiological disagreement (Murre-van den Berg 2005, 315). Coming from a tradition which had developed a sense of its ecclesial jurisdiction derived at least in part from its missionary exploits (and these as proof of the patriarch's authority), Sulaqa likely saw little need to accept the juridical authority of the contemporary pope and to defer to him indefinitely.

Origins and early development 19

This is disputed by contemporary Chaldean scholars, however. Albert Abouna suggests that Sulaqa and his associates were well aware of the expected requirements for communion with the Latin church being 'not simple people'. The decision to engage with Latin representatives was preferred to those of the Byzantine church because the Latins were considered to be more similar theologically (Abouna 2013).[5] The contacts between the Byzantines and members of the Church of the East were, by the sixteenth century, likely limited due to geographical distance and the complications of Ottoman occupation. Byzantine expansion in Central Asia was not unheard of, so there were some possibilities of connections with the East Syriacs at this juncture (cf. Dauvillier 1953, passim).

East Syriac perspectives on the Petrine See

As East Syriac expansion until the fourteenth century had largely been eastward was there still, by the sixteenth century, an accurate and reliable awareness of the distinctive features of both East Syriac and Latin ecclesiologies and their appreciations of the Petrine ministry? According to the nineteenth century Chaldean patriarch Ebedjesu V Khayyath (1894–1900), there was a consistent awareness of Petrine primacy derived from several Syriac sources. Initially from St Ephrem, insofar as he greatly remarks on the significance of St Peter in his works, and in Narsai (late fourth–late fifth centuries), who compares the authority endowed on Peter as akin to that of Moses. The editor of Khayyath's work concludes that 'l'Église nestorienne a toujours cru, sans jamais varier sur ce point, à la primauté de juridiction de saint Pierre sur toute l'Église'. These comments come from an author compiling his arguments at a time of consolidating an Eastern Catholic Chaldean identity strongly supportive of the Tridentine ecclesiological model of a Catholic of Church rites, under the leadership of a Supreme Pontiff. The comments are indicative that Petrine primacy was recognised in East Syriac texts even if there was not widespread awareness or acceptance of these arguments (Khayyath 1896, 137–41).

An account of earlier Church of the East-Holy See interaction which mirrored, to an extent, Sulaqa's case, is the thirteenth-century travelogue of Rabban Sawma, an East Syriac Turkic monk, during his visit to Rome (Budge 1928). Sawma's account provides some indication of contemporary East Syriac ecclesiological concerns regarding the Petrine office and the Christology of the church in the West. Sawma's visit came at a time when the Church of the East was still a significant institution in the socio-political life of Eurasian societies especially under the Mongols.[6] Sawma was a senior monk and was accompanied by his colleague Markos as they journeyed from their residence in northern China throughout Asia with the intention of visiting Jerusalem. Markos was elected patriarch – as Yahballaha III – during their travels. The new patriarch asked Sawma to continue his sojourn and visit Rome (Budge 1928, 172–3ff.; Labourt 1908a, 559).

Following his arrival, Sawma met initially with a group of cardinals and latterly Pope Nicholas IV (1288–1292) (Budge 1928, 56–63, 75–83). A key aspect of the meetings was Christological discussion. The summary of proceedings in Budge's

20 *Origins and early development*

translation shows both sides calling into question the accordance of the others' beliefs with their understanding of orthodox Christology as derived from church councils to the fifth century. Murre-van den Berg, following a Syriac text of the Chaldean Vincentian priest Paul Bedjan, infers that during these meetings the cardinals largely accepted the rectitude of Sawma's beliefs (Murre-van den Berg 2006b, 383 nn. 34, 390, 391 75; Bedjan 1895):

> During that same discussion Rabban Sauma produced a traditional 'Nestorian' confession, in which two qnume (besides two natures and one person) are distinguished in Jesus Christ, a statement which surprisingly goes unnoticed by the cardinals.
>
> (Murre-van den Berg 2006b, 383)

This is curious and indicative that the Latin surprise at receiving an East Syriac cleric perhaps overrode their desire to be very particular about his community's theological persuasion. During the meetings, discussion also encompassed the filioque clause – the belief that the Holy Spirit proceeds from the Father and the Son – in the Creed which the East Syriacs traditionally did not include in their professions of faith. This was, according to Budge's translation, not aggressively debated. Perhaps there was insufficient interest in questioning the Christology of a community whose representatives showed great deference to the pope. Ecclesiological perceptions were emerging of a sister church geographically if not theologically distant. The Latin community was aware of the distinctiveness of the Byzantine ecclesiastical identity from the Latin, but this did not necessarily mean a difference existed between it and the East Syriac tradition. The perceived remoteness and age of the community in Mesopotamia and beyond was indicative of its holding fast to traditions and Christology from a time prior to substantial ecclesial division in the Christian world.

It is not made apparent, however, as to the extent of Latin awareness of the Christological context of Sawma's beliefs. The conversation did not touch on Nestorius, for example, which emphasised both contemporary Latin understanding of what the Church of the East was and represented and East Syriac self-identity at the time. Furthermore, Pope Nicholas IV gave communion personally to Sawma on Palm Sunday 1288, which is indicative of a perception of the genuinely apostolic, valid and licit nature of Sawma's beliefs and clerical status and the community which he represented. It may have been the case that the Latin perspective in the thirteenth century was to bring Sawma into communion with the Holy See, and there was no clearer way of affirming this than through receiving the Eucharist from the Pope. Taking communion was a first step and with a long-term plan to firmly bring East Syriac Christological perspectives into accordance with those held by the Latin Church.

The culmination of the engagement with the Holy See appears to have been a union confirmed in a letter of 7 April 1288 but, as I have noted previously, this did not last (J. Richard 1977, 109). From the Latin perspective it may simply have been granting the benefit of the doubt to Sawma for his acceptance of the pope as head of the church in the West and thus someone with whom normatively the Latin church should be in communion.

Sawma presumably considered that the pope's authority and jurisdiction could extend only to the church in the West alone (Murre-van den Berg 2006a, 390 n. 74). This disavowal of the Petrine primacy of jurisdiction should be seen in the context of the then still extant reach of the Church of the East's ecclesiastical organisation throughout Asia, the geographical distance of these ecclesial provinces from Rome and the limits of papal ability to extend ecclesial influence into those areas in which the Church of the East was sole bearer of the Christian tradition. The expectation of the Holy See to affect the Church of the East's ecclesiology and its understanding of where the highest authority in the universal Christian oikumene subsisted, and the acceptance of the pope as this source of jurisdiction and authority, may well have seemed a rather obtuse issue of limited relevance to the day-to-day administration of the East Syriac community.

Furthermore, there does not appear to have been a sustained consensual view of the nature of primacy within the East Syriac *milieu*. One of the most comprehensive assessments comes from Murre-van den Berg's work on the international nature of the Church of the East (2005). She considers that the Church of the East held to a multiplicity of perspectives on the place of primacy in the universal Christian community and that no one East Syriac position was defined and maintained from the Late Antique to early modern periods. However, Murre-van den Berg affirms that prevailing themes were consistently present: first, the necessity of some form of union with the Roman Patriarchate as one of the great sees of the early Christian world. However, within this relationship the contemporary Catholicos-Patriarch of Seleucia-Ctesiphon would retain the *de facto* if not *de jure* supremacy of honour and authority. Second, the framing of their ecclesiastical relationship in a way that the link with the Roman patriarch was perceived to be more significant than with any other such as Antioch or Alexandria. This was perhaps largely due to the awareness of the limited ecclesial or temporal influence which these patriarchates held within Muslim-dominated societies. Third, there was no apparent notion that the varying Christological emphases of the patriarchates was a central issue of concern as to permit or deny communion. Nevertheless, these themes and their implementation as essential ecclesiological aspects of East Syriac identity were dependent on the strength of contemporary East Syriac ecclesiastical organisation, the interests of the contemporary religious élite and their ability to enforce these views, the East Syriac patriarch's interests and style of managing the community – whether more monarchical or conciliar in approach – and the degree of interaction with the Holy See and interest in its ecclesiological model.

If in 1553 Julius III and his advisers had a strong awareness of the precedent set by Nicholas IV for engaging with East Syriac leaders, then they may have built on that thirteenth-century model for gaining the adherence of the Sulaqite community in the sixteenth century. The Latin approach could be summarised as engagement through points of issue on ecclesiastical organisation and then subsequently to encourage consideration of why the Holy See's position on Christology

22 *Origins and early development*

and theology in general was essential for those in union with the Holy See to hold. Fourth, leading to a gradual accretion of aspects of ecclesiology and identity to reflect the standards and model which was expected by the Holy See.

From the East Syriac perspective, it may have been that the status of the Catholicos-Patriarch as head of all the churches of the east was considered a similar position as that possessed by the Holy See as patriarch of the Western Christian oikumene. This view seems to have been emphasised by Rabban Sawma in his meetings in Rome when 'Mar Papa' Nicholas IV himself noted the leadership role which the institution of the papacy purported to hold over the universal Christian community (Budge 1928, 177–8, 191, 196). This in contrast to Byzantine ecclesiology, which affirmed that ecclesial authority was manifested through an ecumenical council and not in the office of one man.

Nevertheless, some deference to the papacy as an institution appears to have been believed to be necessary, as the pope gave Sawma a bull permitting the East Syriac patriarch to govern the Christians of the East and confirmed Sawma as the Visitor-General in the patriarch's jurisdiction (Budge 1928, 196). Whether this was, from Sawma's perspective, a mere formality or expression of goodwill from the pope may never be known, but it shows the inter-relation between the jurisdictions of West and East could be reaffirmed with relative ease. It also indicates that Nicholas IV, Benedict XI and their advisers assumed the Church of the East as holding to a complementary view of the other's ecclesial community as a partner in international Christian life.

The early Chaldean Catholic community and Sulaqa's legacy

The confirmation of Sulaqa as patriarch and the necessary ceremonies to affect this were not concluded immediately following his arrival in Rome in November 1552. In fact, it was not until February 1553 that he made a profession of faith which was considered to be in accord with Latin Tridentine belief (Habbi 1966, 107–8). The entire process was concluded in April 1553 when Sulaqa was elevated to the patriarchate.

An open and largely unknown question is what Sulaqa hoped to achieve in the long term when he was in a situation of seeking rectification of his clerical position but not necessarily of desiring an all-encompassing commitment to the Holy See's vision for ecclesial organisation. Once the latter process was set in motion, there was effectively no turning back other than breaking with the Holy See's vision.

In attending upon the pope, Sulaqa gained a source of legitimisation for clerical rank sufficient to act as head of the East Syriac community. This link with the contemporary pope by extension granted Sulaqa and his successors partnerships with Latin institutions which became substantial influences upon the development of the Chaldean community and of the East Syriac tradition as a whole. Furthermore, it granted him at least theoretically a degree of protection by the Holy See over his activities: he had become the pope's man in Mesopotamia. The granting of senior ecclesiastical rank to Sulaqa was vital to shore up his position for his return home

Origins and early development 23

as – unbeknownst to the Holy See at the time of his consecration – the legitimate, if hereditary, patriarch Shemon VII still held office. It had been conveyed to the pope that Shemon was incapacitated (Wilmshurst 2011, 299; Baumer 2006, 248). This situation implied that Sulaqa and his supporters were very determined to wrest authority over the Church of the East away from those who held power.

The licit nature of Chaldean activity was given strength through the consecration of new bishops. Also, it legitimised the Chaldean community in the sight of local Ottoman administrators. Retrospectively, the Holy See was concerned by the lawfulness of raising Sulaqa to the patriarchate given it had been thought justified owing to the death of the contemporary Patriarch of the Church of the East. When it was discovered that this was not the case – he was still alive – it caused some consternation, especially as it supposed the Holy See had, as a result, acted in an illegitimate manner and to the detriment of the emerging Latin-East Syriac relationship. It is possible that it was considered acceptable to proceed in this way, as the established method of hereditary succession to the patriarchate was itself contrary to canon law.

Nonetheless, I suggest that perhaps the Sulaqites sought a return to a more just and stronger model of church governance: when the number of suitable patriarchal relations declined in the line of hereditary succession, the church's centralised authority could weaken (cf. Baumer 2006, 233). I also suggest the reduction in the geographical sphere in which the church operated led to altered perceptions of what was attainable for the community with fewer resources. A smaller geographical sphere in which to organise the church also would lead to the growth of more intensified and varied personal relationships. These rivalries were heightened due to hereditary succession and limited the opportunities for clergy to advance to the highest office and senior episcopal positions (cf. Baumer 2006, 247). The rôle of monastic involvement is also significant, as during the church's missionary expansion they were at the forefront of nearly all activities. By the time the church had declined, the monks perhaps sought to restore their positions of influence. Moreover, as they were somewhat isolated by nature, the opportunity for dissent towards the authority could have been co-ordinated in their more closed monastic environment. Ambitious clergy seeking to gain office to direct the church and unable to avail themselves of the usual opportunity for advancement in the episcopate would at least have a base for personal spiritual and educational advancement within the monastery.

In summary, we can note Sulaqa sought rectification of his ecclesial position but it seems unlikely to have understood this as becoming a new ecclesial identity. He was to be the leader of the East Syriac faction in union with the Holy See, and with the long-term plan to aggregate all the East Syriac dioceses and people to the remit of his leadership. This type of arrangement came to characterise the Chaldeans into the present as part of the East Syriac tradition and distinguished chiefly by their, at least official, acceptance of the status of the pope as head of the universal church.

When Sulaqa engaged with the Holy See, he likely did not envisage the development of a different type of East Syriac community and that which existed in the

24 *Origins and early development*

ecclesiological space between the Church of the East and Latin church. However, his meetings in Rome had lasting impact into the twenty-first century and, as a result, two churches emerged: the Church of the East and the Chaldean Catholic Church. Both largely share very similar Christological and theological beliefs and liturgical practices but remain set apart in ecclesiastical organisation through two patriarchal lineages.

Chaldean Catholic identity development in the sixteenth century

A separate ecclesial organisational identity among the East Syriac community, as so far as such existed from the 1550s, may have formed and been diffused among those loyal to Sulaqa. The dioceses of Salmas, Urmia and Erbil which supported him were all traditionally strong centres of East Syriac religious life. Sulaqa's position was further reinforced by the fifty doctors of the East Syriac élite who attended him in his travels via Jerusalem to Rome (Murre-van den Berg 2009, 155; Babakhan 1900, 489). However, the construction of a specifically Chaldean religious identity did not take place at the same time as the establishment of the Sulaqite patriarchal line other than to form in opposition to the Church of the East and to identify with the Holy See as a link of episcopal legitimacy.

The formalisation of the Latin perception about the Chaldeans as a distinct ecclesial identity was held in the context of the term *natio*. It should not be understood as the Holy See having an awareness of the specific national or ethnic character of those who became Chaldeans. *Natio* was used from a Latin perspective to describe a group which had a shared ecclesial identity drawn from a distinctive cultural *milieu* and according to the geographical and political circumstances in which it was found. The term was linked also to that of *ritus*, *traditio* and *Ecclesia* which were, in the post-Tridentine era, used interchangeably (Faris 2002, 283).

Natio had a wider application in the context of the Ottoman Empire which Heyberger outlines: 'Le terme de <<nation>> désignait indifféremment des groupes qui se distinguaient par leur costume, leur religion, leur langue, leur organisation sociale, leur mode de vie ou par pleusieurs de ces critères' (Heyberger 1994, 63). In this sense, it was not a term exclusive to Christian communities and could be equally applied to Kurds, Arabs, Jews and so forth. *Natio* was – if nothing else – an attempt at sociological classification of the plurality of Ottoman society to ensure a means to administer such diverse communities. *Natio* was reinforced through the millet system, under which non-Muslims were governed by the Ottomans. Here it attained a meaning which, in the context of Eastern Christians in union with the Holy See, aided the adoption of the Tridentine concept of a universal Catholic Church of rites – which were largely coterminous with *natio*.

Sulaqa's successors

Despite the initial enthusiasm for Sulaqa's consecration, support was found only in Amid and Mardin for Yohannan VII on his return to Mesopotamia (Baumer

Origins and early development 25

2006, 248). Support was particularly strong in Amid, from where the Capuchin Franciscans organised their missions and where Yohannan VII established his patriarchal headquarters (Teule 2011c). Perhaps, in his absence, some were found lukewarm in their earlier support for upsetting the *status quo*. Despite the despatch of two Dominican advisers to assist in the consolidation of Sulaqa's work, ecclesial separatism declined in popularity (Tisserant 1931, cols 228–9). Sulaqa came to an ignominious end in 1555 when he was murdered by being drowned. It was later alleged that Shemon VII had bribed the Ottoman authorities 200 gold pieces to carry out the deed (Baumer 2006, 248; Babakhan 1900, 489). Whether this was, in fact, the exact set of circumstances, such an accusation is indicative of the strength of feeling and intensity of relationships among contemporary East Syriac factions. The event continues to have resonance, as Sulaqa is regarded as a martyr by many Chaldeans.

Sulaqa's successors who attempted to maintain a link with the Latin missionaries and communion with the pope were (cf. Wilmshurst 2011, 345, 477):

- Abdisho IV (1555–1570)
- Yahballah IV (1570–1580)[7]
- Shemon IX (1580–1600)
- Shemon X (1600–1638)
- Shemon XI (1638–1656)

There was a strong Latin missionary interest in maintaining the Sulaqite line, with Abdisho IV closely controlled by the Holy See. This was perhaps in recognition of his intelligence and ecclesiological knowledge (cf. Lemmens OFM 1926b, 18–19). Nonetheless, as Abdisho was invited to present his profession of faith at the Council of Trent, this would seem to deny any suggestion of disloyalty to the pope either in jurisdictional or theological terms (Le Coz 1995, 329; Labourt 1908a, 559; Dib 1914, 25).

However, the movement of successive patriarchs to residences in remote locations around northern Mesopotamia inhibited their contacts with Latin missionaries. Abdisho initially established the patriarchal residence in the monastery of Mar Jacob the Recluse near Seert, whilst Shemon IX moved to Salmas, and his successor, Shemon X, left for Kochanes in the Hakkari mountains. He did this despite expressing a desire to visit Rome to express his loyalty to the pope and to ensure the education of his clergy in the Papal States (Teule 2011a; Le Coz 1995, 329; Wilmshurst 2011, 317; Labourt 1908a, 560).

Wilmshurst suggests the gradual geographical retreat was to avoid representatives of the legitimist patriarch and the Holy See engaging with the Chaldeans (Wilmshurst 2011, 322–3). Baumer argues it was to avoid Ottoman persecution for having brought into their Empire agents of the dominant socio-religious actor in Europe, and a combination of these factors was likely to have been the catalyst (Baumer 2006, 248). Labourt's suggestion that the Turco-Persian Wars of the early seventeenth century limited the patriarch's freedom of movement and caused interruptions in communication with Latin representatives is perhaps

26 *Origins and early development*

the most likely (Labourt 1908a, 560; Wilmshurst 2000, 25; Murre-van den Berg 1999, 235).

One effort to retain the Holy See's confidence came from Shemon XI, who wrote to Pope Innocent X (1644–1655) in 1653 stating that 40,000 families were loyal to him across twenty-eight 'districts' (Wilmshurst 2011, 349; Lampart 1966, 233). This attempt to impress the pope does not seem to have had the desired effect, however, and as the Latins became aware of the illegitimate way in which the Sulaqa line originated (through contacts with the legitimist East Syriac patriarchal line), there was likely far less concern for advancing the Sulaqite patriarchal claimant as the lawful East Syriac leader. In 1672, the Sulaqites finally ended attempts at communion.[8]

I suggest there was, for the Sulaqites, no religious reason not to return to the belief patterns of the Church of the East. The development of a separate ecclesial identity was not sufficiently observed to ensure the widespread acceptance of post-Ephesian Christology and Latin ecclesiological beliefs as defined at the Council of Trent. Instead, the Sulaqite community retained its traditional position and became a narrowly focused group extremely limited in their geographical reach and religious influence. This was the case until a resurgence from the nineteenth century following the intervention of Anglican, Latin, protestant and Russian missionaries.

It should be emphasised that from 1553 to 1650, the Chaldean ecclesial structures were weakened through little notion of how an Eastern Christian community in union with the pope was supposed to develop. The main other example of an emerging Eastern Catholic ecclesial community of a Syriac tradition were the Maronites. The Maronite example may have provided a basic outline for the construction of a Chaldean Eastern Catholic rite ecclesiology which could be adapted to the particular requirements of the Mesopotamian Christian *milieu* (Heyberger 1994, 232–9).

Nevertheless, the creation of ecclesial structures with a Chaldean ethos remained challenging. This was based on a lack of interest in maintaining 'Chaldean-ness' from those East Syriacs who had initially sought support from the pope (Valognes 1994, 433). The East Syriac leadership's efforts in attaining union with the pope and pursuing a distinctive Chaldean identity were not always met with support from the laity or other clergy: Shemon XII's correspondence with Pope Alexander VII (1655–1667) in 1658 was strongly criticised by his congregations (Labourt 1908a, 560; Badger 1852, I:149). The acceptance of Tridentine beliefs for the governance of the universal church and the derivation of ecclesial authority from the Holy See appears to have been a key stumbling block. This was an issue which detracted from the independence that the Church of the East had enjoyed for most of its existence.

The acceptance of contemporary Christological and ecclesiological trends by the East Syriac-Chaldean faction's leadership was a requirement by the Holy See for their being accepted into communion. Also, there was a sense that personal loyalty to the contemporary pope was obligatory, as epitomised by the Chaldean patriarchal claimant's normative attendance in Rome to receive the pallium. This

Origins and early development 27

personal interaction with the pope was an opportunity for the Holy See to impress the need for an avowed Tridentine ecclesial identity among the Chaldeans (cf. Lemmens OFM 1926a, 214–15). Nevertheless, was this such an apparently simple procedure? Would the Chaldean leadership have viewed affirming a Latin Credo and receiving the pallium as bestowing them authority and communion with the Holy See? If the Chaldean patriarchal claimants were fully aware of the traditional status of their forbears and the influence they wielded throughout Asia, did they consider they lacked true apostolicity, valid clerical orders or the authority to assert their own jurisdiction? How could the Chaldeans become, in effect, a junior partner in an ecclesial community whose leader purported to be the Vicar of Christ on Earth given their forbears had once held a far wider geographical jurisdiction than the Latin church? Further, the pope viewed the Chaldean community not as a church but as an ecclesial rite under his overarching jurisdiction.

I suggest that rapprochement on issues of ecclesiastical organisation and Christology became the focus of Latin missionary work from the late sixteenth century. This was in order to combat any doubts as to the superiority of the Tridentine paradigm and in attempts to align East Syriac with Tridentine ecclesiology. By the late nineteenth century, an Eastern Catholic Chaldean rite fully cognisant of such a Tridentine influenced identity was moulded through sustained education as to what was considered acceptable ecclesiology.

However, Latin efforts were complicated because missionaries were unlikely to have been entirely certain of the normative nature of the Chaldean community. The intention was *not* to create more Latin Christians, but to pursue union with those outside of the jurisdiction of the pope whilst ensuring they retained their liturgical practices and aspects of ecclesial identity which were in accord with Tridentine ecclesiology. The close ecclesial bond which the Chaldean Church came to have with the papacy was, and is, a key marker of its identity. Further, it is suggestive that this bond originated as a result of a desire to transcend any theological controversies by instead promoting the more simplistic ecclesiological link with the pope as the means to form a union.

Latin presence in Mesopotamia (I)

The Latin presence in Mesopotamia derived from two main factors: (1) the expectation of widespread change of allegiance among the East Syriac population during the mid-sixteenth century to union with the Holy See and (2) the increasingly strong Augustinian and Carmelite presences in Persia and along the trade routes through the Indian Ocean to South Asia and China (F. Richard 1990). The connections with India and Persia reflected the traditional links the Church of the East had in these regions such as Basra, Isfahan and Kerala, which were key points on trade routes and subsequently areas of Latin expansion (Flannery 2013, 78–81).

The impetus of Latin expansion originated from the post-Tridentine zeal for overseas missions and also Trent's focus upon the *Orient* to revivify native Christian communities (Heyberger 1994, 227–8ff.). With the foundation of the Propaganda in 1622, and the establishment of a Latin ecclesial presence in Baghdad

28 *Origins and early development*

in 1632, we may surmise that the missions took on a more organised manner. This establishment also segued with the increasing Ottoman military presence and attempts to definitively wrestle control of Mesopotamia from the Safavid Persians. Growing Ottoman dominance and relative openness to Western powers meant Latin agents could proceed into Mesopotamia.

Timoteo Perez (1632–1639), first Latin Vicar for Babylon (Baghdad), represented the Holy See's interests in Mesopotamia and held tentative oversight for Latin engagements with the East Syriac communities (Filoni 2008, 24). Latin efforts to gain adherents to a Chaldean ecclesial identity were particularly successful in the regions surrounding Mosul and Amid from the mid-seventeenth century (Wilmshurst 2000, 26). Nevertheless, given the internecine conflicts occurring within the groups, and the small number of persons involved, low level political clashes and the influence of one cleric over a village affected the populace's religious affiliation and meant the Holy See's general missionary policy was difficult to direct.

It is not clear what Latin missionary policy was in the late sixteenth and early seventeenth centuries, and whether adoption of a set of theological views or a different type of ecclesiastical organisation was of greater significance to the East Syriacs. The Propaganda granted support in a general sense and encouraged mutual support between each missionary order, but on a practical basis this would vary. Those on the ground would be operating on an independent basis and following pragmatic approaches (cf. Flannery 2013, 81–2).

One may note from the missionaries' actions, coming from a post-Tridentine Catholic perspective affirming the Pope's primacy, that it was viewed as normal to approach the East Syriac patriarch in order to convince him of the rectitude of the Catholic Faith. If this goal was not reached, a focus then shifted to a lower level of bishops and priests and subsequently to the community at large (Valensi 1997, 263–4ff.).

Legitimist line of patriarchs (1591–1700)

By the early seventeenth century, the hereditary line of patriarchs who resided in and around Mosul became as active in contacts with Latin missionaries as their proto-Chaldean peers.[9] From 1610, Patriarch Elias VIII's (1591–1617) engagements resulted in Franciscans visiting him to investigate the possibility of union with the Holy See. This was followed by an invitation to the Franciscan superior at Aleppo, Tommaso da Novana, to a synod held at Amid in 1616 with the apparent purpose of initiating union (Murre-van den Berg 1999, 244; Abdoulahad and Chabot 1896, 69). If a union was created formally, it did not last beyond Elias' death the next year, most likely due to his continued public appreciation of Nestorius (Frazee 1983, 143; cf. Badger 1852, I:149).

Discussions continued under Elias IX (1617–1660), who accepted a Latin creed but commemorated Nestorius in the liturgy and denied the title of Theotokos to the Blessed Virgin (Murre-van den Berg 1999, 245). In an attempt to curry favour with the Latins, Elias IX withheld the appointment of a hereditary successor to demonstrate his desire to alter church governance in conformity with Latin practice in the appointment of bishops (Murre-van den Berg 1999, 245; Wilmshurst 2011, 326). Possibly the nature of church governance could have been overlooked were the legitimists to disavow their support for the two Christological points of contention.

Elias X (1660–1700) attempted some contact with the Holy See in 1669 but on the basis of requests for a chapel at the Holy Sepulchre in Jerusalem and an East Syriac seminary in the Papal States (Wilmshurst 2011, 326; Murre-van den Berg 1999, 246). This was perhaps an attempt to reclaim the Chapel of the Crucifixion in the Holy Sepulchre, which was permitted for East Syriac use since at least 1607 (Brock 2006, 189–90, 198).

Ottoman administrative influence

As the Church of the East consolidated its position following the attacks of Tamerlane, so the Ottomans expanded their empire in the Mediterranean and south-west Asia. The Ottomans occupied Mesopotamia in 1534, remaining in control until 1919. Their political and social influence were lasting upon all the East Syriac factions. However, from 1501–1732, the Shia Safavid dynasty in Persia was strong enough to pose as an existential threat to the Sunni Ottomans. Subsequent wars between the two empires caused a divide in the work of the East Syriac patriarchs, as dioceses were split by Ottoman-Safavid jurisdictions (Baumer 2006, 248). The divide also prevented a contiguous attempt by Latin missionaries to obtain the ecclesial allegiance of the East Syriac communities and develop a homogeneous Chaldean community.

The impetus for Latin political and religious advances in the Ottoman Empire were reinforced through the Catholic European military victories at Lepanto (1571), Vienna (1683) and Belgrade (1716). These successes were only partly responsible for these advances, as Latin missionaries gained the opportunity to act in the Ottoman Empire. In 1569, France concluded a series of treaties with the Sublime Porte, known as the 'Capitulations', to the mutual benefit of the two powers. One aspect of the treaty was to grant freedom of movement to Latin agents within Ottoman territories, which extended French influence in the Levant and Mesopotamia (Frazee 1983, 67).

The Ottoman Empire's multi-confessional nature presented the ruling élite with the challenges of maintaining superior legal status for Muslims whilst also providing a framework to administer non-Muslims. The non-Muslim communities were divided, according to confession, into *millets* and granted the right to govern themselves with their own customs and practices.

The Church of the East was placed under the Armenian millet in 1461. The Armenian millet extended into those areas of the eastern Ottoman Empire where East Syriac communities could be found. This perhaps seemed a reasonable administrative alteration, especially given the relatively small size of the East Syriac communities (Le Coz 1995, 311–12). The effects of such a system upon the East Syriac community had been experienced under the Sasanian Empire. In

30 *Origins and early development*

the early fifth century, Shah Yazdgard I (399–420) granted the Church of the East status as a 'legitimate minority group' and the patriarch the authority to govern the community according to their own customs (Gillman and Klimkeit 1999, 113). Following the Arab invasions, such a system of control for each non-Muslim community continued and was reinforced by the Islamic *dhimma* concept. The *dhimma* paradigm encompasses those 'people of the book' in Islamic jurisprudence whose religious liberties are guaranteed in law following the payment of the *jizya* (poll) tax. Quite apart from the economic disadvantage, the gradual deterioration of Christian communities resulted from the emphasis upon their lower status – being considered qualitatively different in legal matters – and regular, if not consistently violent, incidents of persecution experienced under Ottoman rule.

Ottoman Mesopotamia was divided into three major provinces centred on the cities of Baghdad, Mosul and Basra. The northern area of Ottoman jurisdiction – the province of Sharizoor – was administered largely by autonomous Kurdish tribes (Tripp 2007, 8–9). Ottoman administration should not necessarily be considered as detrimental to East Syriac life. A renewal in Christian literary production from the seventeenth century is perhaps evidence of the benefits which the combination of Ottoman rule and a Latin missionary presence engendered (Ainsworth 1841, 52; Rassam 2010, 105; Murre-van den Berg 2006a, 10–11). Further, the Chaldeans and other Eastern Catholics were protected to an extent, as the Holy See's influence via the French diplomatic corps could alleviate the position of the communities. However, at a local level, some compromises with the Ottoman authorities were very difficult to escape, and were viewed by some Christians as a means of advancement.

The establishment of the Josephite patriarchal line in Amid

For the Chaldeans, the era of 1670–1750 was defined by the establishment of a third line of claim to the East Syriac patriarchate at Amid under Capuchin Franciscan direction, alongside the existing Sulaqite and hereditary lines, with each purporting to represent the heritage of the undivided Church of the East. Initially, the rejuvenation of the Latin presence in Amid was intended to restore a previously strong Chaldean diocese which had fallen back under the Church of the East's influence (Badger 1852, I:150). With missionary success came the intention of developing a stable patriarchal line for the Chaldeans loyal to the Holy See and under close Capuchin direction. Capuchins were present in northern Mesopotamia from 1636, and having consolidated their mission in Mosul were in a position to expand their activities by the 1670s (Fiey OP 1965, I:56).

Shimun XIII Denha (1662–1700) had ended the Sulaqite relationship with the Holy See in 1672 (Baumer 2006, 248; Bello OAOC 1939, 5). Thus, until 1681 and the formal establishment of the new Chaldean patriarchal line, a nine-year gap existed whereby there was no patriarch, recognised by the Holy See, among the potentially Chaldean parties. The increasing preponderance of Latin missionaries ensured the Chaldeans were not without any spiritual support and direction during this period. It is quite probable that some returned to the allegiance of the Church of the East, but the exact nature of this remains unknown. It should be thought neither that a Chaldean identity existed only among those who had entered into communion with the Holy See nor that those who were in communion had completely disavowed their beliefs which accorded with their background in the Church of the East. The Chaldean community was not created *ex nihilo*, but primarily through gaining the allegiance of those within the East Syriac community who were sympathetic to the idea of union with the Holy See and/or the advantages which association with the Latin missionaries might bring them.

Aside from restoring the Chaldean patriarchate, the expansion of the Capuchin mission in Amid also took place in the context of the recent centenary of the conclusion of the Council of Trent in 1663, and the consolidation of Eastern Catholic populations in the Levant. The perception that it was an opportune time for a rejuvenation of the Chaldean community seems likely to have been a theme not far from the minds of the Capuchins (Lampart 1966, 87–90). There was perhaps also a level of competition between the Latins working in the Levant, Mesopotamia and Persia to advance the cause of their own religious orders.

The leader of the new patriarchal line was Joseph, the legitimist Metropolitan of Amid. His intention of entering into union with the Holy See is found in a letter he wrote in October 1670 affirming his full accord with Tridentine ecclesiological and Christological views (Lampart 1966, 95–7). He proved zealous for advocating for a Chaldean community, and as of 1672, he was active outside of his own diocese, visiting the East Syriacs of Mardin to this end (Lampart 1966, 98).

Following Metropolitan Joseph's affiliation with a Chaldean identity, he and the Capuchins came into conflict with the legitimist patriarch, Elias X. Elias sought to overthrow Joseph through the intervention of the Ottoman authorities. Nonetheless, Joseph was granted recognition by the civil power in 1677 as head of the Chaldean community.[10]

Following secular approval, Joseph was granted religious authority from the Holy See as 'patriarch of the Chaldean nation deprived of its patriarch' in 1681 (Abdoulahad and Chabot 1896, 71–7). The somewhat unclear nature of this title, and the authority and/or jurisdiction which it granted, reflected the contemporary ecclesiological theory particular to the East Syriac situation. It appears to have been based in the notional hope that at a future time the two patriarchal lineages within the sphere of Latin missionary activity – legitimist and Josephite – could be reconciled into a single line. (Wilmshurst 2011, 331) The legitimist patriarch retained the cachet of *legitimacy*, and this lawful status was greatly valued by the Latins. Perhaps it was considered that, were the legitimist patriarch to die, his community could be persuaded to enter into union with the Holy See under the Josephite claimant. Or, alternatively, that the legitimist patriarch could himself be brought into union with the Holy See and the need for the Josephite line would cease (cf. Badger 1852, I:150). The patriarchal title also reflects the Holy See's desire to care for those Chaldeans who had previously been loyal to the Sulaqite patriarchal claimant. With Shimun XIII Denha ending his relationship with the Holy See in 1672, those who still desired union with the Holy See were *the Chaldean nation deprived of a patriarch.*

32 *Origins and early development*

As of the 1670s, the Tridentine paradigm imbued and expressed by Latin missionaries appears to have ensured that the Josephite line had a greater sense of purpose, self-awareness of what was required of an Eastern Christian community in union with the pope, and likelihood of success. I suggest this was the time by which it was well understood that the ideal formation of a universal church was one with a plurality of ecclesial rites. This stands opposed to one consisting of a communion of churches under the oversight of the pope as had been advanced in Latin ecclesiology prior to Trent. Joseph I's letter to the pope of October 1670, for example, emphasises especially the union with the Holy See and submission to the pope's authoritative jurisdiction. Albeit written under the guidance of the Capuchins, the letter reflects also their awareness of Tridentine ecclesiology:

> Praetera firmiter credo et suscipio quaecumque docet Ecclesia Catholica Romana et tradit circa septem Sacramenta novae legis et amplector omnia Concilia et omnia quaecumque constituerent in eis Patres ex voluntate Summi Pontificis Capitis Ecclesiae . . . Et tandem ipsum Deum deprecor ut me dignetur adiuvare et faciat ut teneam quod dixi et scripsi firmiter exequendo, et Ecclesia redeat ad gremium matris suae pristinae et oves ad Pastorem qui est Summus Pontifex sedens in Ecclesia Romana.
>
> (Lampart 1966, 97)

The pursuit of a Tridentine influenced Chaldean identity was strongly pursued under the new patriarch and his successors Joseph II (1696–1713) and Joseph III (1713–1757). This was an identity expressed, for example, through Latin devotions such as the Rosary (Murre-van den Berg 1999, 258). It seems Latin efforts were aided by the Josephite patriarchs' leadership qualities: Joseph I's charismatic personality attracted Christians from as far as Baghdad to hear his preaching; Joseph II was remarkable for his pastoral efforts during an outbreak of plague in 1713 and died whilst ministering among the faithful (Abdoulahad and Chabot 1896, 86–7; Wilmshurst 2011, 331).

During Joseph II's rule, Latin theological trends were firmly established due to his interest in their application to the Chaldeans. He outlined his thought in the *Book of the Magnet* and the *Book of the Polished Mirror*. These works emphasised a Tridentine ecclesiology and the necessity of East Syriac union with the Holy See (Teule 2011b, 435–6). Latin influence was also seen in his consideration of sacramental theology, where he emphasised the distinction between mortal and venial sins which was uncommon in the Church of the East (Teule 2004, 235).

Joseph II's expositions were related to the influence of precise delineations in theology, which were expected of all clergy in union with the Holy See after the Council of Trent. A Scholastic approach was considered necessary to defend and uphold the Faith due to protestant attacks and a desire to distinguish between the theology of the Byzantine patriarchates and the Holy See (Teule 2011b, 436; Heyberger 1994, 435).

The Josephite patriarchs' openness to Latin theological influence extended further than any earlier Chaldean group due to frequent visits of their clergy to

Europe, especially the Papal States. Joseph I, for example, spent five months in Rome in 1675 as he grew in his position of responsibility for the Chaldeans of Amid prior to his elevation as patriarch. From 1694 until his death in 1707, he resided in Rome, as he was too ill to conduct his office (Abdoulahad and Chabot 1896, 84–5). He must have absorbed the culture and nature of Tridentine ecclesiology and would have gained a greater understanding of what was proposed for Eastern Catholics.

Whilst Latin efforts focused on the Josephites, the relations with the legitimist line continued under the tutelage of the Discalced Carmelites and Dominicans (Frazee 1983, 210; Coakley and Taylor 2009, 1–2). The Latins presumably maintained this level of presence throughout Mesopotamia to ensure the Chaldean project succeeded in some form. The ties of family and tribe were powerful influences in the retention of association with one or other East Syriac community. It is telling, for example, that in the absence of a key Josephite leader men should revert to the Church of the East. Whilst Joseph III toured Europe in the 1720s to gain funds for the Chaldeans, in Mesopotamia, the legitimist patriarch was able to gain the affiliation of East Syriacs in Seert. Joseph appears to have made little effort to stamp his authority over the Chaldeans, leaving much work up to the Capuchins (Wilmshurst 2011, 332; Frazee 1983, 210).

This example suggests that the Catholicity of the communities was limited when not directly supported by leaders staunchly in favour of union with the Holy See and the adoption of Tridentine ecclesiology. Moreover, circumstances could change very dramatically: at the death of Joseph III in 1757, only one Josephite Chaldean bishop remained (Wilmshurst 2011, 332). Another problem for the Josephite line was securing consistent financial support. Despite the extensive European fund raising efforts of Joseph III and his successor Joseph IV (1757–1780), there was always a shortfall. It is not clear whether this was a direct result of a shortage of funding from the Holy See or the result of the further payment of taxes and bribes to the Ottoman authorities. Joseph IV, for example, was imprisoned by the Ottomans in the 1780s due to an unpaid debt of 20,000 piastres (Frazee 1983, 212).

By the 1770s, the patriarchal leadership began to stagnate, and Joseph IV appears to have lacked the stamina or desire to remain in office, gradually withdrawing from public life and resigning the patriarchate in 1780. The Holy See appointed him patriarchal administrator, and he spent the last five years of his life in Rome. This development suited both Joseph IV and the papacy, as the latter was permitted to wind down the Josephite line as pressure increased on the legitimist patriarch to enter into union with the Holy See. Due to growing popular support among the legitimists for engaging with the Latin missionaries, by the 1720s, the Patriarch Elias XII (1722–1778) was persuaded of the viability of pursuing a Chaldean identity (Frazee 1983, 210–11).

The Josephite line, for all its advantages as the first Chaldean community formed under direct Latin instruction in Mesopotamia, lacked numerical strength and legitimacy. The original patriarchal line still occupied the See of Mosul and the contemporary patriarchal residence of Rabban Hormizd monastery (Wilmshurst 2011,

34 *Origins and early development*

333). The travels and absences of patriarchs Joseph III and IV across the Middle East to Europe emphasised the very large amount of day-to-day religious work to be carried out by the lower ranking Chaldean clergy and Latin missionaries.

Joseph III's absence in particular was to the Chaldeans' detriment. They required patriarchal leadership to counter the increasingly effective missionary efforts of the Church of the East under Elias XII (Wilmshurst 2000, 27). Moreover, despite the Latin missionaries' preferences for working with the Josephites, the legitimists at least maintained their patriarch resident in Mesopotamia. However, if we consider the Chaldean project's success in the long term, this period of international travelling helped to emphasise to the Holy See and the Propaganda the vitality and persistence of the Chaldeans in looking to achieve success for their mission. If Joseph III and IV did not appreciate it at that time, they were providing a foundation on which to build the Chaldeans' future as a presence at the heart of Catholic life. The importance of supporting a literary revival, for example, should not be underestimated, especially in the context of an increasingly cosmopolitan Chaldean population throughout the Middle East from the beginning of the nineteenth century. Joseph IV assisted in the publication of liturgical works such as a Syriac-Arabic Chaldean missal (Joseph IV 1767).

Why be a Chaldean?

As Chaldean ecclesial identity emerged as an aspect of the East Syriac tradition, adherence to the faction in union with the Holy See gradually increased in popularity. I suggest there were three key factors which underpinned East Syriac interest in Chaldean identity and union with the Holy See.

First, the argument from authority and the status which the Holy See was perceived to hold within the universal church. Regardless of whether East Syriacs would accept its jurisdiction, the See of Rome, which the contemporary pope represented, was regarded to have authority derived from the apostolic era. If the concept of papal supremacy was consistently challenged by East Syriac leaders, the significant position of the Holy See in international Christian affairs was not disputed (Murre-van den Berg 2005, 306–9). Following exposition of Latin beliefs regarding authority in the universal church, unity through communion with the contemporary pope grew as an important distinguishing marker for those who asserted a Chaldean identity (Khayyath 1896, 146–8).

Second, the earnest desire to adhere to the Christian tradition as preached by Latin missionaries and to be part of the Tridentine Catholic vision. The Chaldean identity formation was an extended process from the sixteenth to nineteenth centuries, yet the maintenance of a Chaldean identity explicitly differentiated from the Church of the East was at least not initially clear for many of those East Syriacs who aggregated to the Chaldean community.

For those who had a Western-led education, and thus a broader appreciation of the Holy See's ecclesiology and Christology, the assent to enter into union with the Holy See may have been more from intellectual conviction than from spiritual, emotional or familial causes. It appears also that many were sincere in their desire

Origins and early development   35

to be in union with the papacy, and held a genuine conviction of the rectitude of Tridentine ecclesiology. Patriarch Joseph II is one example (cf. Teule 2004; Rassam 2010, 111–12).

However, with a lack of contemporary accounts (or a window into others' souls), one will unlikely ever conclusively prove if a conversion of the heart took place among Chaldean believers on a widespread scale. Such a conversion was a point of no return, and the time from which a previous affiliation was shed in favour of a new one.

In the present era, much emphasis is placed on the desires and interests of the individual, and it is more difficult to comprehend the influence which community leaders can have over a group's beliefs. Indeed, as Maggiolini notes regarding the formation of Syrian Catholic identity: 'The particularly clannish and tribal structures were in fact favouring mass conversions sustaining the fast development of new local religious communities (2012, 262). Thus, for the Chaldeans, I suggest the most likely process of conversion was assent by East Syriac leaders to the Tridentine Catholic vision of faith as preached by Latin missionaries. This was followed by the diffusion of such beliefs among the respective tribe or villages associated with each leader.

It seems likely that the conversion of the heart was limited to a few individuals, with the majority accepting the status quo for pragmatic reasons. Nevertheless, some would have had an experience related to their personal beliefs which no longer permitted them to vacillate in their allegiance: either to adhere to the Chaldean ecclesial vision or remain solely within the religious milieu of the Church of the East.

The third major factor in adherence to the Chaldean faction, and as indicated by Murre-van den Berg, was the growing separation between Aramaic and Arabic speaking East Syriacs (2009, 157). Maurice Briere's translation of a Syriac history of the monastery of Rabban Hormizd gives an example of a monk who is said to have separated from the Church of the East partly as a result of learning Arabic. The distinction in the text from his actually becoming a true Christian (from the perspective of the Chaldean author) by becoming a Catholic is clear: 'Il vécut avec des chrétiens et se mit à étudier la langue arabe; après avoir appris la lecture de l'arabe, il renonça à sa religion et devint chrétien' (Gĕ'dan 1910, 414). This separation has been maintained to the present day, as in general, Arabic speakers form a larger proportion of the Chaldeans and Syriac speakers of the Church of the East (Petrosian 2006, 127).

Those Eastern Catholic communities in the Middle East which had been established during the eighteenth century were specific conduits of Western Christian knowledge via the mediums of French, Latin and Arabic. These included the Melkite Catholic (1724), Coptic Catholic (1741) and the Syrian Catholic (1781). The spread of the use of a common language such as Arabic or Latin among the Chaldeans to engage with other churches in the Middle East permitted an exchange of ideas. This process was vital for the importation of Latin theological ideas and Western cultural and social innovations from other Eastern Catholic communities especially the Maronites.

36 *Origins and early development*

These material and intellectual benefits continued East Syriac engagement with the Holy See (Murre-van den Berg 2008, 321–2). This factor in membership of the Chaldean community also tied in with the economic advantages which membership of the Chaldeans granted in Mosul. Khoury argues, 'The most prominent among them [Christian urban elites] embraced Catholicism as a marker of affluence' (Khoury 1997, 148): affluence which was often closely tied to the use of Arabic as a means to expand one's mercantile activities.

Latin presence in Mesopotamia (II) and the unification of the Chaldean communities

From the mid-eighteenth century, Latin missionary efforts to expand the Chaldean community across Mesopotamia were increasingly successful. Wilmshurst highlights the conversion of the Metropolitan of Salmas, Shemon (1777–1789): 'Taking with him most of the Nestorians of Khosrowa and the other Christian villages in the Salmas plain [in north-eastern Mesopotamia]. Only one village, Ula, remained stubbornly Nestorian' (Wilmshurst 2000, 28, 2011, 328). The concentration of Capuchin, Dominican and Carmelite missionaries created an environment in which the Chaldean project could come to fruition (cf. Habbi 1971, 128–30).

General Latin missionary policy for the seventeenth and eighteenth centuries in Ottoman territory appears to have been directed at improving standards of clerical education among the Eastern Catholic communities and advancing a wider appreciation of their history through the collation of existing literature. The Council of Trent obliged every Catholic hierarchy to maintain seminaries and support the professional development of the clergy as an élite class which likely influenced these educational efforts in Mesopotamia and the Levant.[11]

With the increase in the Chaldean community's size, material and intellectual development, the legitimist patriarchs engaged strongly with the Latins to consider what opportunities a closer relationship with the Holy See might offer. Patriarch Elias XII, through his contacts with the Dominicans, had a profession of faith approved via the auspices of Emmanuel, the Latin Archbishop of Babylon in 1771 (Labourt 1908a, 560). Meanwhile the Sulaqite line patriarch Shemon XV (1740–1780) resident in Kochannes, also affirmed a Latin Christology (Dauvillier 1942, 373). Sulaqite allegiance was not retained beyond Shemon XV's death in 1780; his desire for union with the Holy See seemingly poorly supported among his community.

The next fifty years of East Syriac history focused on familial disputes within the legitimist line and Josephite reluctance to cede leadership of the Chaldeans as required by the Holy See. From the 1770s, explicit Christological and ecclesiological disputes, whilst used to smear opponents for political advantage, seem not to have been at the heart of contentions between the Josephites and legitimists (Baumer 2006, 248, 250). Disputes instead concentrated on the emerging claims of Yohannan Hormizd as patriarch of a united East Syriac community in union with the Holy See.

Origins and early development 37

Yohannan was born in Alqosh in 1760 and rose to influence as the *Natar Kursya* to Elias XII. Yohannan had replaced the original successor to Elias, Isho'yab, in 1776, who Yohannan asserted:

> Joined himself to the holy Church [of Rome], and six times he recanted, and the oftener he left the orthodox faith the more he used to blaspheme, and that from covetousness, and a love of money which were inherent in him.
>
> (Badger 1852, I:151)

Isho'yab also sought to gain the Holy See's support to displace his uncle, and after Elias XII's death, he became patriarch of the legitimist line as Elias XIII (1778–1804). Upon taking office, he restored the hereditary succession procedure but gained favour with the Latin missionaries by asserting a post-Ephesian Christology (Wilmshurst 2000, 29, 2011, 335), However, his Latin sympathies were merely a façade for advancing his own interests. He abandoned them as soon as the Ottomans granted him the civil recognition of patriarchal authority (Bello OAOC 1939, 11).

Yohannan became Metropolitan of Mosul in 1780 and held the Holy See's approval following his adherence to Tridentine ecclesiological and Christological norms from 1778. Subsequently, those legitimists with sympathies for union with the Holy See supported him as a patriarchal candidate in resistance. Yohannan's efforts to undermine his cousin's patriarchal leadership saw the start of a fractious twenty-year period of competition by both leaders for diocesan bishops' loyalties (Habbi 1971, 134–5; Wilmshurst 2011, 335).

Although Yohannan affirmed an apparently strong belief in post-Ephesian Christology and Tridentine ecclesiology, the Holy See declined to grant him patriarchal authority, instead naming him as patriarchal administrator (Badger 1852, I:152). Following this apparent snub, from 1783 to 1830 Yohannan's ecclesial loyalty fluctuated from a close relationship with the Holy See to a near complete withdrawal of support, with some accusations that he was still 'nestorien de coeur'.[12]

Divisions between the East Syriacs were complicated by the interventions of the local Ottoman authorities, who patronised one or other patriarchal claimant with a view to political and financial gain (Badger 1852, I:156). Thus, when a supporter of Yohannan visited an area under the control of an Ottoman leader supporting Elias, imprisonment and corporal punishment followed (Badger 1852, I:153). Fortunately for Yohannan, Elias XIII died in 1804. However, his position was not assured. Further challenges emerged from within the Chaldean community from the Josephite line patriarchal claimant Augustin Hindi and the lay leader Gabriel Dembo.

Joseph IV died in retirement in Rome in 1796, and his nephew Augustin Hindi acted as *de facto* patriarch to the Josephite Chaldeans from that time until his death in 1827. Hindi was a strong threat to Hormizd's potential advancement. Bello presents East Syriac population figures for 1796 and Hindi's supporters included at least twenty-five percent of the entire community, and a third of the priests.[13]

Gabriel Dembo sought to reinvigorate the East Syriac monastic tradition through occupying the monastery of Rabban Hormizd and establishing the religious order of the Chaldean Antonians of the Congregation of St Hormisdas (OAOC). This

38 *Origins and early development*

order was similar to that founded among the Maronites in the seventeenth century (Gĕ'dan 1910, 410, 415). The Maronite Antonians were a well-established group from a similar linguistic environment in whose footsteps it was relatively easy to tread – Dembo having become familiar with their community in Aleppo (Bello OAOC 1939, 41–5).

Dembo's independent work was met with suspicion by Yohannan. Dembo was potentially a very dangerous threat to his position because he was a 'new man' with organisational acumen gained from his earlier life as a merchant which, perhaps paradoxically, granted him opportunity to make a success of rejuvenating monastic life (Bello OAOC 1939; Gĕ'dan 1910, 423). Independent organisation, well planned and with a professional ethos, was difficult to reconcile with the nepotistic control maintained, however unofficially, within East Syriac communities.

From 1808, Dembo's efforts focused on a pedagogical system which embraced a syllabus of Arabic, logic and liturgical studies (Badger 1852, I:162). This was not remarkable *per se*, as East Syriac monasteries had been centres of higher learning during the church's missionary period (c. 400–1300) (Brock 2009, 66–70; Teule 2002, passim). What was remarkable was delivering this quality of education into the East Syriac heartland in the modern era. Despite the clerical formation offered by Latin missionaries and some Chaldean clergy travelling to the Papal States for advanced study, these influences were not yet sufficiently diffused for the benefits to be spread throughout the community. Thus, Dembo offered an alternative means of advancement in education for many eager students.

Dembo was founding his congregation at the right time. The local Latin missionaries were, in fact, limited in activity in the early nineteenth century and were not necessarily available to train new clergy:

> De 1800 à 1811 il n'y eut que deux PP. Dominicains en Chaldée et le dernier quitta Mossoul en 1815; il n'y revinrent qu'en 1841. À Diarbékir la mission des Capuchins fut abandonnée de 1803 à 1808; elle reprit ensuite pour deux ans, en 1828 pour quelques mois, enfin elle fut reconstituée à Mardin en 1841. Même pénurie de personnel à Bagdad que le dernier Père Carme quitta en 1825.
>
> (Bello OAOC 1939, 25)

The possibility of influence in ecclesial affairs gained ground outside of the traditional clerical groups. This was an issue of contention for Yohannan, with monks chosen as bishops and thus patriarchs in the East Syriac tradition (Bello OAOC 1939, 37). Therefore, Rabban Hormizd's redevelopment was also a threat to maintaining the future premier status of the leading clerical family – the monastery was a historic centre of East Syriac spiritual life and had an aura of respectability to which others looked with interest.[14]

Dembo and Yohannan as opposition figures

Dembo's community expanded rapidly: in 1808, Dembo had two others with him, and by 1827, there were ninety-three monks (Wilmshurst 2000, 263–4). However,

Origins and early development 39

these efforts were not free from the injudicious methods which some East Syriac factions were prepared to utilise for political gain: accusations of corruption and misuse of position were made by Dembo's supporters against Yohannan in 1812 which saw him suspended by the Holy See as patriarchal administrator, with Augustine Hindi placed in control over both Chaldean patriarchal lines (Bello OAOC 1939, 17–18). Yet in 1816, the Latin Vicar Apostolic for Mesopotamia wrote to the Propaganda in support of Yohannan which eventually resulted in a formal reconciliation between he and Pope Leo XII (1823–1829) in 1826 (Habbi 1971, 140). Despite the conflict between Dembo and Yohannan, the reinvigoration of monastic life at Rabban Hormzid was of long-term benefit to the Chaldean community throughout the rest of the nineteenth century. The level of education among the monks was of a high standard and saw them raised up as future church leaders such as Patriarch Joseph VI Audo (1847–1878).

In an attempt to consolidate his position, Augustine Hindi consecrated five new bishops and received the pallium in 1818. However, recognition from the Holy See as patriarch did not come (Habbi 1971, 138). It has been suggested the pallium was instead given as a reward for his administrative efforts during the discord among the Chaldean communities (Wilmshurst 2011, 333). Nevertheless, Hindi considered it as confirmation of his status as patriarch and from then until his death considered himself Patriarch Joseph V.

Three of Joseph V's newly consecrated bishops attempted the creation of a new clerical group in opposition to Yohannan, and it would seem also against Joseph V. This situation continued from 1822 to 1827 and ended with the Holy See's intervention following the death of Joseph V in 1827 (Badger 1852, I:163). This the opportunity the Latin missionaries had sought, and as Wilmshurst argues about Yohannan: 'Despite his many faults, [he] was a good Catholic, or at least could be presented as one' (Wilmshurst 2011, 338). Thus, the apparent patriarchal authority which the see at Amid had been granted was definitively withdrawn and by 1830, through the intervention of the vicar apostolic in Mesopotamia, Yohannan was granted the title of Chaldean patriarch. Yohannan VIII must have had extraordinary ambition to maintain his efforts over the half century which it took him to gain patriarchal office given he was seventy-four at the time of his acknowledgement by the Holy See (Wilmshurst 2011, 339). It therefore seems likely that his agitation was derived at least in part from a vocational calling and a hope for union with the Holy See and not just a desire for advancement within the East Syriac community. Having been named *Natar Kursya* at the age of sixteen, this event surely made a lasting impression on his early psychological and religious formation and as to why he regarded his pursuit of the patriarchate as lawful.

Notes

1 Unless otherwise noted, dates given after names refer to length of time in office as bishop, king, pope and so forth.
2 Latin influence over the East Syriac community appears to have been substantial and the then resident East Syriac metropolitan, Elias, entered into union with the Latins in 1340, but at this juncture the term *Chaldean* was not used (Wilmshurst 2000, 63).

40 *Origins and early development*

The large East Syriac church in Famagusta was built in 1359 and, as such, suggests the community's presence in the Cypriot *milieu* was maintained even so. Bacci argues that the church was likely, in fact, used by a Miaphysite or Melkite community given the iconography emphasises the role of Mary as the Mother of God *(theotokos)* – something with which the Church of the East would, normatively, have been largely uncomfortable (Bacci 2006, 218–20). Nonetheless, it is possible that it was a mixed Syriac group who made use of the church. Alternatively, the other Eastern Christian communities present may have influenced the local East Syriac community and led to their veneration of the Blessed Virgin as *theotokos* as a result.

3 Franciscans were originally established in the Holy Land in 1217 from which time they became the dominant Latin religious order in the Levant. Their influence became such that Pope Clement VI (1342–1352) in 1342 gave them the responsibility for guardianship of the Holy Places. The chief Franciscan of the Holy Land held substantial oversight in regional Catholic affairs, appointment as the 'Guardian of Mount Zion in Jerusalem' and the office of the Latin Patriarch of Jerusalem (Labourt 1908b, 231).

4 One aspect which serves as example of this comes from the 1553 papal bull officially outlining Sulaqa's status. Perhaps unremarkable at the time but with possible connotations for the present-day Chaldean patriarch's authority, the bull set the limits of patriarchal jurisdiction to Mesopotamia and also 'les autres pays soumis a la juridiction habituelle du patriarche et les monasteres situes dans la Chine at dans les Indes' (Dauvillier 1942, col. 368).

5 Abouna is one of the oldest living Chaldean priests – in his tenth decade as of 2016 – and has had a long scholarly career.

6 A significant and strong relationship between the Holy See and the Mongol khans emerged in the thirteenth and fourteenth centuries with hopes for widespread Mongol conversions to Christianity. Such a relationship perhaps also influenced East Syriac perceptions of the papacy and acted as an encouragement to engage more closely with the Latin community. The Il-Khanid rulers Gazan (1295–1304) and his brother Oljaitu (1304–1316) had both been baptised as children, for example, with the latter's baptismal name *Nicholas* given in honour of Pope Nicholas IV (Ryan 1998, 416 n. 33; Baum and Winkler 2003, 96–7; cf. Morgan 2014, xv–xvii; Budge 1928, 174).

7 Some authors suggest another patriarch – Abraham – led the Chaldeans from 1570–1577. This was, however, disproved by the two most recent scholars to consider East Syriac patriarchal lineages in some depth (Wilmshurst 2011, 345; Murre-van den Berg 1999, 251–2ff.).

8 The East Syriac communities of India engaged with the Latin church at a different pace to those in Mesopotamia, with the context of Portuguese imperial ambitions in South Asia and the Indian Ocean seeing the eventual enforcement of Latin ecclesiological norms from the mid-sixteenth century over resident East Syriacs.

9 From the fourteenth century, the East Syriac patriarch resided in the vicinity of Mosul. Ecclesiastically, Mosul had been a joint metropolitanate with Erbil from the ninth century, but in the thirteenth century, these were separated, owing to a decline of the Christian presence. Despite Tamerlane's invasions of the late fourteenth and early fifteenth centuries, the Mosul region was unaffected, as its governor surrendered directly on his advance, thus for a time preserving the city's safety. From the mid-fifteenth century, the patriarchal residence shifted to the monastery of Rabban Hormizd, about thirty miles north of Mosul in the vicinity of the town of Alqosh. Thus, it is common to find the legitimist line described as the Mosul patriarchate or as resident in Alqosh (Wilmshurst 2011, 286–8; Harrak 2003, 293–4).

10 In 1672 when Joseph's position had been earlier disputed by Elias X, an Ottoman governor in Amid was called upon to discern his legitimacy as the leader of the local East Syriac community (Abdoulahad and Chabot 1896, passim). In this instance, the governor upheld Joseph's position.

Origins and early development 41

11 An exemplary type of this new clerical class was the Maronite J. S. Assemani (b. 1687 d. 1768) who greatly aided the furtherance of knowledge of the Syriac churches through his work *Biblioteca Orientalis* (Assemani 1719).

12 A first-hand account by Yohannan is found as an English translation from the Syriac original in Badger (1852, I:150–60); cf. Bello OAOC (1939, 12).

13 'Patriarcat de Diarbekir [Josephite]' thirty-five priests and 1,061 families and 'Patriarcat de Babylone' sixty-four priests and 2,962 families – totalling ninety-nine priests and 4,033 families (Bello OAOC 1939, 13).

14 The monastery had been established in the seventh century by the monk Hormizd, an influential contemporary East Syriac religious figure renowned among the community for holiness and also for success in opposing West Syriac expansion (Bello OAOC 1939, 62; Budge 1902, II, pt. 1:85–90, 117–18, 134–41).

Bibliography

Abdoulahad, [Chaldean Archbishop of Amid], and Jean-Baptiste Chabot, eds. 1896. 'Les origines du patriarcat chaldeén: Vie de Mar Youssef Ier premier patriarche des chaldeéns (1681–1695)'. *Revue de l'Orient chrétien*, Series 1, 1 (2): 66–90.

Abouna, Rev. Fr Albert. 2013. Chaldean history Interview by Kristian Girling. Face-to-face with written notes, Erbil, Iraq. Translated by Suha Rassam.

Ainsworth, William. 1841. 'An Account of a Visit to the Chaldeans, Inhabiting Central Kurdistán; and of an Ascent of the Peak of Rowándiz (Ṭúr Sheïkhíwá) in Summer in 1840'. *Journal of the Royal Geographical Society of London* 11: 21–76.

Assemani, Joseph. S. 1719. *Biblioteca orientalis Clementino-Vaticana in qua manuscriptos codices Syriacos, Arabicos, Persicos, Turcicos, Hebraicos, Samaritanos, Armenicos, Æthiopicos, Græcos, Ægypticos, Ibericos, & Malabaricos, jussu et munifecentia Clementis XI Pontificus Maximi ex oriente conquisitos, comparatos, avectos, & Bibliothecæ Vaticanæ additicos recensuit, digessit, et genuina scripta à spuriis secrevit, addita singulorum auctorum vita*. 3 vols. Rome: Bibliotheca Vaticana.

Babakhan, Jacques. 1900. 'Deux Lettres d'Élie XI, Patriarche de Babylone'. *Revue de l'Orient Chrétien* 5: 481–91.

Bacci, Michele. 2006. 'Syrian, Palaiologan, and Gothic Murals in the "Nestorian" Church of Famagusta'. *Δελτίον Της Χριστιανικής Αρχαιολογικής Εταιρείας [=Proceedings of the Christian Archaeological Society]* 27: 207–20.

Badger, George Percy. 1852. *The Nestorians and Their Rituals: With the Narrative of a Mission to Mesopotamia and Coordistan in 1842–1844, and of a Late Visit to Those Countries in 1850: Also, Researches Into the Present Condition of the Syrian Jacobites, Papal Syrians, and Chaldeans, and an Inquiry Into the Religious Tenets of the Yezeedees*. Edited by John Mason Neale. Vol. I. 2 vols. London: Joseph Masters. https://archive.org/details/nestorianstheirr01badg.

Baum, Wilhelm, and Dietmar W. Winkler. 2003. *The Church of the East: A Concise History*. Translated by Miranda G. Henry. London: RoutledgeCurzon.

Baumer, Christoph. 2006. *The Church of the East: An Illustrated History of Assyrian Christianity*. London: Tauris.

Bedjan, P., ed. 1895. *Tashlitha de-Maran Yahb-alaha = Histoire de Mar Jab-Alaha, patriarche, et de Raban Sauma*. 2nd Edition. Leipzig: Harrassowitz.

Bello OAOC, Stéphane. 1939. *La Congrégation de S. Hormisdas et l'Église chaldéenne dans la première moitié du XIXe siècle*. Orientalia Christiana analecta 122. Rome: Pont. Institutum Orientalium Studiorum.

42 *Origins and early development*

Brock, Sebastian. 2006. 'East Syriac Pilgrims to Jerusalem in the Early Ottoman Period'. *Aram Periodical* 18: 189–201. doi:10.2143/ARAM.18.0.2020728.

———. 2009. 'The Cultural Contribution of Monasticism in Iraq'. In *The Christian Heritage of Iraq: Collected Papers From the Christianity of Iraq I–V Seminar Days*, edited by Erica C. D. Hunter, 64–80. Gorgias Eastern Christian Studies 13. Piscataway, NJ: Gorgias Press.

Bruns, Peter. 2013. 'Mar Jahballaha und eine römische Kirchenunion aus dem Jahre 1304'. *Journal of Eastern Christian Studies* 65 (3–4): 151–66. doi:10.2143/JECS.65.3.3011239.

Budge, E. A. Wallis, ed. 1902. *The Histories of Rabban Hôrmîzd the Persian and Rabban Bar-'Idtâ*. Translated by Ernest Alfred Wallis Budge. Vol. II, pt. 1. London: Luzac and Co. https://archive.org/details/historiesrabban00budggoog.

———, trans. 1928. *The Monks of Kûblâi Khân, Emperor of China, or the History of the Life and Travels of Rabban ṢâWmâ, Envoy and Plenipotentiary of the Mongol Khans to the Kings of Europe, and Marḳôs Who as Mâr Yahbhallâhâ III Became Patriarch of the Nestorian Church in Asia*. London: The Religious Tract Society.

Coakley, J. F., and David G. K. Taylor. 2009. *Syriac Books Printed at the Dominican Press, Mosul*. Gorgias Handbooks 14. Piscataway, NJ: Gorgias Press LLC.

Dauvillier, Jean. 1942. *'Chaldeén (Droit)'. Dictionnaire de Droit Canonique: Contenant Tous Les Termes Du Droit Canonique Avec Un Sommaire de L'histoire et Des Institutions et de L'etat Actuel de La Discipline*. Paris: Libraire Letouzey et Ane.

———. 1953. 'Byzantins D'Asie centrale et D'Extrème-Orient au moyan age'. *Revue des études byzantines* XI: 62–87.

———. 1979. 'La paputé, l'union des Églises et les missions en Orient durant le moyen age: A propos d'un ouvrage récent'. *Revue d'histoire ecclésiastique* LXXIV: 640–51.

Dib, Pierre. 1914. 'Une mission en Orient sous le Pontificat de Pie IV'. *Revue de l'Orient chrétien* 19: 24–32, 266–77.

Dickens, Mark. 2009. 'Syriac Gravestones in the Tashkent History Museum'. In *Hidden Treasures and Intercultural Encounters: Studies on East Syriac Christianity in China and Central Asia*, edited by Dietmar W. Winkler and Li Tang, 13–49. Wien: LIT Verlag. http://eprints.soas.ac.uk/10309/.

Faris, John D. 2002. 'The Latin Church Sui Iuris'. *Jurist* 62: 280–93.

Fiey OP, Jean Maurice. 1965. *Assyrie Chrétienne – Contribution a l'Étude de l'Histoire et de la Géographie Ecclésiastiques et Monastiques du Nord de l'Iraq*. Vol. I. 3 vols. Recherches publiées sous la direction de l'Institut de Lettres Orientales de Beyrouth, XXII. Beirut: Imprimerie Catholique.

———. 1969. 'Le pèlerinage des Nestoriens et Jacobites à Jérusalem'. *Cahiers de civilisation médiévale* 12 (46): 113–26. doi:10.3406/ccmed.1969.1480.

Filoni, Fernando. 2008. *La Chiesa nella terra d'Abramo: Dalla diocesi di Babilonia dei latini alla nunziatura apostolica in Iraq*. Milan: Biblioteca Universale Rizzoli.

Finnerty, John L. 1907. 'Andrew of Rhodes'. In *The Catholic Encyclopedia*. New York: Robert Appleton Company. www.newadvent.org/cathen/01474b.htm.

Flannery, John. 2013. *The Mission of the Portuguese Augustinians to Persia and Beyond (1602–1747)*. Studies in Christian Mission 43. Leiden and Boston, MA: Brill. https://books.google.co.uk/books?id=Nz5TO9BNFH8C&lpg=PA73&pg=PP1#v=onepage&q&f=false.

Frazee, Charles A. 1983. *Catholics and Sultans: The Church and the Ottoman Empire 1453–1923*. London: Cambridge University Press.

Galleti, Mirella. 2003. *Cristiani del Kurdistan, Assiri, Caldei, Siro-Cattolici e Siro-Ortodossi*. Rome: Jouvence.

Gë'dan, Paul. 1910. 'Histoire du couvent de Rabban Hormizd de 1808 a 1832'. Translated by Maurice Briere. *Revue de l'Orient chrétien*, Series 2, 15 (4): 410–24.

Gill SJ, Joseph. 1959. *The Council of Florence*. London and New York: Cambridge University Press.

Gillman, Ian, and Hans-Joachim Klimkeit. 1999. *Christians in Asia Before 1500*. Richmond: Curzon Press.

Goormachtigh OP, Bernard Marie. 1896. 'Histoire de la mission dominicaine en Mésopotamie et en Kurdistan depuis ses premières origines jusques à nos jours'. *Analecta Sacri Ordinis Fratrum Praedicatorum* 2: 271–83, 405–19.

Habbi, Joseph. 1966. 'Signification de l'union chaldéenne de Mar Sulaqa avec Rome en 1553'. *L'Orient Syrien* 11: 99–132, 199–230.

———. 1971. 'L'unification de la hiérarchie chaldéenne dans la première moitié du XIXe siècle'. *Parole de l'Orient* II (1–2): 121–43, 305–27.

Harrak, Amir. 2003. 'Patriarchal Funerary Inscriptions in the Monastery of Rabban Hormizd: Types Literary Origins, and Purpose'. *Hugoye: Journal of Syriac Studies* 6 (2): 293–309.

Heyberger, Bernard. 1994. *Les Chrétiens Du Proche-Orient Au Temps de La Réforme Catholique (Syrie, Liban, Palestine, XVIIe-XVIIIe Siècles)*. Rome: École Française de Rome.

Joseph IV, ed. 1767. *Missale Chaldaicum Ex Decreto Sacræ Congregationis de Propaganda Fide Editum [Readings From the Epistles of S. Paul, in Syriac, With an Arabic Translation in the Syriac Character; Followed by the Liturgy of the Blessed Apostles, in Syriac, and by the Gospels in the Peshito Syriac Version, With an Arabic Translation in the Syriac Character]*. Rome: Sacræ Congregationis Typrographia.

Khayyath, Georges Ebed-Jesus V. 1896. 'Doctrine de l'Eglise chaldeenne sur la primaute de saint Pierre'. Edited by D. Emmanuel OSB. *Revue de l'Orient chrétien*, Series 1, I (2): 137–48.

Khoury, Dina Rizk. 1997. *State and Provincial Society in the Ottoman Empire: Mosul, 1540–1834*. Cambridge Studies in Islamic Civilization. Cambridge: Cambridge University Press.

Labourt, Jérôme. 1908a. 'Chaldean Christians'. In *The Catholic Encyclopedia*. New York: Robert Appleton Company. www.newadvent.org/cathen/03559a.htm.

———. 1908b. 'Note sur les schismes de l'Église nestorienne du XVIe au XIXe siècle'. *Journal Asiatique* 11 (April): 227–35.

Lampart, Albert. 1966. *Ein Märtyrer der Union mit Rom : Joseph I., 1681–1696, Patriarch der Chaldäer*. Einsiedeln: Benzinger.

Langdale, Allan, and Michael J. K. Walsh. 2007. 'A Short Report on Three Newly Accessible Churches in the Syrian Quarter of Famagusta'. *Journal of Cyprus Studies* 13 (33): 105–23.

Le Coz, Raymond. 1995. *L'Église d'Orient : Chrétiens d'Irak, d'Iran et de Turquie*. Cerf-Histoire. Paris: Editions du Cerf.

Lemmens OFM, Leonhard. 1926a. 'Notae criticae ad initia unionis Chaldaeorum ca. 1551–1629'. *Antonianium* 1: 205–18.

———. 1926b. 'Relationes inter nationem Chaldaeorum et custodiam Terrae Sanctae, 1551–1629'. *Archivum Franciscanum Historicum* 19: 17–28.

Maggiolini, Paolo. 2012. 'Bringing Together Eastern Catholics Under a Common Civil Head: The Agreements Between the Syriac and Chaldean Patriarchs and the Civil Head of the Armenian Catholic Church in Constantinople (1833–1871)'. *Journal of Eastern Christian Studies* 64 (3–4): 253–85. doi:10.2143/JECS.64.3.2961412.

44 Origins and early development

Meinardus, Otto. 1967. 'The Nestorians in Egypt'. *Oriens Christianus* 51: 112–29.

Messmer, Sebastian. 1907. 'Archbishop'. In *The Catholic Encyclopedia*. New York: Robert Appleton Company. www.newadvent.org/cathen/01691a.htm.

Missick, Stephen Andrew. 1999. 'The Assyrian Church in the Mongolian Empire'. *Journal of Assyrian Academic Studies* 13 (2): 85–104.

Morgan, David. 2014. 'Introduction to the New Edition'. In *The Monks of Kublai Khan Emperor of China: Medieval Travels From China Through Central Asia to Persia and Beyond*, ix–xviii. London and New York: I.B. Tauris.

Murre-van den Berg, Heleen L. 1999. 'The Patriarchs of the Church of the East From the Fifteenth to Eighteenth Centuries'. *Hugoye: Journal of Syriac Studies* 2 (2): 235–64.

———. 2005. 'The Church of the East in the Sixteenth to the Eighteenth Century: World Church or Ethnic Community?' In *Redefining Christian Identity: Cultural Interaction in the Middle East Since the Rise of Islam*, 301–20. Orientalia Lovaniensia Analecta 134. Louvain: Peeters.

———. 2006a. '"I the Weak Scribe" Scribes in the Church of the East in the Ottoman Period'. *Journal of Eastern Christian Studies* 58 (1–2): 9–26. doi:10.2143/JECS.58.1.2017734.

———. 2006b. 'The Church of the East in Mesopotamia in the Mongol Period'. In *Jingjiao the Church of the East in China and Central Asia*, edited by Roman Malek and Peter Hofrichter, 377–94. Collectanea Serica. Sankt Augustin: Institut Monumenta Serica.

———. 2008. 'Classical Syriac, Neo-Aramaic and Arabic in the Church of the East and the Chaldean Church Between 1500 and 1800'. In *Aramaic in Its Historical and Linguistic Setting*, edited by Holger Gzella and Margaretga L. Folmer, 311–27. Veröffentlichungen Der Orientalischen Kommission 50. Wiesbaden: Harrassowitz.

———. 2009. 'Chaldeans and Assyrians: The Church of the East in the Ottoman Period'. In *The Christian Heritage of Iraq: Collected Papers from the Christianity of Iraq I–V Seminar Days*, 146–64. Piscataway, NJ: Gorgias Press.

Petrosian, Vahram. 2006. 'Assyrians in Iraq'. *Iran & the Caucasus* 10 (1): 113–47. doi:10.1163/157338406777979322.

Rassam, Suha. 2010. *Christianity in Iraq: Its Origins and Development to the Present Day*. New Edition. Leominster: Gracewing Publishing.

Richard, Francis. 1990. 'Carmelites in Persia'. In *Encyclopædia Iranica*. New York: Encyclopædia Iranica Foundation. www.iranicaonline.org/articles/carmelites-in-persia.

Richard, Jean. 1977. *La papauté et les missions d'Orient au Moyen Age (XIIIe-XVe siècles)*. Collection de l'École française de Rome 33. Rome: École française de Rome.

Ryan, James D. 1998. 'Christian Wives of Mongol Khans: Tartar Queens and Missionary Expectations in Asia'. *Journal of the Royal Asiatic Society*, Series 3, 8 (3): 411–21.

Teule, Herman. 2002. 'La renaissance syriaque (1026–1318)'. *Irénikon* 95: 174–94.

———. 2003a. 'Gregory Barhebraeus and His Time: The Syrian Renaissance'. *Journal of the Canadian Society for Syriac Studies* 3: 21–43.

———. 2003b. 'Saint Louis and the East Syrians, the Dream of a Terrestrial Empire: East Syrian Attitudes to the West'. In *East and West in the Crusader States: Context – Contacts – Confrontations*, edited by Krijnie Ciggaar and Herman Teule, 3:101–22. Orientalia Lovaniensia Analecta 125. Leuven and Dudley, MA: Peeters.

———. 2004. 'Joseph II. Patriarch of the Chaldeans (1696–1713/4), and the Book of the Magnet. First Soundings'. In *Studies on the Christian Arabic Heritage: In Honour of Father Prof. Dr. Samir Khalil Samir S.I. at the Occasion of His Sixty-Fifth Birthday*, edited by Herman Teule and Rifaat Y. Ebied. Eastern Christian Studies 5. Leuven: Peeters.

———. 2011a. '"Abdisho" of Gazarta'. In *Gorgias Encyclopedic Dictionary of the Syriac Heritage*, edited by Sebastian Brock, Aaron Michael Butts, George A. Kiraz, and Lucas Van Rompay. Piscataway, NJ: Gorgias Press.

———. 2011b. 'Yawsep II'. In *Gorgias Encyclopedic Dictionary of the Syriac Heritage*, edited by Sebastian Brock, Aaron Michael Butts, George A. Kiraz, and Lucas Van Rompay. Piscataway, NJ: Gorgias Press.

———. 2011c. 'Yoḥannan Sullaqa'. In *Gorgias Encyclopedic Dictionary of the Syriac Heritage*, edited by Sebastian Brock, Aaron Michael Butts, George A. Kiraz, and Lucas Van Rompay. Piscataway, NJ: Gorgias Press.

Tfinkdji, Joseph. 1913. *L'Église Chaldéenne Catholique Autrefois et Aujourd'hui*. Paris: Bureaux des études ecclésiastiques.

Tisserant, Eugène. 1931. 'L'Église Nestorienne'. In *Dictionnaire de Theologie Catholique*. edited by Alfred Vacant, Eugène Mangenot, and Emile Amann, Paris: Letouzey et Ané.

Tripp, Charles. 2007. *A History of Iraq*. Third Edition. Cambridge: Cambridge University Press.

Valensi, Lucette. 1997. 'Inter-Communal Relations and Changes in Religious Affiliation in the Middle East (Seventeenth to Nineteenth Centuries)'. *Comparative Studies in Society and History* 39 (2): 251–69.

Valognes, Jean-Pierre. 1994. *Vie et Mort Des Chrétiens d'Orient: Des Origines à Nos Jours*. Paris: Fayard.

Weltecke, Dorothea. 2011. 'Crusades'. In *Gorgias Encyclopedic Dictionary of the Syriac Heritage*, edited by Sebastian Brock, Aaron Michael Butts, George A. Kiraz, and Lucas Van Rompay. Piscataway, NJ: Gorgias Press.

Wilmshurst, David. 2000. *The Ecclesiastical Organisation of the Church of the East 1318–1913*. Corpus Scriptorum Christianorum Orientalium ; Subsidia, vol. 582. tomus 104. Lovanii: Peeters.

———. 2011. *The Martyred Church: A History of the Church of the East*. Sawbridgeworth, Hertfordshire: East and West.

Yacoub, Joseph. 2004. 'La reprise à Chypre en 1445 du nom de <<Chaldéens>> par les fidèles de l'Église de l'Orient'. *Istina* XLIX: 378–90.

2 Political change in Mesopotamia and the origins of the modern Chaldean Church (1830–1918)

From the final Ottoman conquest of Mesopotamia in 1704 until 1831 and the assertion of direct Ottoman rule, the Mesopotamian provinces were administered by a series of pseudo-independent Georgian mamluks.[1] By 1749, the Georgians had so consolidated their power that the Sultan was obliged to accept their effective autonomy. There was little to which the Ottomans could be opposed, as the Mamluks could be relied upon to secure the region against threats from Persia or the Russian Empire. Such was the strength of their leader, Daud Pasha (1816–1831), that he refused Sultan Mahmud II's (1808–1839) request to leave his post when requested in 1830. Direct Ottoman military intervention followed in an attempt to prevent complete political autonomy for Mesopotamia as Mohammed Ali had pursued in Egypt.

The 1830s were a difficult time for northern Mesopotamia. A plague of 1831 had severely affected the economy, and the Kurds viewed the disruption caused by the changing patterns of rule in Mesopotamia as an opportunity to assert their independence via a series of revolts. These negatively impacted the surrounding populations, including the East Syriac communities. Alqosh was attacked, for example, and severely damaged in 1832 (Bazzi 2008, 11).

This period of political difficulty segued with the modern Chaldean community's emergence, but did not see Yohannan VIII usefully employed in consolidating his flock.[2] He sought to maintain the practice of hereditary succession, to place his chosen candidate as the next patriarch and to continue his feud with Gabriel Dembo. This feud ended only after Dembo's death during a Kurdish raid in 1832 (Wilmshurst 2011, 383; Gë'dan 1910, 410, 1911, 355). However, Bishop Joseph Audo, who would go on to be the future patriarch, Joseph VI, conspired with Rabban Hormizd's monks to gain their tithes, which should have been paid directly to the patriarch rather than Audo as the local bishop. The ensuing row was brought to the Holy See's attention, which sent the apostolic vicar of Aleppo to consider the matter directly. Eventually, the vicar ruled in favour of Yohannan VIII. But by this time in 1835, Yohannan was increasingly frail and resided in Baghdad until his death in 1838 (Wilmshurst 2011, 383–5).

Ecclesiological discourse and developments

Prior to the formalisation of ecclesial relationships between the East Syriac communities and the Latin church, an underlying question remained unresolved: what was the East Syriac Christological paradigm? Was it an expression of extreme dyophysitism akin to what was perceived to be the heresy of Nestorianism, or, was it, in fact, in accord with the Latin understanding of Christ's human and divine natures? I suggest that for many of those who became members of the Chaldean community, that discourse on Christology was a topic far removed from their day-to-day lives and that the issue was not of principal importance to their affiliation to one or other East Syriac community.

If we accept, following Wilmshurst, that the latest and most authoritative Christological statements of the Church of the East come from Abdisho, Metropolitan of Nisibis, in his 1298 work *The Pearl*, then this likely remained their standard Christological outline for several centuries.[3] Abdisho's work confirmed the 'formula of [Theodore of Mopsuestia] two natures in two hypostases and one person' (Wilmshurst 2011, 273–5, 281). It is not clear, however, if, by the time of the Chaldean faction's emergence in 1552, the level of knowledge among the East Syriac community still extended far enough to debate in detail on theological disputes apart from the rudiments of their faith. It is possible that it was only from the nineteenth century and encounters with Latin, Anglican, protestant and Russian missionaries that scholarly efforts in the explicit Christological traditions of the Church of the East were revived.

Indeed, as Wilmshurst outlines throughout his work *The Ecclesiastical Organisation of the Church of the East 1318–1913* (2000), at least from the sixteenth century until the nineteenth century scholarly output focused on copying manuscripts and not original works. The protestant missionary Asahel Grant observed in the 1830s that in the Sulaqite community only the patriarch had a complete text of the Bible, which was split into several volumes and lent out to the clergy (1841, 65).

It is not clear whether the Latin missionaries acknowledged the variation of depth in theological education prevalent among the East Syriacs. It is possible the Latins may have worked from the assumption that all East Syriacs expressed a Nestorian Christology and based their proselytising efforts from this premise. I suggest that owing to a lack of ecclesial distinctiveness it was at least until the unification of the claims to the leadership of the Chaldean Church in 1830 a relatively informal procedure to move between the East Syriac communities.

It appears that, for those Chaldeans who had received a more advanced education, there was acknowledgement of the doctrine preached by the Latins of *extra ecclesiam nulla salus* (Smith and Dwight 1833, II:252). However, when a rudimentary level of education was relatively widespread, ecclesial jurisdiction or Christological nuances would have had little impact as arguments when approaching someone to discuss papal primacy. This being said, the increasingly distinctive liturgical and para-liturgical practices which the Latin missionaries introduced whether through praying the Holy Rosary, the celebration of feasts such as Corpus Christi or the devotion to the Five Sacred Wounds of Christ, would have contrasted the differences between the communities (Gĕ'dan 1910, 422).

It appears that until an ecclesial distinctiveness became readily apparent, the Holy See adopted a cautious approach to conclusively support the Chaldean community, as indicated by the reluctance to grant titles to Augustine Hindi

48   *Political change in Mesopotamia*

and the intention to gain the legitimist patriarchal line's allegiance (cf. Labourt 1908, 230).

From the late 1830s, confidence appears to have risen among the Latins that the Chaldean project was on the right path, with the Chaldean episcopate increasingly free of the parochial culture which appeared to exist among the community. The Latin confidence was summarised by Asahel Grant:

> The Papists in Mesopotamia have assured me that no effort will be spared to convert the whole of the Nestorian Church to their faith; and this report is confirmed by letters since received from Bagdad, one of which says that three bishops and priests, educated at the Propaganda, were 'about going to Mosul to hold a convention to devise measures to bring over all the Nestorians to the Romish faith!' [*sic*].
>
> (1841, 47–8)

These attempts to gain the adherence of the entire East Syriac population were complicated by the Latins' desire to do so in a manner that assumed the existing limits of East Syriac dioceses. This was a potentially complicated procedure that involved competition with claims from the Sulaqite patriarch: one diocese professed loyalty to him and another to the Holy See. This was never settled and, in practice, determined on a village-by-village basis instead (Badger 1852b, I:172–3).

The heritage of the undivided Church of the East

From the 1830s, the Chaldean patriarchal lineage represented the unified East Syriac communities who had been associated with either the legitimist patriarchate or that of the Josephite patriarchate. However, from the 1830s, the Sulaqite patriarchal line (i.e. the original East Syriac faction to enter into union with the Holy See in 1553) and its community represented the traditions of the Church of the East as they had existed prior to the development of the Chaldean community in the sixteenth century.

The Church of the East, as it exists in the twenty-first century, may be sensitive to highlighting this quirk of historical ecclesiastical development. Nonetheless, it would not regard this as denying it legitimacy or status as *the* manifestation of the Church of the East and as descended from the Synod of Dadisho which advanced the church's autocephaly from 424. Sulaqa's successors largely returned to an explicitly East Syriac ecclesial independence and identity but, as has been shown, varied in their interest in engaging with the Holy See. Historically, the Church of the East, in some instances relied on engagement with the Chaldeans in order to revivify their ecclesial life. This would be acknowledged by contemporary members of the Church of the East. For example: East Syriac liturgical works were produced by Latin printing presses intended for use by the Chaldean clergy but also used by the Church of the East (Royel 2014, 20 n. 48). Such a type of relationship suggests that once the concept of some form of union with the Holy See had become a widespread concept among the East Syriac communities, it was difficult to develop entirely independent of the Latin milieu.

These issues being noted, Chaldeans would likely also have perceived of themselves as acting entirely in and as part of the heritage of the undivided Church of the East. Their conception, however, reflected the view of the necessity of best expressing membership of this tradition through union with the Roman See. In essence, the Chaldeans *were* (and are) East Syriac in their beliefs and practices, yet accepted that union with the Pope obliged them to introduce particular Latin concepts which were to become a normative aspect of their ecclesial identity.

Nicholas I Zaya

Nicholas I Zaya (1838–1847) was appointed by the Holy See to succeed Yohannan VIII. This intervention did not endear either him or the papacy in the person of Pope Gregory XVI to the Chaldean hierarchy, who regarded this as a grave imposition (Wilmshurst 2000, 33; Badger 1852a, II:165). Moreover, as Nicholas was a Persian subject, there may have been some concern as to his suitability to lead an increasingly Mesopotamian-focused Chaldean community. The monks of Rabban Hormizd, under the tutelage of the emerging leadership of Joseph Audo, were also antagonistic towards Nicholas. He had to work extensively to gain their approval (Wilmshurst 2000, 33; cf. Badger 1852b, I:168–9). Nicholas' difficulties were compounded in 1843 following his suggestion to introduce the Gregorian calendar, but the level of opposition became so strong that the plans were withdrawn (Badger 1852b, I:170).

A success arrived in 1845 as Nicholas gained the support of Rabban Hormizd's monks. Together they attempted to improve their financial arrangements by restoring some agricultural properties in and around Alqosh to their ownership (Badger 1852b, I:171). However, this was opposed by disaffected parties who sought Nicholas' overthrow via accusations of corruption to the Holy See (Wilmshurst 2000, 34; Badger 1852b, I:170–2). The Holy See was not in a position to have access to a full account of events, and sought to investigate Nicholas' activities. Instead of facing this ongoing and further pressure on his position, Nicholas resigned from the patriarchate in 1847 and died in 1855.

Changes among the Ottomans

From October 1844, the Chaldean-Ottoman relationship altered on an administrative level. The Chaldeans were brought within the structure of the millet system under the aegis of the Armenian Catholic millet, whose patriarch acted on the Chaldeans' behalf in administrative matters (Gaunt 2006, 13; Maggiolini 2012, 271). Legitimising the Chaldean position came in the context of Ottoman social and legal reform introduced by Sultan Abdulmecid I (1839–1861). The changes, known as the *Tanzimat*, were implemented to bring the Empire in line with contemporary military, social, economic and political trends prevalent among the European powers, whose dominance in the Mediterranean was increasing at a rate

50   *Political change in Mesopotamia*

the Ottomans were nearly unable to match. The most significant change came in the standardisation in bureaucratic and administrative structures over and above arbitrary use of power manifested via patronage networks (Ceylan 2010, 69–71).

The greatest benefits to the Empire's Christians came in the pronouncement of the *Hatti Serif* (1839) and *Hatti Humayun* (1856) which gave explicit equality in law to all Christian communities. The latter also effectively ended the use of *sharia* and the millet system. However, legal equality brought with it the Muslim populations' ire. The change in social status for Christians threatened Muslim-led judicial and statutory paradigms from which most existing Ottoman laws derived (Movsesian 2010, 2). The reforms saw, amongst other aspects, the prohibition of the slave trade, universal conscription (including of non-Muslims), the introduction of a post office system and the establishment of secular law courts. All of which required significant financial backing to follow through, complete and maintain against the recalcitrance of the established power groups (cf. Davison 1954, 859).

The reforms' implementation slowed due to internal opposition. With the effects of the Panic of 1873 international financial crisis, the Ottomans were unable to sustain the Tanzimat due to insufficient tax revenue. From 1878, Sultan Abd al-Hamed II (1876–1909) reconsolidated the sultanate's powers and re-instituted an explicitly Sunni cultural and social paradigm throughout the Empire.

From the 1870s, the Chaldeans were increasingly dependent on how the Ottomans conceived Christian status within the Empire in general. The changing social circumstances moving towards and away from greater social mobility saw Christians throughout the Middle East expedite their efforts to self-improvement, as they recognised that education, vocational training and commercial development were vital to ensure their retaining a position of something approaching the higher social status of the Muslim population.

Concurrent with Mesopotamian Christian advancement was the consolidation of the Mesopotamian Shia population which had undergone a revival from the late 1700s following widespread conversions among the southern tribes (Ceylan 2010, 35; Nakash 2003, 28–9). Such a situation did not necessarily imply a volatile or sectarian situation, but as religious affiliation defined community paradigms it also led to reconsideration of the social order and as to who ought to control political affairs. The question of political control was brought to the fore with the Young Turks' accession to power in Constantinople from 1908. Mesopotamia's ethnic and religious plurality did not concur with the views of the Young Turks, who fomented a zeal for a supposed Turkish ideal of ethnicity and culture and as the supreme race in opposition to any other within the Empire. Christian engagement with Western political ideals through their education or mercantile activities saw them increasingly involved in Arab nationalist groups.

The foundations of modern Arab nationalist thought were constructed by a significant proportion of Christian intelligentsia. Christian involvement was related to opposing the political dominance of Sunni Islam and limiting the role of religion in public life. There was also a genuine belief in nationalism's vitality as an ideal to overcome sectarian mentalities and Turkish domination of the Arab Middle East.

Eastern Catholic consolidation, the Chaldeans and the First Vatican Council

From the 1850s, the Chaldean Church's strength and identity as an ecclesial organisation relied on the ecclesiology developed by Nicholas I's successor Joseph VI Audo. Audo asserted a vision of effective church governance through strengthening the apostolic zeal and level of religious education among the Chaldean clergy and laity (cf. Wilmshurst 2011, 386). Audo was convinced of the need for a close ecclesiological relationship with the Holy See, but this did not prevent his desiring ecclesial autonomy and attempting to justify this whenever possible. Valognes appraises Audo's position thus: 'Une personnalité incontestée, sincèrement attachée au catholicisme, mais qui ne fait pas mystère de sa fidélité à la tradition orientale' (Valognes 1994, 434).

Audo's pursuit of autonomy was brought into focus when, in apparent contravention of papal jurisdiction, he consecrated bishops for the East Syriac congregations in India in 1860, 1874 and 1875 (Pius IX 1872, passim). The Indian East Syriacs had a consistently challenging relationship with Latin missionaries who entered the sub-continent from the sixteenth century under the auspices of the Portuguese Empire.

Traditionally, the Indians had been under the jurisdiction of the Patriarch of Seleucia-Ctesiphon and were reliant upon him for episcopal consecrations. Following the Chaldean community's foundation, the Indians looked to Yohannan Sulaqa and his successors for episcopal replacements. The Holy See opposed this arrangement primarily due to the papacy having reserved the right to choose bishops for India since the sixteenth century. It was also opposed due to the increasing strength of the Portuguese *Padroado*[4] in India and the assertion of Latin jurisdiction over all the Christians of the region regardless of pre-existing ecclesiastical organisation (Habbi 1980, 86). The situation was further complicated by the Indians asserting a more independent character than their continuing relationship with the Mesopotamian-based East Syriacs would suggest, with a strong desire expressed to retain Malabarese cultural distinctiveness (see, for example, Podipara 1970; cf. Habbi 1980, 84). Those East Syriac rite Indian communities in union with the Holy See came to be known as the Syro-Malabarese which reflected their religious, linguistic and geographic origins.

By the eighteenth century, and despite the long-term Portuguese imperial presence and Latin jurisdiction, the significance of receiving bishops from Mesopotamia had not been lost on the Malabarese. The last Mesopotamian appointed bishop died at the end of the sixteenth century, but communal memory of traditional practices remained strong and supportive of their continued implementation. The Malabarese sought the Chaldean hierarchy's assistance in 1796 with a delegation visiting Mosul, but the responsibility of the Chaldeans for the provision of clergy – as opposed to their appointment by the Holy See – was not conclusively resolved at that juncture, most likely due to the contemporary factionalism prevalent among the Chaldeans (Habbi 1971, 131–2). Joseph VI, when

52 *Political change in Mesopotamia*

called upon from 1860, however, considered episcopal consecrations for India as within his remit.

Joseph VI's concern for the status of the Malabarese East Syriac Christians and the Holy See's response was indicative of ongoing and under-considered issues in the Chaldean-Latin relationship. First, it demonstrated the contemporary significance of traditional procedures for appointing bishops and for the relevance to day-to-day ecclesiastical administration by the patriarch. Second, it was an aspect of the legacy which the Chaldeans assumed from the Church of the East and which Audo regarded as within his responsibilities. Third, it marked the contrasting perspectives on how Eastern Catholic ecclesiology should develop: whether formed at the discretion of Latin missionaries or as annunciated by Eastern Catholics who wished to retain existing customs. Fourth, the situation showed that the identity of the East Syriac tradition could not be confined to the peoples, cultures and customs of Mesopotamia alone but must retain its plural and international character.

The Holy See's concern for the situation in India related to the extent to which an Eastern Catholic patriarch could unilaterally provide episcopal consecrations for a group operating within an environment dominated by the Latin clergy. I suggest, as the Chaldean situation developed vicariously from the 1550s, the implications of the Holy See's rôle in Malabarese and Mesopotamian affairs was likely little considered. Furthermore, in asserting his jurisdiction over the Indian territories, Audo perhaps did not realise the extent to which the Holy See considered the appointment of bishops as its own prerogative.

In view of attempting some standardisation of practices among Eastern Catholics, Pope Pius IX (1846–1878) had implemented changes in ecclesiastical administration. The Chaldeans were affected by the implementation of the ecclesiastical constitution 'Reversurus' through the bull of 1869 'Cum ecclesiastical disciplina'. The latter permitted the Holy See to confirm who was and who was not to be appointed as bishop in every diocese, and confirmed to the Chaldeans their position as a community directly reliant on the Holy See in these matters (Baumer 2006, 252). In the 1830s, with the unified Chaldean community's establishment, it is not clear whether this was an issue of discussion. Perhaps due to satisfaction with the co-operation of the Chaldeans, the issue was overlooked. Alternatively, it may have been discussed and accepted at the time with less thought given to its future implications.

Audo's relationship with the Holy See came to a head at the First Vatican Council (1869–1870). He regarded with deep concern the definitive extension of papal authority over all other bishops in union with the Holy See, as well as to the detrimental influence which the dogma of papal infallibility might have on the continuation of local traditional practices for the management of Eastern Catholic ecclesiastical organisation (Bury 1930, 100). Audo, for example, considered it impossible for patriarchal rights to be withdrawn by the Holy See and further argued that the position of the Eastern Catholics was in such disarray that any Latin intervention to alter this could cause further difficulties in gaining Eastern Christians' allegiance (Frazee 1983, 235).

On the question of papal infallibility, Audo chose not to vote at the Council and instead temporarily departed (Frazee 1983, 235–6). Pius IX was reportedly

Political change in Mesopotamia   53

extremely angered by this. However, as Audo was of an advanced age – by this time in his eighth decade – we may suppose that Pius was slightly more well disposed to his attitudes than if opposed by a younger and potentially longer living rival. Nevertheless, the publication of the 1872 papal encyclical 'Quae in Patriarchatu' was directed at him and the Chaldean clergy. It was based around Audo's reluctance to conform to the *padroado*'s conditions, and his preference for dealing with the situation himself. Also, Pius was concerned over the status of Eastern Catholic rites and the nature of papal infallibility.

The encyclical gave an outline of historical relations between the Holy See and Chaldeans and emphasised for Pius IX as to 'what remain[ed] to be done to drive away those dangers threatening Catholic faith and unity' (Pius IX 1872, para. 1). The pope, in this instance, was concerned that despite finally achieving unity among the Chaldeans, the patriarch still did not concur with the expected Eastern Catholic ecclesiological position: union with the Holy See and acceptance of papal jurisdiction in ecclesial matters.

The core issues of contention were hereditary succession – referred to as 'the disgrace' – and the widespread nature of Nestorianism perceived by the Holy See as still present among East Syriac communities, which, they viewed, could influence the Chaldean faithful (Pius IX 1872, para. 2). Pius IX's aim was to assert that he as pope was the final arbiter in Chaldean ecclesial life, and eventually Audo was reconciled with papal policy (Wilmshurst 2011, 387–8ff.; Pius IX 1872, para. 11). Pius' actions, whilst perhaps appearing overly authoritarian, especially concerning whether Audo could lawfully appoint his own candidates for bishops, were meant to ensure the lasting stability and security of the community which had been so fragile until the early nineteenth century.

Despite Audo's eventual submission to the Holy See in all matters, the relationship with the papacy was never essentially resolved until the emergence of a separate Syro-Malabarese hierarchy from 1887 (Pius IX 1872, paras 4–6; Wilmshurst 2011, 388–9). Audo, whilst a very able leader, was never of one mind with Pius IX. Indeed, shortly before his death Audo was nearly excommunicated. Yet, his activities were carried out with a concern for those who came to him seeking assistance and to maintain Eastern Catholic rites and customs after the Vatican Council. Audo's final statement on the matter came at the end of his life:

> Je veux mourir obéissant fils de la Sainte Eglise catholique, soumis au Saint-Siege. Ce que j'ai fait contre le n'a pas été par Siège St. esprit de rébellion, mais que j'ai cru c'était pour le bien de la nation. J'ai été condamné, je me demande pardon j'en soumets.
>
> (Martina SJ 1990, 107)

Consolidation prior to the First World War

Audo's zeal for the consolidation of the Chaldean community was continued by his successor Elias XII Peter Abulyonan (1879–1894). Abulyonan sought the adherence of the Sulaqite East Syriac communities, but during his tenure was

54 *Political change in Mesopotamia*

faced with increased competition from Anglican and protestant missionaries (Wilmshurst 2011, 391).

The Anglicans regarded the Church of the East as a natural ally and as a community which adhered to similar beliefs as the Church of England. Their approach was to encourage and sustain the perceived similarities with the Anglican Communion – such as opposition to papal jurisdiction and a broadly aniconic approach to church art – and to ensure the revivification of the East Syriac church apart from the influence of the Holy See and Latin missionaries. Conversely, in approaching the East Syriac communities, protestant missionaries sought converts to their particular denomination and a definitive change in ecclesial affiliation and identity.

However, the patriarchs of the Sulaqite lineage were cognisant of the relative merits and drawbacks of adhering to protestant beliefs or association with the Anglican communion. Patriarch Shemon XVIII Rubil (1861–1903) affirmed it would be far better to become a member of the Chaldean community than any other Christian group (Coakley 1992, 172).

This suggests that the Chaldeans continued to hold a very similar ecclesial *identity* even if their ultimate ecclesial *allegiance* was to the Holy See. Further, the long-standing encounter with the Latin milieu ensured it was more readily understood and appreciated by way of comparison with Anglican or protestant paradigms. It seems likely that the apostolic heritage of the Roman See and its greater international status and breadth of presence in the Middle East also swayed East Syriac sympathy in its favour.

Abulyonan, after the colourful lives of Joseph VI Audo and several of his predecessors, can comparatively be regarded as a more conservative patriarch. He is notable for having been one of the youngest Chaldean patriarchs at the time of his election in 1879 – at most in his late thirties (having been born c. 1840). This indicated that he was a talented man, especially considering he had been consecrated a bishop only in 1874. I suggest he was selected at the recommendation of the Apostolic delegate for Mesopotamia, Eugène-Louis-Marie Lion (1874–1883), who likely sought a complete break with the influence of a traditionalist East Syriac *milieu* as exemplified by figures such as Audo.

After his premature death from typhoid fever, Abulyonan was succeeded by Georges Ebedjesu V Khayyath. Despite leading the Chaldeans for only five years, he made several contributions to an increase in studies of East Syriac history and literary culture (Tisserant 1931, col. 247). He is also an interesting figure for having written a defence of papal primacy whilst Chaldean archbishop of Amadiya. It seems likely this work was largely formulated as a result of his studies at the Propaganda (Oussani 1901, 84–5; Khayyath 1870; Tisserant 1931, col. 247). For the Holy See, there could have been little more satisfaction than that found in the rise of an erudite leader supportive of a central pillar of Tridentine ecclesiology. This was in the context of having had to contend with Chaldean leaders who were opposed to such ideals. Khayyath's short but significant rule marked the consolidation of a new era of co-operation with the Holy See.

Khayyath's rule was also marked by the start of widespread massacres of the Christian communities in and around eastern Asia Minor and northern Mesopotamia

Political change in Mesopotamia   55

from 1894. These massacres were presaged by a minor Armenian revolt against the levying of a double rate of tax on their community. This was repressed by Kurdish militia and affected nearly the whole of the local Armenian community. The East Syriacs may not have been affected directly, but the situation laid the foundations of an atmosphere of insecurity surrounding non-Muslims' status in the Ottoman Empire.

Chaldean missions to the Church of the East

In the early twentieth century, the Chaldean hierarchy's support for their communities and continued missionary efforts were extensive. Ratel provides an example of a significant body of converts to the Chaldean community in 1903 resulting from missionary activities begun in late 1899. The group consisted of:

> Mgr Ichoïale, évêque de Douré, du mélik Nemroud, neveu de Mar-Schémoun, de l'archidiacre Joseph et de quatre autres, tous de la famille patriarcale; et, en outre, de quatre prêtres et de trente cheïks, représentants des principales tribus nestoriennes.
>
> (Ratel 1904, 290)

Indicating that success builds on success, the Chaldeans were in a position to increase their numbers from influential members of the East Syriac population.

As Chaldean identity strengthened from the nineteenth century, we can note that to return to the Church of the East if one had become Chaldean was considered a grievous incident. One monk of the monastery of Rabban Hormizd who did so is referred to as: 'Henàni sô est mort au milieu des païens après être devenu nestorien' (Gë'dan 1910, 420). This was an indication of the level of reaction against those who returned to what was perceived as error. Such devotion to the Chaldean cause was likely popularly held and outwardly demonstrated by the use of easily identifiable Catholic customs such as devotion to the Holy Rosary, to which was ascribed miraculous deliverance in times of danger (Gë'dan 1910, 421).

A study of the Chaldeans which highlights the extent of conversions was providentially undertaken in 1913 by Fr Joseph Tfinkdji and built on the previous work of Khayyath (Tfinkdji 1913; Khayyath 1896). An awareness of Chaldean identity was present in Tfinkdji's mind, and he speaks highly of those in leadership positions in the Chaldean community expressing links with the Holy See. Quite apart from the remarkably comprehensive documentary project which he produced, what is particularly notable is his choice of words for the book's title: *L'Eglise Chaldéenne*. The purposeful use of the term *Church* to describe the Chaldeans indicates there was some concept of the semi-autonomous nature of the community set apart from the Catholic Church, even if not formally acknowledged as such by the Holy See. This would later be officially adopted at the Second Vatican Council.

As of 1913, the Chaldean community consisted of twelve dioceses in Mesopotamia as well as thirteen patriarchal vicariates serving outlying Chaldean

56 *Political change in Mesopotamia*

communities (Tfinkdji 1913, 34–7). Total population estimates vary, but in considering the figures collected on the Chaldeans, we should note from Ceylan that the Christian populations were often the most under accounted for in Ottoman census records (Ceylan 2010, 36). Such a state of affairs was not necessarily shared among the Latin and Chaldean clergy, who it seems documented their communities in some detail and an overall picture does begin to emerge.

Oussani affirms the Chaldean population as 100,000 in 1901 but later increased this estimate to 150,000 (Oussani 1901, 81, 1921, xxiv–xxv), whereas Paulin Martin in 1867 and Khayyath and Chabot in 1896 put the figures nearer to 70,000–80,000 (Wilmshurst 2011, 400; Khayyath 1896, 453; Martin 1867, 205–10). With the discrepancy in the figures, it seems likely the aforementioned difficulties of accessing reliable information did have an effect.

The largest areas of Chaldean population were in Mosul and Salmas, with the vast majority based in and around Mosul, with approximately 30,000 Chaldeans (Khayyath 1896, 436; Wilmshurst 2000, 199). Before the First World War, the future of the Chaldean community appeared to be assured: of 199 'Chaldean' villages, approximately 180 had their own priest according to data collated by Wilmshurst. Where the Church of the East had one priest for every 400 community members, the Chaldeans had approximately one priest for every 300 people (Wilmshurst 2011, 401).

Massacre without remorse: 1915–1918

Ottoman entry to the First World War was a turning point in Chaldean history. The community experienced a period of extreme persecution under the cover of the conflict, and several dioceses were destroyed. One significant outcome was to see the Chaldeans emerge as the dominant church in Mesopotamia-Iraq from 1919.

Infrequent but increasingly brutal attacks against East Syriacs took place from the mid-nineteenth century. These events could have been attributed to intercommunal rivalries resolved through extreme methods of coercion, especially as they derived much of their intensity from living in proximity to the Kurds. However, during and after the First World War, the massacres were characterised by anti-Christian rhetoric which depicted Syriac and Armenian Christians as a threat to Ottoman Imperial security. Further justification for attacks was derived from fears of Christians' potential rôle as fifth columnists acting in support of Britain, France and the Russian Empire.

Prior to 1915, Mesopotamian Muslim perceptions of Christians varied. In areas such as Basra or Kirkuk, apparently amicable relations were built around shared mercantile interests. In contrast, Muslim attitudes in Mosul or Amid were often hostile. The British Vice-Consul in Mosul, writing in 1909, described communal relations:

> The attitude of the Moslems towards the Christians and Jews, to whom . . . they are in a majority of ten to one, is that of a master towards slaves whom he treats with a certain lordly tolerance so long as they keep their place. Any sign

of pretension to equality is promptly repressed. It is often noticed in the street that almost any Christian submissively makes way even for a Moslem child.

(Wilkie Young 1971, 232)

Wilkie Young was writing in reference to an area outside of the direct reach of the subsequent massacres. However, the treatment, even there, was extremely harsh. The local population still strongly remembered the persecutions of the nineteenth century (G. Bell 1909).

Kurdish and Arab attitudes to Christians were complicated by the commitment among the modernising Young Turk movement for an exclusive ethnic vision for the Ottoman Empire. Originally, the movement had favoured a pan-ethnic notion of Turkish identity. However, following a 1913 coup in Constantinople, the Committee for Union and Progress (CUP) emerged as the strongest political faction in the Empire. The CUP altered the modernising position to instead focus on a Turkification of the entire population and the reduction of the social status of Ottoman subjects of non-Turkish ethnicity. The influence of minorities was to be dispersed through ethnic cleansing (Gaunt 2006, 40–1). These policies served only to increase more fractious relations between the Kurds and the Christians, as both were on the edges of the new political vision.

First World War and start of massacres

A *jihad* was declared in conjunction with the Ottoman declaration of war against the Entente powers. The purpose of the former was to advance the cause of the latter. The *jihad*'s declaration was also pragmatic: it was advanced in order to garner support from those subjects of the Sultan increasingly disillusioned by the apparent modernisation and secularisation of the Empire under the direction of the CUP. It was also hoped to encourage support for the Sultan from among the substantial Muslim populations under British, French and Russian Imperial governance (cf. Allawi 2014, 48).

Violence did not begin *en masse* with the declaration of *jihad* in November 1914, but from this time onward until the conclusion of the Treaty of Lausanne in 1923, consistent intense attempts were made by the Turks and the Kurds to destroy or deport the Christian populations in northern Mesopotamia and eastern Asia Minor (Baumer 2006, 261).

East Syriac-Russian relations

Prior to the massacres, increasingly cordial relations had developed over the course of the nineteenth century between members of the East Syriac communities and the Russian Empire and Church. These encounters centred chiefly on the East Syriac populations in Urmia, north-west Persia. The geographical proximity of Russia and its status as a Christian empire meant association with its ecclesial institutions was valued by members of the Church of the East as a potential interlocutor comparable to the Holy See.

58   *Political change in Mesopotamia*

As had occurred in the development of East Syriac relations with the Holy See, initially small groups or individual clerics aggregated to membership of the Russian church. These engagements appeared to encourage the Sulaqite line patriarch Shemon XVIII Rubil to write to Tsar Alexander II (1855–1881) in 1868 seeking ecclesial and material support (Joseph 1961, 99). However, nothing was formally achieved at that time.

Nonetheless, ongoing interest remained strong among the East Syriacs in Urmia. In May 1897, two priests of the Russian church were despatched to consider the possibility of receiving the entire Diocese of Urmia into communion.

It is not clear as to the extent which Patriarch Shemon XVIII Rubil approved of this, but according to Abramtsov's account of events, the East Syriac population sought to commit themselves wholeheartedly to the Russian Orthodox paradigm. This was most strongly evidenced in the petition of reception which the community drafted to clarify their beliefs to the Russian Synod. Its referral to the community as 'the Syrio-Chaldean people, followers of Nestorius', acknowledges a separation between their church and the Orthodox since the fifth century and that 'the signers accepted and believed . . . all the [post-Ephesian] doctrines regarding the Person of Christ, the Theotokos . . . and generally the doctrines held by the Church Catholic' (Abramtsov 1960, 159).

The eventual outcome was the formal reception of the Bishop of Urmia, Mar Jonas, and three other clerics into the Russian Church, in St Petersburg on the Feast of the Annunciation of the Blessed Virgin Mary (25 March, Old Style calendar) in 1898. The bishop and his colleagues returned to Urmia, and by 1905, up to 70,000 Christians of East Syriac heritage are asserted to have converted to Russian Orthodoxy (cf. Tisserant 1931, col. 260). This was the first mass demonstration of political and religious loyalty to the Russian Empire, and its 1909 occupation of the Urmia region appeared to create a secure region for East Syriac residents (Baumer 2006, 259–60).

However, in the long term, this level of co-operation with the Russians gave credence to the Turkish and Kurdish fear of Armenian and Syriac Christian communities seceding entirely from the Ottoman Empire and becoming a direct threat to the success of the war effort. It is perhaps understandable that the Church of the East's hierarchy desired to militarily support their only ally. Nevertheless, Russian imperial concerns regarding the East Syriacs were never defined. Notwithstanding the apparent conversion of patriarch Shemon XIX Benjamin (1903–1918) and some of the community in 1914, the number of converts was immaterial to the Russian military's decision as to whether they would or would not defend the East Syriacs in the context of war with the Ottomans.[5] The Urmia region was of relatively low strategic importance to the Russians in contrast with the rest of the Caucasus (Baumer 2006, 261).

Start of the Massacres

Massacres of the East Syriac population began in January 1915 but were effected more strongly following a formal declaration of war by the Church of the East

Political change in Mesopotamia 59

against the Ottoman Empire (Baumer 2006, 262). The declaration came as a result of overconfidence of the Church of the East's elites, who concluded that they could expect Russian military support in the near future. The massacres proceeded from west to east as the Turks gained ground against the Russians during 1915. Turkish and Kurdish attacks were uniform in nature, and there was no alternative for Christians but to flee, starve to death, be killed outright or be enslaved.

Following the withdrawal of Russian protection in 1915, many Christians took the opportunity to enter Russian territory. However, this resulted in the deaths of up 15,000 East Syriacs during extremely arduous winter conditions (Baumer 2006, 261, 261 n. 46). Two of the most badly affected Chaldean groups were in Amid and Seert. In these areas, every Chaldean village was destroyed and the Archbishop of Seert, Addai Scher, was beheaded in June 1915. He was a noted scholar and his loss was a great blow to the Chaldeans (Scher 1910; Brock and Kiraz 2011). The extent of destruction for other dioceses was no less significant, and Mardin, Gazarta,[6] Van, Salmas and Urmia[7] were effectively destroyed as ecclesial entities (Wilmshurst 2011, 423, 2000, 83).

In permitting this ethnic cleansing, Ottoman leaders appear to have been motivated by strategic necessity – they perceived it as imperative to remove those actively or sympathetically opposed to Turkish hegemony. This was a conventional strategy by the standards of late nineteenth and early twentieth century warfare, which viewed forced displacements from areas of operations as a normative procedure: the Russians also conducted a similar process in the Caucasus. However, the Turkish efforts to remove sections of the Christian populations eventually consisted of death squads targeting whole Christian communities and not relocations (Gaunt 2006, 65). Also as Gaunt highlights, in Amid, 1,600 people were offered life were they to convert to Islam, indicating there was, in this especially badly affected area, a specific anti-Christian motive (Gaunt 2006, 162). Wilmshurst outlines another instance from the village of Dilman:

> [this] predominantly Chaldean community . . . about 800 strong, was massacred when the town fell to the Turks. Some of the Chaldeans were offered their lives if they converted to Islam, and were killed when they refused. Eyewitnesses noted that Muslim villagers joined in the looting, and that while most of the killing was done by the Kurdish irregulars, regular Turkish officers made no effort to stop them.
>
> (Wilmshurst 2011, 416)

The Holy See was not inactive in attempts to provide some succour to Ottoman Christians. Pope Benedict XV attempted to influence Sultan Mehmed V (1909–1918) during 1915. The response and policy of Mehmed and his government was to continue to favour collective punishment due to the apparent difficulty of distinguishing between supposed Armenian rebels and peaceful subjects (cf. Gaunt 2006, 151).

Attempts to defend the East Syriac population via military means were focused around the Syriac leader Agha Petros. It appears he was well acquainted with the

60   Political change in Mesopotamia

different powers in the region, having been educated at a European school and later working for the Ottomans as a civil servant. However, he was a controversial figure accused of permitting violent excesses by the soldiers under his command. Despite his military successes he was unpopular, as he sought to lead the East Syriac community instead of the patriarch (Wilmshurst 2011, 420–1). Petros' military activities were largely welcomed, but his efforts further incited the Ottomans and gave expression to their fears of the Church of the East operating as an independent power within the region (Gaunt 2006, 123, 128).

By February 1917, the Russian Empire faced internal political division, and the Ottomans were succumbing to British military victories in the Arabian peninsula and Mesopotamia. At that time, it was unclear whether Christians could hope for French and British support, and in March 1917, the Church of the East entered into a partnership of convenience with the Kurdish leader Agha Simko. This arrangement was encouraged by the Russians, who sought means to secure their position from then still active Turkish forces. Once the Russian government had fallen in the winter of 1917, the provincial areas of the Empire were left to attend as best they could to their own security. In this case, the Kurds saw an opportunity to remove their East Syriac enemies and murdered Patriarch Shemon XIX in March 1918.[8]

Impact on the Chaldeans

For the Chaldeans, this period was perhaps the most trying encountered in their history.[9] Their situation was particularly tragic, as they had avoided political agitation prior to the war. The distinctive nature of each Syriac church was not clear to outside observers, and the collective guilt of all Christians, regardless of involvement in any anti-Ottoman activity, was assumed by Ottoman forces. If we accept that attacks by Turks and Kurds against Syriacs (Chaldean, Syrian Orthodox, Syrian Catholic and Church of the East) led to either death or emigration for fifty to sixty percent of these populations overall, one might have assumed as a contemporary observer that the churches would have gravely struggled to recover. Oussani and Naayem suggest a total Syriac Christian population pre-1914 of 700,000 and up to 250,000 killed by 1918 (Baumer 2006, 252; Oussani 1921, xxiv–xxv; Naayem 1921, xxx).

Fortunately for the Chaldeans, some of their population was quite far removed from the immediate areas of massacre. South of Mosul, life was far less affected, notwithstanding the ongoing military campaign in Mesopotamia between the British and the Ottomans. As the British Imperial forces firmly established themselves in Basra, the Chaldeans were protected from Ottoman depredations, and the Ottoman *wali* of Baghdad, Suleyman Nazif, forbade killing of Christians in his *wilayet* (Gaunt 2006, 305).

Wilmshurst, who has collated available data on the Chaldeans for this era, suggests that approximately ten to fifteen percent of the pre-war Chaldean population were killed (c. 10,000–15,000 of 100,000) (Wilmshurst 2011,

436–7, 446). After the massacres, according to the Holy See's statistics – which Wilmshurst presents – there were approximately 44,000 Chaldeans in 1928. This figure is contrasted with that of Stephen Kajo in 1937, who suggested 140,000. Between the lower figure suggested by the Holy See and the higher figure of Kajo, it can be suggested that there were approximately 80,000 Chaldeans present in Iraq just before the start of the Second World War (Wilmshurst 2011, 444).[10]

Thus, even despite the loss of a significant proportion of the community, the Chaldeans appear to have begun to recover to pre-massacre levels by the 1930s. Nevertheless, this growth may not have been organic *per se* – through births – but derived from the necessary readjustments many East Syriacs made after the war to access pastoral care from Chaldean clergy in the absence of those of the Church of the East. In 1920, there remained six bishops in the Church of the East including the patriarch, who was himself only eleven years old. Of the laity, perhaps as many as a third were killed during the war (Wilmshurst 2011, 423, 440–1). The circumstances for the Church of the East were extremely difficult, and it appears to have been uncertain whether the church could continue to function as an independent ecclesiastical institution.[11]

In making an assessment of this era, the variable quality of extant information needed to determine the exact number of Chaldeans affected should be noted. Whilst there is a range of academic and popular literature, these works often refer to non-Armenian Christians of the region as Assyrians (Petrosian 2006, 114, 117). There is no conventional way to distinguish between Chaldeans, members of the Church of the East or members of both churches who have affirmed an Assyrian identity. This is largely due to the wide variety of writers, the lack of a definition as to the specific nature of each title and as to whether they are mutually exclusive. Thus, sources from this period can be confused and ignore further the distinction between the Syriac Catholics and Syrian Orthodox.

It may have been an issue that a comprehensive report was not conducted after the massacres by or on behalf of the Chaldeans. This was inhibited by the lack of stability in the new Iraqi state: a nation-wide uprising occurred in the context of British attempts to assert their rule in 1920. Further, a sense of exhaustion was experienced by the Chaldeans in the aftermath of the massacres. A perception emerged that rebuilding the community and creating a new *status quo* should come before assessment of the immediate past.

Notes

1 Mamluks were freed slaves trained originally as a military force by Muslim rulers in the Middle East. The most famous dynasty of which ruled Egypt and Syria during the mid-thirteenth to early sixteenth centuries.
2 Nevertheless, Tfinkdji does write highly of him: 'La conversion de Jean VIII Hormez inaugurait une nouvelle phase de prospérité et de bonheur pour l'Eglise chaldeénne' (Tfinkdji 1913, 15).
3 Badger provides an English translation (1852a, II:380–422).

62 *Political change in Mesopotamia*

4 The *Padroado* was an arrangement formed between the Portuguese Empire and the Holy See. It granted the Empire *de facto* control over Latin religious communities within its territories. Numerous conflicts of interest arose, but it had the advantage, from the perspective of the Holy See, of ensuring the consolidation of Catholicism among one of the largest and most influential Empires of its time (cf. Teles e Cunha 2011, 53–4).

5 That relatively little is known about the extent of the Russian mission relates to the dispersal of the community during the First World War and the destruction of public Christian life under Soviet rule. There was limited scope for the revival of the mission. Were a full account of the mission's history to be made known more widely, it could alter the contemporary appraisal which sees East Syriac life in the nineteenth century dominated by Latin, Anglican or protestant interlocutors.

6 Phillippe-Jacques Abraham OAOC, Bishop of Gazarta was martyred in August 1915.

7 Of which only Salmas and Urmia were to return to a state of normal ecclesial functioning later in the twentieth century. Amid remains a titular diocese with jurisdiction over Chaldeans resident in the Republic of Turkey.

8 His immediate successor, Mar Shemon XX, was his brother, Polos, who died in 1920. Polos was succeeded by his nephew, Eshai, who took the name Mar Shemon XXI. N.B. this was, following a recalculation in the patriarchal lineage, changed to XXIII (Coakley 1996, 181, 181 n15).

9 At least until the 2003 invasion of Iraq.

10 It seems unlikely that the figure of 44,000 Chaldeans can be considered authoritative and perhaps can be accounted for by the relative lack of infrastructure in many areas of Iraq and the difficulty of conducting a census. Indeed, this is an issue which continues to affect the Chaldeans into the twenty-first century, with the Holy See presenting figures with substantial variations and apparent discrepancies: tens of thousands of people 'appearing' and 'disappearing' over a period of twenty years. See, for example, the Chaldean population statistics of 1990, 2000 and 2010 in Roberson CSP (2010).

11 Coakley notes: 'It is hard to imagine a worse state of affairs for the leadership of the church [of the East] at the beginning of the 1920s: the patriarch a boy with a very small contingent of supporters, and three of the other four bishops more or less disaffected' (1996, 183).

Bibliography

Abramtsov, David F. 1960. 'The Assyrians of Persia and the Russian Orthodox Church'. *One Church* 6: 155–69.

Allawi, Ali A. 2014. *Faisal I of Iraq*. New Haven, CT and London: Yale University Press.

Badger, George Percy. 1852a. *The Nestorians and Their Rituals: With the Narrative of a Mission to Mesopotamia and Coordistan in 1842–1844, and of a Late Visit to Those Countries in 1850: Also, Researches Into the Present Condition of the Syrian Jacobites, Papal Syrians, and Chaldeans, and an Inquiry Into the Religious Tenets of the Yezeedees*. Edited by John Mason Neale. Vol. II. 2 vols. London: Joseph Masters. https://archive.org/details/nestoriansandth00nealgoog.

———. 1852b. *The Nestorians and Their Rituals: With the Narrative of a Mission to Mesopotamia and Coordistan in 1842–1844, and of a Late Visit to Those Countries in 1850: Also, Researches Into the Present Condition of the Syrian Jacobites, Papal Syrians, and Chaldeans, and an Inquiry Into the Religious Tenets of the Yezeedees*. Edited by John Mason Neale. Vol. I. 2 vols. London: Joseph Masters. https://archive.org/details/nestorianstheirr01badg.

Political change in Mesopotamia 63

Baumer, Christoph. 2006. *The Church of the East: An Illustrated History of Assyrian Christianity*. London: Tauris.

Bazzi, Michael J. 2008. *Tilkepe Past and Present*. Edited by Michael J. Bazzi. Translated by Galia Kizi-Thomas. First English translation with updated information. San Diego, CA: Venus Printing.

Bell, Gertrude. Letter to Florence Bell. 1909, April 28. Gertrude Bell Archive. www.gerty.ncl.ac.uk/letter_details.php?letter_id=1692.

Brock, Sebastian, and George A. Kiraz. 2011. 'Scher, Addai'. In *Gorgias Encyclopedic Dictionary of the Syriac Heritage*, edited by Sebastian P. Brock, Aaron Michael Butts, George A. Kiraz, and Lucas Van Rompay. Piscataway, NJ: Gorgias Press.

Bury, John Bagnell. 1930. *History of the Papacy in the 19th Century (1864–1878)*. London: Macmillan.

Ceylan, Ebubekir. 2010. *The Ottoman Origins of Modern Iraq: Political Reform, Modernization and Development in the Nineteenth Century Middle East*. Library of Ottoman Studies 22. London: Tauris Academic Studies.

Coakley, J. F. 1992. *The Church of the East and the Church of England: A History of the Archbishop of Canterbury's Assyrian Mission*. Oxford: Clarendon Press.

———. 1996. 'The Church of the East Since 1914'. *Bulletin of the John Rylands University Library of Manchester* 78 (3): 179–98.

Davison, Roderic H. 1954. 'Turkish Attitudes Concerning Christian-Muslim Equality in the Nineteenth Century'. *The American Historical Review* 59 (4): 844–64. doi:10.2307/1845120.

Frazee, Charles A. 1983. *Catholics and Sultans: The Church and the Ottoman Empire 1453–1923*. London: Cambridge University Press.

Gaunt, David. 2006. *Massacres, Resistance, Protectors: Muslim-Christian Relations in Eastern Anatolia During World War I*. Piscataway, NJ: Gorgias Press.

Gĕ'dan, Paul. 1910. 'Histoire du couvent de Rabban Hormizd de 1808 a 1832'. Translated by Maurice Briere. *Revue de l'Orient chrétien*, Series 2, 15 (4): 410–24.

———. 1911. 'Histoire du couvent de Rabban Hormizd de 1808 a 1832'. Translated by Maurice Briere. *Revue de l'Orient chrétien*, Series 2, 16 (4): 346–55.

Grant, Asahel. 1841. *The Nestorians; or, the Lost Tribes: Containing Evidence of Their Identity, an Account of Their Manners, Customs, and Ceremonies; Together With Sketches of Travel in Ancient Assyria, Armenia, Media, and Mesopotamia; and Illustrations of Scripture Prophecy*. London: John Murray. https://archive.org/details/nestoriansorlos00grangoog.

Habbi, Joseph. 1971. 'L'unification de la hiérarchie chaldéenne dans la première moitié du XIXe siècle'. *Parole de l'Orient* II (1–2): 121–43, 305–27.

———. 1980. 'Les Chaldéens et les Malabares au XIX siècle'. *Oriens Christianus* 64: 82–107.

Joseph, John. 1961. *The Nestorians and Their Muslim Neighbors: A Study of Western Influence on Their Relations*. Princeton Oriental Studies 20. Princeton, NJ: Princeton University Press.

Khayyath, Georges Ebed-Jesus V. 1870. *Syri orientales, seu Chaldaei, Nestoriani et Romanorum pontificum primatus: commentatio historico-philogico-theologica, adjeetis textibus citationum genuina lingua propriisque litteris exaratis*. Rome: Typis S. Congregatinis de Propaganda Fide. https://archive.org/details/syriorientalesse00khay.

———. 1896. 'Etat Religieux des dioceses formant le Patriarcat Chaldeen de Babylone au 1er janvier 1896'. Edited by Jean-Baptiste Chabot. *Revue de l'Orient chrétien*, Series 1, 1 (4): 433–53.

64 *Political change in Mesopotamia*

Labourt, Jérôme. 1908. 'Note sur les schismes de l'Église nestorienne du XVIe au XIXe siècle'. *Journal Asiatique* 11 (April): 227–35.

Maggiolini, Paolo. 2012. 'Bringing Together Eastern Catholics Under a Common Civil Head: The Agreements Between the Syriac and Chaldean Patriarchs and the Civil Head of the Armenian Catholic Church in Constantinople (1833–1871)'. *Journal of Eastern Christian Studies* 64 (3–4): 253–85. doi:10.2143/JECS.64.3.2961412.

Martin, Jean Pierre Paulin. 1867. *La Chaldée: esquisse historique: suivie de quelques réflexions sur l'Órient*. Imprimerie de la Civiltà Cattolica. https://books.google.com/boo ks?id=bCIYAAAAYAAJ&pg=PA37#v=onepage&q&f=false.

Martina SJ, Giacomo. 1990. *Pio IX (1867–1878)*. Miscellanea Historiae Pontificiae 58. Rome: Editrice Pontificia Universita Gregoriana.

Movsesian, Mark L. 2010. 'Elusive Equality: The Armenian Genocide and the Failure of Ottoman Legal Reform'. *University of St. Thomas Journal of Law & Public Policy* 4 (2): 1–17.

Naayem, Joseph. 1921. 'Author's Preface'. In *Shall This Nation Die?*, edited by Joseph Naayem, xxvii–xxxi. New York: Chaldean Rescue. https://archive.org/stream/shallthisnation d00naay.

Nakash, Yitzhak. 2003. *The Shi'is of Iraq*. 2nd paperback Edition. Princeton, NJ: Princeton University Press.

Oussani, Gabriel. 1901. 'The Modern Chaldeans and Nestorians, and the Study of Syriac Among Them'. *Journal of the American Oriental Society* 22: 79–96.

———. 1921. 'An Historical Essay on the Assyro-Chaldean Christians'. In *Shall This Nation Die?*, edited by Joseph Naayem, xv–xxvi. New York: Chaldean Rescue. https://archive.org/stream/shallthisnationd00naay.

Petrosian, Vahram. 2006. 'Assyrians in Iraq'. *Iran & the Caucasus* 10 (1): 113–47. doi:10. 1163/157338406777979322.

Pius IX. 1872. 'Quae in Patriarchatu – On the Church in Chaldea'. Holy See. www.papalen cyclicals.net/Pius09/p9quaein.htm.

Podipara, Placid J. 1970. *The Individuality of the Malabar Church*. Palai: St Thomas Press.

Ratel, A. 1904. 'L'Église nestorienne en Turquie et en Perse'. *Echoes d'Orient* 7: 285–92, 348–52.

Roberson CSP, Ronald G. 2010. 'The Eastern Catholic Churches 2010'. www.cnewa.org/ source-images/Roberson-eastcath-statistics/eastcatholic-stat10.pdf.

Royel, Mar Awa. 2014. 'The Pearl of Great Price: The Anaphora of the Apostles Addai & Mari as an Ecclesial and Cultural Identifier of the Assyrian Church of the East'. *Orientalia Christiana Periodica* 80 (1): 5–22.

Scher, Addai. 1910. 'Episodes de l'Histoire du Kurdistan'. *Journal Asiatique*, Series 10, 15 (February): 119–39.

Smith, Eli, and Harrison Gray Otis Dwight. 1833. *Researches of the Rev. E. Smith and Rev. H. G. O. Dwight in Armenia; Including a Journey Through Asia Minor, and Into Georgia and Persia, With a Visit to the Nestorian and Chaldean Christians of Oormiah and Salmas*. Vol. II. 2 vols. Boston, MA: Crocker and Brewster. https://archive.org/details/ researchesofreve02smit.

Teles e Cunha, João. 2011. 'Confluence and Divergence: The Thomas Christians and the Padroado c. 1500–1607'. *Journal of Eastern Christian Studies* 63 (1–2): 45–71. doi:10.2143/JECS.63.1.2149613.

Tfinkdji, Joseph. 1913. *L'Église Chaldéenne Catholique Autrefois et Aujourd'hui*. Paris: Bureaux des études ecclésiastiques.

Tisserant, Eugène. 1931. 'L'Église Nestorienne'. In *Dictionnaire de Theologie Catholique*. edited by Alfred Vacant, Eugène Mangenot and Emile Amann Paris: Letouzey et Ané.

Valognes, Jean-Pierre. 1994. *Vie et Mort Des Chrétiens d'Orient: Des Origines à Nos Jours*. Paris: Fayard.

Young, Wilkie. 1971. 'Mosul in 1909'. *Middle Eastern Studies* 7 (2): 229–35.

Wilmshurst, David. 2000. *The Ecclesiastical Organisation of the Church of the East 1318–1913*. Corpus Scriptorum Christianorum Orientalium ; Subsidia, vol. 582. tomus 104. Lovanii: Peeters.

———. 2011. *The Martyred Church: A History of the Church of the East*. Sawbridgeworth, Hertfordshire: East and West.

3 Re-discovering the Chaldean narrative in modern Iraq (1918–2003)

Outlining Chaldean history in the context of the establishment of the modern state of Iraq in 1921 is a novel area of study. There is a lack of pre-existing methodology in place to consider the Chaldeans in the full light of their status as an Eastern Catholic church, their relationship with the Holy See, and the relationship between the office of Chaldean patriarch and the Iraqi state. Furthermore, there is a lack of ecclesiastical history written by Chaldeans in the modern period. We may be justifiably surprised at the lack of works written since 1921 given that reflection on relationships with the temporal power and chronicles of church affairs were so regularly produced by East Syriac authors in Late Antique and Medieval eras (see Wood 2013; Debié 2010, 71–2; Becker 2008, 40–5; Brock 1979).

The account of Israel Audo, Chaldean Bishop of Mardin, on the massacres and how they affected his diocese and the Chaldeans more widely was one of the few historical accounts produced, for example, on this topic.[1] An absence of self-reflection in this context is perhaps unsurprising given that from the 1930s to 1960s, the Chaldeans were in an era which focused on integration into the new Iraqi society. There was an emphasis on looking forward instead of retrospective glances into painful events of which many, by the 1960s, would have had no experience or recollection.[2] Why would ecclesiology and ecclesiastical history be discussed other than among community members with a particular interest or for the purpose of instruction of students and seminarians? Population displacement, urbanisation and engagement with modern political ideologies all also provided distraction from a need or desire to consider Chaldean identity and history.

Ecclesiastical history and ecclesiological discussions altered somewhat with the establishment of the Syriac Corporation of the Iraqi Academy and the production of ecclesial journals such as *Fikr al-Masihi* and that of the Syriac Corporation itself. Nonetheless, these developments relied upon the driving interests of Iraqi and non-Iraqi Christian intelligentsia (e.g. Abouna; Brock; Cheikho SJ; Fiey OP; Habbi; Youssif) and were largely not popularly led. Moreover, there was and still does exist a lack of widespread interest in the historical experience of the Chaldeans in the era between 1921–2003 among the community.[3]

A contiguous Chaldean culture so deeply rooted in northern Mesopotamia and eastern Asia Minor could not easily be reconciled to the new Iraq and its different cultural and geographical environments. The incarnation of Chaldean life had to be reaffirmed and structured so as to meet the needs of a community whose position was irrevocably altered. Where previously ecclesiological identity was central to their lives, multiple and, in some instances, competing levels of attachments and identities emerged whether to the state, their perceived ethnicity or economic foci.

This is a wider historiographical issue raised, for example, by Borrut and Cobb in their work on the Umayyad dynasty which governed the Levant and Mesopotamia from the mid-seventh to mid-eighth centuries. They note: 'Sensitive students inevitably confront the question . . . how do we know what we think we know about the Umayyads?' (Borrut and Cobb 2010, 2). This is a question which may just as easily be applied to the Chaldeans as to our comprehension of their history. We are left in a situation where in many instances we just do not know the definitive answers to many questions, which will likely remain the case for the indefinite future.

Building on current scholarship

The modern religious history of Iraqi Christianity especially from the 1930s onward is a developing genre in scholarship. A lacuna, for example, in the historiography, is the lack of studies on Patriarch Emmanuel II Thomas (1900–1947). This is a surprising gap given his time in office is one of the longest periods of patriarchal tenure since the establishment of the Chaldean community. By way of comparison, the first European language biography of King Feisel I (1921–1933), the first Iraqi monarch, was published only in 2014 (Allawi 2014).

If Thomas' rule has lacked scrutiny, this could reflect the church's distressed nature during the second decade of his patriarchal career and the political neutrality which he encouraged among the Chaldeans. He advanced a quietist approach with the intention of safeguarding the community more securely from accusations of treachery and thus persecution.[4] Thomas was keenly aware of the tragedy which had befallen the Church of the East during the 1915–1918 massacres as a result of acquiescing to a political narrative which set their community apart from surrounding Ottoman and Kurdish society. Such a path was rejected by Thomas and, I suggest, his entry into Iraqi political life through membership of the Iraqi senate was perceived as a more efficacious means to retain Christian influence at the élite level of the state.[5] This also mirrored the example of East Syriac-lay élite interaction under the Abbasids.

Generally, in the historiography, there is a large body of literature which considers Iraqi Christianity from different perspectives of scholarly, personal and professional interests. However, there is less discussion of Christian relationships with the governments of the republican and especially Baath administrations from 1958. Most recently, Wilmshurst (2011), Valognes (1994), Yacoub (1996) and Rassam (2010) have redressed this balance, but their works in the former two instances lack a specificity to the Chaldeans or Iraq in one volume, whilst the latter two come from quite a partisan perspective towards the East Syriac communities. O'Mahony (2009, 2004a, 2004b) and Audo (2012, 2008, Audo

68 *Re-discovering the Chaldean narrative*

et al. (2005) have made several contributions whilst Teule (2015, 2012, 2008) and Hunter (2014a, 2014b) probably come closest to beginning an assessment of the socio-political involvements of Iraqi Christians, but their works in these instances tend to focus on the situation post-2003.

Difficulties have existed in general in pursuing a comprehensive approach to Iraqi historical studies which encompass all religious, political and ethnic communities. A major edited volume that has emerged since 2003, which seeks to revivify modern Iraqi historical studies despite being over 500 pages in length with thirty-three articles in total, provides no essay which considers the challenges of writing the history of the non-Muslim inhabitants or that of non-Arabs or non-Kurds. The work is greatly welcomed for discussing a range of methodological issues, but fails to recognise the normative plurality of Iraq and to attempt to encourage a history of Iraq that is a more purely historical account and not conveyed through the lens of political science, political history, sociology or anthropology. This absence is somewhat surprising given that the introduction, co-authored by two of the editors, notes:

> With Iraq facing the danger of implosion, which groups – or even segments of the population with their own sub-Iraqi and trans-border references – will be able to impose their visions of history? Is Iraq facing an unavoidable 'fragmentation of collective memory'?
>
> (Bocco and Tejel 2012, xiii)

More widely, we can note, in one of the standard texts on Iraqi political history, Tripp in his otherwise useful *A History of Iraq*, refers to Christians on nine occasions – as per the index – with only the briefest explanations of their roles and mainly in relation to the political aims of those who associated with an Assyrian identity (2007). Whilst Simons, who also offers a very useful broad introductory history of Iraq, lacks consideration of more than a passing nature of the Christian segments of the population (2004). These works are contrasted with the concise but excellent outline of Christian contributions to Iraq in Abdullah's work which provides an indication of how a history of Iraq can account for its plural character (2003). Stansfield also has a good, if brief, assessment of how the Christian communities were affected by Iraqi political discourse (2007).

This trend of avoiding mention of the Christian population in Iraq and the wider Middle East is disappointing given the available scholarship on the Christians and the emphasis in recent and contemporary academic studies for considering the place of minorities (so-called) in Middle Eastern societies.[6] By way of comparison, there has been a growing interest in the former Jewish populations of Mesopotamia-Iraq in the last fifteen years which raise awareness of Iraq's former plurality and ensure that a bipolar Sunni-Shia discourse does not dominate (Masters 2001; Rejwan 2004; Snir 2006; Gavish 2010; Somekh 2012).

Among scholars of Western Christian background there is a general uncertainty towards how to treat the works produced by Christians of the East Syriac tradition. This is perhaps due to concomitant difficulties in comprehending what process of theological or ecclesiological engagement should be taken towards the East Syriac churches due to the relative lack of expertise which the dominant Latin and protestant discourses have concerning them. Nevertheless, through the growth of the modern ecumenical movement, the increasing importance of Iraq to regional and international politics and the growth of diaspora groups in the West, practical and theological engagement has increased and seen a boom in studies especially from the 1960s. Brock (1982, 1996, 2004, 2009) and Fiey (1959, 1970, 1993, 1994) led scholarship in this area. Thus, the Christians of Iraq have come to be well served in general, but lacking has been an assessment of their relations with the Baath party and Saddam Hussein. It appears from present scholarship that there are hints at and awareness of aspects of this relationship but a lack of concentrated discussion (White 2007, 5–8). There is little if any discussion, for example, on the rôle of Tariq Aziz, his religious identity and the effects of this on Baath policy. The extended interview with Aziz conducted by Bouvet and Denaud contains only a few pages concerning his religious identity and no discussion of how this affected his position in government (2000). The churches and their relationship to international communities is also lacking. The Holy See's place within Iraqi history has a limited assessment, which is remarkable especially considering the strong interest with which popes John Paul II and Benedict XVI had in the Middle East (Filoni 2008; Toulat 1992).

In considering the Chaldeans in and of themselves, we do well to recall how they have been viewed by the Muslim populations: Christians were often and still are considered a homogeneous group by the government and many non-Christian Iraqis. From 1921, the churches in Iraq were largely engaged with through the office of the Chaldean patriarch. His position as *primus inter pares* among the church leaders resident in the country granted him this rôle. This suggests the Muslim precept that 'unbelief constitutes one nation' has had a lasting influence even among more secularised rulers in the Arab Middle East (Masters 2001, 81).

A new political order: 1918–1947

In the new Middle Eastern order established after the First World War, the Chaldeans experienced a period of initial uncertainty, but saw a growth of hope for a secure place in Iraq. This uncertainty derived from fears of what future status they would have in an Arab Sunni-dominated state, and how they were to consolidate their church structures and communities after the massacres. Chaldean hopes for the future also centred on British Imperial influence in Iraq. Iraq's legal system and constitution were formulated with British oversight and intended to ensure that, in the fullness of time, Iraqis would be accepting of pluralism in public life and equal social status in law for all citizens (Natarajan 2011, 806).

The state of Iraq was formed officially for the first time following the 1920 Treaty of Sèvres. The treaty guaranteed Britain control over the Mesopotamian region via a League of Nations mandate until 1932. The mandate was given legitimacy through the establishment of a constitutional monarchy. The first king was, in fact, the son of the Sheriff of Mecca, Feisel, who governed from 1921 until

70 Re-discovering the Chaldean narrative

his death in 1933. His successors were kings Ghazi (1933–1939) and Feisel II (1939–1958).

The plebiscite which formally established Feisel as monarch had a return of over ninety percent, causing some doubt as to its validity. This doubt is unsurprising when we consider Feisel had no geographical or personal ties with Mesopotamia. Moreover, as he was Sunni, it was supposed he would likely bring with him an élite of similar background even if this would be regarded with concern by the largely Shia population.

The British thinking behind suggesting Feisel for the monarchy was astute, however, and based on the popular appeal he attained during the First World War through his involvement in the Arab Revolt and his family's alleged line of descent from the Islamic prophet, Mohammed. Initially, Christians appear to have opposed Feisel's introduction given his Hijazi origins, with Dawisha noting that 'the thriving Christian and Jewish communities of Iraq [did not] find palatable their incorporation into a Muslim-dominated Kingdom ruled from Mecca' (2005, 39). However, as the realities of his character and rule became apparent, and following the loss of Mecca and his territories in the Hijaz to the Saudis, fears of an overtly Muslim state faded.

Any thoughts of complete Iraqi independence were largely quashed by the 1922 Anglo-Iraqi Treaty which saw several areas of administration given British advisers in order to maintain the economy in line with the financial imperatives of the Empire (HMSO 1925, 4, 9). A new version of the treaty was made in 1930 which again favoured the British. Military facilities were made available to their forces for a twenty-five year period, which safeguarded their access to Iraq's oilfields. Thus, when considering Iraq from 1918–1930, we should see it as an economic vassal state to the British Empire as opposed to a novel independent Arab constitutional monarchy (cf. Tripp 2007, 51). The conflicting dynamic between the British imperatives for the Empire's economy in the free flow of oil and the Iraqi élites was only to be effectively resolved following the withdrawal of British military forces in the 1950s.

Chaldean state and inter-communal relations

As the new state had been artificially created, it was some time before there began a coagulation of interests to sustain it. Major opposition to British imperial influence and the direction of Iraqi affairs by a monarch from the Hijaz were first manifested during the 1920 rebellion. As the Arab Revolt helped expedite the end of Ottoman rule, so such a rebellion fuelled the imaginations of Mesopotamian residents who perceived a similar effort could be made to remove the British. Despite British military dominance in the southern Levant, Egypt and peninsula Arabia, their hold on Mesopotamia appeared tenuous by comparison. There, British victory against the Ottomans had been extremely costly.

The rebellion was largely focused in mid- and southern Iraq. Popular support derived justification from Islamic jurisprudence and the question as to whether Muslims – Sunni or Shia – could be justifiably ruled by an infidel power such as the

British (Nakash 2003, 67). Such a state of affairs had long existed for Muslims in other regions, whether in the Caucasus under the Russian Empire or French North Africa. That such a state of affairs began to exist in what many Muslims considered the heartland of their religion was, however, a direct threat to their social dominance in the central Middle East and could be religiously interpreted as an indication of a fatal decline and/or punishment. Therefore, rebellion brought together for a short time the Sunni and Shia Arab populations of Mesopotamia-Iraq. The renewed call to *jihad* was considered as a very dangerous threat by the non-Muslim populations. Even if such rhetoric was not directed at them, it ensured that from the foundation of Iraq in 1921 Christians, Jews, Mandeans and Yazidis were sensitive to the necessity of a stable Iraqi social order.

Eventual British victory did not rely solely on military intervention but also upon the conservative nature of a sufficient proportion of the native population. There was every hope among tribal and landowning élites to see the restoration of order so as to begin to rebuild their economic and social dominance regardless of who laid claim as the civil power. There also existed a proportion of the population largely disinterested in the coercive attempts by any one faction to establish themselves as dominant. With many residents of Basra and Baghdad having extended interactions with the British from the mid-nineteenth century, an awareness existed of the likely inevitability of British Imperial success in the power vacuum left following the defeat of the Ottomans. No one of the Iraqi factions had sufficient capabilities to emerge victorious, with the new Iraq appearing to require an authoritative leadership figure and institutions around which the new ideal of Iraqi patriotism could be anchored.

The Chaldeans were not opposed in principle to a co-opted monarchy under British supervision and remained acquiescent to the stabilisation of the social order (Rutledge 2014, 185). The British recognition of the Chaldean patriarch's influence bolstered this support. Emmanuel II Thomas was given a position on an advisory council of ministers under British supervision in 1920, and, from the formation of the state in 1921, he was a member of the Iraqi Senate (Tripp 2007, 44). The early drafts of the first Iraqi Constitution had also provided for set numbers of minority members in the Chamber of Deputies as an attempt to support their position within a unitary Iraqi state (Joseph 1983, 115). These proposals were rejected by the Chaldeans, however, for fear of appearing to set themselves apart from the rest of society.

The military élite and the Assyrians

Although the monarch was the head of state, Iraq's governance – outside of British intervention – was largely determined by the prime minister, his cabinet and the competing factions who held sway among contemporary ministerial appointments. The cabinet became dominated by the military but their political affiliations were further divided by strength of adherence to nationalism, socialism and Islam.

As the military élites came to consolidate control over Iraqi politics from the 1930s, the army became the primary means of coercion utilised by Sunnis

72 Re-discovering the Chaldean narrative

to maintain their privileged status. The military saw the maintenance of Iraq's borders as established from the Treaty of Sèvres as a foundational principle of the state, and would not countenance opposition by any group who attempted to undermine this *status quo*. Thus, during times of perceived or actual threat decisive action was taken and the Kurds, Yezidis and Shia were all repressed between 1933–1936 and 1936–1941 (Nakash 2003, 123). The acts of force the armed forces' leadership used to maintain their position derived from the lack of economic or religious influence they could otherwise exert to influence or coerce the population.

In such circumstances, the creation of a more secure socio-religious situation for Christians was not aided by British reliance on levies recruited among members of the Church of the East and other numerically minor communities. These Church members and communities were used to quell uprisings against British influence especially in northern Iraq (Petrosian 2006, 120; Bet Shlimon 2012, 95). As some East Syriacs had begun to assert an ethnic and cultural link to the Assyrian Empire of antiquity, these assertions were transformed into political action in the twentieth century as they agitated for an autonomous Assyrian region in Iraq. The levies were perceived by Assyrian nationalists as a potential means for advancing this end.

It appeared to many Iraqis that the Assyrians acted in concord with the British and were favoured through links established between the British High Commissioner and Patriarch Mar Shimun XXIII (Husry 1974, 166). Plans for secession culminated in the publication of an Assyrian Officer Manifesto in 1932 which outlined the formation of an autonomous region in the Nineveh plains. (Husry 1974, 167). In pursuing such an agenda, the Assyrians were in opposition to the king, the British and Iraq's Arab population who had little desire to see any form of devolution or the potential loss of a buffer zone with Turkey and Syria. The military élite were particularly concerned given the Assyrian independence movement coalesced concurrent with campaigns against Kurdish separatists (Husry 1974, 168).

The mutual antagonism between the army and the levies increased and in 1933 the Simele tragedy occurred. The circumstances of the incident became heavily politicised over time and according to authors' biases have led to either one or other side being blamed for the outcome of events (Husry 1974, 175; Main 1933, 664).

The essential event leading up to Simele was the release of levies from British service in 1933. Each levy following his demobilisation was permitted to retain a rifle and ammunition and thus a highly trained independent military force was established totalling nearly 10,000 men. When we consider the Iraqi army had only 30,000 soldiers at this time, we can note a potentially serious strategic threat (Main 1933, 667). For many levies returning to their homes in northern Iraq, independence in some form was seen as a realistic option. The Iraqi Army sought initially to disarm the ex-levies, and, following confusion as to how and whether this could take place and Assyrian fears of physical danger, it appears plans were made on both sides to intervene militarily against the other.

The main incident focused on the village of Simele and involved only the soldiers of each side. However, violence soon extended to surrounding Christian villages which saw civilian massacres. Estimates as to the total number killed vary, but a figure of approximately 1,000 casualties appears to be the most likely (Main 1933, 672).

Regardless of the extent of the attacks and whatever actually led to and took place during the incident, the outcome for Assyrian nationalists and for the Church of the East was deleterious and ecclesiologically decisive. In 1933, Mar Shimun XXIII was exiled from Iraq. He initially moved to Cyprus and later settled in Chicago from 1940 (Baumer 2006, 269). This marked the first time since the consolidation of the Church of the East at the Synod of Dadisho in 424 that its patriarch was not officially resident in Asia. The events reinforced the Chaldean position as the senior Christian community in Iraq but gave credence to a popular assumption of the potential disloyalty of Christians. It would be an exaggeration to characterise the Assyrian nationalist cause as one inherently unsettling for the majority of Christians and other numerically minor religious groups in their relationship with Muslim communities and the government of the day. However, through aggrandisement for secession, the Assyrians influenced the general perception of and beliefs about Christians' political intentions: to establish an autonomous region intent on limiting Muslim led political hegemony.

Emmanuel II Thomas (1900–1947)

From the foundation of Iraq, Thomas recognised that the future security of the Chaldeans and the Christian population more widely was linked to (1) accepting the government of the day – so far as its activities did not interfere with Chaldean religious practices, (2) supporting modernist political ideals of the separation of religion and the state and (3) a commitment to an Arab national identity. These three concerns became the cornerstone of the Chaldean interaction with the contemporary political élite, a type of interaction which only altered following the 2003 invasion of Iraq. This position was in contrast to that of the Church of the East, which lost its patriarch to exile and lacked the intellectual and material resources to formulate a coherent plan for their position in the new state (cf. Husry 1974, 166).

Thomas' efforts were not particular to the Chaldeans, as all Iraqi religious leaders during the 1920s–1930s were obliged to assess and engineer a secure leadership position in the new political and social environment (Lukitz 1995, 108). However, Thomas was fortunate to make his mark on political culture through his membership of the Iraqi senate and in his personal relationship with Feisel I. Thomas' privileged position supported the integration of Chaldeans into Iraqi society in general. This integration was popularly based in the educational and economic advancement which many Chaldeans attained and which the patriarch and hierarchy strongly encouraged.

Admiration for Catholic forms of education, and the religious communities which maintained schools, should not be underestimated, given that until the First

74 Re-discovering the Chaldean narrative

World War, literacy extended to only five percent of the Mesopotamian population (Abdullah 2003, 123). A European observer writing in 1927 noted:

> How backward the conditions still are . . . is shown by the fact that one Government secondary school in Baghdad, with a boarding section, is sufficient to meet the demand for secondary education for boys in the capital, and that the total attendance at the five Government secondary schools in the whole of Iraq is 562 pupils.
>
> (Conway 1927, 334)

However, the Christian advantage gradually began to decline as Muslims grew to compete economically and socially in the professions with significant investment in all levels of state education (Lukitz 1995, 109–10). Nevertheless, the quality of Chaldean life from 1921–1947 generally improved, which related to Thomas' willingness to work within a society in which Sunni and Shia law and custom were cultural and societal norms. As a graduate of the Jesuit University of St Joseph in Beirut, he had received formative training in a religiously plural region, which had permitted engagement with the Eastern Catholic and Arab literary and cultural revival from the late nineteenth century. The transfer of Thomas' Levantine experiences to Iraq served to reinforce his commitment to maintain a plural Iraqi socio-religious *status quo* united with an openness to Arab culture.

Thomas' success was demonstrated most clearly by the overall expansion of the Christian population which more than doubled in Baghdad, Basra and Kirkuk between 1932 and 1957 (Betts 1979, 105). The rapid change in urban demography was remarkable, and the concentration of Chaldeans in Baghdad altered the focus of a community whose traditions had largely been sustained in and around Mosul for the previous 600 years.

Movement to Baghdad entailed some change in identity for Chaldeans. Through participation in urban life in the capital, engagement increased with the Iraqi Baath and Communist parties. There was also a shift away from agricultural based employment towards artisanal, technical or professional rôles. There had long existed a core of Christian urban intelligentsia, but the population shift from Mosul and the Nineveh plains was the first time since the Abbasid era that East Syriac life had been so far advanced in Baghdad.

The Chaldean position in Baghdad was further reinforced through the departure of the Jewish population during the 1940s and early 1950s. The displacement of the Iraqi Jewish population came following the foundation of the state of Israel in 1948, with many Iraqi Muslims encouraging their expulsion. This was a significant departure from the views which Feisel I had espoused during his rule concerning the Semitic root of life in Mesopotamia as a common bond between the Jews, Muslims and Christians of Iraq (Snir 2006, 382). Indeed, given the anti-Zionist and pro-Iraqi discourse pursued by many Jewish Iraqis, their departure is even more remarkable (Snir 2006, 383–4; Ben-Yaacob et al. 2007).

With the Chaldeans entering the social gap which the Jews left, it was, for many Muslim Iraqis, a first opportunity to come into contact with Christians on a regular basis. It was recognised that their interventions in public discourse came not in an ostentatious manner but relied on being a humble (but not silent) presence by maintaining a living Christian witness in a challenging majority Muslim environment. The Chaldean experience of Iraqi society was also influenced by their increasing interactions with the Shia population. Formerly, the Chaldeans had mainly encountered the Sunni communities, whether Arab or Kurdish, who predominated in northern Mesopotamia. As demographic change and geographical foci shifted, a generally amenable relationship developed with the Shia and also, for those in Baghdad, with the large Jewish population.

A significant feature of Thomas' rule during the inter-war era was the start of Chaldean emigration from the Middle East. Economic opportunities in urban areas of North America, for example, could not be ignored by those eager to improve their conditions during the Ottoman Empire's decline. Iraqi society did give freedom for Christian communities to expand in areas of public life. This was especially the case in the professions and skilled labour, but some areas of work were still limited by an unofficial bar on Christians entering them, such as administrative and managerial positions (Rassam 2010, 140). The draw of emigration was also due to the opportunity to reside in what were perceived to be Christian countries in which religious life would be far less affected by societal pressures.

Nevertheless, at Thomas' death, the Chaldeans in Iraq were in a relatively comfortable situation, as the latter years of his leadership segued with the consolidation of the petroleum industry. The subsequent growth in the economy reached to such a level that Coptic, Armenian and other Christian migrants were keen to move to Iraq to take advantage of the situation where their skills in engineering and medicine were very well received (Hambye SJ 1968, 84; cf. Rassam 2010, 134–5).

Iraq as a nation and Chaldean involvement in political activity

Regardless of the Chaldean population's involvement in forming a new plural Arab led society, the majority of religious or ethnic communities was not as strong supporters of the new state. Indeed, it would be hard to describe Iraq as a stable country prior to the late 1920s, and in 1932, Feisel I voiced his concerns:

> The inhabitants of Iraq have not sufficient national cohesion to admit of Government agreeing to any differentiation between sects or classes, and that the policy must first be for all classes to realize they are Iraqis.
>
> (Quoted in Husry 1974, 169)

Such a *status quo* was exacerbated by internal and external powers' actions. The finalisation of Iraq's border with Turkey came only in 1932, with the Turkish state seeking to annex Mosul and its environs from the end of the First World War. These ambitions were prevented only through British military intervention and the commitment of the League of Nations to favour Iraqi ownership from

76 *Re-discovering the Chaldean narrative*

1924. Whilst in Basra, the religiously mixed merchant class were unified in their attempts to develop the city as the main port hub in the Persian Gulf in competition with Kuwait (Visser 2007, 25; Nakash 2003, 63).

A key point of contention was what constituted an Iraqi patriotic identity. Patriotic concepts were split between those who supported an Iraqi particularist paradigm, which was also supported by the British, and those who sought a more pan-Arabist emphasis on union with other Arab peoples in the surrounding region. Thus, the distinction of who could be considered within the state was radically different: for the pan-Arabists, the Kurds, for example, could not be fully considered to fit within the future Arab collective. As Ottoman rule had been relatively benign until the mid-nineteenth century, and had limited social impact outside urban areas in central and southern Mesopotamia, a unifying Mesopotamian identity in opposition to their rule had not developed (Marr 2010, 18–20). Implementing a national identity relied on the acceptance of the new political and geographic boundaries and sufficient coagulation of sectional interests to ensure an identity was widely held. Without the enforcement of the Arab monarchy on the state and their support for an Iraqi patriotism however abstract or ill defined, the pluralism of the Iraqi *milieu* would likely have retreated into more regionally based political groupings because no other overarching body existed around which to form a point of unity in the new state.

The Chaldeans' situation was complicated by their location – whether rural or urban – and their ability to cope within what became a predominantly linguistically Arab state: rural dwellers were generally Syriac speakers and urban residents were Arabic speakers (Masters 2001, 45). Those who remained resident in more rural northern Iraq were, for example, generally more affected by the challenges of adjusting to the use of Arabic as the state's official language.

Until the 1950s, Chaldean community members largely avoided political activism and concentrated on economic and social activities. Limited direct engagement in politics was shaped by the dominant role which the clergy held in determining the relationship of the entire community with the state. I suggest there was an unwillingness to cede political influence to the laity, as the hierarchy had controlled East Syriac relations with the state for nearly 1,500 years.

Thomas' position as a member of the Iraqi senate from 1921 reinforced the dominance of the patriarchal office in determining the community's relationship with the state. Thomas' position in the senate was perhaps not initially conceptualised as that of an essentially political rôle, but instead as an advisor with some oversight into the application of new statutes on the Chaldean population. Such an arrangement reflected the intermediary rôle of the patriarch between the state and community. This was drawn from the precedent of East Syriac patriarchs in the Sasanid, Abbasid and Mongol Empires who regularly engaged the contemporary ruling elites to ensure their community's security.

The clergy's dominance did not entirely preclude lay Christian involvement in the state. Yusif Ghanima[7] and Rafael Buti were the ministers of Finance and State, respectively (Betts 1979, 183). Christian integration into senior positions followed a pragmatic approach from successive governments. Christians were appointed to roles where their often more cosmopolitan upbringings could be put to good use with, for example, Najib Sa'igh being made Iraqi ambassador to the Lebanon (Betts 1979, 184).

Joseph VII Ghanima (1947–1958) and the end of the monarchy

Thomas' successor was Joseph Ghanima. He had been born in 1881 in Mosul and was ordained in 1904. Having lived through the era of the massacres, he was well aware of the necessity of securing the community's position in Iraqi society via a co-operative relationship with the government. Moreover, he had been present with the League of Nations delegation who were to determine whether Turkey had a right to annex Mosul in the 1920s. He was used to the political difficulties consonant with the independent Iraqi state. He latterly served as an auxiliary bishop in the dioceses of Mosul and Baghdad in the role of Thomas' secretary prior to his appointment as patriarch. It was unfortunate that such a well-qualified candidate to lead the Chaldeans died in 1958, the same year as the monarchy was overthrown.

The transfer of the patriarchal headquarters to Baghdad from Mosul in 1950 was an example of Joseph VII Ghanima's desire to ensure the Chaldeans were not dismissed from political and social life in Iraq. This was a significant change, but one which was not without precedent (Petrosian 2006, 125; Seferta 2008, 14). The Abbasid dynasty's capital of Baghdad was host to the East Syriac patriarchs on a consistent basis, and under Ottoman rule Baghdad had been the *de facto* centre of administration in Mesopotamia. The Chaldean Patriarch entered the centre of Iraqi political power and strengthened his claim to the See of Seleucia-Ctesiphon and the Chaldean claim to the heritage of the undivided Church of the East.

Ghanima was fortunate to lead the Chaldeans during a period of relative political stability in Iraq and to consolidate a neutral and, to a certain extent, privileged position for the community which effectively emerged as the national church of Iraq. This was a national church in an Islamicised culture, of a minority of the population and with limited direct influence on the government's political thought.

Joseph VII also furthered Chaldean life more widely: he consecrated a new Cathedral in Tehran in July 1950 and a church in Egypt in 1951 (*The Catholic Herald* 1950, 1951). He also took steps to improve clerical standards by confirming the necessity for priests to complete a formal seminary education (*The Catholic Herald* 1952). Ghanima was, in effect, completing much of the prodigious work which Thomas had instigated.

Thomas had seen the need for further improving the standards of Christian education and, with the support of the Iraqi government and the Holy See, a Jesuit school – Baghdad College – was established in 1932 (Girling 2016, passim). This institution was open to all Iraqis regardless of religion and welcomed for its modern pedagogy. In starting the school at an early stage in Iraqi history, it ensured that a Christian education, if not overt Christianity, could be found supporting the new élites.

78 *Re-discovering the Chaldean narrative*

Baghdad College's success permitted the establishment of the Jesuit-led al-Hikma University in 1955. Both institutions provided a very high standard of education for many future Iraqi leaders and were a means for Iraqi Catholics to demonstrate their loyalty to the state. Further, they emphasised that Christianity was not a detrimental influence on Iraqi society and that Christian methods of education could dramatically improve the quality of the professional classes.

The naming of the university indicated the traditions which the Jesuits and government wished to respect, with the title chosen for the mutual Christian and Muslim association with King Solomon and that of the ninth century discussions between Patriarch Timothy I and Caliph al-Mahdi in the context of the centre of scientific and philosophical research known as Bayt al-Hikma in Abbasid Baghdad (D'Ancona 2013). The opportunity for regular debate came freely with a mixed student body of approximately fifty percent Christian and Muslim from 1956–1968 (MacDonnell SJ 1994, 175).

In 1968, following the Baath government's establishment, all non-state schools were closed. In the case of Baghdad College and al-Hikma, concerns were expressed over the threat the schools posed to the maintenance of pan-Arabist ideals in student formation and over the more *catholic* paradigm which they endeavoured to provide for their education. These concerns were not because they were Christian, but instead arose due to fears of participation in Anglo-American imperialism, as they were led by American Jesuits (MacDonnell SJ 1994, 251 and 235–7). Until 1968, I suggest the educational contribution which the Jesuits and Catholics more widely made may have offset an emerging politicisation of Iraqi schools dominated by a strong Sunni influence. Non-Arabs and non-Sunni communities were thus well equipped to work as political and economic actors with as great legitimacy as Sunni Arabs (cf. Lukitz 1995, 113).

1958 rebellion against the Iraqi monarchy

As a result of Anglo-German rivalry to take strategic control of south-west Asia, the British reintroduced direct rule to Iraq for the duration of the Second World War due to the pro-Axis leanings of Iraqi Prime Minister Rashid Ali. At this time, Iraqis were not greatly desirous of supporting any European power. However, many Arab nationalists believed that a German victory over the British Empire would see Iraq prosper more abundantly and gain independence sooner, and worked to popularise this view.

Until the reaffirmation of ties with Britain in foreign and defence policy under the 1948 Portsmouth Treaty, there was relatively limited interest in Iraq to agitate towards a change in the method of government from constitutional monarchy to a republic. However, the Treaty's ratification saw the consolidation and popularisation of the views of Iraqi nationalist and socialist factions who regarded the monarchy as little more than a means to maintain British strategic hegemony in the region and secure access to Iraqi natural resources (HMSO 1948).

By the late 1940s, Chaldean involvement in Iraqi political parties had become more commonplace, and the interest in seeing the maintenance of monarchical

Re-discovering the Chaldean narrative 79

means of government declined among the politically active groupings. In the 1920s, Chaldean social life had been eased by the monarchy's open attitude towards maintaining their presence, whereas the underlying political instability of the 1930s and 1940s, in the short term, led to vacuums of power, with the armed forces acting as guarantors of law and order in periods of change between governments. I suggest the lack of legitimacy with which the monarchy had been regarded – as both a Sunni imposition on majority Shia state and a British institution – left the Chaldean hierarchy in an uncertain position concerning how they could claim the community's legitimate place in public life given their reliance on the support of the King. The monarchy represented stability and authority and provided the basic unifying point for Iraqi national life. To suggest removing this institution implied a generalised loss of societal stability, and it was far from certain that an alternative means of government would be as open to the Chaldean patriarch's public rôle.

I suggest, in this context, that the Chaldean hierarchy tended more strongly towards favouring retention of the monarchy, whilst the laity desired more radical changes which they perceived could come about through involvement with political parties. Nonetheless, the hierarchy's support for the monarchy could not be considered unassailable and did come at some cost. For example, per an Iraqi law of 1947, the Minister of Justice had the right to oversee the religious courts of Christians and Jews (Joseph 1961, 216). Furthermore, the head of these communities was required to be an Iraqi citizen of good standing. As the Church of the East's patriarch had been exiled in 1933, he was barred from ruling his own church at least in Iraq (Joseph 1961, 216–17). Such a level of control indicates that the shadow of the Ottoman millet system was not yet removed from Iraqi life.

Ghanima's death, in 1958, marked the start of a qualitative shift in the Chaldean hierarchy's relations with the government. It is possible that had he pursued a more distinctive policy towards the government the Chaldean community could have emerged in a stronger position in Iraq from 1958. Ghanima perhaps neglected societal issues related to the popular desire for a more equitable economic order which were pertinent to Iraqis as a whole. If he had been vocal in annunciating the Chaldean contributions to Iraqi society, he may have garnered more widespread support for the intermediary role of the patriarchal office in political and social affairs and the Chaldean community in general. Nevertheless, his position is understandable when we consider that Ghanima had lived much of his life in Thomas' shadow as his secretary. As a result, it was difficult for him to develop a distinctive pro-active approach as patriarch.

With British imperial influence in Iraq re-impressed through the Portsmouth Treaty and the 1955 Baghdad Pact, the end of constitutional monarchy moved closer. That the treaties obliged the Iraqi government to maintain their national defence policy in line with British imperatives and to maintain their military infrastructure through links with British industry until 1973 was widely regarded as deeply patronising. Furthermore, by the mid-1950s, Iraqi nationalist feeling had grown in the context of Nasser's success in Egypt and the British failure at Suez (Marr 2010, 24). The monarchy's downfall was further expedited through

80 *Re-discovering the Chaldean narrative*

weak efforts to advance a more equitable programme of land tenure and economic reforms in general. In summer 1958, the army acquiesced to a republican coup and the royal family were executed.

The monarchy, during its existence, offered a veneer of legitimacy to the idea of a stable Iraqi social order. Yet, in actuality, it was far more heavily stratified and weaker than realised. The monarch's rôle was as an authoritative national figure, even if the monarchy wielded little real power and was used by competing factions for their own personal aggrandisement and advancement. This position of the office of the monarch, as somewhat set apart from the real power interactions of the day, contrasted with that of the Chaldean leader. The patriarch, in real terms, could directly influence a segment of the Iraqi population through his office, something which the monarch in Iraq struggled to achieve.

Paul II Cheikho, the Iraqi state and the new Catholic ecclesiology of the Second Vatican Council

Ghanima died just six days before the murder of King Feisel II and his family in July 1958. The physical and psychological impact of the disintegration of the political order on Ghanima prior to his death will likely never be known, but I suggest he was cognisant of substantial changes afoot and likely feared for the future of the Chaldean community.

Ghanima was succeeded by Paul II Cheikho (1958–1989), whose leadership was contiguous with much of Baath party rule. As Emmanuel II Thomas had set the tone for the consolidation of the Chaldean community in the 1920s and the creation of a modern state, so Cheikho had to contend with the re-creation of political, economic and social life as Iraq was transformed into an authoritarian police state controlled by Saddam Hussein. Valognes also rightly emphasises the significant regional and international events which were to affect Iraq during Hussein's leadership which included the petrol boom of the 1970s, the Kurdish revolts from the 1960s onward and the Iran-Iraq War from 1981–1988 (Valognes 1994, 436). To this should be added the effects of the Second Vatican Council upon Chaldean ecclesial character as a *sui juris* church and the development of a new form of relations with the Holy See.

The new ecclesiology for the universal Catholic church from 1965 was to be a communion of churches in union with the Holy See (Green 2002, 244). It was an attempt to move towards a model in which the Holy See acted as *primus inter pares*, with the pope as chief bishop 'presiding in love' over the others. The change in Catholic ecclesiology facilitated a new form of Eastern Catholic union with the Holy See. All particular Catholic ecclesial communities became *sui juris* churches: self-governing and with the responsibility to determine their ecclesiology insofar as it remained in accordance with existing traditions. Galadza characterises *sui juris* ecclesial identity as:

> distinguished not only by their worship, but also by indigenous theologies, spiritualities and canonical traditions. Each of them is also to incarnate in unique

fashion the unity, holiness, catholicity and apostolicity of the one Church, with the Bishop of Rome serving as the touchstone of this unity and continuity.

(Galadza 2007, 291)

This new form of overarching ecclesiology was an attempt to devolve ecclesial power and restore latent jurisdictional powers essential to the authority of the bishop who heads each *sui juris* church. This model was perceived to be more in keeping with that which existed prior to the Council of Trent and was considered to have existed in the early centuries of the Christian oikumene.

It appears a new ecclesiological identity took time to develop, and it was many years before all church members grasped the implications of the new model. The use of the vernacular in the liturgy, which some Eastern Catholic churches introduced after the Second Vatican Council – including the Chaldeans – had far greater impact on the way in which the church operated and expressed its identity than through more abstract ecclesiological theories.

For the Chaldeans, the other major change to take place in the aftermath of the Council was the creation of the dioceses of Ahvaz (in Iran), Erbil and Sulaymaniya between 1966–1968. It is unlikely the impetus to do so derived solely from the Council, however, and in actuality, took place in the context of general ecclesiastical reorganisation which saw the establishment of the dioceses of Aleppo, Beirut and Alqosh from 1957–1960.

Christian involvement with revolutionary movements

The establishment of republican government did not impact directly on the conduct of religious affairs. Nevertheless, a setback to the Christian position in national affairs was the Chaldean patriarch's removal from the senate and thus a decline in influence over the legislature. Although from 1958 all religious leaders were barred from involvement in legislative affairs, the effect on the Chaldeans, and by extension all Christians, was greater than the Muslim populations. This was due to the Christian community's size compared with the Sunni and Shia and the lack of Christian communal cohesion outside of a religious framework: they could not, like the Kurds for example, express unity through ethnic identity.

To retain their voice at the highest level of the Iraqi state, Christians were obliged to have one authoritative point of contact with the contemporary political élite. A divergence of opinions expressed via political parties, whilst attractive for those Christians interested in pursuing a modern Western-style parliamentary democracy, detracted from the recognition of Christians as an essential part of Iraqi society because they lacked a figure who represented their interests in a comprehensive manner. Whether or not such a position was desirable, the traditional paradigm of Mesopotamian-Iraqi society as divided by religious affiliation had existed in some form since the Sasanid era. Each religious community represented by one figure or a small dedicated group was, perhaps, the most efficacious way in which to ensure the continued presence of the Chaldean *difference* in Iraqi society and popular recognition of such.

82 Re-discovering the Chaldean narrative

In some respects, and due to the republicans' desire to establish a more secularist paradigm for the Iraqi state, the seizure of power by General Abd al-Karim Qasim and Colonel Abdul Salam Arif benefited the Chaldeans. Legal reform, for example, limited the rôle of the *sharia*. It seemed also for a time that there might be an end to the dominance of the Sunni minority (Baram et al. 2010, 6). Furthermore, it was initially thought that Qasim's mixed ethno-religious heritage of Sunni Arab and Shia Kurd might endear him to a greater cross section of the population and serve as a unifying aspect to Iraqi political life. Nevertheless, he could not maintain his hold on power, and in a 1963, coup led by his former ally Colonel Arif, Qasim was deposed and executed (Kirmanj 2010, 49).

Qasim's death was not especially detrimental to the Chaldeans, but at times of internal upheaval in the republican era, they were often on dangerous ground as political scapegoats due to substantial Christian involvement with the Communist Party. This was exemplified during Qasim's tenure when Christians were implicated in a communist rising in 1959 in Mosul and from 1959 to 1960 in attacks against conservative pan-Arabist Muslims. Despite the Chaldean Patriarchate's transferral to Baghdad in 1950 and Chaldean migration to the city, a significant Christian population remained in Mosul. 30,000 Christians were displaced following violent traditionalist Muslim reaction to the 1959 rising and Qasim's attempts to introduce socialist socio-economic policies (Betts 1979, 185). The upset, caused at a national and regional level by Christian involvement, was strong. Many families avoided attacks by confining themselves to their homes. Rivalries and perceived threats between socio-religious groups in northern Iraq were often more intense than those in central and southern Iraq, with a greater number of groups competing for dominance and which challenged stable political order (Betts 1979, 106).

A significant minority of East Syriac Christians saw the Iraqi Communist Party (ICP) as an avenue for radical change in a society which they viewed as continuing in the traditions of power for the very few, and assumed that a Marxist inspired political system would resolve these differences. That those involved in the instigation and maintenance of the party were often middle class urban intellectuals (a group which coalesced with many Christians) was a trend found throughout the Arab Middle East. The first ICP general secretary was Yusuf Salman Yusuf of East Syriac heritage, who had become involved with Soviet Russian activists during the 1920s and helped form the ICP's first iteration in 1935 but was executed in 1949 as a result of his involvement in anti-government activity (Betts 1979, 148, 184).

Christian activists in the ICP came to represent as much as ten percent of the total membership, and the Chaldean hierarchy considered their involvement as highly dangerous. Joseph Gogue, Chaldean Archbishop of Basra, and Cheikho all but formally prohibited participation in ICP activities (Betts 1979, 185). Such condemnations were necessary to disavow Muslim Iraqis of the notion that Christians favoured an anti-religious party gaining influence in government. This was a difficulty shared with the Shia religious leadership, as communism appealed to many as a means to alleviate their political minority status (Nakash 2003, 132–4).

Conversely, from the late 1950s, some Shia gravitated towards a rejuvenation of their religious identity as the preferred means to affect change through an Islamic Revolution and, given their proportionate size in the population, this seemed likely to succeed (Nakash 2003, 135). For the Chaldeans, a popular militant religious identity which could affect such change was not a realistic path given that it lacked historical precedent in the East Syriac tradition and support from a sufficiently large section of the Chaldean population.

Republican governments and the rise of the IBP

The party which was to dominate Iraq from 1968–2003 had its origins in Syria in 1943. The Baath was established under the tutelage of a religiously mixed group of intelligentsia. One of the figures who was to remain a key Baathist theorist was the Syrian philosopher Michel Aflaq, who came from an Antiochian Orthodox family. With its message of Arab unity, freedom from Western influence and a more equitable socio-economic order under a socialist system, the Baath Party proved very popular and had a captive audience especially among students, young professionals and eventually the armed forces in Iraq.

Saddam Hussein became involved in the party from the early 1950s and emerged as a militant leader. In 1959, he made a failed assassination attempt on General Qasim. With the failure of the attack, Hussein spent the next four years in exile. During this time, he developed the Iraqi Baath Party (IBP) as the chief vehicle of the 'Arab Revolution' in Iraq. He sought to ensure that the mistakes made in pursuing this agenda by other revolutionary parties would not be repeated and created a hardened cadre of activists to facilitate IBP success (Sassoon 2011, 19–29ff.).

The Baathists came to predominance initially in the 1963 coup which overthrew Qasim. The Baathists were unable to take power at that time due to a lack of sufficient military and popular support to maintain their momentum. By contrast, their success in 1968 relied on the consolidation of the party membership and a rise in popularity. The Baath came to be viewed as the only party capable of upholding an independent Iraq and which could form an effective counter to the perceived threat of the state of Israel, Iran and the US to the Arab states. It was also perceived that the IBP would more efficaciously utilise the national petroleum revenues. Despite a rapid increase in the standard of living from 1958 to 1968, there was continued hope for a more equitable and meritocratic economic settlement especially among the new and growing urban middle class.

After consolidating their initial political success, the 1958 coup leaders sought to remove perceived injustices in Iraq by weakening the influence of socio-economic élites principally through land redistribution. However, as the republicans were unable to break the entrenched patronage networks which the land owners and tribal leaders controlled, so were they unable to meet the demands of a rising middle class caught up in a wave of economic development. This transformed Iraqi infrastructure and the hope among the peasantry for land redistribution (Mansfield 1982, 70).

84 *Re-discovering the Chaldean narrative*

It should be noted that Baathist control of the government and state was not conclusively completed upon taking power in 1968. IBP control extended gradually, and the period to 1979 was reliant on building a broader base of support which involved the Kurdish Democratic Party (PDK) and ICP in government under the grouping titled the National Progressive Front. Efforts were also made to deal with the Kurdish question, but a 1974 law granting autonomy was viewed as insufficient to assuage the PDK's aspirations and they began to agitate for separation by military means. In 1976, the ICP was repressed along with a purge of independently minded military officers (Luizard 2002, 84, 90–1). All these events served as means to advance IBP status. The purge in the military particularly indicated the substantial power which the IBP wielded: the army had been the key faction determining the contemporary government since the establishment of the modern state of Iraq. Baathist capability to alter the existing political *status quo* without alienating the general public was determined by the use of petroleum revenues to make good on their ideological promises to create a more equitable socio-economic order (Luizard 2002, 94–5).

Political change impacts on the Chaldeans

The effects of political changes during the 1960s on the Chaldeans varied by geographic location and socio-economic position. However, I suggest an overarching trend was a loss of confidence in the ability of traditionally influential institutions, such as the patriarchate, to secure the Chaldeans' position in Iraqi society. This was exemplified when, with the loss of authoritative political leadership and societal stability, the Chaldean hierarchy organised for the migration of those in their communities who so desired via Turkey to the West (Interview, Chaldean community member, Amman, May 2013). Nevertheless, the Chaldean commitment to the ideal of Iraq as a nation state did not disappear, and Sengstock suggests the opportune circumstances for the Chaldean community's integration in a national cause facilitated by the IBP (Sengstock 1974, 201, 202). Until Mesopotamia became Iraq, Christians tended towards regionalism with trans-regional identities tied to church membership. This changed following the creation of an independent state where all were expected to contribute to the nation state and its development. The hope for greater socio-economic development and the advancement of a lay-state paradigm were aspirations shared between Chaldeans and modernist Muslims. The Baath offered this, and the party avoided the potentially dangerous effects of overtly anti-religious socialism favoured by the ICP. However, the overall development for the poorer urban and rural classes which the Christian intelligentsia favoured could still be acted upon. As Mansfield notes:

> The socialist content in Ba'thism is not very specific. It is less a set of socio-economic principles than a rather vague means of national improvement. Saddam says that only certain broad basic conditions need to be fulfilled for a system to be called socialist.
>
> (Mansfield 1982, 69)

I suggest Chaldean participation in the IBP brought with it an increased respectability for the party and the appearance of a wider base of support. Christian involvement declined only after the increasing prevalence of Baathist identity and ideology to the exclusion of any other in national politics, the militarisation of Iraqi life and the implementation of authoritarian security structures.

Regardless of the new government's secularising and social-nationalist intentions, the new 1970 Iraqi constitution established Islam as the state's religion but guaranteed religious freedom (Yacoub 1996, 28). At the core of Baathist ideology was the acceptance of the advent of Islam as one of the most important events in Arab history. However, it was accepted only for its spiritual foundations – the political structures which grew up around Islam were to be ignored. Instead the political order was to be based on modern ideals of nationalism and a self-reliant industrial economic order (Dawisha 1983, 115). Different religious identities were permitted, but were to be deprecated for the progression of the greater Arab cause. This Arabist discourse had been influenced and formed by Christian leaders within and outside Iraq. Michel Aflaq, for example, considered himself an Arab first and a Christian second (Kelidar 1974, 22).

Religion was not hidden under IBP rule. It was acceptable insofar as it was not *political*, which was suppressed. The state, as directed by the party, was the only arena in which political development of national policies and national identity was to take place. External to this arena activity could occur, as long as ideology derived from alternative religious, political or cultural sources did not attempt to affect change on a national level or weaken the IBP hold on the means of coercion in the state. Such a separation of the overall direction of Iraqi society goes deeper than the English term *secularism* implies, which more emphasises attempts to suppress overt displays of religion in public life. The French term *laïcité* is perhaps more appropriate in the context of the IBP's attempts to separate political direction of society from influence by non-party institutions and to reduce the influence of religious movements determined to affect widespread political change. Moreover, it marks the distinction between the lay element of society and the party élite who assumed the direction of society from all other organisations who previously would have had a voice and influence in the direction of national affairs. The desire to advance such a paradigm of *laïcité* was linked not just to fulfilling Baathist ideological imperatives but also due to the need to present a societal mentality which could unite the Iraqi population to oppose the rise of revolutionary Shia groups (Luizard 2002, 99–103).

The suppression of overt displays of religious identity was challenging to enforce given religion formed a chief distinguishing marker of communities in Iraq. Public and private Chaldean displays of religious practice were discounted as a threat by the government as they were, in general, disinclined to be involved in political agitation. This is a point emphasised by Sengstock, who noted that the 'Chaldeans have lived politically as "marginal men"' (Sengstock 1974, 202; Pacini 1998, 15).

86 *Re-discovering the Chaldean narrative*

Mesopotamian identity

The Christian rôle in twentieth century Iraqi society held precedent from earlier periods in Mesopotamia during the rule of the Sassanids, Abbasids or Mongols, who permitted Christians to act as integral contributors to developing Arab and Mesopotamian societies. To an extent, such pluralistic concerns were supported by Saddam Hussein, who was enamoured by pre-Islamic Mesopotamian history. He attempted to consolidate the history of the ancient Akkadian, Assyrian and Babylonian Empires under the aegis of a unique Arab Iraqi-Mesopotamian discourse (Baram 1983, 435–7). This was brought into public life through cultural events such as the Mosul Spring Festivals:

> The Festivals were meant to get across to the dwellers of the Mosul district – Arabs, Kurds and Turkomans, Muslims, Christians – and to all Iraqis, essentially three ideas. First, that each part of Iraq, north, centre, and south, had a history to be proud of somehow connected to the dwellers of those regions in present-day Iraq. Second, that all these histories should be regarded as an Iraqi heritage and third, that the recognition of this heritage should encourage everyone 'to strengthen internal Iraqi unity.
>
> (Baram 1983, 429)

Hussein, however, supported a plural society only in the context of attempts to make Iraq appear unique among Arab countries as the legitimate successor to the Semitic empires of ancient history. Further, he hoped to emphasise internally and to the world the superiority of Iraq as the best-suited country to lead the Arab peoples. The emphasis on an Arab national identity was implicitly supported by the Chaldeans, with those who supported an Assyrian identity setting themselves apart. These Chaldeans were exposed to accusations of treachery by the state.

Cheikho, the Baath and Saddam Hussein

Cheikho was born in Alqosh in 1906 and ordained priest for the diocese of Mosul in 1930. Like Thomas and Ghanima, his background introduced him to the challenge of accommodating refugees from northern Iraq after the Ottoman massacres and the demands for political autonomy raised by the Assyrian nationalists in the 1920s and 1930s. Cheikho received a sound formation for future patriarchal office as Bishop of Akra from 1947 to 1957 and was a graduate of the Pontifical Oriental Institute. Cheikho also oversaw the establishment of twenty-five new Baghdadi Chaldean parishes and the construction of a new seminary in Dora in 1962 – the region of the capital which would go on to become known as the 'Vatican Quarter' (O'Mahony 2005, 29; *The Catholic Herald* 1962). The continuing growth in the city was a remarkable rise given that until the First World War only three Chaldean churches existed there. It also emphasises the rapid ecclesiological and demographic changes with which successive patriarchs had to contend.

Cheikho was also responsible for interpreting and implementing the new *sui juris* ecclesiological identity and, having been named a member of the Sacred Congregation for the Oriental Churches in 1963, he was at the forefront of the future direction of the development of Eastern Catholic identity (*The Catholic Herald* 1963). It is possible that maintaining a close relationship with the Holy See was a reason for his pastoral work being largely unhindered during Hussein's rule. Too heavily damaging this relationship potentially limited the Holy See's voice of mediation in regional and international affairs with which Iraq became entangled.

Saddam Hussein became President of Iraq in July 1979 following the resignation of his predecessor, Ahmed Hasan al-Bakr. Hussein had prepared for his ultimate accession to power since the 1968 coup through extending IBP influence into nearly all Iraqi institutions. Chaldean ecclesial life was perhaps one of the least impacted, but even in this arena informers and security service agents were prevalent. Nonetheless, a greater modicum of free action was permitted. This was perhaps due to the Church being perceived as a non-state institution which could be effectively influenced by the state because the Chaldean patriarch was resident in Iraq unlike the patriarchs of the Syrian Orthodox (Syria), Syrian Catholics (Lebanon) and Church of the East (US).

The position of Chaldeans in relation to the Baath, whilst formally directed by Cheikho, was heterogeneous and affected by three main factors: location, social position and strength of adherence to the nationalist ideal of a separate Assyrian region in the north of Iraq (Rassam 2012). For Chaldean residents of central and southern Iraq, there was a general acceptance of the Baathist *status quo* especially due to its restrictions on Islamic jurisprudence and customs in public life.

Due to the ongoing conflict between the state and the Kurds, those Chaldeans resident in northern Iraq were faced with the need to agitate for their communities' defence. This scenario was complicated by those Christian political exiles who gained relative freedom of operation among the Kurds of northern Iraq. These activists viewed Christian political autonomy as necessary for their security. Chaldean residents and political exiles were brought together under the auspices of the Assyrian Democratic Movement (ADM) which emerged as the leading proponent of an independent Christian political and ethnic identity in Iraq. Such Assyrian and Kurdish separatist movements affected the Baathist view of northern Iraq which came to regard the region as the abode of political enemies. Such a state of affairs was of great sorrow to Cheikho, whose regard for northern Iraq stemmed from his own origins there and tenure as bishop of Akra. Cheikho had to be pragmatic in his leadership, as he dealt with radical alterations to Iraqi culture and society. I suggest reluctance to intervene on behalf of the northern Chaldeans during times of Iraqi military incursion was perceived as necessary to ensure stability for the majority who resided in central and southern Iraq. Nonetheless, this was, ultimately, detrimental to Chaldean ecclesial identity, which was so strongly associated with the north.

The Iran-Iraq War 1980–1988

From the mid-1970s, Iraqi foreign policy focused on the traditional rivalry between Arabs and Iranians to become the leading power in West Asia, in the competition between the Baath state and the Pahlavi monarchy. It is a remarkable coincidence that 1979 saw Hussein's rise to power and the success of Ruholla Khomeini's Islamic revolution in Iran.

The Iranian Chaldean community was challenged by the introduction of militant Shiism as the formal ideology of the state and society. The Chaldeans lost a large proportion of their support, as all foreign Latin clergy were obliged to leave Iran in 1979. After their departure, only six (Iranian) members of the previous 150 Latin clergy and religious remained (Baumer 2006, 276). Chaldeans in Iraq had a genuine fear of the impact which an expressly Shia political revolutionary ideology could have on their society were Iran to invade. Youhannan Issayi, Chaldean Archbishop of Tehran (1970–1999), noted in 1983: 'Christians began to feel the need for a religious revision of their lives and a return to God' (Hebblethwaite 1983, 1042). Such a statement perhaps indicated detachment from a traditional Chaldean identity in which life centred on the parish and ecclesial institutions in rural villages. Modernity, urbanisation and engagement with political parties and the state had weakened this lifestyle.

In this context, those united by religion were divided by geography and nationality, with Chaldeans serving in both Iranian and Iraqi armed forces during the Iran-Iraq War. Iraqi Chaldeans were found to be as committed supporters of the War as any other Iraqi community, and their subsequent military service largely reflected that of the general population (O'Mahony 2004b, 443).

The war saw high casualties among the Christian communities, which some accord to the purposeful placement of Christian soldiers in exposed positions at the front. However, this could have been a result of Christians' attempts to prove their worth to their fellow soldiers rather than a politically motivated military order (Petrosian 2006, 128). In general terms, the War served as a means to improve the Chaldeans' social status: until the 1980s, unofficial barriers to Christian progression in state apparatus continued to exist. This derived from the continued stereotype of Christian desire for separatism and the Sunni reluctance to cede power to any other community. As a result of Christian participation, the highest ranks in the military were opened to them which positively affected how they were perceived in wider society (O'Mahony 2003, 6).

It is difficult to assess Chaldean beliefs and perceptions about the war, as no survey of Christian Iraqi military veterans has taken place. If we are to take the opinions of the highest ranking Chaldean in the political order as shared by the populace, we can note that Tariq Aziz referred to the Iranians as 'savages' and stated he would have used nuclear weapons to defeat them if they were available (Takeyh 2010, 376). Such language indicates the intense and personal nature of the conflict in Iraqi society and the persistent Christian fear of revolutionary Shia Islam. Such rhetoric and the dehumanisation of the Iranians was a theme pursued under the Baath, with Saddam Hussein's uncle writing in a propaganda leaflet entitled *Three Creatures*

God never created – Persians, Jews and flies: 'The Persians are animals given human form by God. Their morals are bad, they have a mean nature . . . Brother Arabs, the Persians are the number one enemy!' (Quoted in Luizard 2002, 100). In Aziz's case, his views of the Islamic Republic were coloured by its attempted assassination of him in 1980.

Tariq Aziz

It has been suggested that those Chaldeans who accepted membership of the IBP were in some way collaborators with the state. This casts Chaldean commitments to the party in an entirely pejorative light and views all the actions of the state as being directed by Hussein (cf. Wilmshurst 2011, 438). In actuality, membership was no more or less a marker of collaboration than party membership of any other authoritarian government, such as the Communist in the USSR or the NSDAP in Germany during the 1930s and 1940s. If one wished to work in the civil service or the military, membership was mandatory.

Tariq Aziz rose to prominence during the first Baath coup in 1963, but he, along with many other IBP members, were forced into exile until their ultimate triumph in 1968.[8] Aziz had been a strong influence on party thought and activity since working as editor of the party newspaper, later rising to become Minister of Information in the 1970s before attaining the position of deputy prime minister and foreign minister and becoming one of the most powerful men in Iraq.

Aziz's initial interest in the IBP came from a desire to reform Iraqi society and to ensure complete independence from the British Empire. This inspiration was later transformed into fulfilling the political aims of Hussein and developing Iraq into a modern industrial state. Aziz's Christian origins were never denied during his political career, yet despite being baptised Mikhael Yohannan he utilised a *nom de plume* to escape the explicit connotations of his name in order to support his political success (Spencer 2010). His subsequent career was an unusual but not an impossible trajectory for a Chaldean. It is not clear to what level he consistently associated himself with the Christian faith or a Chaldean identity: he stated in 2000 that he did not practice religion but his wife did and that all his children had been baptised (Bouvet and Denaud 2000, 80). Aziz's religious background was not detrimental to Saddam and the IBP's popular support. However, if on occasion there was criticism towards the government or a failing in Aziz's area of responsibility, this could be referred to as the damaging influence of his Christianity[9] (Interview, Chaldean community leader, Erbil, October 2013).

Prior to Aziz, Christians had assumed high office: Dr Hanna Khayat was the first Iraqi health minister and Rafael Butti was propaganda minister in 1953. Chaldeans also still maintained a substantial influence in the professions from the 1970s onward, and their contributions reinforced the notion of the Christian community's value to Iraqi society.

Aziz did intervene for Christians on occasion, but this was never over issues that would alter their social status. In June 1992, the Missionaries of Charity were in disagreement with Iraqi state bureaucracy over whether they had a right to

90 *Re-discovering the Chaldean narrative*

continue working in the country. Patriarch Raphael I Bidawid appealed to Aziz to resolve this issue favourably, and the religious sisters were permitted to remain (*Catholic News Service* 2010). That he did consent to act following appeals from a church leader indicates he must have retained some sympathy for Christians in general, however far he may have moved away from the Chaldean *milieu*. Indeed, Aziz likely considered them as his natural constituency within Iraqi society.

The Christian communities since 2003 would perhaps not have made such efforts to highlight Aziz's position to an international audience during his trial, sentencing and subsequent imprisonment on death row, if he had not been in a position to ameliorate their situation during Baathist rule. Georges Casmoussa, the Syrian Catholic Archbishop of Mosul, noted in 2010: 'Tariq Aziz was not in security, he was a civil minister. Of course he was part of the regime of Saddam, but that does not mean he was responsible for everything that happened'. (*Catholic News Service* 2010). That until the 2003 invasion of Iraq, Aziz maintained his position as a high-profile figure in Hussein's immediate coterie was due, partly, to the political expediency of a high-ranking non-Muslim presence in government to present an image of plurality to the wider world. Aziz's Chaldean identity also facilitated the Iraqi state's relationship with the Holy See and Vatican diplomatic corps under Hussein. This relationship, from the 1980s, became a means to develop Iraqi interests in a broader context and to consolidate Holy See-Iraqi relations.[10]

The Kurdish rebellions and Christian involvement

If as one contemporary author suggested 'it is in Iraq that the Kurds have the fairest treatment [by comparison with other states in which they reside]', Iraq also presented the most opportune circumstances for a Kurdish rebellion to succeed given the disintegration of the political *status quo* from 1958 to 1968 (Edmonds 1958, 147). Instability at the executive level inhibited the construction of a sustained policy for dealing with Kurdish aspirations, and the Iraqi army was relied upon to contain them. Such a turn of events led to the association of Iraqi policy for dealing with the question of Kurdish autonomy with a primarily military answer for most of the next four decades. In contrast, the formulation of a political resolution for meeting Kurdish demands was perceived as a denial of Iraqi territorial sovereignty and nationhood.

Regardless of the Chaldean influx to southern Iraq as a result of the massacres in the First World War and later Kurdish rebellions, substantial communities remained in the northern towns of Akra, Alqosh, Erbil, Duhok, Kirkuk, Mosul, Sulaymaniya and Zakho. Each were key centres of Chaldean life and, from the 1960s and the return of the Kurdish leader Mustapha Barazani from exile in the USSR, increasing foci of Kurdish attempts to gain independence.

Some Christians resident in the northern provinces supported Kurdish military and political activities with, it appears, the majority of activists drawn from the Church of the East and a significant minority of Syrian Orthodox (Donabed and Mako 2009, 75). Betts and Schmidt indicate that at the final dissolution of the Assyrian Levies in 1955, many of the highly trained fighters turned their loyalties from the British to the Kurdish separatists. Schmidt described one Kurdish military unit he came across being formed of 200 militiamen of whom 30 were Christians (Betts 1979, 186; Schmidt 1964, 71). The Kurds were viewed as a suitable body upon which to attach themselves to advance the cause of Assyrian nationalism, with both seeking to aggregate their power under a government which had no interest in their political independence (Hazen 1979, 49). It was paradoxical, however, to see the ethnic ideal of Assyrian nationalism pursued through support from a group which had previously massacred Christians during the First World War. This reflected the rapidly changing pragmatic alliances which existed in the region (Joseph 1961, 37; Donabed and Mako 2009, 75). Nevertheless, I suggest, through becoming part of Kurdish political discourse, Assyrian nationalists detrimentally affected their relations with other Christians. The nationalist approach of the Assyrians contradicted the traditionally multi-ethnic communities which formed the East Syriac churches (cf. Hastings 1997, 185). Furthermore, the Assyrians sought to control the discourse on nomenclature among the Christian communities utilising 'Assyrian' as a suitable title for all Christians so that the supposed link to the Assyrian people of the Ancient World could be maintained and give credence to their agitation for an independent state (Teule 2011, 313–14).

Nature of combat and effects on Chaldeans

During the Iraqi army pacification campaigns, no discrimination was made between the intended target – the Kurds – and other communities, including the Chaldeans, members of the Church of the East and Yezidis all of whom were affected by the conflict. The Chaldeans suffered particular persecution during military operations in 1963 in Amadiya and during the Anfal campaign of the 1980s (Wilmshurst 2011, 438). Chaldean life was also undermined due to the Arabisation policy pursued by the IBP. This process involved the movement of Sunni Arabs from southern and central Iraq to the villages of Kurdistan. Combined with the continuing effects of military activity, this policy saw further Christian migration from the north to central and southern Iraq.

The experience of day-to-day Christian life across northern Iraq was not uniform. The geographic and social variations across the region precluded the development of a consistent narrative. Nevertheless, during the Kurdish rebellions, nearly all the Christians of the region were affected in some way. The Chaldean village of Inishke provides a useful example of the population's changing fortunes and the long-term effects of the clash of Kurdish demands for independence with Arab nationalist ideology on the region's ethnic and religious make-up.[11]

As of 2017, Inishke is a small settlement in Duhok province under the administration of the Kurdish Regional Government and is ecclesiastically part of the Chaldean Diocese of Zakho-Amadiya. In the 1950s, a stable Chaldean presence was based around the parish church of Mart Shimuni and Her Holy Sons. From the 1958 revolution, the situation deteriorated, and as military action against the

92 Re-discovering the Chaldean narrative

Kurds began, the Chaldeans started to migrate. This period was also contiguous with an increase in the number of Kurdish nomads settling and turning to agriculture, which appears to have led to competition for the use of land suitable for agriculture (Edmonds 1958, 149). The Chaldeans became so pressurised as a result of residing in the conflict zone, that in 1961 a Mosul-based priest sent buses to bring the women and children from Inishke to the city. Nearly all Christian villages in the Duhok area faced similar difficulties, and it was only in late 1973 that former villagers began to return as redevelopment began in the area.

What was most striking from the information gained during the interview was the Chaldean community's resilience and attachment to their village. Despite a separation of over ten years for many of the residents, every effort was expended to secure the earliest safe opportunity to return. The sense of stewardship over the village, regardless of ongoing political and military conflict, emphasised that geographical ties to the land are integral to Chaldean identity.

From the late 1970s onward, the restoration of political order encouraged more families to return and, with the Church's support, resumed the norms of daily life. Indeed, the area became popular with Arab tourists, especially from the Gulf states, who took advantage of the cooler summer climate which the higher altitudes offered. The area's reputation grew to the extent that Saddam Hussein visited in 1979 and built several vacation palaces for his close associates. Hussein's favour for the village did not benefit the Chaldeans, as it greatly increased the security forces present in the area and complicated the livelihoods of local farmers. As the Arabisation policies of the late 1970s and early 1980s were vigorously implemented, some of the most fertile land was appropriated for Hussein's own purposes, while other tracts were given for use by Arab migrants from central and southern Iraq.

Although Arabisation of Iraq had been ongoing since the British mandate, the Baathist implementation of the policy was the first time population movement had been encouraged so comprehensively to the detriment of the population of northern Iraq (Marr 2010, 20). The intentions of the policy were, through social and economic activities, to re-engineer northern Iraqi society, which led to three main outcomes. First, the nationalisation of arable/pastoral land; second, non-Arabs were denied access to their previously owned property and third, resettlement of northern Iraq with Sunni Arabs from the economically unproductive al-Jazira desert (Muscati and Bouckaert 2009, 19).

The difficulties for Christians who lived in and around the areas of Kurdish autonomy were further exacerbated by the violence used during the Anfal campaign from 1987–1988:

> By the end of August [1988], all organised resistance was at an end the Iraqi armed forces were in control of the whole of the Kurdish autonomous region, roughly 80% of all the villages had been destroyed, much of the agricultural land was declared 'prohibited territory' and possibly 100,000 people had lost their lives.

(Tripp 2007, 236)

Christians became the 'collateral damage' in a campaign prosecuted with extreme violence.[12] That many Christians and Yazidis identified at least officially as Arabs and were at worst politically ambivalent towards the Baath state was ignored. Approximately 150 Christian and Yazidi villages were destroyed, along with twenty-four churches, monasteries and an orphanage. Clergy were not exempt from attack, and several were alleged to have been killed, either among the civilians in the conflict area, or targeted directly by the Baath security services ('Iraq: Continuous and Silent Ethnic Cleansing. Displaced Persons in Iraqi Kurdistan and Iraqi Refugees in Iran' 2003, 40–2, 55). A particular concern for the continuation of ecclesial life was the destruction of monastic property, which saw the transferral of personnel to the Chaldean monastery of St Anthony's in Baghdad (Seferta 2008, 23).

The effects of forced displacement were not just in the immediate aftermath of events. In 1991, up to two million Kurds left northern Iraq. Even where this was temporary, it created an irruption in the social order (Luizard 2002, 108). Where were Chaldeans to place themselves while they became more exposed as wider Kurdish society withdrew? Later, when Kurds returned, and especially after 2003 with the rejuvenation of Kurdish identity, how could Chaldeans continue to maintain a place in the social order without being reduced to a group holding to a paradigm of *dhimmi* status? The Kurdish rise to determine political affairs in northern Iraq prevented another outcome. In advancing their own cause as a minority in Iraq, other minorities were reduced in significance and came to exist in Kurdish society as Kurdish subjects reliant upon Kurdish goodwill to maintain an active presence in the region.

The difficulties faced in northern Iraq during the 1970s–1980s were not shared by those Chaldeans resident in central and southern Iraq. Those in Baghdad were often inclined to discount military attacks and government policies as exaggerated or affecting only those Christians directly involved in anti-government activity. This may seem surprising given the uniting bond of church membership and familial connections with the northern populations. However, these were tempered by the relief for their overall security situation away from the northern difficulties, and the belief that Chaldean involvement in anti-government activity was a direct threat to the *status quo*. A mentality prevailed that Hussein in particular had been 'good for us Christians', implying that criticism of government actions or anti-Christian persecutions should be limited if voiced at all (This paragraph from discussions with Chaldean community members, London, 2012–2014).

The Kurdish situation came to a denouement only after the 1990–1991 Gulf War and the Coalition efforts to shackle Iraq's economy and inhibit Iraqi armed forces from continued punitive actions in the north. As a result, the Kurds established their *de facto* autonomy and a parliament was formed in 1992. Five of the 105 members were Christians, with four seats won by the ADM and the other by the Union of Christians of Kurdistan (O'Mahony 2003, 7; Teule 2012, 181–2). The Kurdish parliament in 1996 remarkably recognised 7 August (date of the massacres at Simele in 1933) as a national holiday in the region, which granted the Assyrian nationalists hope that they were recognised as an accepted community

94 *Re-discovering the Chaldean narrative*

within the Kurdish *milieu* (Teule 2011, 315). This success for Christian representation and their social stability was complicated, however, by the continuing political and tribal inspired violence between the PUK and KDP, who did not reach a truce until 1998.

Raphael I Bidawid (1989–2003)

Cheiko's time as patriarch can be characterised initially by the difficulty of establishing a new paradigm for Chaldean state relations under the republican governments of 1958–1968. The political shocks which Iraq experienced until the stabilisation in central government under the Baath from 1968 weakened the patriarch's capability to formulate an effective narrative for church-state relations.

Cheikho was succeeded by Raphael I Bidawid. Bidawid was born in Mosul in 1922, and was marked out from a young age for advancement to a leadership position. He entered the Dominican run minor seminary in 1933 and was then sent for further formation at the Vatican from 1936 to 1946. He received such a thorough formation that, by 1956, he had completed two doctorates in theology and philosophy.[13] The extended formation in the Vatican led to accusations later in life of his being a partisan of Latin theological and liturgical trends. Yet, this formation also ensured that Bidawid was better able to gain influence within the Holy See and its associated institutions once he had assumed office as patriarch in 1989.

After his time in Europe, he served as the vice-rector of the Chaldean seminary in Mosul and as chaplain to the Chaldean workers of the Iraqi Petroleum Company before receiving consecration as Bishop of Amadiya in 1957, at only thirty-five years of age. Bidawid spent a long period of his life as Chaldean Bishop of Beirut (1966–1989). His experiences in the Lebanon gave him insight as to how to consolidate the Chaldean *status quo* within the confines of long-term conflicts.

As patriarch, Bidawid saw the Chaldeans' status begin to radically alter within Iraq. By 1989, Iraq had been at war or on a total war footing for nearly a decade and faced significant economic difficulties, having exhausted most of the foreign currency reserves which had been built up from petroleum production in the 1970s. Further, the long-term physical effects of the conflict were telling and caused deep social trauma:

> Iraq suffered over 400,000 dead and wounded . . . By the time of the ceasefire, [in 1988] more than 50 percent of Iraq's males between the ages of 18 and 45 were in the military . . . Many young men, those who did not qualify for special exemption, spent eight of their most productive years in armed service.
> (Mylroie 1989, 61)

A normal sense of inter-personal relations which did not rely on shared experience of military life, conflict or socio-economic deprivation, was very difficult to restore. An especially problematic issue was the passing on of such disturbed communal experiences to the next generation of Iraqis. Collective communal memory of eight years of war and its effects was not limited just to those who died or returned physically or mentally scarred but also to their families and children. This phenomenon, owing to Iraq's relative inaccessibility for research, can only be estimated, but seems likely to be under assessed.

The Chaldean experience during this period mirrored that of other Iraqis, but was tempered by the existence of the wider Middle Eastern and Western diaspora which opened opportunities for migration. Bidawid encouraged Chaldeans to remain even despite difficulties. His working relationship with the government and Hussein played a substantial part in this, as did his reputedly charismatic personality (Seferta 2008, 18). This relationship the patriarch had to navigate carefully, and especially in the context of another major war from August 1990.

Second Gulf War 1990–1991 and migration

Bidawid was strong in his condemnation of the Coalition invasion, and at least officially supported Iraq's annexation of Kuwait. A Christian Peace Conference modelled after one held by Iraqi Muslim leaders earlier that year was staged in December 1990. As the title of the conference suggested, the Iraqi churches were present to pursue a peaceful resolution and support Hussein's plan for a negotiated settlement to the crisis. This was couched in terms of defeating foreign threats to the Arab nationalist struggle (Long 2004, 131). Hussein also drew upon religious rhetoric to support resistance to the Coalition forces: he contrasted the righteousness of Iraq's cause with the blasphemous betrayal of Christian values which U.S. President George H. W. Bush pursued by attempting to intervene militarily in the situation (Long 2004, 132).

During and after the war, Bidawid's choice of words, on occasions, may have been injudicious. In January 1991, he stated that chemical weapons might be used by Iraq as a last resort if invaded and, for example, called Hussein a 'real gentleman' (*The Tablet* 1991, 110; Corley 2003). In other instances, he unequivocally referred to Coalition preparations for entering Kuwait as a crime, and that the Baathist annexation of Kuwait was justified in view of the economic warfare (viz. the manipulation of oil prices) by which Iraq had been affected in the preceding two years (*The Tablet* 1991, 110). Yet Bidawid was also realistic about the effects another conflict could have upon Iraqi society with the potential of widespread anti-Christian feeling developing through accusations of proximity to Western interests. I suggest Bidawid considered his statements in support of the Baath government to be the most utilitarian means to secure and even advance the Chaldeans' position post-conflict. Indeed, it should be recalled that the outcome of the American-led war against Iraq was considered to be far from a foregone conclusion at the time. Iraq's military was one of the largest in the Middle East, and had gained substantial combat experience over the previous decade.

Post-war Iraq

The immediate effects of the January–February 1991 Coalition invasion were restricted to Iraqi soldiers and the populations of Baghdad and Iraq south of the

96   Re-discovering the Chaldean narrative

capital. However, the entire population of Iraq suffered from the subsequent effects of infrastructure destruction and the state's inability to rebuild following the implementation of comprehensive punitive sanctions. In this context, migration from Iraq was a popular option for the Chaldeans. The professional classes were in the best position to leave the country or, if they remained, escape from the effects of inflation and limited material resources due to higher salaries. The most severely affected were those Chaldeans too poor to afford the costs of migration or alleviate their position in the face of rising inflation.

It seems likely that the loss of a critical mass of Chaldeans in Iraq was not apparent until after the end of the 1991 Gulf War. Prior to the War, the construction of a new Chaldean cathedral in Baghdad had been planned, with capacity for 5,000 people, and a new Christian higher education institute, Babylon College, had opened in 1990 (Yacoub 1996, 32–3; Rassam 2010, 175). Thus, despite the Iran-Iraq War, the Chaldean presence was regarded as likely to continue. Also, in general, Iraq was perceived to have sufficient resources to redevelop from 1988. The destruction of infrastructure in 1991, and the status accorded to Iraq as a pariah state in the aftermath, radically changed this situation.

The quality of Christian life in Iraq declined further and rapidly from the mid-1990s with four major catalysts: (1) the implementation of a more hard-line state security policy, (2) the decline in quality of healthcare, (3) the bombing of Iraq by Coalition forces during Operation Desert Fox in 1998 and (4) the end of the state's neutrality policy in religious affairs, which saw Hussein seeking the support of Islamist groups as a result of his loss in support from other sections of Iraqi society.

In response to the new Iraqi reality and the difficulties which Christians throughout the Middle East were facing from economic difficulties, Bidawid pushed for greater co-ordination between the churches. He assisted the foundation of the Council of Catholic Patriarchs and Bishops (in the Middle East) and a Council with a similar purpose for the clergy in Iraq (Rassam 2010, 172). To continue the Chaldean tradition of contributing to wider society, Bidawid established *Caritas Iraq* – a charitable organisation to alleviate difficulties Iraqis experienced as a result of sanctions (Rassam 2010, 172). It seems likely Bidawid's vision for shoring up the Chaldean position can be credited to his time ministering to Lebanese Chaldeans: the awareness he gained of the realities of social and military conflicts in a quasi-functional and multi-confessional state equipped him well to deal with similar difficulties which Iraq experienced.

One immediate aspect of the war's aftermath was the defeat of an anti-government rebellion by the Iraqi armed forces. The rebellion's suppression was intended as a marker of Hussein's reaffirmation of control over the state. Chaldeans were not widely involved in the rebellion, but there had existed a widespread assumption that the government would be overthrown. It appears that political forces external to Iraq attempted to influence Chaldeans to become more closely involved with the rebellion in order to gain an advantageous position in a post-Baathist Iraq (O'Mahony 2003, 7).

To avoid any implications of collusion with foreign powers, Kurdish nationalist aspirations or an association with a proposed Assyrian state, Bidawid was opposed to asserting a particular ethnic identity for the Chaldeans. Rather, he proposed that one can have a national affiliation apart from Iraqi – if so desired – and also be a Chaldean (Petrosian 2006, 115–17). This view was based on two factors: political and social difficulties, but also a recognition of the limits placed on the Church's ecclesiology by asserting an ethnic affiliation. The Chaldeans could not affirm to belong to the multi-ethnic and missionary-orientated heritage of the East Syriac tradition if the limits of the community relied on a particular ethnic identity. Moreover, as the Chaldeans grew in size in the diaspora and expanded their work in the modern ecumenical movement, a paradigm of mutual aid between the Syriac churches and more widely among the Eastern Churches began to form. This paradigm was antithetical to those who asserted a particular ethnic nature of religious identity.

However, Bidawid had to manage the expectations, status and safety of the Chaldeans in what was becoming two distinct state entities: the Kurdish administered region and Iraq proper. Joseph relates how during a visit to northern Iraq in 1998, Bidawid stated: '[Christians and Kurds] are the sons of this land; we have a joint history. I can even say, more than this: We have common blood' (Joseph 2000, 221). Such a view seems unlikely to have been endorsed by Saddam Hussein, but I suggest there was perhaps recognition within the Baath administration that the patriarch was not just the President's 'man' but a leader of an international community to which he had diverse responsibilities.

Chaldean migration 1991–2003

The Melkite priest Jean Corbon identifies a process of *delocalisation* during the twentieth century whereby a church has origins or long-term residence in one place but subsequently the community migrates in whole or in part to one or more locations, often some distance from their place of origin (Corbon 1998, 98). The Melkites are a prime example of this: with a global population of 1.6 million, nearly half of all Melkites live in South America. Causes of population displacement inherent to delocalisation range from economic decline to persecution, and such a process can even be placed in the context of the normative Christian missionary impulse resulting from geographical displacement. The process permits the revivification of ecclesial life in new environments, and the development of an ecclesiological vision which more effectively meets the needs of an international church.

There are strong precedents for the delocalisation of the Chaldeans. This is derived, for example, from the East Syriac tradition's missionary work throughout Central Asia as well as Joseph VI Audo's attempts to maintain jurisdiction over the East Syriac communities in India. The difference of conception between delocalisation and that of missionary activity could be considered as one more of terminology than of nature. Migration can provoke interest in the religious identity and practices of a migrant community among native residents much as active missionary work does.

During the internationalisation of the Chaldeans in the twentieth century, the chief barrier to delocalisation becoming an active missionary process were the

98 *Re-discovering the Chaldean narrative*

negative connotations attached to the causes of migration. Chaldeans departed Iraq from a context of persecution, extended conflict and socio-political disenfranchisement. By contrast, the spread of East Syriac Christianity from the fifth to thirteenth centuries came during an era of particularly active propagation of the faith, from a community proportionately larger in size and with greater resources during a sustained era of the expansion of socio-economic development throughout Asia. The level of hardening of religious communal boundaries in the twentieth century, the militant Muslim opposition to the spread of Christianity in Central Asia and the Middle East and the ambivalence of populations in the West to Christianity caused active missionary work to be more challenging than any time since the Apostolic era.

The greatest Chaldean concentrations outside of the Middle East came to reside in the US, with Detroit, MI, becoming one of the first and subsequently most long-lasting diaspora hubs (Bacall 2014, passim). Detroit was a focus for manufacturing industries for skilled and unskilled labour, and appealed to a variety of Catholic migrants from Chaldeans and Maronites to Ukrainians and Irish. The Chaldeans were supported by the Maronites from the outset of their arrival, and attended their Liturgy before the arrival of their first permanent priest in 1947 (Seferta 2004). The lack of a priest and dedicated religious institutions from the first arrival of Chaldeans to Detroit in 1889 was far from unusual among early Arab migrants to the US, who were reluctant to establish churches and mosques, as they considered their stay to be a temporary one (Seferta 2004; Kayyali 2006, 87). The possibility of a return to the Middle East was then not far from their minds, with perhaps a perception that Western social and technological changes would soon have their effect in their homelands. This viewpoint altered as attachment to the Middle East declined, stronger ties to the West developed and recognition grew that their position in the West allowed for an explicitly Christian culture to develop more abundantly (Swan and Saba 1974, 89).

Migration from 1991 continued to favour the US as a final destination, but increased in geographical spread, with concentrations established in Scandinavia, Germany, France, the Netherlands, Jordan, Syria, Greece, Britain, Georgia and Australasia.

In the European diaspora and the Middle East (outside of Iraq), the emphasis in ecclesial life has been on shared activity with other Syriac churches (especially the Syrian Catholics and Church of the East) and/or attendance at the Latin liturgy. The Syriac Orthodox Church, Church of the East and Ancient Church of the East all have one or more dioceses in Europe.[14] However, the Syrian Catholic and Chaldean Catholic churches have only, at most, patriarchal vicariates or apostolic visitors.[15] In North America and Australasia, Chaldean jurisdictions have been present since 1982 and 2006, respectively. It is perhaps easier to establish dioceses in contiguous states, whereas in Europe the Chaldeans are spread widely across a variety of jurisdictional boundaries, both ecclesial and national.

Nevertheless, the lack of Chaldean dioceses in Europe is surprising. Where the Chaldeans are not granted sufficient ecclesial support, this encourages engagements with other Syriac churches. Across the whole of Britain, for example, there

Re-discovering the Chaldean narrative 99

has only ever been one Chaldean priest available to work on a variety of projects to support the community and to form and maintain a sense of Chaldean ecclesiological identity. These responsibilities are also quite apart from the necessity to provide the sacraments.[16]

Until the 1990s, motivation to migrate largely derived from hope for social stability and economic advantage and a desire to live within a more Christian cultural environment (if migrating to the West). Following Kurdish *de facto* independence from the 1990s, northern Iraq, with its traditional status as a centre of East Syriac activity, also proved increasingly popular as a destination for families from Baghdad, Basra and Kirkuk. Migration into Kurdistan was not universally viewed as necessary or desirable by Chaldeans, but substantial changes were taking place. Baghdad lost up to half of its Chaldean population between 1990 and 2000 (Roberson CSP 2014, 3). The ecclesiological and social implications of this cannot be underestimated. For those who remained, life became harder as the social space left by the departed Chaldeans was filled by other influences and factions. Baghdad, which had formed the centre of Chaldean life since the 1950s, was reduced in significance and the status of the patriarch weakened. Without a sufficiently large community to refer to, the patriarch's ability to represent, to the Baath élite, that Christian affairs were integral and essential to Iraqi society, was negated.

Meeting the varied needs of the Chaldeans

Tensions existed between clergy and laity over delocalisation in a strategic context and how they should contribute to the Church in the long term. From 1991, the hierarchy emphasised the need for the community to remain in the regions from where their ecclesiastical culture developed to ensure that its character and contributions to Iraqi society were sustained (Cherubini 1995a, 46; *Asianews.It* 2013). There continues to exist an underlying fear, which is not widely acknowledged, of the switch between ecclesial identities by migrants whether in the West or the Middle East. This is not necessarily a process migrants enter into willingly, but does suggest that the Chaldean clergy in the diaspora are unprepared to maintain a Chaldean ecclesial identity because of the rapid changes in population which have occurred since 1991. An example of such a challenge is found in the Hashemite Kingdom of Jordan, where perhaps up to 30,000 Iraqi Chaldeans have resided prior to further onward migration from 2003 to 2013. Despite this large Iraqi Chaldean population, there has only ever been one Chaldean chaplain in Jordan at any one time (Conversations with Latin and Chaldean community members, Amman, May 2013).

The Latin community in Jordan is considered by Iraqi migrants and refugees to have a particularly welcoming atmosphere, where being a Christian is the main aspect of identity (Conversations with Latin and Chaldean community members, Amman, May 2013). Thus, an explicitly Chaldean identity is diluted through taking part in religious life in such a *milieu*. The number of *de facto* conversions to the Latin church by Eastern Christians appears also to have been and continues to be quite high as a result of the economic and charitable support available, but also

100 *Re-discovering the Chaldean narrative*

due to Latin social and educational institutions. However, no statistics are kept even of *de jure* conversions due to the controversial nature of such conversions in the current environment of attempts to maintain the survival of churches, which are much smaller numerically and financially than the Latin community in Jordan. Chaldean clergy are right to speak up on migration. Yet, if measures are not put in place to secure an identity more heavily influenced by the East Syriac tradition, the number of these Latin-Chaldeans will almost certainly continue to increase.

This is a broader issue than just a religious concern, with the Christians becoming lost among the refugee populations in the Levant. Those who would normally be most active in sustaining Iraqi society are denied opportunities to commit to the societies in which they come to reside due to difficulties attaining visas or residence status. At the time of their departure, migrants are often of a younger age and better qualified (though not necessarily all the young are better qualified and *vice versa*), thus increasing the average age of the community in Iraq with fewer persons able to replace the rôles of adults who travel abroad for work (cf. Sabella 1998, 152). The Chaldean refugee population in Jordan appears oversupplied with talented and well-qualified workers. This was reflected in the variety of professions among the people encountered during research visits in May and June 2013 including engineers, university lecturers, self-made businessmen and businesswomen, architects and NGO workers. Their available skills were not always being put to good use in Jordan where, for example, many work as restaurant staff for a minimal salary often as low as eighty Jordanian dinars a week.[17]

The particular difficulties which Christian Iraqis have experienced are seen in the disparity between their size in Iraq by contrast with the entire Middle East. As of 1998, 3.2 percent of Iraqis were Christian, whereas for the whole of the Middle East, the Christian population was 6.3 percent (Pacini 1998, 15, 22). The larger Christian proportion of the populations of Lebanon, Syria and Egypt notwithstanding, this was still a significant demographic difference affected by the outcome of the 1991 war and subsequent sanctions. This was reflected in refugee statistics collated prior to the invasion in 2003. These showed that, in 2001, of all officially registered refugees, Iraqis were the third greatest population globally and, in 2000, the second largest group seeking asylum in economically developed countries (Chatelard 2002, 1).

Final years of Hussein and Bidawid

The Chaldean situation in Iraq and abroad was complicated during Bidawid's last five years in office (1998–2003) due to ill health. In and of itself, the Chaldean patriarchal rôle was difficult. But, when coupled with attempting to restore its status in a declining economic atmosphere, and faced with antipathy by major powers in and outside of the Middle East, this factor became significant. Bidawid sought medical treatment in the Lebanon which, whilst necessary given the parlous state of healthcare in Iraq, was criticised by many in the Iraqi Chaldean community.[18]

Nevertheless, Bidawid continued his work as far as he was able, which included acting as an intermediary – either himself or another senior cleric – between the

Iraqi government and the Holy See. This relationship, in turn, formed a channel to opening Chaldean relations with Western political leadership. Further, it demonstrated both the plurality which still existed in Iraq, and that not all Iraqi life was determined by Saddam Hussein.

The strength of goodwill which Hussein built up with the Holy See saw plans laid for a visit by Pope John Paul II to Iraq in 2000 (Mostyn 1999). The visit was eventually cancelled due to fears over ensuring the pope's security, and the potential for Baathist embarrassment were anything untoward to occur. There also existed wider diplomatic concern that the pope might make statements which could be detrimental to the US as the force behind the sanctions or critical of Baathist policies (O'Mahony 2005, 37). Nevertheless, meetings continued between senior members of the Congregation of the Oriental Churches and Baathist leadership. The presence of high-ranking clergy in Iraq reflected the Holy See's continued interest in the well-being of the Christian population and reinforced to the international Catholic community that Iraqi Catholics were an integral part of the universal church. Their long-standing relationship with the Holy See also assisted the Chaldeans in justifying their presence in a Western environment when they were and are so little acknowledged by the Western churches in general. The presence of St Thérèse of Lisieux's relics in Iraq in 2002 was a sign of the Iraqi Catholic population's continued commitment to the universal and multifaceted international Catholic community. (*ZENIT News Agency 2002*). Given that St Thérèse is also one of the patrons of Catholic missions, I suggest this also marked a point of reflection on the challenging environment for the Catholic community's growth in Iraq.

Modern ecumenism and Chaldean involvement

Bidawid's engagement with political powers was reflected in his efforts to advance modern ecumenism with other churches, as derived from the decrees of the Second Vatican Council 'Unitatis Redintegratio' and 'Orientalium Ecclesiarum'. Bidawid had been an early supporter of such modern ecumenical sentiments stating at the Council:

> Omnes Christifideles in mea Eparchia, precibus petunt et vota faciunt ut hoc Concilium Oecumenicum unitati Ecclesiae praesto sit, ut sint unum ovile et unus pastor.
>
> (Cherubini 1995b, 14)

Modern ecumenical discourse affirmed the necessity of developing relations with Eastern Christians not in union with the Holy See and in particular recognising their historic mission and witness (Paul VI 1964, secs 5, 24). The purpose of engaging with other Christians changed from one of direct attempts at conversion to the Catholic Faith and submission to the Holy See, to a focus on reconsidering theological disagreements with a hope for reconciliation (Girling 2012, 38–40).

102 *Re-discovering the Chaldean narrative*

The Chaldeans have pursued ecumenism especially vigorously. Their situation in Iraq is unmatched in the Arab Middle East since the Second World War for the rate of decline of a Christian population, perhaps with the exception of the churches in occupied Palestine. The encouragement for engagement with other Eastern Christians had been, prior to the 1960s, supported in Baghdad at the Carmelite 'Centre' under the direction of Frs Robert Beulay and Raymond Charbonnier from 1956 (Hansbury 2007). The appeal of ecumenism was to give Iraqi Christians an apparent means to forge a united front to inform the rest of Iraqi society of their contribution to the country, to consolidate available resources between communities and to act as a mediating influence, however unofficially, between Sunni and Shia.

Regional discussions were formalised from 1974 and took place within the context of the Middle East Council of Churches (MECC), the chief inter-Christian ecumenical body in the region. MECC had been formed as an extension of the World Council of Churches to pursue debate specifically resonant with the local churches especially regarding the issue of relations with Muslims on a temporal and religious level.[19] The other main arena for dialogue is within the Syriac tradition at the *Pro Oriente* forum. The forum was founded in 1964 with a view towards implementing the principles of ecumenical reconciliation of 'Unitatis Redintegratio' among the Eastern Christian communities in particular. From 1993, the Church of the East was invited to take part in dialogue with the Chaldeans, and further to share Catholic academic and pastoral resources which resulted in the Holy See granting clergy of the Church of the East the opportunity to study in Chaldean institutions in Baghdad and Vatican universities (see, for example, Soro 2004; Youssef 1996).

As a result of these engagements, significant changes were brought about in the East Syriac communities' relationship through the completion of agreements in 1997 and 2001. The former agreement saw the establishment of co-operation at an official level between the two churches in pastoral areas and the latter saw permission granted for inter-communion at the Divine Liturgy between the churches (Mar Raphael I Bidawid and Mar Dinkha IV 1998, 185–8). The growth in the diaspora populations suggests that co-operation between the churches may become a more frequent activity, as resources are dissipated so widely in North America, Australia and Europe. The diaspora outside of the Middle East had, as of 2000, become the new homeland for approximately twenty-five percent of Chaldeans. By the end of the 1990s, at least one third of all Christians had left Iraq. The numbers only increased following the approach to the Second Gulf War (Roberson CSP 2010; Petrosian 2006, 114).

Prelude to the invasion of 2003

Reflecting now, nearly fifteen years after the 2003 invasion, it appears war was inevitable once the Coalition powers had determined the need to expand their strategic positions in the Middle East. The strength of anti-war feeling exhibited by the populations of the invading countries was ignored: the largest worldwide public demonstrations for decades had no impact on the resolve of the Coalition governments to invade Iraq. With such a scenario, Bidawid's efforts to shore up the Chaldean population and Iraqi society in the face of war may now appear to have been futile. Yet, at the time, they were underpinned by belief in a Divine Hope: that war could be averted. This was reinforced by the awareness that the removal of Saddam Hussein presaged not just a change of political order but also a loss of Iraq as a national entity.

Reflections by Christians since the invasion of March 2003 have compared the relative quality of life under Saddam Hussein to their post-war situation, which often sees them as refugees or unable, for the most part, to sustain livelihoods in their own country. One Christian interviewed in 2007 argued that Hussein was 'a secular leader especially good for Christians, as long as they stayed out of the way . . . "When Saddam was in power there was no fighting. Saddam loved the Christians"' (Sudilovsky 2007, 1). Whilst we may not go so far as to support the interviewee's understanding of Hussein's admiration for Christians – his personal Chaldean cook notwithstanding – the human cost of the occupation of Iraq indicates the preference which they had for his rule is not without merit. There appears to have been an understanding that religious and political instability leading to sectarian conflict would destroy their position in society. Nevertheless, Iraqi Christian life during the twentieth century should not necessarily all be viewed via the prism of a decline in well-being, loss of status or near permanent migration. As Betts notes of the 1970s: 'The combined advantages of affluence, education, higher health standards, and a strong sense of community worked to create an enviable social image for Christians' (Betts 1979, 136). Furthermore, large proportions of Christians remained in Iraq regardless of internal political changes and with no desire to leave. We should recall that in the Iraqi Kurdistan region, since the establishment of permanent semi-autonomy from 1992, that the Christians were regarded as net contributors to society. However, the overall mindset of Christians altered, even in Kurdistan, and saw the development of a communal melancholia from March 2003.

Notes

1 An English translation of which is currently being prepared by Andrew Palmer, Radboud University, Nijmegen.
2 As of the Second Vatican Council (1962–1965), Thomas Reis, Chaldean bishop of Zakho (1957–1965), noted the religious indifference of the youth and the detrimental affects of Communism and Freemasonry upon the retention of religious practice and identity (Cherubini 1995a, 46–7).
3 Observed among conversations with a range of Chaldeans – laity, clergy, young and old – during research visits in northern Iraq (October 2013), London (2012–2014) and Jordan (May–June 2013). Only very few of the community cognizant of the importance of discoursing on Chaldean history.
4 Such a quietist approach to patriarchal leadership is similar to that which is associated with Iraqi Shiite clerics. For example: during the career of Grand Ayatollah Ali al-Sistani in the late twentieth and early twenty-first centuries (Petrosian 2006, 125; Rahimi 2004, 12–14).

104 *Re-discovering the Chaldean narrative*

5 Thomas was a native of Alqosh (b. 1852) but also gained wide experience of Chaldean life outside of Mesopotamia: he trained for the priesthood in Beirut (ordained 1879) and served as Bishop of Seert from 1892–1900. It seems likely that the brutal murder of his successor in Seert – Addai Scher – during the Seyfo in 1915 and the loss of the diocese as an ecclesial entity was an influential factor in Thomas' subsequent drive to consolidate the Chaldean community in Iraq as part of a plural religious society.

6 This section and following will refer to religious minorities in Iraq. It should not be thought that because the Christians, Yazidis, Mandeans and so forth are numerical minorities that they are in any sense less legitimately or intimately involved in the development of modern Iraq. Their historical contributions to the Mesopotamian region preclude them being considered as a minor influence. The Shia, despite their overwhelming majority in the Iraqi population, were a *de facto* minority given their limited political and social roles in modern Iraq.

7 Not to be confused with Chaldean patriarch Yusif VII Ghanima (1947–1958).

8 He was born in 1936 in the northern Iraqi town of Telkef – one of the most culturally Chaldean towns of Iraq.

9 There is a remarkable lack of information in general or academic literature available on Aziz, and studies on his religious identity and influence on Saddam Hussein and the Baath government would be a very useful contribution to scholarship.

10 Aziz died whilst still imprisoned in June 2015.

11 The following information gathered in an extended interview with the parish priest of Inishke in October 2013.

12 The effects of the Iraqi-Kurdish conflict on the residents of northern Iraq should not be underestimated. Some estimates suggest up to 1,000,000 people were forcibly displaced or departed as refugees (cf. Joseph 2000, 215).

13 Respectively on East Syriac patriarch Timothy I and Sunni philosopher Al-Ghazali (b. 1058 d. 1111).

14 The Ancient Church of the East is a community which emerged from the Church of the East in 1964. The Ancient Church can be broadly considered to hold to a traditionalist perspective on East Syriac ecclesial life. The chief cause for its emergence was the replacement of the Julian by the Gregorian calendar. The patriarchal see is in Baghdad, and since 1972, the Church has been led by Mar Addai II. Its total membership worldwide is c. 100,000 people.

15 Since November 2016, Saad Sirop, titular bishop of Hirta and formerly auxiliary bishop in Baghdad, has been the Chaldean apostolic visitor *in* Europe. This is, to my knowledge, the first time a cleric of episcopal rank has been appointed to this position *and* resident in Europe.

16 Fr Habib Jajou (from 2014, bishop of the Archdiocese of Basra) had as of 2012 approximately 500 families to minister to, many of whom do not reside near to the main community in London but across Britain. Of those outside his immediate remit, many attend the Latin liturgy to fulfil their Sunday obligation (Interview, London, November 2012).

17 Roughly equivalent to £90 as of 2017.

18 Such a situation following him to the grave with his 2003 funeral held in Beirut.

19 The Church of the East has yet to join the MECC, with accusations of heresy related to a perceived Nestorian Christology still raised.

Bibliography

Abdullah, Thabit A. J. 2003. *A Short History of Iraq From 636 to the Present*. Harlow: Pearson Education.

Allawi, Ali A. 2014. *Faisal I of Iraq*. New Haven, CT and London: Yale University Press.

Asianews.It. 2013. 'Patriarch Sako Calls on Christians Not to Flee Iraq', August 27. www. asianews.it/news-en/Patriarch-Sako-calls-on-Christians-not-to-flee-Iraq-28849.html.

Audo SJ, Antoine. 2008. 'Les chrétiens d'Iraq – Histoire et perspectives'. *Etudes. Revue de culture contemporaine* 408 (2): 209–18.

———. 2012. 'The Current Situation of Christianity in the Middle East, Especially Syria, After the Synod of the Middle East's Final Declaration (September 2012) and the Papal Visit to Lebanon'. In *Living Stones Yearbook 2012*, edited by Mary Grey, Duncan Macpherson, Anthony O'Mahony, and Colin South, 1–17. London: Living Stones of the Holy Land Trust.

Audo SJ, Antoine, Louis Sako, Fadel Sidarouss, and Michel Sabbah. 2005. *Églises au Moyen-Orient: défis et espérances*. Cahiers de l'Orient chrétien 3. Beirut: CEDRAC.

Bacall, Jacob. 2014. *Chaldeans in Detroit*. Charleston, SC: Arcadia Publishing.

Baram, Amatzia. 1983. 'Mespotamian Identity in Ba'thi Iraq'. *Middle Eastern Studies* 19 (4): 426–55.

Baram, Amatzia, Achim Rohde, and Ronen Zeidel. 2010. 'Iraq: History Reconsidered, Present Reassessed'. In *Iraq Between Occupations: Perspectives From 1920 to the Present*, edited by Amatzia Baram, Achim Rohde, and Ronen Zeidel, 1–12. Basingstoke: Palgrave Macmillan.

Baumer, Christoph. 2006. *The Church of the East: An Illustrated History of Assyrian Christianity*. London: Tauris.

Becker, Adam H., ed. 2008. *Sources for the Study of the School of Nisibis*. Translated by Adam H. Becker. Translated Texts for Historians 50. Liverpool: Liverpool University Press.

Ben-Yaacob, Abraham, Nissim Kazzaz, Hayyim J. Cohen, and Avraham Yaari. 2007. 'Baghdad'. In *Encyclopaedia Judaica*, edited by Michael Berenbaum and Fred Skolnik. Detroit: Macmillan Reference USA. Gale Virtual Reference Library. http://go.galegroup. com/ps/i.do?id=GALE%7CCCX2587501872&v=2.1&u=imcpl1111&it=r&p=GVRL&s w=w&asid=0457988c18ce05ffb7afc15a7d8c796c.

Bet Shlimon, Arbella. 2012. 'Kirkuk, 1918–1968: Oil and the Politics of Identity in an Iraqi City'. Ph. D. thesis, Harvard University, Cambridge, MA.

Betts, Robert Brenton. 1979. *Christians in the Arab East: A Political Study*. Rev. Edition. London: S.P.C.K.

Bocco, Riccardo, and Jordi Tejel. 2012. 'Introduction'. In *Writing the Modern History of Iraq: Historiographical and Political Challenges*, edited by Jordi Tejel, Peter Sluglett, Riccardo Bocco, and Hamit Bozarslan, xi–xvii. Hackensack, NJ: World Scientific.

Borrut, Antoine, and Paul M. Cobb. 2010. 'Introduction: Towards a History of Umayyad Legacies'. In *Umayyad Legacies: Medieval Memories From Syria to Spain*, edited by Antoine Borrut and Paul M. Cobb, 1–22. Islamic History and Civilization: Studies and Texts 80. Leiden and Boston, MA: Brill.

Bouvet, Béatrice, and Patrick Denaud. 2000. *Tarek Aziz: le diplomate de Saddam Hussein*. Des hommes et des conflits. Paris: Harmattan.

Brock, Sebastian. 1979. 'Syriac Historical Writing: A Survey of the Main Sources'. *Journal of the Iraqi Academy (Syriac Corporation)* 5: 1–30.

———. 1982. 'Christians in the Sasanian Empire: A Case of Divided Loyalties'. In *Religion and National Identity*, edited by Stuart Mews, 1–19. Studies in Church History 18. Oxford: Blackwell for the Ecclesiastical History Society.

———. 1996. 'The "Nestorian" Church: A Lamentable Misnomer'. *Bulletin of the John Rylands Library* 78: 23–35.

106 *Re-discovering the Chaldean narrative*

———. 2004. 'The Syriac Churches in Ecumenical Dialogue on Christology'. In *Eastern Christianity: Studies in Modern History, Religion and Politics*, edited by Anthony O'Mahony, 44–65. London: Melisende.

———. 2009. 'The Cultural Contribution of Monasticism in Iraq'. In *The Christian Heritage of Iraq: Collected Papers From the Christianity of Iraq I–V Seminar Days*, edited by Erica C. D. Hunter, 64–80. Gorgias Eastern Christian Studies 13. Piscataway, NJ: Gorgias Press.

The Catholic Herald. 1950. 'Persian Cathedral', August 4.

———. 1951. 'Church Near Home of Holy Family', February 16.

———. 1952. 'Vocations from Baghdad', November 21.

———. 1962. 'Chaldean Seminary', March 9.

———. 1963. 'Pope John Names Six Patriarchs to Top Posts', March 29.

Catholic News Service. 2010. 'Vatican Says It Hopes Iraq Does Not Execute Tariq Aziz', October 27. www.catholicnews.com/data/stories/cns/1004407.htm.

Chatelard, Geraldine. 2002. 'Jordan as a Transit Country: Semi-Protectionist Immigration Policies and Their Effects on Iraqi Forced Migrants'. Working Paper 61, New Issues in Refugee Research, United Nations High Commissioner for Refugees, Florence, Italy. www.unhcr.org/refworld/docid/4ff3fcbe2.html.

Cherubini, Roberto. 1995a. 'La Chiesa Caldea Cattolica Al Concilio Ecumenico Vaticano II, Parte I'. *Studi e Ricerche Sull'Oriente Cristiano* XVIII (1/2): 41–7.

———. 1995b. 'La Chiesa Caldea Cattolica al Concilio Ecumenico Vaticano II, parte II'. *Studi e Ricerche sull'Oriente Cristiano* XVIII (3): 13–47.

Conway, Agnes. 1927. 'Education in Iraq, 1927'. *Journal of the Royal Central Asian Society* 14 (4): 334–39. doi:10.1080/03068372708724980.

Corbon, Jean. 1998. 'The Churches of the Middle East: Their Origins and Identity, From Their Roots in the Past to Their Openness to the Present'. In *Christian Communities in the Arab Middle East: The Challenge of the Future*, edited by Andrea Pacini, 92–110. Oxford: Clarendon Press.

Corley, Felix. 2003. 'Patriarch Raphael I Bidawid'. *The Independent*, July 12. www.independent.co.uk/news/obituaries/patriarch-raphael-i-bidawid-36756.html.

D'Ancona, Cristina. 2013. 'Greek Sources in Arabic and Islamic Philosophy'. In *The Stanford Encyclopedia of Philosophy*, edited by Edward N. Zalta. Stanford, CA: Center for the Study of Language and Information. http://stanford.library.usyd.edu.au/entries/arabic-islamic-greek/.

Dawisha, Adeed. 1983. 'Invoking the Spirit of Arabism: Islam in the Foreign Policy of Saddam's Iraq'. In *Islam in Foreign Policy*, edited by Adeed Dawisha, 112–28. Cambridge: Cambridge University Press.

———. 2005. *Arab Nationalism in the Twentieth Century: From Triumph to Despair*. First paperback printing. Princeton, NJ: Princeton University Press.

Debié, Muriel. 2010. 'Writing History as "Histoires": The Biographical Dimension of East-Syriac Historiography'. In *Writing 'True Stories': Historians and Hagiographers in the Late Antique and Medieval Near East*, edited by Arietta Papaconstantinou, 43–75. Cultural Encounters in Late Antiquity and the Middle Ages 9. Leiden: Brill. www.academia.edu/474627/_Writing_History_as_Histoires_The_Biographical_Dimension_of_East-Syriac_Historiography_in_Writing_True_Stories_Historians_and_Hagiographers_in_the_Late_Antique_and_Medieval_Near_East_A._Papaconstantinou_ed._in_collaboration_with_M._Debi%C3%A9_H._Kennedy_Leiden_Brill_Cultural_Encounters_in_Late_Antiquity_and_the_Middle_Ages_9_2010_p._43–75.

Donabed, Sargon, and Shamiran Mako. 2009. 'Ethno-Cultural and Religious Identity of Syrian Orthodox Christians'. *Chronos: Revue d'Histoire de l'Université de Balamand* 19: 71–113.

Edmonds, Cecil John. 1958. 'The Place of the Kurds in the Middle Eastern Scene'. *Journal of the Royal Central Asian Society* 45 (2): 141–53. doi:10.1080/03068375808731634.

Fiey OP, Jean Maurice. 1959. *Mossoul Chrétienne: Essai Sur l'histoire, l'archéologie et l'état Actuel Des Monuments Chrétiens de La Ville de Mossoul*. Recherches Publiées Sous La Direction de l'Institut de Lettres Orientales de Beyrouth 12. Beirut: Imprimerie Catholique.

———. 1970. *Jalons pour une histoire de l'Église en Iraq*. Corpus Scriptorum Christianorum Orientalium, v. 310. Louvain: Secrétariat du Corpus SCO.

———. 1993. *Pour un oriens christianus novus: répertoire des diocèses syriaques orientaux et occidentaux*. Beiruter Texte und Studien 49. Beirut: Franz Steiner Verlag.

———. 1994. 'The Spread of the Persian Church'. In *First Non-Official Consultation on Dialogue Within the Syriac Tradition*, edited by Alfred Stirnemann and Gerhard Wilflinger, 97–105. Syriac Dialogue 1. Vienna: Pro Oriente.

Filoni, Fernando. 2008. *La Chiesa nella terra d'Abramo: Dalla diocesi di Babilonia dei latini alla nunziatura apostolica in Iraq*. Milan: Biblioteca Universale Rizzoli.

Galadza, Peter. 2007. 'Eastern Catholic Christianity'. In *The Blackwell Companion to Eastern Christianity*, edited by Ken Parry, 291–318. Malden, MA: Blackwell.

Gavish, Haya. 2010. *Unwitting Zionists: The Jewish Community of Zakho in Iraqi Kurdistan*. Raphael Patai Series in Jewish Folklore and Anthropology. Detroit, MI: Wayne State University Press.

Girling, Kristian. 2012. 'Engaging "the Martyred Church" – the Chaldean Catholic Church, Assyrian Church of the East and the Holy See in Ecumenical Dialogue 1994–2012 and the Influence of the Second Vatican Council'. In *Living Stones Yearbook 2012*, edited by Mary Grey, Duncan Macpherson, Anthony O'Mahony, and Colin South, 38–64. London: Living Stones of the Holy Land Trust.

———. 2016. 'Jesuit Contributions to the Iraqi Education System in the 1930s and Later'. *International Studies in Catholic Education* 8 (2): 179–92. doi:10.1080/19422539.2016.1206400.

Green, Thomas J. 2002. 'The Latin and Eastern Codes: Guiding Principles'. *Jurist* 62: 235–79.

Hambye SJ, Édouard René. 1968. 'Two New Archdioceses for the Catholic Chaldeans'. *Eastern Churches Review: A Journal of Eastern Christendom* II (1): 84–5.

Hansbury, Mary. 2007. 'Professor Robert Beulay, OCD (1927–2007)'. *Journal of the Canadian Society for Syriac Studies* 7: 99–102.

Hastings, Adrian. 1997. *The Construction of Nationhood, Ethnicity, Religion and Nationalism*. Cambridge: Cambridge University Press.

Hazen, William E. 1979. 'Minorities in Revolt: The Kurds of Iran, Iraq, Syria, and Turkey'. In *The Political Role of Minority Groups in the Middle East*, edited by Ronald D. McLaurin, 49–75. New York: Praeger Publishers.

Hebblethwaite, Peter. 1983. 'The Synod on Social Sin'. *The Tablet*, October 22.

HMSO. 1925. 'Treaty of Alliance Between Great Britain and Iraq, Signed at Bagdad October 10, 1922; and Protocol to Treaty of Alliance Between Great Brtiain and Irak of October 10, 1922, Signed at Bagdad, April 30, 1923; Together With Agreements Subsidiary to the Treaty of Alliance Between Great Britain and Irak of October 10, 1922 Signed at Bagdad, March 25, 1924'. His Majesty's Stationery Office, London. www.galeuk.com/iraq/pdfs/Treaty%20of%20alliance%20btw%20GB%20&%20Iraq%2010%20Oct%201922%20CO%20730%20167%201.pdf.

108 *Re-discovering the Chaldean narrative*

———. 1948. 'Treaty of Alliance Between His Majesty in Respect of the United Kingdom of Great Britain and Northern Ireland and His Majesty the King of Iraq'. His Majesty's Stationery Office, London.

Hunter, Erica C. D. 2014a. 'Coping in Kurdistan: The Christian Diaspora'. In *Religious Minorities in Kurdistan: Beyond the Mainstream*, edited by Khanna Omarkhali, 321–38. Studies in Oriental Religions 68. Wiesbaden: Harrassowitz Verlag.

———. 2014b. 'The Holy Apostolic Catholic Assyrian Church of the East'. In *Eastern Christianity and Politics in the Twenty-First Century*, edited by Lucian Leustean, 601–20. Routledge Contemporary Russia and Eastern Europe Series 54. London: Routledge.

Husry, Khaldun S. 1974. 'The Assyrian Affair of 1933 (I)'. *International Journal of Middle East Studies* 5 (2): 161–76.

'Iraq: Continuous and Silent Ethnic Cleansing: Displaced Persons in Iraqi Kurdistan and Iraqi Refugees in Iran'. 2003. Paris: International Federation for Human Rights (FIDH) and The International Alliance for Justice (AIJ). www.fidh.org/IMG/pdf/iq350a.pdf.

Joseph, John. 1961. *The Nestorians and Their Muslim Neighbors: A Study of Western Influence on Their Relations*. Princeton Oriental Studies 20. Princeton, NJ: Princeton University Press.

———. 1983. *Muslim-Christian Relations and Inter-Christian Rivalries in the Middle East: The Case of the Jacobites in an Age of Transition*. Albany: State University of New York Press.

———. 2000. *The Modern Assyrians of the Middle East: Encounters With Western Christian Missions, Archaeologists, and Colonial Power*. Studies in Christian Mission 26. Leiden: Brill.

Kayyali, Randa A. 2006. *The Arab Americans*. The New Americans. Westport, CT: Greenwood Press.

Kelidar, A. R. 1974. 'Religion and State in Syria'. *Asian Affairs* 5 (1): 16–22. doi:10.1080/03068377408729692.

Kirmanj, Sherko. 2010. 'The Clash of Identities in Iraq'. In *Iraq Between Occupations: Perspectives From 1920 to the Present*, edited by Amatzia Baram, Achim Rohde, and Ronen Zeidel, 43–59. Basingstoke: Palgrave Macmillan.

Long, Jerry M. 2004. *Saddam's War of Words: Politics, Religion, and the Iraqi Invasion of Kuwait*. Austin, TX: University of Texas Press.

Luizard, Pierre-Jean. 2002. *La Question Irakienne*. Paris: Fayard.

Lukitz, Liora. 1995. *Iraq: The Search for National Identity*. London: Frank Cass.

MacDonnell SJ, Joseph F. 1994. *Jesuits by the Tigris – Men for Others in Baghdad*. Boston, MA: Jesuit Mission Press. https://archive.org/details/jesuitsbytigrism00macd.

Main, Ernest. 1933. 'Iraq and the Assyrians – 1932–33'. *Journal of the Royal Central Asian Society* 20 (4): 664–74. doi:10.1080/03068373308725285.

Mansfield, Peter. 1982. 'Saddam Husain's Political Thinking: The Comparison With Nasser'. In *Iraq: The Contemporary State*, edited by Tim Niblock, 62–73. Beckenham: Croom Helm Ltd.

Mar Raphael I Bidawid, and Mar Dinkha IV. 1998. 'Joint Synodal Decree for Promoting Unity Between the Assyrian Church of the East and the Chaldean Church 15th August 1997'. In *Third Non-Official Consultation on Dialogue Within the Syriac Tradition*, Edited by Alfred Stirnemann and Gerhard Wilflinger, 185–88. Syriac Dialogue 3. Vienna: Pro Oriente.

Marr, Phebe. 2010. 'One Iraq or Many: What Has Happened to Iraqi Identity'. In *Iraq Between Occupations: Perspectives From 1920 to the Present*, edited by Amatzia Baram, Achim Rohde, and Ronen Zeidel, 15–41. Basingstoke: Palgrave Macmillan.

Re-discovering the Chaldean narrative 109

Masters, Bruce. 2001. *Christians and Jews in the Ottoman Arab World: The Roots of Sectarianism*. Cambridge: Cambridge University Press.

Mostyn, Trevor. 1999. 'What Will the Pope Tell Saddam?' *The Tablet*, October 9.

Muscati, Samer, and Peter Bouckaert. 2009. *On Vulnerable Ground Violence Against Minority Communities in Nineveh Province's Disputed Territories*. New York: Human Rights Watch. www.hrw.org/reports/2009/11/10/vulnerable-ground-0.

Mylroie, Laurie A. 1989. 'After the Guns Fell Silent: Iraq in the Middle East'. *The Middle East Journal* XLIII: 51–67.

Nakash, Yitzhak. 2003. *The Shi'is of Iraq*. 2nd paperback Edition. Princeton, NJ: Princeton University Press.

Natarajan, Usha. 2011. 'Creating and Recreating Iraq: Legacies of the Mandate System in Contemporary Understandings of Third World Sovereignty'. *Leiden Journal of International Law* 24 (4): 799–822. doi:10.1017/S0922156511000380.

O'Mahony, Anthony. 2003. 'Iraq's Christians on Edge'. *The Tablet*, March 15.

———. 2004a. 'Christianity in Modern Iraq'. *International Journal for the Study of the Christian Church* 4 (2): 121–42. doi:10.1080/1474225042000288939.

———. 2004b. 'The Chaldean Catholic Church: The Politics of Church-State Relations in Modern Iraq'. *The Heythrop Journal* 45 (4): 435–50. doi:10.1111/j.1468-2265.2004.00265.x.

———. 2005. 'Life and Death of a Patriarch: Mar Rouphael I Bidawid, Patriarch of Babylon, and the Chaldean Catholic Church in Iraq'. *Sobornost* 27 (1): 26–46.

———. 2009. 'Christianity in Iraq: Modern History, Theology, Dialogue and Politics (Until 2003)'. In *The Christian Heritage of Iraq: Collected Papers From the Christianity of Iraq I–V Seminar Days*, edited by Erica Hunter, 237–84. Gorgias Eastern Christian Studies 13. Piscataway, NJ: Gorgias Press.

Pacini, Andrea. 1998. 'Introduction'. In *Christian Communities in the Arab Middle East: The Challenge of the Future*, edited by Andrea Pacini, 1–24. Oxford: Clarendon Press.

Paul VI. 1964. 'Orientalium Ecclesiarium – Decree on the Catholic Churches of the Eastern Rite'. Holy See. www.vatican.va/archive/hist_councils/ii_vatican_council/documents/vat-ii_decree_19641121_orientalium-ecclesiarum_en.html.

Petrosian, Vahram. 2006. 'Assyrians in Iraq'. *Iran & the Caucasus* 10 (1): 113–47. doi:10.1163/157338406777979322.

Rahimi, Babak. 2004. 'Ayatollah Ali Al-Sistani and the Democratization of Post-Saddam Iraq'. *Middle East Review of International Affairs* 8 (4): 12–19.

Rassam, Suha. 2010. *Christianity in Iraq: Its Origins and Development to the Present Day*. New Edition. Leominster: Gracewing Publishing.

———. 2012. Iraqi Christian life late twentieth century to pre- Gulf War 1990/1 era. Interview by Kristian Girling. Face-to-face interview with own short hand notes, Thames Ditton, England.

Rejwan, Nissim. 2004. *The Last Jews in Baghdad: Remembering a Lost Homeland*. Austin, TX: University of Texas Press.

Roberson CSP, Ronald G. 2010. 'The Eastern Catholic Churches 2010'. www.cnewa.org/source-images/Roberson-eastcath-statistics/eastcatholic-stat10.pdf.

———. 2014. 'The Eastern Catholic Churches 2014'. Annuario Pontificio. www.cnewa.org/source-images/Roberson-eastcath-statistics/eastcatholic-stat14.pdf.

Rutledge, Ian. 2014. *Enemy on the Euphrates: The British Occupation of Iraq and the Great Arab Revolt, 1914–1921*. London: Saqi Books.

Sabella, Bernard. 1998. 'The Emigration of Christian Arabs: Dimensions and Causes of the Phenomenon'. In *Christian Communities in the Arab Middle East: The Challenge of the Future*, edited by Andrea Pacini, 127–54. Oxford: Clarendon Press.

110 *Re-discovering the Chaldean narrative*

Sassoon, Joseph. 2011. *Saddam Hussein's Ba'th Party: Inside an Authoritarian Regime*. Cambridge and New York: Cambridge University Press.

Schmidt, Dana Adams. 1964. *Journey Among Brave Men*. Boston, MA: Little Brown.

Seferta, Joseph. 2004. 'Iraq's Catholic Exiles'. *The Tablet*, September 4.

———. 2008. *The Chaldean Church of Iraq – a Story of Survival*. Chapel-en-le-Frith: Blackfriars Publications.

Sengstock, Mary C. 1974. 'Traditional and Nationalist Identity in a Christian Arab Community'. *Sociological Analysis* 35 (3): 201–10.

Simons, Geoff. 2004. *Iraq From Sumer to Post-Saddam*. Third Edition. Basingstoke: Palgrave Macmillan.

Snir, Reuven. 2006. ' "Religion Is for God, the Fatherland Is for Everyone": Arab-Jewish Writers in Modern Iraq and the Clash of Narratives After Their Immigration to Israel'. *Journal of the American Oriental Society* 126 (3): 379–99.

Somekh, Sasson. 2012. *Life after Baghdad: Memoirs of an Arab-Jew in Israel, 1950–2000*. Brighton and Portland, OR: Sussex Academic Press.

Soro, Bawai. 2004. 'The Eucharist in the Church of the East: A Means to Unity'. In *Sixth Non-Official Consultation on Dialogue Within the Syriac Tradition*, edited by Peter Hofrichter and Gerhard Wilflinger, 189–202. Syriac Dialogue 6. Vienna: Pro Oriente.

Spencer, Richard. 2010. 'Tariq Aziz: A Profile'. *The Daily Telegraph*, October 26. www.telegraph.co.uk/news/worldnews/middleast/iraq/8088253/Tariq-Aziz-a-profile.html.

Stansfield, Gareth R. V. 2007. *Iraq: People, History, Politics*. Hot Spots in Global Politics. Cambridge: Polity.

Sudilovsky, Judith. 2007. 'Life Was Better under Saddam, Say Christian Refugees'. *The Catholic Herald*, March 9.

Swan, Charles L., and Leila B. Saba. 1974. 'The Migration of a Minority'. In *Arabic Speaking Communities in American Cities*, edited by Barbara C. Aswad, 85–110. New York: Center for Migration Studies of New York.

The Tablet. 1991. 'War in the Gulf', January 26.

Takeyh, Ray. 2010. 'The Iran-Iraq War: A Reassessment'. *Middle East Journal* 64 (3): 366–83. doi:10.3751/64.3.12.

Teule, Herman. 2008. *Les Assyro-Chaldéens: Chrétiens d'Irak, d'Iran et de Turquie*. Fils d'Abraham. Turnhout: Brepols.

———. 2011. 'Christianity in Iraq: The Development of Secular Christian Political Thinking'. *One in Christ* 45 (2): 312–20.

———. 2012. 'Christians in Iraq: An Analysis of Some Recent Political Developments'. *Der Islam* 88 (1): 179–98. doi:10.1515/islam-201100010.

———. 2015. 'Christians in Iraq: An Analysis of Some Recent Developments'. In *Christsein in Der Islamischen Welt: Festschrift Für Martin Tamcke Zum 60. Geburtstag*, edited by Sidney H. Griffith and Sven Grebenstein, 587–94. Wiesbaden: Harrassowitz Verlag.

Toulat, Jean. 1992. *Le Pape contre la guerre du Golfe*. Paris: OEIL.

Tripp, Charles. 2007. *A History of Iraq*. Third Edition. Cambridge: Cambridge University Press.

Valognes, Jean-Pierre. 1994. *Vie et Mort Des Chrétiens d'Orient: Des Origines à Nos Jours*. Paris: Fayard.

Visser, Reidar. 2007. 'Basra, the Reluctant Seat of "Shiastan" '. *Middle East Report*, no. 242, The Shi'a in the Arab World (Spring): 23–8.

White, Andrew. 2007. *Iraq: Searching for Hope*. New Edition. London: Continuum.

Wilmshurst, David. 2011. *The Martyred Church: A History of the Church of the East*. Sawbridgeworth, Hertfordshire: East and West.

Wood, Philip. 2013. *The Chronicle of Seert: Christian Historical Imagination in Late Antique Iraq*. Oxford Early Christian Studies. Oxford: Oxford University Press. http://fdslive.oup.com/www.oup.com/academic/pdf/openaccess/9780199670673.pdf.

Yacoub, Joseph. 1996. *Babylone chrétienne : géopolitique de l'Église de Mésopotamie*. Paris: Descle de Brouwer.

Youssef, Pierre. 1996. 'Christ in the Liturgical Tradition of the Church of the East'. In *Second Non-Official Consultation on Dialogue Within the Syriac Tradition*, edited by Alfred Stirnemann and Gerhard Wilflinger, 173–85. Syriac Dialogue 2. Vienna: Pro Oriente.

ZENIT News Agency. 2002. 'St. Thérèse's Relics Arrive in Iraq – Sign of Hope for Peace for Christians Who Fear War', November 21. www.zenit.org/en/articles/st-therese-s-relics-arrive-in-iraq.

4 The Chaldean Church in the new Iraq (2003–2013)

This chapter provides a history of the Chaldean Church during the ten years following the 2003 invasion of Iraq. I focus on the effects of conflict and socio-economic change on Chaldean ecclesiology and ecclesiastical organisation. Source material was collated largely during a research visit to northern Iraq in October 2013. The material chiefly consists of baptismal, marriage and population records from Chaldean parish and diocesan archives. Information was also provided by Chaldean clergy in central and southern Iraq – regions inaccessible due to constraints on freedom of movement – who supplied information from their own records. Discussions and interviews with Chaldeans were also conducted ranging from political activists and historians to clergy and physicians.[1]

As this is a growing and unexplored area of study, much work remains to be done. However, the research for this study is fortunate to have been completed in 2013 prior to the rise of Da'esh. Further accumulation of data, even via e-mail correspondence from June 2014, has proven very difficult due to the direct ethnic cleansing of the Christian populations in northern Iraq. Whether a similar study can be conducted again in the future remains to be seen, but the research findings presented here document the Chaldean Church at a crucial crossroads in its history.

Chaldean identity post-invasion

From the 1990s, Iraqi Christian identity became more fluid and less denominationally bound, with a more generic identity beginning to emerge among the communities in Iraq. This identity has been expressed largely either as *Iraqi Christian* or *Assyrian Christian*, and confusion as to nomenclature can occur. This can lead to ignorance of the ecclesial differences which still exist but have not always been consistently recognised in existing secondary literature. Nonetheless, it is important to recall, as nearly all Iraqi Christians encountered during my research still held a strong attachment to, and identification with, the church in which they were baptised. But, since the invasion, this identity was in tension with their identity as Iraqi citizens and their perceived ethnic identity, whether Arab, Assyrian or other.

I suggest, in the post-invasion era, Iraqi Christians have been obliged to provide a definition of communal and personal identity as a result of residing in a society

The Chaldean Church in the new Iraq   113

with competing notions of what constitutes membership of the Iraqi nation. This has been further complicated by the confines of the Islamic Arab *milieu*, in which a variety of opinions exist as to how non-Muslim Iraqis should be treated in law. Christians have had to attempt to re-justify their presence despite their heritage and to re-instil confidence in the churches as legitimate influences upon Iraqi society.

Historical Overview (2003–2008)

From March 2003 to March 2013, Iraq saw an immediate socio-economic and political decline, with a gradual growth in stability of a sort in some provinces. This stabilisation was especially notable for those, including many Chaldeans, resident in the northern Iraqi provinces of Duhok, Sulaymaniya and Erbil administered by the Kurdistan Regional Government (KRG). By the mid-1990s, the three provinces had effectively become an independent Kurdish-led state defended by the Coalition-imposed no-fly zone over northern Iraq, and backed by claims to the oil reserves present in the provinces or in proximity to the border with Iraq proper. This *status quo* continued into the twenty-first century, with the Kurdish armed forces (Peshmerga) facilitating the 2003 Coalition invasion.[2]

The KRG is largely pro-Western in its foreign and economic policies, with commitments from the political élite to protect numerical minority groups especially Christians. Unofficially these commitments vary by location, but the general level of freedom from violence and economic opportunities offered by the KRG saw thousands of Chaldean families move from central and southern provinces to northern Iraq.

Radical alteration of life expectations

Through removing the rule and state apparatus of Saddam Hussein and the Baath Party, the Coalition removed those elements which had coerced, regulated and controlled nearly all aspects of Iraqi life. Thus, as for all Iraqis, Chaldeans have seen a radical reorientation of life expectations. The change from life under Hussein to life in the new republic has provided few tangible benefits to the Chaldeans. Their perceived proximity to Western ideals and political agendas has led to persecution. A sustained atmosphere of security in which all Iraqi citizens could exercise a normal life remained elusive, with regular sectarian violence between Shia militias and Sunni Islamist factions a threat to even the most basic of day-to-day activities.

These difficulties were intensified once the initial stages of occupation were completed. The Coalition Provisional Authority (CPA), which was the body acting as the Iraqi government in the time prior to which elections could be held for the Iraqi parliament, disbanded the Iraqi armed forces and police on 23 May 2003 (Bremer 2003). The CPA considered it a political imperative to remove IBP influence from the coercive arms of the state, but gave little consideration to the impact of such changes. The lack of native security forces was disastrous for the

114 *The Chaldean Church in the new Iraq*

maintenance of law and order, and exacerbated the situation for the Christians. They rarely resorted to organising a community militia for self-defence, as was the case for many Muslim or even Yezidi groups.[3]

Another difficulty for the Chaldeans at the time of the invasion was a leadership crisis. Patriarch Bidawid died in July 2003 and his successor – Emmanuel III Delly – was ultimately selected by the Holy See after the Chaldean synod of bishops had failed to reach a decision. Antoine Audo SJ, Bishop of Aleppo, emerged as a prominent candidate, but was perceived to suffer from a lack of direct contemporary experience of Chaldean life in Iraq. That no decision was reached to choose such a well-qualified candidate, I suggest, was indicative of the loss of direction towards the end of Bidawid's life and the limited influence he had in the choice of his successor. The Holy See, in being obliged to determine the successor and in choosing Delly, demonstrated a somewhat surprising lack of forethought in what the Chaldeans required for their leadership at a time of qualitative change in Iraq. Indeed, there was a degree of short-sightedness on the part of the Holy See in selecting a leader who was not well integrated with extended church networks in the Middle East or with a strong understanding of the institutions of the contemporary papacy.

We should recognise both the difficult legacy which Delly assumed from Bidawid and his own status as a compromise candidate, which inhibited developing an authoritative leadership position that could have been granted by a clear victory at the patriarchal election. Delly *was* a fortunate choice insofar as he had an excellent knowledge of internal Chaldean affairs and the ecclesiastical organisation of the Church in Iraq down to the parish level. Yet he lacked that sense of communal confidence which is derived from successful transitions between leaders. I suggest this was the foundation for a sense of long-term disappointment among many Chaldeans in the patriarchal office, with church leaders neglecting to outline a comprehensive approach to meeting the demands of the new Iraq. This set of circumstances perhaps also led to a consolidation of diocesan identities with individual bishops being obliged to become *de facto* leaders of 'churches'. It is possible that a patriarch with a stronger personality could have withstood better the competing demands of the Iraqi dioceses, the demands of the increasingly autonomous Chaldean dioceses of the United States and the overall decline of Iraqi socio-economic life. These factors should be borne in mind when considering the following assessment of recent Chaldean history.

The effects of the invasion by Coalition forces in 2003 on the Chaldean community and initial attempts to reconstruct civil society

In attempting to enforce democracy on Iraq, the CPA followed the same essential processes as the British had attempted in the 1920s in establishing Iraq as a state for the first time. This included the creation of new executive, legislative, judicial and military branches of the state. These developments were generally dictated by what was perceived necessary to meet the needs of the occupying power rather than changes which would have been best suited to the native population. This was seen in the composition of the Iraqi Governing Council (IGC), established in July 2003. Its twenty-five members were to advise the CPA and consisted of thirteen Shia, five Sunni, five Kurds, one Turkmen and one Assyrian (Tripp 2007, 284). Whether this was more than a mere veneer of supposed legitimisation of the occupation is open for question, but it at least supposed an attempt to better reflect the ethnic and religious groups who composed the Iraqi nation.

The major differences between the two reformulations of Mesopotamia-Iraq were the available technology, highly increased destructive power of weaponry and, as a result of previous Coalition interventions, increased enmity between Iraqis and the invading forces. It would appear, therefore, the potential for the successful establishment of a republican democracy under the United States' tutelage was far less likely than that of a constitutional monarchy encouraged by the British. In the Chaldeans' case, at least, the British had recognised the significance of including their patriarch within the legislature from 1921.

In 2003, Chaldean cognisance of their vital role in the historic and future development of Mesopotamia-Iraq extended to a formal letter of the hierarchy addressed to the CPA's head, Paul Bremer. The bishops requested acknowledgement of their tradition of contributions and further, to permit them a formal rôle in redeveloping Iraqi national life (Emmanuel III Delly et al. 2003). This appears to have been ignored and Christians were to be frozen out of making a meaningful contribution to nation formation. It appears the CPA were at a loss as how to engage with the non-Muslim populations, and were pursuing a policy of ameliorating communal divisions in Iraq focused on the Sunni-Shia religious and Arab-Kurdish ethnic dichotomies with little awareness of Iraq's plurality.

It may appear in retrospect that the Iraqi situation was without any likely resolution and that the Chaldean attempts to reaffirm their presence and commitment was futile at this juncture. It was, however, considered even worse were they to do nothing entirely. The bishops' letter was submitted at a time when it was thought that development of a positive nature could still occur prior to the start of intensified Shia-Sunni conflicts, the rise of Al-Qaeda in Iraq and the massive migration of the Chaldean community (Emmanuel III Delly et al. 2003).

Christians speaking with one voice?

The Chaldeans faced the challenge of protecting their own community and maintaining their leadership rôle among the Iraqi churches and as the largest non-Muslim community. However, as we have noted in earlier chapters, political and denominational divisions among the churches existed for much of the twentieth century. Only with the start of ecumenical engagements was unity of action recognised as a means to consolidate the security of Iraqi Christians into the future (Lamani 2009, 11).

An attempted consensus among Christians emerged in 2003, when the ADM discussed the descriptive term *Chaldo-Assyrian* for use in the new state's constitutional and legal framework when referring to the Christian population. Efforts at unified nomenclature were complicated by the requirement to cover so many

116　*The Chaldean Church in the new Iraq*

competing interests, and the conflicting views regarding the appropriate future rôle of the churches and Christian political organisations. The ADM's efforts were initially supported by many churches including the Chaldeans. However, the Chaldean hierarchy later withdrew support, largely due to fears that the ADM and their preferred aggregate term would be used as part of a push for the establishment of an autonomous Christian region in Iraq, something to which the Chaldean hierarchy remained opposed (Teule 2011, 315–16). The situation in Iraq by mid-2003 was such that unity of any kind may have been preferable in order to be better engaged in the state re-formation process. Yet in the context of Bidawid's death and subsequent patriarchal election, it was very difficult for the Chaldeans to provide a definitive commitment to such inter-Christian initiatives.

I suggest the churches were reluctant to engage with ostensibly Christian political parties owing to continuing disputes over who could better represent the community on a national level and whether religiously or politically directed identity was a better means for securing the Chaldean community in Iraq. The former identity emphasised Iraqi citizenship and a plural society. The latter identity often emphasised the imperative of an autonomous Christian region and a withdrawal from engagement with wider Iraqi society. Nevertheless, Chaldean leaders were obliged to retain working relationships with Christian politicians and their positions within Iraqi representative bodies, as they were able to directly assist the Christians through facilitating the provision of housing, the resolution of legal disputes – especially with the KRG – and the granting of government funding (Teule 2012, 187).

The rise of violence against Christians

Intimidation of Christians began with videos of beheadings being left outside homes in Mosul in Spring 2003 whilst Patriarch Delly received, in June 2003, a letter accusing him of collaboration and demanding he leave Iraq (Rassam 2012, 13; Gunn 2009, 10). Such a focus on the patriarch three months after the invasion indicating a developed awareness of the Chaldean presence among Islamist factions.

The first, most comprehensive attack against the Christian population took place on 1 August 2004 when five churches were bombed in Baghdad and Mosul, with eleven people killed and fifty injured (Glatz 2004; Hirst 2004b). The focus of these attacks on Catholic churches (Armenian, Syrian and Chaldean) was justified by blaming 'the Pope for leading an anti-Muslim crusade' (Hirst 2004a, 25). The spurious reasoning provided by the Islamist group was an attempted justification for ongoing criminal and terrorist behaviour manifested as religiously motivated violence against Christians in general. Bombing attacks against churches continued in October and December in Baghdad, with increasingly co-ordinated, short and intense campaigns aimed at removing the Christian presence.

From a regional perspective, attacks on the Chaldeans were largely confined to Baghdad, Kirkuk, in and around Mosul and nearby Christian villages of the

The Chaldean Church in the new Iraq 117

Nineveh plain. Basra had a significant Chaldean presence, but saw fewer anti-Christian attacks, which can perhaps be accounted for by the lack of an intensified Sunni-Shia conflict due to the Shia dominance in southern Iraq. Regardless of their geographical location, the Chaldeans maintained the *status quo* of their religious life as best they could even as it became more dangerous to do so and migration from central Iraq rapidly increased.

It is notable that anti-Christian actions were undertaken long before Pope Benedict XVI made comments which were perceived to criticise Islam in 2006. This indicates that the reasoning for violence was established among Muslim attackers, and marks out the papacy and the connected churches in Iraq as a particular target (Benedict XVI 2006). Moreover, that the Holy See had been one of the leading voices most ardent in opposing the invasion seems to have gone unheeded (*ZENIT News Agency 2002*).

Social and psychological affects after the end of Baath party rule

Despite Iraq's socio-economic decline during the Iran-Iraq and Gulf wars, the state's security apparatus and general stability remained largely the same and ensured that existential threats to Hussein's rule were removed. This was demonstrated most strongly in the defeat of the 1991 popular rebellion, and a widespread belief existed among many Iraqis of the necessity of Hussein's rule. Therefore, to go from such a situation to the consistently disturbed society from March 2003 required of Chaldeans a reassessment of personal, ecclesiological and political paradigms to determine one's place within the new order. This new order, however, brought with it only new competing social tensions with which to contend.

The psychological shock among the Chaldean population was immediate and, to an extent, paralysing. It affected the Church's ability to cope with the change inflicted and to contend with the ferocity of persecution. In the longer term, it imprinted a fear of other Iraqis and a destructive pattern of self-doubt and disassociation of their patriotic attachment to the Iraqi nation. This psychological development, resulting from cultural and social change, was highlighted by the Latin Archbishop of Baghdad, Jean Sleiman OCD (2001–present). Speaking in London in September 2008, he referred to the intensification of the outlook of *Dhimmitude* among the Christian population, whereby they have been considered less than full members of society regardless of Muslim affirmations to the contrary since the seventh century. Such an outlook which, Sleiman stated, is 'not [necessarily] reflected in the laws of the land but it is very present in the culture and psychology of the people' (Sleiman OCD 2008). Bosworth noted from a longer term historical context:

> It is surprising that, in the face of legal and financial disabilities . . . and of a relentless social and cultural Muslim pressure, if not of sustained persecution, that the dhimmī communities survived as well as they did.
>
> (Bosworth 2012, 161)

118 *The Chaldean Church in the new Iraq*

Such similar effects and stipulations began to be implemented in all but name against Iraqi Christians, which saw the emergence of a popular awareness not just of martyrdom of individual Christians or of different churches, but **a martyrdom of the Christian narrative and presence in Iraq** and a denial of non-Muslim contributions to Mesopotamian-Iraqi history.

Physical and legal persecution has been a consistent threat faced by East Syriac Christians throughout their history. However, aside from events after 2003, martyrdom as a theme in the Chaldean Church had not been so resolutely impressed upon the entirety of the Chaldean communal memory other than during the Ottoman massacres of 1915–1918. For the period 1921–2003, the martyrdom narrative appears to have been suppressed, and attempts were made to play down the anti-Christian connotations which some events appeared to have. This happened through more senior members of the Church recommending to those affected that issues of contention in business dealings be dropped, or that the motivations in the murder of Chaldeans could be ascribed to non-religious reasons. The intention to downplay these events as specifically anti-Christian was to ensure that the secure social position which Iraqi Christians had attained in general terms could be extended indefinitely. Furthermore, the Chaldean desire to suppress the martyrdom concept at the level of communal memory among older generations was also derived from a desire to forget the traumas experienced during the 1915–1918 massacres, subsequent forced displacement and the severe loss of ecclesiastical, cultural and material heritage.[4]

The reawakening of the presence of the martyrdom theme came in the context of the post-2003 scenario of societal collapse and eventual civil war. A fixed narrative of marginalisation of Christians emerged which could not be challenged by the churches: **at a society-wide level, the decline of the Christian presence was ignored, considered acceptable or inevitable**. The lack of concern for the Christians by other Iraqis became so prevalent that it destroyed societal plurality and saw the lived reality of Christian life alter to one of consistent social and material deprivation. A means of attempting to redeem this experience was to emphasise the process as one of martyrdom. In theory, this provided some comfort, with the notion of the Chaldeans experiencing the lived reality of the Christian notion of long suffering in times of extreme trial. Yet for a population which had been in a state of sustained decline since the 1990s and subsequently faced a final push out of wider Iraqi societal consciousness, theological reflection offered little practical comfort. The Chaldeans were being rejected on a nation-wide level for the first time in Mesopotamia-Iraq.

Detrimental changes to Christians' psychological outlook increased through the lack of resources available to deal with the traumas to which the invasion and subsequent persecution were witness. Due to the extent of these difficulties, the Chaldean hierarchy looked to support their community as far as they were able and introduced training for seminarians and priests in order to recognise and engage with community members who were suffering from Post-Traumatic Stress Disorder (PTSD) and other mental health difficulties. This training was vital to deal with the growth in mental health problems among the communities, as it is

The Chaldean Church in the new Iraq   119

approximated that PTSD arising from conflict situations often emerges five to ten years after the event which causes symptoms to develop.

A new constitutional order *and* Chaldean involvement?

Regardless of the unstable social situation, it was hoped that the implementation of a new constitution might bring about some normalisation in Iraqi social interactions. Christians were wary of accepting the new constitution due to the limited opportunity they had to influence the drafting of the document: Christians had only one meeting in August 2005 to air their concerns (Yacoub 2010, 179). Nonetheless, the new fundamental law of Iraq received approval from the CPA and IGC on 28 August 2005, with a popular referendum ratifying it in October 2005.

The constitution granted some hope for the remembrance of non-Islamic contributions to Mesopotamia-Iraq. The Preamble referred to both the temporal and religious pre-Arab Mesopotamian heritage and the production of the first law code under the Babylonian king, Hammurabi (Yacoub 2010, 174, 175 n. 4). Such sentiments are in contrast with the rest of the document which ignore mention of non-Islamic contributors. Overall, this is paradoxical, as from the outset, the constitution indicates support for democracy, rights of minorities and freedom of worship but is framed by the assertion that no new law can contradict the *sharia* and that the Federal Supreme Court was to be based around Islamic jurisprudence, a knowledge of which was required for all judges (Yacoub 2010, 176).

By comparison, the preferences of the Chaldeans from March 2003 were for a lay state. They emphasised the importance of patriotic citizenship, the rights of women and the disabled and opposition to a state based on ethnic divisions (Yacoub 2010, 179–80), whereas many Iraqi Muslims sought a state which countered the secular paradigm that Hussein had enforced until the last few years of his rule. The Islamic revival in West Asia from the 1970s often emphasised the implementation of *sharia* norms in tension with 'matters of women, religious freedom, and co-existence with non-Muslims' (Hefner 2014, 642). The Chaldean preferences reflected the precedents set at least officially under the rule of the IBP. By comparison they were similar to the paradigm still then experienced in Syria under the leadership of another Baathist president, Bashar al-Assad. Antoine Audo SJ, contemporary Chaldean bishop of Aleppo, outlines the situation thus:

> Accustomed to a single and comfortable discourse at every level of the institutions of the state, especially the army, education and the single party, the Syrian people, despite their ethnic, religious and geographical differences, enjoyed a certain stability, with the comfort and progress which that brought. The country's Christians . . . found in this regime considerable security and a reining in of all religious extremism. We might even say that Christians prospered: in universities, manufacturing, business, etc.
>
> (2012, 13)

120   *The Chaldean Church in the new Iraq*

In theory, the new Iraqi constitution provided the opportunity for Christians to participate in a *comfortable discourse* with the government and its infrastructure, and supposed they could remain contributors in Iraqi society with the opportunity to practice their faith. Constitutional articles which are particularly relevant to the Chaldean population include the following:

- 2: Freedom of worship
- 10: Freedom to worship at places of religious significance
- 35c: State guarantee against religious coercion
- 36a: Freedom of expression
- 40: Freedom of belief
- 41: State forbidden to interfere in administration of religious groups
- 41b: 'Protection of places of worship' ('Final Draft Iraqi Constitution' 2005).

These concepts are further supported throughout the document with guarantees of rights for different ethnic and religious groups to self-administration and cultural and educational independence (Yacoub 2010, 175). In practice, however, these guarantees have been extremely difficult to maintain. This is due to widely held and ingrained Muslim religious and cultural views regarding the lower worth attached to Christianity and other non-Muslim religions not just on a spiritual level, but on the necessity of their legal status as subordinate to Muslims (Taneja 2007, 26; 'Final Draft Iraqi Constitution' 2005, sec. 1, art. 2). The increasingly assertive Islamic groups which came to dominate Iraqi political and social life reinforced views and actions which had, to a large degree, been kept in check by Saddam Hussein's government and were instead freely able to attempt to establish an idealised new Iraq in which significant minorities of the population would be repressed. The revivification of the distinct legal status of Christians in a Muslim-dominated country was a product of the long-term *dhimmi* conditioning which they had experienced over centuries and was derived from Koranic and *sharia* based stipulations as to their treatment (Hefner 2014, 639). These stipulations, however loosely they were enjoined upon the Christians throughout the history of Mesopotamia, were never removed from Muslim Iraqi legal discourse into the twenty-first century (Mallat 1988, 700).

Other difficulties associated with the formal wording of the constitution have arisen for the Chaldeans. We can note, for example, the greater status in law which groups are granted who have a cohesive and explicitly expressed ethnic identity (Yacoub 2010, 175–6). As the Chaldean hierarchy did not consistently support the idea that their community was an ethnic group, it was not evident how their position as a separate religious group would be protected. This distinction is important, for it purports a secondary tier to which the Chaldeans are ascribed – as merely a minority religious group – within the hierarchy of the nation. This forms a precedent for future considerations of Iraqi society as delineated by a sectarian *milieu*. However, if they asserted a particular Aramaic, Syriac or Assyrian ethnicity, they would appear in law to have a stronger claim to the resources of the state and a more 'genuine' position in a social order. This 'social order' grew

The Chaldean Church in the new Iraq 121

accustomed to a paradigm that suggested an explicit ethnic identity was necessary to achieve this position.

A veneer of democracy, rights for numerical minorities and national unity as exists in the new Iraq is dangerous, for it presupposes that there is some commitment among the state bureaucracy and government towards the manifestation and maintenance of these political ideals. As the Iraqi situation as of early 2017 is less unified and more fragmented politically, we can share Byman's view that a democracy can exist in theory, but often in practice exists with values determined by the faction which has the strongest control over the means of coercion. In effect, this leads to the exclusion of certain parties (Byman 2003, 54). Moreover, the decisive influence of leaders who support the implementation of Islamic legal and cultural practices would appear to prevent the development of a lay-state paradigm, which had been perceived as a goal in the introduction of representative democracy to Iraq. As noted earlier, the Preamble of the new constitution states that Islamic values cannot be contradicted by any law yet commits Iraq to a republican, federal, democratic, pluralistic system (Seferta 2005, 10; 'Final Draft Iraqi Constitution' 2005, Preamble). Given the multiplicity of interpretations of Islam within Iraq and the further multiplicity within these interpretations of what constitutes the best means of government, it seems highly unlikely pluralism will be effected in the long term.

The Iraqi civil war (2006–2007) and effects on the Chaldeans

At the end of 2005, the Chaldean communities had declined in size due to migration in the face of socio-economic decline but were not yet at a precipitous level. They appeared to retain a critical mass sufficient to sustain their presence to Iraq indefinitely. However, demographic change increased and was brought into perhaps its most destructive phase from 2006–2007, where areas of Christian residence in Mosul and Baghdad were left significantly depleted following specific anti-Christian campaigns. This is particularly evident from the Chaldean parish registers in Baghdad, which saw on average just under fifty percent reductions in the number of baptisms between 2005 and 2008. A selection of four parishes from across the city provides indication of this in Table 4.1.

Anti-Christian persecution in this period operated in the context of a Sunni-Shia civil war from 2006 to 2007, which saw unprecedented levels of violence. In general, the situation for Christians was as bit part actors in the unfolding sectarian narrative. These two years saw Sunni and Shia groups, for the first time since

Table 4.1 Baptismal records from selected Baghdadi parishes, 2005–2008

Year	Mar Bethune	Sacred Heart	Holy Ghost	St Joseph (Karrada)
2005	39	67	22	59
2006	29	54	22	64
2007	18	18	12	61
2008	19	33	6	37

Source: *Baghdad Diocesan Records*

122 *The Chaldean Church in the new Iraq*

2003, seek to remove the other on a countrywide scale for posing a threat to the other's implementation of a religiously based social order. The period led to a greater change in mindset of the Chaldeans than any since the invasion period in 2003, with it being widely asserted that not only would they seek security by migrating but also that they had no intention of ever returning (Conversations and observations among the Chaldean communities in northern Iraq, October 2013). This change of mindset is notable as, previously, migration could occur on a temporary basis. This period of violence marked the end of hope for a return to normality in their homeland.

The Chaldean position was compounded by the lack of concern for their situation from the wider Iraqi community, and the lack of interest with which the Western mainstream media regarded the Christians' circumstances, outside of one-off special reports. This is a lack of interest which appears to have extended among those NGOs whose role was to alleviate conditions for internally displaced persons and refugees in the Kurdistan region and in Jordan and Syria. In speaking with Chaldean refugees in Amman, it was strongly emphasised that the United Nations High Commissioner for Refugees (UNHCR) offered limited support. Further, the UNHCR had limited awareness of the specific difficulties faced by Christians, in comparison with Muslim Iraqis, which possibly stemmed from the UNHCR's refusal to record the religion of refugees.[5] This, in turn, limited the collection of data by NGOs on the proportional effects of the war between the Christian and Muslim Iraqi populations.

Notably in this period, quotations from an earlier era of Muslim antagonism towards Christian communities were remarked upon by Benedict XVI during the 2006 Regensberg lecture, remarks which saw an intensification of attacks against Christians over a short period.[6] However, attacks at the time did not appear to distinguish among the different Christian groups, as an Iraqi Presbyterian minister was murdered in November 2006. The reasoning behind this event cast it as 'revenge' for what Benedict XVI had said (Hanish 2009, 7). This disconnect between the group who supposedly caused the offence and the actual person affected revealed the ignorance of the attackers. It is unlikely that an average member of an Islamist militia would have a measured perspective on Benedict's remarks. However, by the time these remarks had been popularised and drawn out of all proportion as to their context, they became a convenient means of criticism and advanced the notion that the Crusades to the Holy Land and the native Iraqi Christian presence were linked and were, in fact, an excuse to continue to engage in generic anti-Christian violence.

A direct attack to inhibit the future development of the Chaldean Church was launched in September and December 2006, with the kidnap of the rector and vice-rector, respectively, of St Peter's seminary in Baghdad (*Asianews.It* 2006). These events led to the decision to relocate the institution to the Christian suburb of Erbil, Ankawa, where it reopened in January 2007. The movement of the seminary, though forced due to threat of violence, was also pragmatic given the increasing Chaldean population resident in and around Ankawa. This population grew year to year in the period 2000–2007 from 2,100 to 6,450 families, as can be seen in Table 4.2.

Table 4.2 Number of Chaldean families in
Ankawa 2000–2007

Archdiocesan records	
Year	*Families*
2000	2,100
2001	2,225
2002	2,365
2003	3,615
2004	3,965
2005	4,289
2006	5,465
2007	6,450

Source: *Erbil Archdiocesan Records*

The growing pace of communal change hung heavily over the hierarchy and laity as they increased their efforts to support those in the internal Iraqi diaspora, with new churches constructed along with accommodation, medical facilities and schools. Christians resolved to exist, to adapt and to prosper as far as the situation permitted. At the establishment of a new church foundation in Erbil, Patriarch Emmanuel III Delly stated:

> And as our fathers have shed their blood for the prosperity of this country and its progress in faith and holiness, we should follow their footsteps. Do not be afraid, O small flock, for the Lord is with us until the end of the world despite all the persecutions that we face whether inside or outside. The interior persecution comes at the time when we are working hard for the good of this country believing that we have all the rights as we have all the duties.
>
> (Emmanuel III Delly 2007)

Delly's remarks reflect the hierarchy's concerns about the Chaldean community's future in Iraq, not just as a token group but also as integral to the formation of national political, social and cultural life. His words, however, failed to resonate with the experiences of Chaldeans outside of the Kurdistan region and the rapidly changing circumstances in which Chaldean families lived. Even those areas of traditional Chaldean concentration were becoming irreversibly weakened. June 2007 was most terribly marked by the murders of Fr Ragheed Aziz Ganni and Sub-Deacons Basman Yousef Daoud, Wadid Hanna and Ghasan Bidawid outside the church of the Holy Ghost in Mosul. These murders were explicitly anti-Christian, with demands to the men that they convert to Islam immediately prior to the attacks along with demands for the closure of the church. The ripple effect of the attacks, for months afterwards, was for many to lead to a reawakening and strengthening of their faith, but also a questioning of the practicalities of remaining resident in Mosul. The number of baptisms at Fr Ragheed's church had held strong during his ministry, but dropped off exponentially following his

124   *The Chaldean Church in the new Iraq*

death and 2008–2013 saw only five baptisms celebrated in the church: 2006 had seen forty-nine and 2007 fifteen baptisms (Baptismal register Holy Ghost parish, Mosul, facsimile copy accessed October 2013). The psychological effects were lasting, and changed the Chaldean mindset from one in which it was possible to consider oneself as still part of the Iraqi populace to an alien resident. The new reality appeared to be that, as a Christian, one could no longer act freely without dissimulation or leading an extremely sheltered life.

Fr Ragheed's murder struck at the heart of Chaldean life in Mosul, as he represented the archetype of the Christian in Iraq as committed and loyal to a unified Iraqi state with a plural social basis. He was well qualified as an engineer, and on the way to completing a doctorate in theology in Rome but instead requested to return to Iraq after the invasion to assist in the rebuilding of the country. A very influential priest within the diocese of Mosul, he eventually came to work as secretary to the then bishop, Polos Faraj Raho. Speaking in May 2005 at a Eucharistic Congress in Bari, Fr Ragheed said:

> The terrorists might think they can kill our bodies or our spirit by frightening us, but, on Sundays, churches are always full. They may try to take our life, but the Eucharist gives it back.
>
> (*The Catholic Herald* 2007a)

It appears that such faith, expressed by the parochial clergy, was one of the main means by which the Chaldean hierarchy could be certain of shoring up and keeping the laity strong in resolve to remain resident in Iraq.

Kidnapping as well as physical attacks are issues which, since 2003, have continually affected the community. In many instances, kidnap of Chaldeans was for purely monetary gain by criminals, as opposed to terrorists, with recognition of the relative wealth of Iraqi Christians. For those motivated by their religion, kidnap was a convenient means to weaken the confidence of the Chaldean community in general and the Church's leadership in particular. In the case of Fr Hani Abd al-Ahad, who was abducted and tortured for two weeks in July 2007 in Baghdad, the central focus appears to have been to attempt to forcibly convert him to Islam and to weaken the resolve of his congregation to remain in Iraq. Fr Hani, when interviewed in January 2008, related the particularly anti-Christian nature of the kidnappers:

> They constantly told me that we Christians were infidels. I got a real lesson on how far their hatred for Christians goes, how it motivates their action. They would not kill me because my Christian blood would have fouled the house preventing them from praying there anymore. [*sic*] When they talked to me they always referred to me as 'piece of filth'.
>
> (Rahema 2008)

The kidnappers' remarks are evidence that the Iraq conflict was influenced not just by those who desired an explicitly Muslim society, but one which excluded all non-Muslim communities, especially Christians.

Regional effects of the war and the Chaldean response

2006 and 2007 saw the start of an intensification of attacks against Christians and of large-scale national and international responses to the problems encountered, with increasing support from the Holy See and Catholic charities. Patriarch Emmanuel III Delly encouraged the Coalition forces to take on their moral responsibility of restoring Iraqi society to a more peaceful status insofar as the Coalition, having broken Iraqi society, were beholden to a very large extent to restore it (Yacoub 2010, 189).

The Holy See, to raise awareness of the Chaldeans' particular difficulties and to recognise the significant role which Christians had in Iraqi life, elevated Delly to the rank of Cardinal on 24 November 2007. Benedict XVI emphasised that:

> He was honouring not just the Patriarch of the Chaldean church, but all Iraqi Christians, and wished to show their plight to the world . . . 'They are experiencing in their own flesh the dramatic consequences of an enduring conflict and now live in a fragile and delicate political situation'.
>
> (*The Catholic Herald* 2007b)

The level of faith and commitment to their religion could not be disputed, and led to some rejuvenation in the community, with their resolve transformed into restoring or establishing essential social and educational services. The historically Syrian Catholic town of Qaraqosh (near Mosul) is a useful example which illustrates the situation as it developed from 2003. Following the invasion, it received 1,372 migrant families of which approximately seventy percent were Chaldean. As of October 2013, 485 Chaldean families were still living in the town when previously only a handful of Chaldeans were resident (Statistics provided by the Centre for Christian Affairs, Qaraqosh, October 2013).

Newly arrived migrants were provided with accommodation in a complex of flats. These offered basic but adequate facilities and had 320 families resident. A municipal building was also purchased, which served as a multi-use hall for weddings, baptismal celebrations and community meetings and so forth. As of October 2013, a dispensary was also being constructed along with ongoing renovation work on a medical and dental surgery. Another practical activity indicative of the difficulties for higher education was the opening of part of the University of Mosul in Qaraqosh for security reasons, with the safety of the Christian students who travelled to Mosul being difficult to ensure.

The administrative hub – the Centre for Christian Affairs – recorded the changing demographics. The Centre, whilst particularly well organised in Qaraqosh, was found throughout other towns and villages in some form, with several key personnel working there with a detailed understanding of the requirements of the local community. The staff often consisted of one of the senior community members from a leading family, the sacristan of the local church and secretarial staff (Conversations, Qaraqosh, October 2013 and general observations, Kurdistan region, October 2013). In speaking with the staff, it was clear that Qaraqosh was

126　*The Chaldean Church in the new Iraq*

a preferred place to stay, due to it being well served by the Syrian Catholic and Chaldean churches and maintaining a very strong sense of Christian communal security and identity.

With the emergence of Da'esh/ISIL from June 2014, Qaraqosh was particularly targeted because of its substantial Christian heritage, dating to at least the fifth century, and Christian populations. The entire community of c. 60,000 people departed in August 2014 as Da'esh occupied the town. It was liberated by Iraqi forces in October 2016, but during Da'esh's rule Christian property and churches were universally desecrated and vandalised. As the campaign to defeat the terrorists in the region remains ongoing, as of early 2017, it is not yet possible to confirm if the town will see the revivification of ecclesial and communal life.

The situation in Qaraqosh in late 2013 can be contrasted with that of the town of Telkef on the border between ICG and KRG control. The area is significant for its East Syriac heritage, and features several monasteries, convents and theological centres in the surrounding area. At times, the patriarchal headquarters was also situated in the town. Until the mid-twentieth century, it was home to a large Chaldean population of over 5,000 families.

The first large-scale migration from the town took place not as a result of persecution but due to the greater opportunities for economic development in Baghdad, Basra and the US, especially during the 1960s.[7] Life for the Telkefi Chaldeans was complicated by the Sunni Islamicisation of the area from the 1990s, and from 2003 the growing influence of a Wahabi mosque. The presence of the mosque was a factor leading to greater discontent in their relations with the Sunni Telkefis. For all intents and purposes, the Chaldeans became second class citizens unable to openly practice their religion beyond the confines of their own church.

Due to the growth in persecution from 2006–2008 nearby in Mosul, Chaldeans moved to Telkef. These migrants helped maintain the population, as they replaced those Telkefis who departed. However, as of October 2013, the number of families had shrunk to 365, consisting of only thirty percent of the town's total population. Ten families left during summer 2013, with a further twenty-five announcing their intention to depart by the end of that year. It was predicted that if conditions remained the same in ten years no Chaldeans would remain in the town. Nevertheless, religious practice remained strong, with attendance at daily morning and evening Masses at 350 and 200 persons, respectively, as of October 2013.

The response of the parish priest, Fr Hadil Louis, was to recognise the particular difficulties with which he was faced and to 'take things as they are, this is [his] reality' with the intention to stay regardless of the situation and to lead those parishioners who remained in the town. He was committed also to helping those who remained to develop a business project of some kind to ensure that income can be generated. The town was fortunate to be supported by Dominican nuns, who ran a school and orphanage which aided in the practical unification of the Chaldeans who were dispersed among the Muslim inhabitants (Conversation, Telkef, October 2013).

The church structures had been looked to as foci of social organisation in twentieth-century northern Iraq. During Baathist rule, people relied less on the

The Chaldean Church in the new Iraq 127

churches as the state was looked to for support in times of difficulty. However, as the state broke down and its ability to extend influence during the Kurdish uprisings weakened, reliance on the church increased. As civil relations broke down from 2003, ecclesial institutions again became vital to the alleviation of economic as well as social and religious difficulties.

Historical overview (2008–2013)

In response to the civil war, the Coalition forces pursued a surge of troops policy whereby areas of particular conflict – such as Baghdad and Anbar provinces – were flooded with sufficient soldiers to inhibit escalation of further incidents and to defeat elements committed to undermining the new order. The 'surge' began in January 2007, and was perceived as the only immediate effective means for inhibiting insurgent and terrorist activities. However, the surge's impact could not be retained following the Coalition forces' departure. This suggested that U.S.-directed plans for post-war Iraq had lost initiative, along with a clear method for the long-term resolution of Iraqi affairs. Nevertheless, the surge followed a nuanced approach to counter-insurgency operations, which focused on 'hearts and minds' and the restoration of basic regular services. Such activity went some way to restore stability, with fewer violent incidents by the end of 2007. Yet this derived from effectively holding large swathes of the population at gunpoint and providing Iraqis with few non-coercive incentives to avoid violence (Cockburn 2008).

The trend for American policies towards Iraq as of 2008, however, also reflected a pragmatic approach to rebuilding the structures of the state, such as permitting former IBP members employment in the government or armed forces. Moreover, with stabilisation of security, foreign investment in the oil economy was encouraged, leading to some level of optimism. A stumbling block was found in the level of corruption which affected the oil economy. In and of itself this was not an unusual issue: propensity for fiscal irregularities is far from unheard of in countries producing hard and soft commodities. However, in the Iraqi case, with little notion or desire to support a unifying sense of nationhood among political élites, corruption was effectively unrestricted and divested among far too wide a group to permit some form of control.

With the tendency towards sectarianism and the desire to please one's own constituents, ministerial portfolios became foci of consolidating power and accumulating wealth at the expense of those outside one's own faction. This was particularly problematic in the level of control which Prime Minister Nouri al-Maliki gained through his appointments as minister of interior, defence and national security from 2005. That a Shia political leader held these offices on top of the premiership led to Sunni disenfranchisement, with concerns raised over the security forces' impartiality in their duties and ability to meet the needs of the entirety of the population. These circumstances, combined with an increasingly strong Shia-Kurdish political alliance at national parliamentary level, were concerning to Sunni Arab Iraqis and perceived as a threat to their social status.

128 *The Chaldean Church in the new Iraq*

Chaldean responses to a new Iraqi society

As of 2008, the restoration of Chaldean life to a recognisable standard such as the pre-2003 *status quo* was impossible. Political, social and psychological changes were too substantial to overcome. The patriarchate might remain in Baghdad, but the focus of Chaldean life in Iraq switched to the Kurdish governed provinces of the north, the city of Kirkuk and the Nineveh plain region with responsibilities derogated to the local bishops to oversee this consolidation.

Chaldean political and social disenfranchisement was most clearly evidenced in the lack of concern expressed by non-Christians following the March 2008 martyrdom of Polos Faraj Raho, Archbishop of Mosul. The Archbishop was murdered after his refusal to any longer pay the *jizya* to a Sunni group for the prevention of violence against his congregation. His determination to end the protection racket cost him his life and foreshadowed the strict application of Sunni legal and cultural practices in Mosul.

The 1915–1918 massacres had seen the death of several senior clergy such as Archbishop Addai Scher, but Archbishop Raho's death took place in the context of the Iraqi, not Ottoman, environment. The Iraqi context appeared to have strongly integrated the Chaldeans as an essential part of society and, as a result, for persecution to take place in this context was all the more shocking. The respect which Chaldeans thought they held among other Iraqis no longer existed. I suggest, moreover, the muted response to the murder was a defining indication of the loss of society-wide interest to see Iraq remain a plural social mix.[8]

However, Iraq overall was in a state of greater security, or at least appeared to be so. The civil war's end in 2007 also saw a move away from ephemeral hopes for 'freedom' and 'democracy'. Instead, focus was placed on the basic requirements of medical care, reliable access to potable water and electricity. January and March 2009 saw the lowest number of civilian and US military casualties, respectively, since March 2003 (Iraq Coalition Casualty Count 2015; 'Documented Civilian Deaths from Violence' 2015). This reduction in violence was contemporaneous with al-Maliki's consolidation of position, with his political coalition gaining the largest single percentage of the vote in provincial elections and, in turn, 126 of 440 seats in the provincial councils. So high were the continued hopes for relative stability in Iraq that May saw the formal withdrawal of British forces. However, in the second half of 2009, direct threats to the state's integrity re-emerged in the form of large, well-planned bomb attacks in Baghdad with terrorist incidents across the country – a pattern of violence which continued into 2010.

Iraqi electoral process and government formation (2003–2013)

The transitional Iraqi government was created and held administrative power until the first general election in 2006. From then, and into 2013, political life focused on the leadership of the Arab Shia secretary-general of the Islamic Dawa Party, Nouri al-Maliki.

al-Maliki was born in the Iraqi Shia heartland near Karbala in 1950 but had been exiled from Iraq for the period 1979–2003 owing to involvement in seditious activities against the IBP. al-Maliki's position in the spotlight of post-invasion Iraqi politics derived from his links with the governments of the US and the Islamic Republic of Iran during his time abroad. He became Prime Minister after the 2006 parliamentary election, with his success related to political alliances with other Shia parties and the Kurds. However, in consolidating his power base, it appears he undermined mechanisms of constraint on the prime ministerial office and pursued a militant approach against opponents via the security services. It is possible these actions took place in the context of removing genuine threats to the Iraqi government, but his opponents regarded him as a self-aggrandising authoritarian determined to support only the Shia community. The perceived Sunni exclusion was vocally criticised and, as with the Chaldeans, became a source of disenfranchisement against the ideal of the new Iraq. However, the Sunni population's size and militia organisations permitted direct attempts to challenge Shia hegemony.

In comparison, the Chaldean hierarchy regularly met with Muslim political and religious élites for the purpose of representing the community's concerns. These engagements were multi-faceted but focused on gaining acknowledgement of their legitimate historical presence to Iraq. Clear supportive public statements for Chaldeans' continued presence and their importance to Iraq were made by Sunni and Shia, yet the collective response of the Muslim communities to supporting their presence was minimal (*Asianews.It* 2009). Nonetheless, the Chaldean leadership was obliged to make this effort, as to do nothing would signal their acceptance of their removal from Iraqi society and the end of the 'difference' which they introduced.

Christian political representation

From 2003, Chaldean political engagement was diversified more widely than ever before with the presence of Christian political parties spreading throughout Iraq.[9] Precedent for Christian participation in the national Iraqi electoral process derives from successes in the KRG with a seat in the Kurdish assembly won in 1992 by Sarkis Aghajan Mamendo as a representative of the Christian Union of Kurdistan. Latterly, Yonadem Yousif Kanna was granted the post of Minister of Public Works, Housing and Environment (Teule 2012, 181–2).

With the new republic's establishment from 2003, the most prominent national party to represent Christians – the ADM – moved its headquarters to Baghdad (Teule 2012, 182). The move acknowledged the ADM's need to be active in the centre of Iraqi national political life, were they to best represent their supporters. This mirrored the Chaldean patriarchate's move to Baghdad in 1950, yet the ADM's placement in the city did not carry with it the same significance. The ADM's lack of a support base in the city, to the same degree as the Chaldeans from 1950 to 2003, inhibited their ability to extend their influence given the majority of their supporters were in northern Iraq. I suggest the patriarch's status, as it had existed to 2003, carried with it some political influence and was

130   *The Chaldean Church in the new Iraq*

broadly recognised across Iraqi society even if his rôle and purpose were not widely understood.

Inserting an ostensibly Christian party which agitated for an autonomous region, was perceived to represent explicitly Western values and had an uncertain relationship with the KRG and ICG, did not help facilitate Christian interests in Baghdad. Nor could it be said that the ADM represented Christians in the same way as the patriarch, given that the normative focus of political parties is to gain political ends through political means, representing only parts of the entire Christian community – the attempt to act as a universal influence in Iraqi society was incomparable with that of the patriarch.

As modern Chaldean ecclesiology is tied to the notion of Iraq and its borders, the new structures of government and the electoral processes influenced Chaldean activity. The community preferred a political balance of parties, which ensured the least explicitly Islamic grouping in parliament and, at a local level, allowed Christian politicians to retain a voice on provincial councils to engage with Muslim leaders. This differed to varying levels across Iraq. Under the KRG, greater openness to Western political ideologies and notions of human rights and equality in law were in accord with Chaldean concerns, as they attempted to secure a place as a recognised minority integral to Kurdish society.

Chaldean identity in post-war Iraq

For many Chaldeans in Iraqi Kurdistan as of 2013, their primary and national identity was Iraqi, but they would next affirm their identity to be Chaldean Christian. This was qualified by the remark that the two – Chaldean and Iraqi – were closely linked and could in no way be separated (Conversations with Chaldean community members, Erbil, October 2013). It seems attachment to Iraq was slightly stronger, however, and this, I suggest, was likely caused by the influence of Arab nationalism pursued under the rule of the Baath. The Arab national and ethnic identity permitted Chaldeans to remain a part of an Iraqi plurality as all that made them distinctive was a religious identity. However, this varied among those who favoured Assyrianism as an ethnic and national identity.

There is a further division of identity for Chaldeans – who have grown up within the Kurdistan region or spent their formative years there: an assertion of Christian ethnicity. Such a statement indicates development apart from being Arab or Assyrian and, due to their circumstances, creates an identity which more accurately reflects the character of their communities and which is acceptable to Kurdish society. By coagulating their religious and ethnic sense of self, they can create a group identity of which the Kurds are already cognisant – popularly viewing the Christians as one homogeneous group which avoids the connotations of an Iraqi identity that could be perceived as antagonistic towards an autonomous Kurdish state.

Language could also be a defining factor influencing which identity was asserted. Those urban residents who had migrated to the KRG from central and southern Iraq were predominantly Arab speakers for whom to return to using Sureth as a vernacular was sometimes viewed as a retrogressive step towards lower socio-economic status. These differences were actualised in religious life by the celebration of the liturgy in either Sureth or Arabic or with a mix of both, with priests in a situation of having to meet the pastoral needs of the entire community. The use of two languages within the liturgy has made for some difficulty for priests and seminarians, not all of whom necessarily know Sureth well if, for example, they were raised outside of northern Iraq.

The creation and maintenance of a specific identity is useful to legitimise and define status in Iraq. Further, the manifestation of a communal presence on a national level (via the patriarchal office) inhibits the pursuit of mono-cultural narratives and exclusive claims of one faction to determine the future of Iraq. Moreover, the Christians, whether intentionally or not, inhibit a dichotomy of Sunni-Shia conflict as the political and social discourses of these groups are obliged to take their contributions into account.

The idea of remaining at the heart of Iraqi society is one factor in the Chaldean patriarch's continued determination to remain officially resident in Baghdad. The option for leaving the city has been open since 2003, but the patriarchate has been maintained because of the access to the political system and the capital status of Baghdad. To depart would pre-suppose admitting defeat in the face of those who use coercion to manipulate Iraqi society and undermine the Chaldean ability to act as a mediating influence on national events.

Situating the Chaldean narrative in Iraq and within the wider Catholic community (2010–2013)

The consolidation of the Chaldeans into northern Iraq saw a concomitant decline in their presence to Iraqi society more widely. Public Chaldean representation derived substantially from the efforts of leading clergy such as the Archbishop of Kirkuk, Louis Sako (2002–2013). At a time when Patriarch Delly's influence was waning through age and ill health, Sako was able to exert a strong influence within the Chaldean community.

Sako's efforts were focused in four areas (1) maintaining relations with Muslim leaders in Kirkuk and nationally regardless of the level or type of response, (2) maintaining the norms of communal life insofar as was possible, (3) emphasising the significance of continued links with the international Catholic community and (4) ensuring a wider perspective on events, namely situating the contemporary Chaldean narrative in the full sweep of East Syriac ecclesiastical history.

The last point significant for inhibiting the Chaldean decline as a reminder to the community that previous experiences of martyrdom and social change had been met stoically and in time were overcome. Retaining awareness that succeeding in the face of adversity was possible, was essential to prevent the development of a passive mentality of victimhood (cf. Col. 1:24; 2 Tim. 1:8). Such themes can be lost if we do not take into account the spiritual and theological aspects of Chaldean identity as a Christian church experiencing extended persecution.

The Holy See was far from ignorant of the realities of the suffering of Iraqi Christians, but did not take overt action in Chaldean affairs between 2003 and

132 *The Chaldean Church in the new Iraq*

2013.[10] The trend in Petrine activity was towards recognising the declining state of affairs for the Eastern Catholics in the Middle East, with such activity exemplified by the Synods for the Catholic bishops of the Middle East in 2010 and 2012.

The 2010 synod saw the publication of the apostolic exhortation *Ecclesia in Medio Oriente*, which covered quite general concerns such as ecumenism, Christian-Jewish and Christian-Muslim communal relations and liturgical theology (Audo SJ 2012, 3–7). However, the exhortation did not speak to the Iraqi context. During his visit to the Lebanon in 2012, Pope Benedict did not make particular efforts to highlight conflicts affecting Christians outside the Levant and Egypt even despite these being discussed during the 2010 Synod (Bouwen M. Afr. 2012, 20–1).

When we consider the spotlight of media attention focused on the pope's travels, I suggest there may have been frustration at Benedict's focus to Lebanese and Palestinian affairs instead of attention given to Syria and Iraq. This was indicative of a context in which the Holy See's concerns for Middle Eastern Christians are genuine but lack a wider plan for their implementation beyond charitable efforts which, whilst vital, do not resolve the long-term need to maintain a Christian vision within Middle Eastern societies. The work of the Apostolic Nuncio to the Republic of Iraq is, for example, split with his time spent as Nuncio to the Hashemite Kingdom of Jordan. This is unfortunate given the level of work required to sustain diplomatic engagements in both countries. It is also to the detriment of pursuing foreign relations in two states with variegated Catholic communities which, whilst similar in many respects, also face different socio-economic and political challenges. Looking retrospectively from 2017, it is remarkable to consider why the Iraqi situation was not better comprehended for its volatility and the need for greater and more direct engagement by the Holy See. This, however, fit with the pattern of activity which many states and NGOs observed with the start of widespread terrorist activity in Syria and concern shifting in focus from Iraq. As will be seen, 2010–2013 was largely a period of consolidation in northern Iraq, and migration abroad for the Chaldeans. The situation was not then perceived to be worse than the previous seven years and was a time of coming to terms with a new and relatively stable, if very difficult, *status quo*.[11]

Notes

1 Unless otherwise noted and referenced, analysis and information presented below comes from the aforementioned research sources.

2 The Peshmerga (literally translated as 'those willing to face death') emerged in the 1940s under the leadership of Kurdish nationalist Mustafa Barzani. For much of the rest of the twentieth century, they formed the vanguard of the Kurdish nationalist movement's armed forces in northern Iraq with branches from both the main Kurdish movements: the Kurdistan Democratic Party and the Patriotic Union of Kurdistan. Since 2003, the Peshmerga have been gradually integrated into the armed forces of the KRG, becoming the largest native military force in Iraq, with largely better morale and esprit d'corps, if not training and equipment, than the reformed Iraqi armed forces under Coalition direction (Lortz 2005, 66–72).

3 A situation which has altered since the emergence of Da'esh and which has resulted in the establishment of an array of Christian militias.

The Chaldean Church in the new Iraq 133

4 One older Chaldean man relating how, having visited eastern Asia Minor to see areas once populated by members of the East Syriac churches, he could weep for the pitiful status in Iraq to which the Christians of the region had been reduced (Conversation, Erbil, October 2013).
5 It was also suggested that UN refugee agencies had a deliberate policy of delaying asylum applications in Jordan once it was known that refugees were Christians. This is practically impossible to verify, but several separate incidences were reported at length during a research visit in May and June 2013 to Amman.
6 The words which appear to have led to a strong Muslim reaction being that of the Byzantine emperor Manuel Paleologus (1391–1425): 'Show me just what Mohammed brought that was new, and there you will find things only evil and inhuman, such as his command to spread by the sword the faith he preached' (Benedict XVI 2006).
7 There was a year on year decline between 1960 and 1971 with, in those respective years, 356 and 176 baptisms (Telkef parish baptismal register, facsimile copy accessed October 2013).
8 A similar context also affected the Yazidis. On 14 August 2007, 796 Yazidis were killed and 1,562 wounded in the north-western Iraqi town of Khataniya during successive suicide bombings. This was the second deadliest terrorist attack in modern history – after the 11 September 2001 attacks in the US – but little if any recognition of this was or has been made in or outside Iraq.
9 Generally, all of these parties support the Assyrianist ethnic identity and an autonomous Christian region. For an outline of the Iraqi electoral system (2003–2013) and political structures, see Appendix A.
10 Other than as noted earlier confirming Delly as a compromise candidate to the patriarchate.
11 Aside from serious incidents which greatly influenced the community in general such as the attack on Our Lady of Salvation, Syrian Catholic Cathedral, Baghdad in 2010.

Bibliography

Asianews.It. 2006. 'Another Chaldean Priest Abducted in Baghdad', December 5. www. asianews.it/index.php?l=en&art=7926.
———. 2009. 'In Kirkuk Christian and Muslim Leaders for Dialogue and Reconciliation', August 29. www.asianews.it/news-en/In-Kirkuk-Christian-and-Muslim-leaders-for-dia logue-and-reconciliation-16181.html.
Audo SJ, Antoine. 2012. 'The Current Situation of Christianity in the Middle East, Especially Syria, After the Synod of the Middle East's Final Declaration (September 2012) and the Papal Visit to Lebanon'. In *Living Stones Yearbook 2012*, edited by Mary Grey, Duncan Macpherson, Anthony O'Mahony, and Colin South, 1–17. London: Living Stones of the Holy Land Trust.
Benedict XVI. 2006. 'Faith, Reason and the University Memories and Reflections'. Aula Magna of the University of Regensburg. www.vatican.va/holy_father/benedict_xvi/speeches/2006/september/documents/hf_ben-xvi_spe_20060912_university-regens burg_en.html.
Bosworth, Clifford Edmund. 2012. 'The Concept of Dhimma in Early Islam'. In *Living Stones Yearbook 2012*, edited by Mary Grey, Duncan Macpherson, Anthony O'Mahony, and Colin South, 143–64. London: Living Stones of the Holy Land Trust.
Bouwen M. Afr., Frans. 2012. 'The Synod for the Middle East: First Results and Future Possibilities'. In *Living Stones Yearbook 2012*, edited by Mary Grey, Duncan Macpherson, Anthony O'Mahony, and Colin South, 18–37. London: Living Stones of the Holy Land Trust.

134 *The Chaldean Church in the new Iraq*

Bremer, L. Paul. 2003. 'Coalition Provisional Authority Order Number 2. Dissolution of Entities'. Coalition Provisional Authority. www.iraqcoalition.org/regulations/20030823_CPAORD_2_Dissolution_of_Entities_with_Annex_A.pdf.

Byman, Daniel. 2003. 'Constructing a Democratic Iraq: Challenges and Opportunities'. *International Security* 28 (1): 47–78.

The Catholic Herald. 2007a. 'True Martyrdom in Iraq', June 8.

———. 2007b. 'Pope Elevates Patriarch to Show "Closeness" to Iraq', November 30.

Cockburn, Patrick. 2008. 'Iraq: Violence Is Down – But Not Because of America's "Surge"'. *The Independent*, September 14. www.independent.co.uk/news/world/middle-east/iraq-violence-is-down-ndash-but-not-because-of-americas-surge-929896.html.

'Documented Civilian Deaths From Violence'. 2015. Iraq Body Count Database. www.iraqbodycount.org/database/.

Emmanuel III Delly. 2007. 'The Verbal Speech of His Beatitude Patriarch Emmanuel III Delly, Chaldean Patriarch of Babylon During the Ceremony of Naming St. Qardagh Patron of the Chaldean Church in Arbil in the North of Iraq'. Committee of Culture and Media at the Holy Family Chaldean Catholic Church in Windsor, Ontario. Dr Suha Rassam Archive.

Emmanuel III Delly, Andre Sana, Ramzi Garmou, Thomas Meram, Petros Hanna Harbuli, Michel Kassarji, Micha Pola Maqdassi, Ibrahim Ibrahim, Sarhad Jammo, Andraos Aboona, Stephane Babaca, Yacoub Scher, Antoine Audo SJ, Shlemon Warduni, Jacques Ishaq, Djibrail Kassab, Paulos Farraj Rahho, Abdul Ahad Sana. 2003. 'Declaration of the Chaldean Bishops on the Role of Chaldeans in the New Iraq'. Chaldean Catholic Patriarchate, Baghdad. www.atour.com/religion/docs/20030921a.html.

'Final Draft Iraqi Constitution'. 2005. Iraqi Constitution Drafting Committee. http://portal.unesco.org/ci/en/files/20704/11332732681iraqi_constitution_en.pdf/iraqi_constitution_en.pdf.

Glatz, Carol. 2004. 'At Least 15 Die in Bomb Attacks on Five Iraqi Catholic Churches'. *The Catholic Times*, August 8.

Gunn, Michael. 2009. 'Keys to the Iraqi Deadlock'. *The Tablet*, May 9.

Hanish, Shak. 2009. 'Christians, Yazidis, and Mandaeans in Iraq: A Survival Issue'. *Digest of Middle East Studies* 18 (1): 1–16. doi:10.1111/j.1949-3606.2009.tb00104.x.

Hefner, Robert W. 2014. 'Islam and Plurality, Old and New'. *Society* 51 (6): 636–44. doi:10.1007/s12115-014-9836-4.

Hirst, Michael. 2004a. 'Iraq's Catholics Shaken by Attacks on Churches'. *The Tablet*, August 7.

———. 2004b. 'The Terror Came as They Gathered for Mass'. *The Tablet*, August 7.

Iraq Coalition Casualty Count. 2015. 'Operation Iraqi Freedom'. Accessed April 11. http://icasualties.org/Iraq/index.aspx.

Lamani, Mokhtar. 2009. *Minorities in Iraq the Other Victims.* Waterloo, Ontario: The Centre for International Governance Innovation.

Lortz, Michael G. 2005. 'Willing to Face Death: A History of Kurdish Military Forces – the Peshmerga – From the Ottoman Empire to Present-Day Iraq'. M.A. thesis, Florida State University, Tallahassee, FL. http://diginole.lib.fsu.edu/etd/1038.

Mallat, Chibli. 1988. 'Religious Militancy in Contemporary Iraq: Muhammad Baqer As-Sadr and the Sunni-Shia Paradigm'. *Third World Quarterly* 10 (2): 699–729. doi:10.1080/01436598808420078.

Rahema, Layla Yousif. 2008. 'Iraqi Priest Abducted and Tortured in Iraq Because He Was Christian'. *Asianews.It*, January 8. http://asianews.it/index.php?1=en&art=11193&size=A.

Rassam, Suha. 2012. 'The Chaldean Catholic Church in Modern Iraq'. Unpublished article.

Seferta, Joseph. 2005. 'Caught in the Middle'. *The Tablet*, September 3.

Sleiman OCD, Jean. 2008. *How to Help Iraqi Christians in Turmoil?* London: Westminster Cathedral Hall.

Taneja, Preti. 2007. *Assimilation, Exodus, Eradication: Iraq's Minority Communities Since 2003*. London: Minority Rights Group International.

Teule, Herman. 2011. 'Christianity in Iraq: The Development of Secular Christian Political Thinking'. *One in Christ* 45 (2): 312–20.

———. 2012. 'Christians in Iraq: An Analysis of Some Recent Political Developments'. *Der Islam* 88 (1): 179–98. doi:10.1515/islam-201100010.

Tripp, Charles. 2007. *A History of Iraq*. Third Edition. Cambridge: Cambridge University Press.

Yacoub, Joseph. 2010. 'Christian Minorities in the Countries of the Middle East: A Glimpse to the Present Situation and Future Perspectives'. In *Syriac Churches Encountering Islam Past Experiences and Future Perspectives*, edited by Dietmar W. Winkler, 172–218. Pro Oriente Studies in the Syriac Tradition 1. Piscataway, NJ: Gorgias Press.

ZENIT News Agency. 2002. 'Cardinal Ratzinger Says Unilateral Attack on Iraq Not Justified', September 22. www.zenit.org/en/articles/cardinal-ratzinger-says-unilateral-attack-on-iraq-not-justified.

5 Chaldean ecclesiology and ecclesial organisation in Mesopotamia-Iraq

The main aim of research undertaken in northern Iraq in 2013 was to document the Chaldean Church's contemporary status. Assessment is provided later of the Iraqi dioceses, with a historical account of their origins to October 2013. This builds on the research completed by Khayyath (1896), Tfinkdji (1913), Tisserant (1931), Fiey (1959, 1965a, 1993) and Wilmshurst (2000). This account also builds on the scholarly heritage of other researchers who have considered the development of Eastern Catholic churches from the early modern period such as Whooley (2004), Flannery (2008) and O'Mahony (2008).

What is ecclesiology and how has it been altered?

Ecclesiology can be defined as the study of the relationships between the organisational, theological, liturgical and pastoral practices of a church and how these aspects of ecclesial life, when considered as a whole, express the church's identity to the world and its members. At the heart of a church's ecclesiology is its awareness of what it means to be a member of that community, individual and communal identities and the implications of this for interactions with other groups. Thus, ecclesiological study seeks to reveal the **essence of church life** and what it means on a practical and metaphysical basis to **live** as a member of a particular church. During research, effort was made to record notes on ecclesiastical organisation, social interaction, theological discussions, liturgical and pastoral practices. The necessity to observe and later recall for writing up the research was essential in trying to 'get under the skin' of the Chaldeans and ensure their community is accurately but not uncritically described.

Ecclesiology and its study have, since the Second Vatican Council, become a key focus of academic and general literature on and about Catholicism. This interest is derived from attempts to alter the nature of the Church's borders and organisation. The Catholic Church no longer holds to a model of a unified monarchical institution with distinct juridical boundaries, but a type of communion in which *the* Church of Christ subsists. Such changes are no more greatly impacted than upon the Eastern Catholic communities which, since 1965, have been held as churches self-governing and *sui juris*. Their position in the universal Catholic communion is now affirmed through asserting union with the pope as episcopal *primus inter pares* rather than consistent and direct submission to his jurisdiction and authority. For Eastern Catholics, this was a push towards virtual autonomy with one of the few limits on independent action being the requirement to defer to the Holy See in the final approval of bishops.

Chaldean ecclesiological change has not taken place in a vacuum and has been determined by the dictates of co-operating in the Catholic communion. It has also been influenced by a commitment to achieving full ecclesial union with the Church of the East which, however, may not necessarily be supported by the papacy or understood by non-East Syriac Christians. The Chaldeans have encountered tension between emphasising their membership of the Catholic communion whilst at the same time pursuing autonomy on a greater scale by emphasising their East Syriac ecclesial identity which draws on the heritage of the community as acting independently of the Holy See's oversight from the fifth to sixteenth centuries (cf. Sako 2014). There are few other examples of such a scenario in ecclesiological studies, with other Eastern Christian traditions having remained largely limited to those areas in which they originated and only since the nineteenth century spreading in a truly international manner or beyond the confines of the nations and territories which they purport to represent.

Nevertheless, the development of a closer ecclesiological bond between the East Syriac churches requires a greater theoretical basis than merely a perception that it could be a good or necessary thing given the difficult circumstances with which the churches are faced. Moreover, in outlining such ideals, the Chaldean hierarchy have lacked the opportunity to comprehensively engage with these ecclesiological speculations on a theoretical basis at least since 2003. Nevertheless, and despite ongoing conflict, theoretical underpinnings of the Chaldean-Church of the East relationship have continued within the successor events to the *Pro Oriente* fora: the Colloquium Syriacum conferences since 2009.

Such meetings are also vital in ensuring that the effects of migration upon ecclesiology are taken into account. Until the late twentieth century, demographic shifts were under considered.[1] As Chaldean ecclesiology was closely linked with their presence within the borders of the Iraqi state, the idea of developing an ecclesiology which reflected the international spread of the Chaldeans was challenging. For those outside of Iraq, questions remain open as how properly to engage with them and the best means to retain them as members of the Church. If arrangements are not provided for by the Chaldean hierarchy, many become *de facto* Latin Catholics.

A further influence on Chaldean ecclesiology has been the necessity to take part in some form of exchange with Muslims, whether in Iraq or the diaspora. This process increased in importance following the 2003 invasion. The church's ecclesiology and ecclesial organisation had to account for the behaviour of Sunni and Shia factions' as much as the Chaldeans' own aspirations for the Church's future.

Chaldean *status quo* in northern Iraq (2003–2013)

As of 2013, Chaldean communities in northern Iraq were found in the provinces of Erbil, Duhok and Sulaymaniya which are administered by the KRG. Those

138   *Ecclesiology and ecclesial organisation*

Chaldean towns and villages on the edge of Nineveh province near to Mosul were also considered a part of the northern Iraqi Chaldean presence such as Telkef and Karamles. The status of these rural villages was complicated by border disputes between the KRG and ICG from 2003 until June 2014. These disputes, in turn, led to questions over rightful governmental jurisdiction and Chaldean unease due to their residing in areas of particular political tension. Chaldean residents in urban areas were better able to protect themselves and receive support from the hierarchy following the 2003 invasion. Communities of tens of families are far easier to displace than cities in which thousands of Christians are resident and often part of a wider multi-religious *milieu*. It was only with the emergence of Da'esh from June 2014 that such large-scale displacement occurred.

Another point of context to the northern Iraqi region is its geography, which affects the relationship between the clergy and the local residents, and how the church is governed. For example: the mountainous terrain in which many Chaldean villages in the Diocese of Amadiya-Zakho are located can inhibit the presence of the bishop during inclement weather conditions in winter. By comparison, the Archbishop of Erbil can far more easily engage with his community which is largely centred in a flat and compact city suburb. The former scenario necessitates a more self-supporting mindset among the community and its parish priest and a different atmosphere in internal diocesan life.

Although I consider the history of dioceses in the light of events in the twenty-first century, it should be recalled these territories were once part of a network of ecclesiastical organisation in the Late Antique and Medieval periods which covered much of the geographical area of modern Iraq. Thus, in discussing the history of the dioceses, we should not see them as appearing *ex nihilo* or as foreign to their surroundings. Areas of Iraq now empty of Christians, particularly the central and southern provinces, were once contiguous with populous East Syriac dioceses and monastic foundations.

Due to travel and security constraints, research focused on Erbil, Zakho-Amadiya and Alqosh. Mosul diocese (as opposed to just Mosul city) retained a substantial Chaldean presence, whilst Sulaymaniya and Akra had only a few hundred Chaldean residents and in most other instances would exist as single parishes. I was fortunate to meet with several senior clerics and Christian community leaders in the dioceses of Alqosh, Erbil and Zakho-Amadiya who aided in understanding their status and plans for the future. The context at that time – prior to Da'esh's emergence – being that the development of the Chaldean Church and other churches could be maintained in the long term even despite any difficulties in the execution of their activities. Such qualitative data collected were vital to provide nuance to the quantitative information.

Diocesan study overview

This study builds a survey profile of the Chaldean Church in Iraq as of October 2013. This profile, with the time and resources available, cannot purport to be an authoritative study of East Syriac ecclesiastical organisation similar to that which Wilmshurst (2000) attempted in his work. However, the study provides indication of the effects of the 2003 war and subsequent conflicts upon Chaldean ecclesiology. It also relates how northern Iraq has become the heartland of the Chaldean Church in the Middle East. There is a general popular and academic awareness of the Chaldean numerical and material decline, but the quantitative data collected illustrates the rate of this decline.

The vast majority of the research material gathered for the diocesan study was collected prior to the emergence of Da'esh in June 2014 and the subsequent ethnic cleansing of the Christian populations of the Nineveh plain region. As the area of Da'esh's occupation covered the heartland of the East Syriac tradition, the removal of the Christian population potentially marks a qualitative shift in the East Syriac churches' ecclesiology and identity. However, as the war to defeat Da'esh is ongoing at the time of writing, an authoritative assessment of the effects on the Chaldeans cannot yet be completed. That being said, in the book's conclusion, I offer some analysis of the implications for the Chaldean Church and East Syriac communities in general.

The data collected 'on the ground' during direct research via interviews, conversations, general observations and access to archives are supplemented from information solicited among the wider Chaldean community via e-mail, telephone or in person. Data sent via e-mail from Baghdad, Basra and Mosul give a welcome breadth to a survey which seeks, where possible, to illustrate Chaldean history within the context of the history of the modern state of Iraq.

However, gaps exist in the study, and this is due to five factors. First, data that were lost or not collected in the first instance and never recorded. This was not an issue encountered on a regular basis with Chaldeans cognisant of the importance of maintaining records in an era of substantial change. Nevertheless, in practice, this varied due to type of inclination of individual priests and bishops to pay close attention to record keeping in their jurisdiction. For some parishes geographically distant from episcopal oversight, there was perhaps a disinclination to provide data. Data provided were also split in some instances by diocesan and parish level, with all baptisms for an entire diocese recorded but not specified as from which parish they originated. Whilst at times of direct difficulty in parish life, such as periods of persecution or population displacement, records were disrupted.

Second, data, which were not collected due to the inability to visit a location because of human/time constraints.[2] As research took place over a four-week period, gaining a deep insight to the lived reality of every extant village and town with a Chaldean population was impossible. (Cf Table 5.1) Other areas, such as Kirkuk, a key contemporary Chaldean centre, were not sufficiently secure to visit. From a practical perspective, the visa granted to British nationals on arrival in the Kurdistan region permitted travel only to those areas under Kurdish control and influence. Security measures at the numerous checkpoints in the Kurdish administered regions were also stringent during the visit in October 2013, owing to a terrorist bombing taking place in late September in Erbil. Queues at vehicle checkpoints, for example, could last several hours.

140 *Ecclesiology and ecclesial organisation*

Table 5.1 Principal villages/towns (by diocese) visited during research in October 2013 in which a Chaldean presence was found

Erbil	Mosul	Zakho-Amadiya	Alqosh	Kirkuk-Sulaymaniya
Ankawa-Erbil	Telkef	Aradin	Teleskef	Sulaymaniya
Shaqlawa	Karamles	Duhok	Alqosh	
Armota	Qaraqosh	Zakho		
Qusenjaq		Feshkhabur		
		Inishke		
		Deir Abon		
		Mangesh		

Third, unwillingness of persons to take part in or assist with the study. Being hosted during research by the Chaldean Archdiocese of Erbil, introduction to the Chaldean communities in northern Iraq was greatly facilitated along with the provision of a driver/fixer/translator for transport, meetings and interviews. Nevertheless, this did not mean all difficulties were removed or that research questions were freely answered. Some, for example, were at first somewhat suspicious of the research project and would only on the second or third meeting or after sustained correspondence be willing to participate. All these issues were quite naturally expected in newly formed inter-personal relations. The Iraqi context, the researcher's British nationality and the study's novelty all produced barriers to an openness to engage in some instances.

Fourth, questions to which no one knows the answer. During an era in which population displacement and the interruption of regular livelihoods have become norms, it was a challenge in some instances to find an interlocutor who was willing to answer questions in a direct manner. There were, for example, limited answers given in discussions to questions on patriarchs Joseph VII Ghanima and Paul II Cheikho. The level of questions might not be particularly taxing – queries about the political views or social origins of the patriarchs – but even here, there was limited awareness of or some dispute as to the answer. Combined with the lack of awareness was the propensity for, in many instances, offering opinions about a question and its subject, as opposed to answering it directly with a definitive factual answer. In due course, this led to caution with regards to drawing out answers from conversations and interviews. Composite answers outlined from a variety of sources were developed.

Fifth, reluctance to ask questions or collect data due to the situation at the time. Given the violence which had often expedited Chaldean migration to northern Iraq and the themes of conflict which had so strongly affected Iraqi society since the Iran-Iraq War, it was necessary to be sensitive to and aware of questions in general, but also when asking about events which had directly impacted those with whom I conversed. It might build a fuller historical record, but would it be wise to press a former resident of Mosul on their experience of persecution prior to being forced to leave their home? Some Chaldeans were very open and explicit about their experiences and opinions and were very eager for their story to be related. However, I made it clear that we could end our discussions at any time and without any obligation for the interviewee to explain why they wished to do so.[3]

Archdiocese of Erbil

The city of Erbil is one of the oldest sites of continuous human habitation in the world, dating to at least 6000 BC. It has long been a principal centre of East Syriac Christianity in Mesopotamia. Christians were present in the city by the early second century. According to one tradition Mari – a follower of Addai, one of the seventy disciples – miraculously healed the ruler of Erbil and delivered a child from demonic possession after which the local élites were converted to Christianity (Chaumont 1988, 17).

The expansion of the Christian community was expedited due to Erbil's position on regional and trans-regional trade routes and by the presence of a Jewish community from the first century, following the local rulers' conversion about the time of the birth of Christ (Sellwood 2011; Harrak 2002, 52). At the Synod of Isaac in 410, when the Christians of the Sasanian Empire sought to consolidate their ecclesiastical organisation, Erbil was included in the ecclesial province of Adiabene. The metropolitans of Adiabene came to reside in the city.[4]

By the seventh century, Erbil had grown to be such a focus of ecclesial activity that it was itself raised to metropolitanate status in the Church of the East. However, with Mosul's growth as an East Syriac centre, a joint see was created for the cities (Wilmshurst 2000, 166–7). Erbil became infamous in Christian memory for the 1310 massacre of the East Syriac community by the local Kurdish rulers and, following the invasion of Tamerlane later that century, Erbil and its surrounds were greatly reduced in non-Muslim activity (Fiey OP 1965a, I:88–91, 93).

Erbil's East Syriac ecclesiastical structure still technically existed into the seventeenth century, but from 1318 to 1607, only four bishops are known by name to have been associated with the city (Wilmshurst 2000, 167). As of 1610, legitimist patriarch Eliya VIII affirmed Erbil as within his jurisdictional purview. However, the city itself no longer retained any cachet of substantial ecclesial activity. It was only in the surrounding villages, such as Ankawa, that East Syriac communities were maintained, with these entering into union with the Holy See from 1779 (Fiey OP 1965a, I:95–6; Wilmshurst 2000, 166–8).

From the early nineteenth century, local East Syriac communities were under the close tutelage of Latin and Chaldean missionaries, and foundations were laid for the consolidation of the communities in the region. This consolidation was expedited by the inclusion of Erbil and surrounding villages in the jurisdiction of the Chaldean Archdiocese of Kirkuk (Wilmshurst 2000, 169).

Erbil was re-established as a diocese in 1968 under the leadership of Archbishop Stéphane Babaca, at which time the Chaldean population was c. 7,000 people. The diocese's re-creation should be seen in the context of the successful Baath party coup of that year and the continued and increasingly intense conflicts

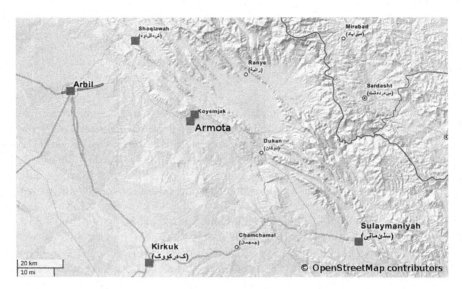

Map 5.1 Erbil and surrounding region

between the Kurds and the Iraqi military in northern Iraq: events which indicated the need to provide greater pastoral care to the Chaldeans. By the end of the twentieth century, the Archdiocesan population stood at over 11,000 people – approximately less than five percent of the global Chaldean population as of 2000. If the bounds of the Archdiocese were not perceived as the most desirable place of residence for Chaldeans, it nevertheless retained some attraction due to the tradition of Christian presence and, from 1991, its status as the *de facto* capital of the increasingly autonomous and prosperous Kurdish administered provinces.

From 2005, the archdiocese lacked direct episcopal oversight until the installation of Archbishop Bashar Warda CSsR in 2010, having experienced a period of *sede vacante* with the death of the last occupant, Yacoub Denha Scher, in 2005. In the intervening period, it was administered by Rabban al-Qas, who was simultaneously bishop of Amadiya. However, Warda's influence in the archdiocese was consolidated from 2007 following the relocation of the Chaldean seminary to Ankawa that year and his appointment as its rector. His subsequent appointment as Archbishop, as a relatively young candidate (age thirty-nine), recognised Iraqi Kurdistan's significance to the Chaldeans and the need for an energetic clerical presence in the Kurdish capital.

Chaldean ecclesiastical life in Ankawa

By 2013, the Chaldean presence had coagulated and performed distinctive functions in Erbil's suburb of Ankawa, which previously would have been the remit of

Ecclesiology and ecclesial organisation 143

activities in the Archdiocese of Baghdad. This has elevated Erbil Archdiocese to a greater significance within the overall Chaldean diocesan structure and linked the future of the Chaldean presence in Iraq with the KRG's success and stability. The Chaldean presence to Ankawa has become unique due to the functions performed there. I suggest that the concentration of religious formation and transfer of population means it has gained the status as *de facto* premier ecclesial body even over and above the patriarchate in the Chaldean community's recent development.

The main Chaldean parishes in Ankawa are Mar Eliya, Mar Gewargis and Mar Qardagh which centre on the cathedral parish of Mar Yusif. Mar Gewargis is the oldest extant church; some aspects of which perhaps date to the tenth century (Fiey OP 1965a, I:171–2).

From the archival material to which access was available it was apparent that Ankawa is regarded as one Chaldean ecclesiastical identity, with the different parishes in each area as adjuncts of the cathedral. Population and baptismal figures for Ankawa were not divided by parish for example.

To confer a greater sense of unity among the Chaldeans, especially the younger members, informal and formal education continued intensively in the provision of youth clubs at the Cathedral to ensure new migrants and the established population engaged with one another. These events were led by seminarians which allowed time for them to gain experience of leadership and engage with their future congregations. Similar activity was also conducted among the seminarians and clergy with a regular football match taking place each week – a means to maintain and build bonds given the severe strain on the community.

The seminary of St Peter, which is now located in the Archdiocese, sits at the heart of the future of the Chaldean Church. Only from 2008 has there been a Chaldean seminary outside of Iraq: Mar Abba in San Diego, California. As high standards of education are regarded as vital to the Chaldean future, and in order to maintain Chaldean traditions and heritage, it was considered imperative to secure the free running of St Peter's following the kidnapping of the rector and vice-rector in 2006 in Baghdad. Notwithstanding their eventual safe return, it was perceived as more suitable to continue the work in Ankawa.

The seminary's relocation has interfered with clerical formation and I suggest will likely lead to the creation of a new outlook among the clergy formed in an environment detached from the political and cultural surroundings and *milieu* of the Iraqi capital. This may limit priests' ability to engage with Iraq as comprehensively, as they have been pushed to the edges of society geographically and culturally. The Chaldeans are faced also with the loss of the minor seminary in Baghdad, which had allowed for the training of younger men in preparation for the priesthood. Nevertheless, the major seminary has become a well-established part of ecclesial life in Ankawa, having seen several ordinations and the continuation of an altered but sustained community and sense of discipleship among the priests. Vocations to the priesthood and religious life have suffered, however. The difficulties which the Chaldeans may have in the future if a larger number of candidates do not enter the seminary was emphasised in conversation with clergy. This was not solely derived from Iraqi cultural-social problems, but also experienced in the US.

144 *Ecclesiology and ecclesial organisation*

The church has been weakened through persecution, but also through the effects of modern irreligious attitudes in the West and the apparent attractions which the world offers and the religious life does not. These are difficulties which are shared by churches worldwide but are of special concern in the Chaldean circumstances.

The Archdiocese appeared to be well supplied in pastoral and spiritual support. The provision of training in counselling to deal with PTSD, for example, and the number of other Chaldeans resident in Ankawa, created an atmosphere in which experiences of displacement and persecution could be shared and dealt with on a communal level. The influx of migrants to the community and their becoming the largest proportion of residents has affected ecclesial identity in the Archdiocese. It is no longer an ecclesiastical body of northern Iraq, but encompasses a multi-regional identity of persons from across the country.

From Graph 5.1, we can note that aside from the First World War era and until 1980, Ankawa saw a trend for growth in real terms for the Chaldeans. The situation in Ankawa during 1914–1918 is suggestive of there being little hope for the restoration of the Chaldean presence to the surrounds of Erbil. From 1900 to 1913, the average annual number of baptisms and weddings stood at 76.43 and 20.21, respectively. During the War years, this dropped to 14.2 and 8.2 but soon was restored. The year 1921 saw a swift return to the pre-war numbers of baptisms, eighty-eight, but with a drop in the number of weddings of which, until 1927, there were only eleven in total. This generally low level of marriages was perhaps due to difficulties in coping with the new system of British rule or the propensity for Chaldean men to travel for work or to build up sufficient material support to provide for a family.

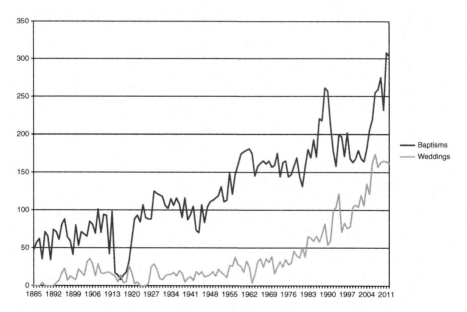

Graph 5.1 Number of Chaldean baptisms and weddings in Ankawa 1885–2012
Source: *Erbil Archdiocesan Records*

Ecclesiology and ecclesial organisation 145

From the 1920s, the Chaldean population grew strongly in Ankawa. Major declines in baptisms and weddings came in the mid-1960s and mid-1990s in reaction to political change and military activities in the surrounding region. Baptismal figures peaked for the twentieth century at 261 in 1989 having risen from the previous high of 193 in 1985. This increase was likely caused by an influx of Chaldeans from the northern Iraqi villages as Kurdish-Iraqi army confrontations took place and as the Iran-Iraq War continued to affect the economies and security of Basra, Kirkuk, Sulaymaniya and Baghdad. It would be useful to compare population statistics of the Archdiocese of Kirkuk and Diocese of Sulaymaniya for the years 1980–1988 to see the extent of change given the proximity of those cities to the border with Iran, but unfortunately such information was unavailable.

As we can note in Graph 5.2 and Tables 5.2, 5.3 and 5.4, the population increase from 2000–2002 was relatively marginal when compared with more recent years.

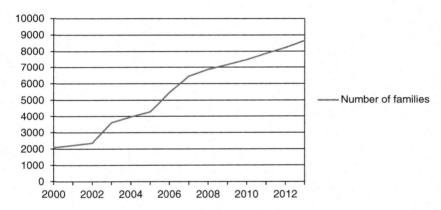

Graph 5.2 Ankawa Chaldean population growth 2000–2013
Source: *Erbil Archdiocesan Records*

Table 5.2 Chaldean population in the Archdiocese of Erbil 1969–2012

Year	Number of persons
1969	7,600
1980	9,650
1990	12,530
1999	12,000
2000	11,492
2001	11,330
2002	11,750
2003	12,000
2004	12,200
2009	20,000
2012	30,000

Source: *Annuario Pontificio (AP)*

146 *Ecclesiology and ecclesial organisation*

Table 5.3 Total number of Chaldean families
in Ankawa by year 2008–2013

Year	Families
2008	6,865
2009	7,160
2010	7,475
2011	7,865
2012	8,240
2013	8,670

Source: *Erbil Archdiocesan records*

Table 5.4 Chaldean population in the dioceses of
Kirkuk and Sulaymaniya 1949–2013

Year	Kirkuk	Sulaymaniya
1949	9,000	–
1966	–	360
1970	6,150	–
1980	4,256	861
1985	–	500
1990	5,470	–
1999	5,050	400
2000	5,115	403
2001	5,050	430
2002	5,095	450
2003	5,040	450
2004	5,700	200
2006	5,600	–
2007	7,000	–
2009	–	550
2010	–	550
2013	7,831	–

Source: *AP*

Nonetheless, those who did move to Erbil were likely motivated by the sanctions' detrimental impact on the Iraqi economy.

The Kurds experienced a period of infighting, with efforts to take control of Erbil by rival factions a focal point of struggle during the mid-1990s. Such instability appears not to have gravely interfered with the Chaldean population – which appears to have remained steady during the entire decade as indicated by the baptismal figures.

The population increases from 2003 to 2007, however, were significantly larger and pertained to the transfer of whole communities and not just a few families.

A terrorist incident in one area of Iraq, for example, could be a cause for the transfer of population to an area perceived to offer greater security. That the number of families increased by 3,000 (c. 13,500–15,000 people) in this period cannot be attributed to a minor migration of population, but entails an entire change in communal make-up in areas of central and southern Iraq. From 2007, the rate of population change slowed but the overall growth in the population increased steadily. This was likely related to the gradual decrease in the number of Chaldeans who transferred to the northern regions with a residual number remaining in Iraq proper.

I suggest that those who had family or business connections to Syria (until 2011), Jordan or Lebanon may have travelled there directly rather than via Erbil. Whilst the city was the 'go-to' point for Chaldeans in the Nineveh plains and Mosul, this did not necessarily relate to the travel plans of those in Basra or Baghdad. Further, I suggest that by 2008, of those resident in the Nineveh plain and Mosul, those who were going to leave had left and it was only in the context of specific events that population movement would again increase such as the 2010 attack on the Cathedral of Our Lady of Salvation in Baghdad or the murder of Archbishop Raho in Mosul in 2008. Indeed, if the present rate of change continued and Erbil remained an attractive destination, the population was only likely to increase with a subsequent decline in the populations resident in central and southern Iraq in the long term.

Parishes outside of Erbil

Outside of the Erbil urban area the Archdiocese consists of three other parishes: Shaqlawa is the largest by population (c. 240 families) and Armota and Qusenjaq are smaller (ninety-five and thirty-five families, respectively). Whilst relatively small, these towns are notable, along with Ankawa, for their association with Chaldean ecclesial identity from the late eighteenth century.

Shaqlawa is about thirty miles north-east of Erbil and had an East Syriac presence at least since the fourteenth century. It is possible that the establishment of these three settlements in the fourteenth century – Qusenjaq, Armota and Shaqlawa – marked a period of population displacement to more remote locations following the massacre of Christians in Erbil in 1310 (Wilmshurst 2000, 168).

Shaqlawa's ecclesial affiliation shifted to become Chaldean in 1779 through the efforts of Yohannan Hormizd and, as of 1913, the town had a Chaldean population of 1,200, with five priests serving the community (Wilmshurst 2000, 171, 176). As can be seen in Graph 5.3, the town saw spikes in baptismal numbers from the mid-1950s. Nevertheless, throughout the Kurdish rebellions and Iran-Iraq War there was relatively little change with only 1974, 1982 and 1983 seeing the number of annual baptisms in the town drop to below forty. This is even more remarkable when we consider the relative proximity of military operations. The town appears to have entered a period of decline from the mid-1990s, only to be gradually restored from 2003. However, since then, population growth appears to have taken place. This was supported by affirmation of local clergy that 'replacements' have filled the gaps in the local population caused by those who moved to

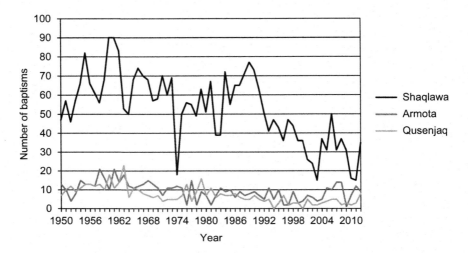

Graph 5.3 Number of baptisms in Armota, Shaqlawa and Qusenjaq 1950–2012
Source: *Erbil Archdiocesan Records*

Ankawa or beyond. Given the distance to Erbil from the towns, it is feasible for people to commute for work. Nevertheless, until 2014, Shaqlawa had a growing tourist industry and local employment was also available.

The Chaldean population of Armota has a history of complicated relations with the local Kurdish population and Iraqi state. The nineteenth century saw extended periods of anti-Christian persecution by Kurds which became so consistently strong that the local residents dug a series of tunnels to remain safely hidden in times of difficulty. Nonetheless, by the 1920s, the town, in terms of its Chaldean population, had consolidated in size and was considered relatively large with ninety families. Until the 1960s, Christians in Armota faced few difficulties of persecution or interference from the government.[5]

During Iraqi army attacks of the 1960s–1970s, sympathies were expressed for the Kurdish attempts at separatism which appeared to segue with Assyrian desires for political autonomy. This sympathy extended in some cases to active support of the Kurds, and during these decades, twenty-three Chaldeans were executed for their involvement in the rebellions. From the parish records, I can suggest a decline in the growth of the Chaldean population – as derived from the number of baptisms – which was (relatively) substantial from 1978 with a return to pre-1970s levels only coming by the mid-2000s. The town was perhaps affected by the successive wars and the difficulty of operating within the context of Peshmerga-Iraqi army operations. That the population growth did not again pick up after the imposition of the no-fly-zone on northern Iraq in the 1990s is surprising but indicative of Chaldeans' desire to reside in the cities of Duhok, Ankawa-Erbil and Sulaymaniya. During the 1970s–1980s, this also included moving to Baghdad or Kirkuk.

Ecclesiology and ecclesial organisation 149

A gradual return of the population took place after the 2003 invasion. However, this was inhibited by Armota seeing limited construction of accommodation. Instead, Qusenjaq has seen more development with apartment communes built for immigrants in 2004 and 2005. Nevertheless, there was some feeling of distance emotionally from Qusenjaq, with those migrants who arrived preferring to move to Armota. This is indicative of the ties of family and location being of greater importance than being provided with accommodation. As a result of forced displacement, Armota has returned to a level of population not seen since the 1920s. The population, by 2013, had become what might be considered a 'traditional' size of population, with ninety-five families resident.

Qusenjaq has, and had, a somewhat smaller Chaldean population than Armota, with sixty families resident by the 1920s, following their settlement in the nineteenth century.[6] The population appears to have remained at a similar size in the aftermath of the massacres, as 300 Chaldeans were resident in 1912 (Chevalier 1985, 44; Wilmshurst 2000, 174). A population shift occurred during the Kurdish rebellions, with half the population estimated to have moved to Mosul during the 1960s (Conversation with Shaqlawan parish priest, October 2013). Such a proportional change in population marked a turning point in the village's Chaldean presence, with only thirty-five families (c. 150 people) resident in 2013.

It is possible that population recovery to pre-1960s levels has still not taken place due to the population's unwillingness to take advantage of traditional local vocations in the agricultural economy. The lure of a better material standard of living in urban areas acted as a draw to the cities and saw the underdevelopment of the rural economy. This has become a lingering problem and inhibits a return to Qusenjaq due to the widespread loss of the skills necessary to be able to return to agrarian life.

It is quite common for northern Iraqi Christians to live and work in agricultural industries or related occupations in small towns and villages. However, this is changing as they engage in areas of economic expansion such as IT, alongside a consistent effort to push for Chaldeans to become members of the professions in accord with a view of what their social status *should* be like. As a result of the shift of the population to southern and central Iraqi cities during the twentieth century, a perception has developed that this predicates a career as a physician, engineer, dentist or academic.

This is a more general issue than that which affects just Qusenjaq. Though many achieved such positions in a time when Iraq was relatively flourishing (1940s–1970s), it has been difficult to maintain expectations of younger generations who desire to achieve the same. This has the knock-on effect of interrupting the Chaldean presence and leading to a decline in Chaldean economic activity in Iraq. Now, the choice for many is to leave the country or at least move to Iraqi Kurdistan. I suggest that those who have relocated from Baghdad can to an extent overwhelm the social make-up of areas of Christian residence in northern Iraq. There is no quantitative data to reflect this, but from conversations and observations in and around Ankawa, for example, it was apparent in the concentration of medical surgeries and the offices of other professions. If this is the case, it is

150 *Ecclesiology and ecclesial organisation*

significant in the long term, as it is unsustainable for all Chaldeans to attain to professional status and/or an urban-centred lifestyle. In reality, the majority of the long-standing Chaldean population in northern Iraq has always tended to come from lower social classes, residing in rural locations and living agrarian lifestyles. It would seem beholden on the Chaldean hierarchy to provide further encouragement for more realistic aspirations if they wish to ensure that Chaldean families can remain in Iraq and that they choose to do so because there are sufficient economic prospects for their residency.

Conclusion: Archdiocese of Erbil

The Archdiocese acts as a focal point of safety in the insulated world of Iraqi Kurdistan, set apart from the rest of Iraq. From June 2014, it was a particular point of refuge for those fleeing attacks by Da'esh. It is remarkable that one archdiocese has become the focus of sustaining the Chaldeans as an ecclesial institution in some form in Iraq, and it is relied upon to secure the safety of a large proportion of those Chaldeans still resident in the country. Being at the heart of Kurdish political and national life also provides a greater level of security than found in other cities, with it implicitly understood among Iraqi and international observers that Erbil's security is vital to the maintenance of stability in the region in the long term.

The protection which the Archdiocese offers is enmeshed with the political stability of the KRG. However, this can detract from the particular Iraqi Chaldean identity which developed in the twentieth century, around which the Chaldean Church focused its ecclesiology: as central geographically and culturally to the Iraqi state. Thus, with the distancing from Iraq proper – in the Kurdish administered provinces – a new identity has in some instances grown among the laity in terms of Assyrian nationalist political aspirations and a disassociation from Iraqi national life.

For Iraqi Chaldeans, the impermanence of the political situation as of 2017 and ethnic cleansing by Da'esh undermines their resilience to physically remain in the country or to continue to pursue a patriotic attachment to Iraq. The Church's northern focused ecclesiastical organisation reflects the new political order, as connections with the patriarchate in Baghdad and dioceses in central and southern Iraq are weakened. Erbil Archdiocese meets the demands of the local Chaldean population whether through the construction of a new hospital, new accommodation for families and the consolidation of the Chaldean seminary to the city. Such developments are emerging outside of the purview of the patriarchal office and the patriarch's direction. We see that the autonomy of the Kurds in the structures of the Iraqi state is mirrored to an extent in the autonomy of the Erbil Archdiocese in the structure of the Chaldean Church.

Archdiocese of Kirkuk-Sulaymaniya

To July 2013 Kirkuk and Sulaymaniya were diocesan centres in their own right. A joint archdiocese was established to consolidate available resources given the Chaldean population's numerically minor size in Sulaymaniya.

Ecclesiology and ecclesial organisation 151

Kirkuk's Christian community can be dated earliest to the second century, following the arrival of a bishop, Theocritos, who constructed a church. The contemporary name of the city was Bet Selok – a reference to its use as a fortress by the Seleucid Empire (Fiey OP 1968, III:20). As with Erbil, the city was likely ripe for Christian expansion, as it was on a key east-west trade route and formed part of the then Jewish-led Kingdom of Adiabene. The ecclesial foundation in the city eventually grew such that the city became the metropolitan see of the ecclesiastical province of Bet Garmai from the early fifth century (Morony 1989, 188).

Kirkuk lost its ecclesial prominence from the second half of the ninth century (Fiey OP 1968, III:42). From the third decade of the ninth century, the Church of the East had been in a period of flux which inhibited attempts to provide contiguous ecclesiastical administration. Timothy I had died in 823 after an over forty-year period as patriarch – the following forty years would see six patriarchs enthroned and two three-year periods of *sede vacante*, one of which (850–853) saw the successive deaths of three of the patriarchs-elect (Fiey OP 1968, III:38). Furthermore, the East Syriac community was also faced with the Abbasid caliph al-Mutawakkil (847–861) who pursued a much more restrictive set of policies towards the non-Muslim residents of Mesopotamia whilst bands of marauders had pillaged much of the Mosul and Bet Garmai regions in the 830s. The extent of the decline was such that Kirkuk lost its status as the metropolitan see and was merged with the adjacent dioceses of Khanijar and Shahrzur during the tenure of patriarch Sergius I (860–872). It appears that Kirkuk continued to be at least a titular diocese into the fourteenth century, with it named jointly with the see of Daquq (Fiey OP 1968, III:36–7ff., 47, 62). Kirkuk returned to prominence, in a Chaldean context, from the 1550s – with some of Yohannan Sulaqa's supporters originating from the city (Wilmshurst 2011, 163, 298).

It appears the first Chaldean ecclesiastical presence to Kirkuk was established in 1789 following Yohanan Hormizd's successful attempt to bring the majority of the town's East Syriac community into union with the Holy See (Fiey OP 1993, 64). However, a Chaldean see – if indeed one was actually established at this juncture – was not physically occupied by a bishop until 1826 (cf. Wilmshurst 2000, 175–6). The years between creation and episcopal appointment segued with the period of intense political and familial rivalry in the Chaldean community, which preceded the unification of Josephite and legitimist patriarchal lineages under Yohannan VIII Hormizd in 1830. By 1913, the archdiocesan population stood at 5,840 Chaldeans. These were served by nine parish churches, with the geographical remit of the archdiocese extending north-westwards to Ankawa and incorporating those towns which, from 1968, were part of Erbil Archdiocese, that is, Shaqlawa, Armota and so forth (Wilmshurst 2011, 401, 2000, 175–6).

In contrast, Sulaymaniya is a modern ecclesial *and* geographical creation. The city was established in 1784 by the Kurdish Baban dynasty, who dominated north-eastern Mesopotamia from the mid-seventeenth to mid-nineteenth centuries and enjoyed a great deal of autonomy from the Ottoman and Safavid empires (Behn 2011). This may have been a cause for the development of the more independent spirit among the Sulaymaniyan population set apart from Iraqi governing powers.

152 Ecclesiology and ecclesial organisation

Sulaymaniya is also one of the least Islamicised of all Kurdish cities. The proximity of the Shia influence from Persia possibly led to the dilution of a militant expression of Islam in the city with a notably plural culture. Until the 1950s, for example, a significant minority of Jews were resident (Ben-Yaacob 2007, 304; Ben-Yaacob et al. 2007, 16). With the Jewish departure and the creation of a social vacuum, the Chaldeans took their place as the largest non-Muslim population.

The primary Chaldean motivation for settling in Sulaymaniya was the expansion of the local agricultural industry and the petroleum industry in north-eastern and eastern Iraq from the 1940s to the 1970s. The establishment of the diocese in 1968 was a response to this migration.[7] However, the diocese only ever received one bishop until its merger with the Kirkuk Archdiocese in 2013. Abdul-Ahad Rabban OSH occupied the see for the years 1982–1998 and was preceded and succeeded by priests who acted as apostolic administrators.[8]

The more recent history of Sulaymaniya has been challenging for the population. In the aftermath of the 1990–1991 Gulf War, the city was besieged, politically independent, occupied and eventually granted autonomous rule by Hussein. This despite it being effectively separated from the rest of the Kurdish-controlled Iraqi territories through an Iraqi army blockade. All these events hampered the sustainability of the urban Chaldean population, who could find a far more amenable standard of living either in Kirkuk or Erbil. This was seen in the subsistence level of population which resided in the city. In 1990 it stood at seventy families, which dropped still further to thirty-five families by 2003. Nevertheless, as Sulaymaniya recovered in the aftermath of the 2003 invasion and returned to a relative level of economic stability, the Chaldean population stood at c. 1,200 persons (250 families) as of October 2013. However, the population was still not viewed as sufficiently large to maintain a separate diocese, and gave justification for merging it with the Archdiocese of Kirkuk in July of that year.

Unfortunately, baptismal, marriage and population figures were not made available during research in Sulaymaniya, and it was not made clear as to the wider context of the causes of this situation in the diocese. However, several key figures were given during discussions with clergy – as indicated earlier and later – which demonstrate the extended and intense displacement of population.

Ecclesial organisation in Sulaymaniya

The Chaldean presence to Sulaymaniya grew only gradually and, it appears, was not at the time of its foundation particularly attractive as a place of residence. The first church – Mart Mariam – was constructed in 1862 and, by 1913, 200 Chaldeans were resident (Wilmshurst 2000, 176). It is possible that a draw of the city had been the relative security which the Baban dynasty was able to provide, along with relative freedom from anti-Christian persecution. In contrast, in the latter half of the nineteenth century Christian residents of the Nineveh plain faced several instances of physical persecution. Mart Mariam continued to be used until 2003, when it was damaged by fire. It is not known if any wider context can be

Ecclesiology and ecclesial organisation   153

attached to this event, but it seems unlikely given the lack of antagonism towards Chaldeans from the Kurds in Sulaymaniya. Subsequently, a new church – Mar Yusif – was used exclusively, having been finished in 2001. The ties to Mart Mariam remain strong, however, with it being used as a shrine on a regular basis by the local residents.

The size of the new church – able to accommodate over 400 persons comfortably – would appear to predispose its use by a far greater population than that present in the city in the early 2000s. However, it has come into more active use with the consolidation of the population during the aftermath of the 2003 invasion. That being said, local clergy indicated concern for the future of the Chaldean presence in the city, specifically in regard to the effects of secularist Western-inspired culture upon the younger members of his congregation. Reducing religious identity and expanding a more laicised outlook permitted greater integration into Iraqi Kurdistan and wider Middle Eastern society.

It is notable that Chaldean identity is often more solidified within areas which face greater threats of physical persecution, whereas Christians resident within a weaker Islamic _milieu_ can tend towards a more ambivalent attitude to the practice of their religion. Notably, Sulaymaniya was the only location in which such an attitude was evident during research. This indifferentist attitude is difficult to counter in Sulaymaniya given only one priest is present to minister to the entire Chaldean congregation. Even with the support of nuns resident in the city, who run an orphanage and encourage community involvement, it is a challenging apostolate.

The unity of the Chaldean community in Sulaymaniya cannot be taken for granted, which hinders further the stability which is hoped for. Over half the population are migrants who have either returned to the city of their family origins or with the hope of taking advantage of the city's political stability. This has led to some friction with long-standing city residents and has only been resolved gradually due to ten 'mixed' marriages. This emphasises that despite religious similarities binding Chaldeans together, human, political, social and economic differences remain regardless of circumstances.

We would be wrong to regard Sulayamaniya's Chaldeans as a forgotten group, but they appear to have struggled for recognition of the particular issues with which they are faced: relative geographical isolation to Kirkuk in the south and Erbil to the west; the growth of religious indifference among the community; and the lack of formalised episcopal oversight. These are issues which are difficult to respond to in a creative manner, as the Sulaymaniyan Chaldeans and their culture have been dispersed throughout Iraq and the diaspora abroad. Indeed, of those who were previously residents in key centres of Chaldean cultural and social life such as Baghdad or Mosul and who travelled to the city, greater onward travel has been registered, with fifty percent estimated to have left Sulaymaniya following their arrival.[9] From 2003, the dissipation of the community slowed to some extent and was evidenced in the few families who left the city to go abroad during 2011–2013 with only seven or eight on average having departed (Conversation, Chaldean community member, Sulaymaniya, October 2013).

Archdiocese of Kirkuk

The twentieth-century history of the Chaldean Archdiocese of Kirkuk is intrinsically tied to the development of the city as one of the major oil producing hubs of Iraq. The city is also a key focus of Kurdish political aspirations with hopes for its integration into a future Kurdish state.

Chaldean aggregation to the city came as part of the communal migration to Iraqi cities from the 1930s and the desire to utilise those vocational skills which they held in proportionately greater quantities than many Arab Muslims and Kurds. Nevertheless, we should not overestimate the Chaldean influence to Kirkuk but recognise it for what it was: a key part of a multi-religious population in which all were seeking to assert the best possible position for their community. Such a process of integration was complicated by the Arabisation policies which were pursued by successive Iraqi governments which undermined Kurdish political and economic claims to the city.

The Chaldean position in this context was to follow the path of least resistance in terms of ethnic identity in order to ensure they could maintain their religious and social freedom in the city. This was an issue which came to be acute under Saddam Hussein because Arab national identity for all Iraqis was the basis of the national political paradigm.[10] During the Hussein era, Kirkuki Chaldeans were discouraged from pursuing an Assyrian identity or any other apart from Arab. The level of adherence to this identity likely varied on a person-by-person basis, but from 2003, Arab ethnic identity began to be discarded in favour of Chaldo-Assyrian. It is not clear how widely supported this was in Kirkuk, but I suggest it proved popular because of the re-emergence of attachment to particular ethno-national identities which had been forbidden for such a length of time during IBP rule, that is, Turkmen, Kurdish and so forth (Discussions with Chaldean Kirkuki migrants to Ankawa, October 2013).

Kirkuki Chaldean population

Fiey noted the numerical decline of Kirkuki Chaldeans to the early twentieth century and how the population was holding on to the heritage of the East Syriac tradition:

> Un maximum de mille Chaldéens survivra dans tout le B. Garmaï en 1914, petit reste de la grande cinquième province de l'Église syrienne orientale, mais aussi levain pour un avenir meilleur dont nous voyons déjà les commencements.
>
> (Fiey OP 1968, III:145)

The earliest estimate for the twentieth century is for 1913, with 800 Chaldeans in Kirkuk. At this time, the city had the third largest Chaldean population in the Archdiocese[11] behind Ankawa (3,000) and Shaqlawa (1,200), with a total population of c. 5,800 people (Wilmshurst 2000, 176). The population presumably grew in Kirkuk following migration after the massacres of 1915–1918. The next

Ecclesiology and ecclesial organisation   155

estimate for the entire Archdiocese was given as 7,620 in 1937. Growth in population in the 1920s and 1930s was organic – through births – but probably was also derived from the assimilation of members of the Church of the East to the Chaldean community (Wilmshurst 2011, 445). Such was the perceived need to aid in consolidating the city's Chaldean population over the next decade that a substantial new church was built in 1949 – St Joseph's – which remained in use until the 2003 invasion, and was subsequently refurbished and reopened in 2014 (cf. Fiey OP 1968, III:49).

According to the Iraqi national census of 1957, 1,509 persons of Syriac ethnicity were present in the city (Anderson and Stansfield 2009, 43). This should perhaps not be viewed as indicative of the Chaldean population, who by that time were asserting an Arabic linguistic and ethnic identity. Furthermore, the number seems somewhat low given the development of the petroleum industry in the area and that the *Annuario Pontificio* gives the total Chaldean population of the Archdiocese as 9,000 in 1949. If the proportion of the diocesan population resident in Kirkuk remained similar to that from earlier eras, it seems likely the Chaldean population almost certainly rose in real terms. Nonetheless, we must note also the countrywide migration of Chaldeans to Baghdad, which had increased in the intervening period, may have caused a drop in population in Kirkuk.

Anecdotal estimates gained during research suggest an increase in population to c. 10,000 Christians by the time of Hussein's rise to power in 1979. This may have declined during the Iran-Iraq War. Nevertheless, and again based on anecdotal evidence, the population appears to have remained the same after the end of the war and until 2003. As of 2013, the Christian population was broken down as follows:

- 1,500 Chaldean families
- 300 Church of the East families
- 100 Armenian families.[12]

A total Christian population of c. 7,500 people out of a total population of c. 750,000.

The level of violence which Chaldeans have faced in Kirkuk is substantially lower than in Mosul or Baghdad but no less consistent in its long-term effects upon the population. It may be that the level of sectarian division is not as strong in Kirkuk because of its historical plurality. However, since 2003, the spread of more intense inter-communal relations has become a concern due to the competing claims of Turkomen, Kurds and Arabs for control of the city.

During the period 2003–2013, the Cathedral of the Sacred Heart was the focus of Chaldean life in the city with five other active parishes ('Msgr Yousif Mirkis, OP Speaks on the Chaldean Church' 2014). The Cathedral had faced a bomb attack in September 2012, but this did not cause major damage. It would seem the bombing was an attempt to reawaken an atmosphere of fear in the city. Despite a number of attacks from 2003, the Chaldean presence was consolidated and a new church, dedicated to St Paul, opened in 2011 to meet the needs of Chaldean migrants to the city (*Al Arabiya News* 2011).

156 *Ecclesiology and ecclesial organisation*

The Chaldean presence was strengthened through Louis Sako's appointment as Archbishop of Kirkuk from 2002–2013.[13] During his Kirkuki apostolate, Sako ensured that the Chaldean voice was represented in local society, and attempted to provide an ideal *type* of Chaldean presence in a post-war Iraqi environment. Sako's efforts were aided due to the greater societal plurality of Kirkuk, his openness to engagement with Muslims and of the need to link the current situation of the Chaldeans to the historic traditions of the East Syriac community.

Sako was cognisant both of the subtle differences which the Chaldeans present to Iraq society and why these differences are of importance. He noted in a 2012 interview that the Chaldean Church 'which, having never been a State Church, carries a rich memory of interaction with Islam and openness towards the East, from Iran to China' (*Agenzia Fides* 2012). This point highlights the integral nature of the Chaldeans to Iraq and that the Chaldeans in principle retain no ideological pretensions of prior associations with particular political systems. Furthermore, it emphasises that the East Syriac tradition should be a normative partner with Muslim residents of Iraq, having incarnated its presence in Mesopotamia in the context of predominantly Islamic societies since the seventh century. Nevertheless, such annunciation of the East Syriac societal position can be lost in the context of civil conflict.

Sako's efforts to sustain engagements with Muslim communities were a practical concession driven by the need to act as a persistent reminder of the Chaldean presence. If Chaldeans do not publicly formulate their status in Iraq, there is no other group which will be inclined to annunciate their integral importance to the country. Sako's most practical encouragement to Muslim-Christian encounter came with an invitation to Fr Paolo Dall'Oglio SJ to establish a religious community in Sulaymaniya. Dall'Oglio's community was to be modelled on that of Deir Mar Musa, near Nabk in Syria where, for many years, he had encouraged the extension of Christian pastoral and spiritual hospitality to Syrian Muslims. The extension of such a religious experiment to Iraq was something which perhaps other Chaldean bishops would have struggled to comprehend or cope with in their jurisdictions – especially following Dall'Oglio's expulsion from Syria by the government owing to his perceived proximity to members of the Syrian opposition. Nevertheless, it appears Sako's invitation was prompted by the necessity of dynamic engagement with Islam, the desire to pursue alternative practical means for resolving societal conflicts and efforts to put into practice Christian precepts of reconciliation even in extremely difficult situations.

Christian culture also continued to be exposed to the wider community of Kirkuk with, for example, the 1600th anniversary celebrations in 2009 of the East Syriac martyrs of Bet Selok in 409. That Sako chose to celebrate such an occasion, which took place during Sasanian Zoroastrian rule, was an astute choice given the lack of connotations of Islamic persecution and which had led to other incidences of martyrdom in northern Mesopotamia (*Asianews.It* 2009). Yet, at the same time, it brought with it a sense of the permanence of the Chaldean community to the city and a reminder to the Muslim communities of the precedent for East Syriac Christian presence and their capabilities to survive in spite of a sustained atmosphere of cultural tension, and legal and physical persecution.

Ecclesiology and ecclesial organisation 157

Conclusion: Archdiocese of Kirkuk-Sulaymaniya

Control of Kirkuk is of significance to the future status of Iraq as a cohesive state. The city has a strong place in Kurdish aspirations for an independent Kurdistan, with the city regarded as a cultural hub alongside its importance as a centre in oil production. With the emergence of Da'esh, Kirkuk's status and character as part of the Arab Iraqi sphere of influence has declined and from June 2014 has been assumed into the jurisdiction of the KRG. It is unclear as to what long-term benefits this may bring to the Christian population, as the overarching political and military situation remains in flux until Da'esh is comprehensively defeated. It is possible that the extension of Kurdish governance may be to the benefit of the Chaldeans if a similar broadly open attitude to the Christian communities is maintained, like that found in Erbil.

Sulaymaniya's place within the Chaldean ecclesiastical organisation appears to be in substantial decline, and it is possible that only a relatively small, or even token, population will remain in the city. This is, perhaps, partly tied to Sulaymaniya never achieving status as a principal centre of Chaldean life and not having a sufficient 'pull factor' for the community by way of comparison with Baghdad or Kirkuk in the twentieth century or Erbil since 2003. It is to be hoped that the consolidation of the two sees – Kirkuk and Sulaymaniya – will also go some way to encourage a consolidation of local Chaldean community life and that the new bishop, Yousif Thoma Mirkis OP (2013–present), will have the opportunity to revivify the East Syriac presence in north-east Iraq.

Dioceses of Zakho-Amadiya and Akra

The northern and north-western regions of Mesopotamia in which the Zakho-Amadiya and Akra dioceses are located became a focus of very active Chaldean life from the late eighteenth century, and were battlegrounds for control by the competing East Syriac patriarchates. These regions had long been associated with the East Syriac tradition. Akra, for example, had previously been part of the Diocese of Marga, with a strong monastic presence. The ninth century Bishop of Marga, Thomas, provides a history in his work *The Book of Governors* (Budge 1893). Nonetheless, it is only with the establishment of the Sulaqite line of patriarchs and competing claims to jurisdiction of East Syriac dioceses that we once again become definitively aware of the Christian presence across these northern regions of Mesopotamia (Wilmshurst 2000, 125, 128; cf. Budge 1893, II:296–7).

Diocese of Akra

The Chaldean see of Akra originated in the nineteenth century as a result of attempts by Yohannan VIII Hormizd to consolidate his position as patriarch as well as confirm his family's prominence in the church hierarchy. Hormizd appointed one of his nephews as the first Chaldean bishop in 1834 as part of an attempt to assert his authority over a region in which the Christian residents largely supported those attached to the Sulaqite patriarchal line (Wilmshurst 2000, 153). The first bishop

158 *Ecclesiology and ecclesial organisation*

appointed with the acquiescence of the Holy See and apart from accusations of nepotism was Eliya Sefaro (1852–1854). Subsequently, the diocese became infamous during the leadership of Yohannan Elias Mellus (1864–1889) (Medlycott 1912). He led the eponymous schism of the 1870s, which had been caused by the development of an independent line of clergy to serve the Malabarese East Syriacs.[14] Despite these circumstances, the diocese had stabilised by the turn of the century and was consolidated under the leadership of Yacoub Yohannan Sahhar (1893–1909) (Wilmshurst 2000, 153).

The town of Akra, like Zakho and Amadiya, served as a garrison for the Ottomans and had a numerically minor Christian population of Chaldeans and Syrian Orthodox, totalling 250 of the 4,700 residents in the late nineteenth century. In 1913, the entire Chaldean diocesan population was estimated at 2,390 people across nineteen villages served by sixteen priests and ten churches (Pétridès 1907, 376; Wilmshurst 2011, 351). For a time, Akra was united with the diocese of Amadiya (1895–1909), but they were later separated. From 1909 to1947, Akra was administered by a patriarchal vicar. Akra diocese presumably did not retain a Chaldean population of sufficient size to necessitate episcopal oversight. More contemporary data on population size emerge from 1958 in the *Annuario Pontifico* (as indicated in Table 5.5) which has figures available from 1958 to 2012.[15]

From 1947, the diocese had stable leadership until 1998 with one of its bishops, the future patriarch Paul II Cheikho, leading the diocese for ten years (1947–1957).[16] Cheikho's previous experience of the diocese was perhaps the cause for his ordering the expansion of the cathedral in Akra in the 1960s, and this despite the relatively small number of Chaldeans then resident in the town: only around 250 in 1961 (Fiey OP 1965a, I:265–6). In 1958, at the end of Cheikho's episcopal tenure, the entire diocesan population stood at 1,636. But by 1970, this had dropped to 550. Why the diocese was not formally amalgamated with another

Table 5.5 Chaldean population in the Diocese of Akra 1958–2012

Year	Number of Catholics
1958	1,636
1970	550
1980	150
1990	245
1999	176
2000	192
2001	263
2002	271
2003	300
2004	310
2006	508
2009	1,051
2012	1,190

Source: *AP*

bordering is unclear: I suggest either the continued political instability in the region prohibited considerations of reorganising ecclesial structures or that it was desirable to retain an appearance of ecclesial strength in the region. The lack of data for the period 1913–1958 inhibits our critiquing the context of Cheikho's pastoral oversight, but given the cathedral's reconstruction, we may suppose he had consolidated the Chaldean community with, for the first time in forty years, permanent episcopal direction. The population decline after Cheikho might be accounted for by the contemporary Iraqi army pacification of Kurdish rebels and the general trend for Chaldean urbanisation in Iraq. Yet, the *Annuario Pontifico* figures for total population of Akra diocese (Catholic and non-Catholic) show a nearly trebling of persons in the region (1958: 32,723; 1970: 85,000). The Chaldean departure for urban areas was perhaps then expedited by the effects of losing their stake in the local social order.

The Chaldean Akran population continued to decline from 1970 to 1990. However, it increased during the Gulf War and then again from 2000 onward. As of 2012, it reached 1,190 people. In the ecclesiastical organisation as a whole, and on a purely numerical basis, Akra has not, in the modern era, held importance. However, its continued operation suggests it holds some ecclesiological significance to and among the Chaldean community.

As of 2013, the remaining centres of population were Akra itself (fifty families), with the rest of the population split between two other villages (c. 120 families) (Clergy of Erbil Archdiocese, October 2013). One of these, Hezarjot is a relatively new settlement established following the displacement of the Church of the East population during the First World War (Wilmshurst 2011, 437). As the total population of the diocese thus amounts to fewer than c. 1,000 persons, it is a diocese in name only in a modern ecclesial context. From the point of view of ecclesial organisation, it would seem appropriate for the Akra diocese to be formally subsumed into Erbil, whose archbishop has current responsibility for the community. Nonetheless, we should recall that retaining a diocese, even for a numerically small community, matches the style of governance historically used in the East Syriac community. A lack of communication, infrastructure and a more insular focus of rural life requires sufficient local clergy to deal with matters arising, with the hierarchy doubling as the civil power on a *de facto* basis in such relatively remote areas.

Zakho-Amadiya ecclesial history

To the late thirteenth century, the geographical region now largely covered by the Chaldean diocese of Zakho-Amadiya and the East Syriac communities resident there had been within the jurisdiction of the Diocese of Bet Nuhadra or, the joint Diocese of Bet Dasen and Ture.[17] Both dioceses had been named suffragan sees of the Metropolitan of Adiabene at the Synod of Isaac in 410, from which time they were occupied to at least the mid-thirteenth century. The last known Bishop of Bet Dasen, Mattai, was present at the consecration of patriarch Yahballah III in 1281 (Wilmshurst 2000, 125; cf. Budge 1893, II:296–7).

160 *Ecclesiology and ecclesial organisation*

During the fourteenth and fifteenth centuries, there were no known bishops for either Bet Dasen or Bet Nuhadra. With the revivification of East Syriac life, especially from the sixteenth century, we find the Amadiyan communities largely loyal to the legitimist patriarchal line. Owing to the concentration of East Syriacs and the ecclesial dependency of Amadiya on Alqosh, the legitimist patriarchal line competed with the Sulaqites for control of the region. In 1784, legitimist patriarch Elias XIII Ishoyab consecrated one his nephews, Hnanisho, as bishop of Amadiya (Wilmshurst 2000, 128).

There had been some earlier success for the Chaldeans, with East Syriac residents of Duhok persuaded of the benefits of union with the Holy See from the seventeenth century. However, it was only from the 1780s that concerted efforts were made to gain East Syriac loyalty more widely in the Amadiyan region. A Chaldean ecclesial structure was established in 1785, and the town of Amadiya and the village of Mangesh emerged as centres of Chaldean activity (Wilmshurst 2000, 125, 134). The strong monastic heritage in the area and its relative proximity to Mosul, where the Dominicans were based, made it an attractive focus for expanding Latin missionary work (cf. Wilmshurst 2000, 125). There was perhaps a desire for the reinvigoration of East Syriac monasticism – which appeared a very real possibility in light of Gabriel Dembo's project at Rabban Hormizd from 1808. To the fourteenth century, at least five major monastic centres were active in the region. However, by the early seventeenth century only one was still in operation (Wilmshurst 2000, 132).

The emerging leadership of Yohannan Hormizd as a potential patriarchal successor for the Chaldeans and competition with Hnanisho for control of the Amadiya region formed a major aspect of local ecclesiastical life until Hnanisho's death in 1813.[18] The competition between East Syriac leaders Elias XIII, Hnanisho, Yohannan Hormizd, Augustine Hindi – titularly Patriarch Joseph V – and Gabriel Dembo from the 1780s to 1820s was seemingly a severe barrier to gaining the sympathy of the Holy See and the Latin missionaries.

With Amadiyan residents caught in the middle of these events, it seems likely there existed a strong awareness of the instability pertaining to the leadership of the community, as well as a fluctuating sense of Chaldean identity and sense of the purpose of the patriarchal office. With no one clear patriarchal leader of the East Syriac communities from the death of Elias XIII in 1804 to Yohannan's patriarchal appointment in 1830, to what church would East Syriacs be converting or to whom would they be switching their ecclesial affiliation? That the ecclesial functioning of the communities continued was testament to the subsidiarity of action among the East Syriacs in the operation of their affairs and, I suggest, a lack of concern as to jurisdictional boundaries as borders between Chaldean, legitimist or Sulaqite communities. An overarching sense of East Syriac identity broadly prevailed among community members at the time, with loyalty to one faction not necessarily implying an exclusive relationship with it and its clergy.

The competition between the Church of the East and the Chaldeans for control of the East Syriac populations in the area only saw an end in the aftermath of the massacres of the First World War. Displaced members of the Church of the East

Ecclesiology and ecclesial organisation   161

from Asia Minor migrated to northern Mesopotamia and assumed membership of the Chaldean community due to a shortage of their own church infrastructure and clergy. An attraction of Amadiya to new residents was its historical reputation as a centre of Christian life and geographic location as a key point of economic exchange between the Kurds of the highland regions and the merchants of Mesopotamia-Iraq proper (Streck 1913, 324).

A Chaldean episcopal presence to the Zakho region was established in the 1830s and consolidated in 1851 through the aggregation of villages which had been within the remit of the neighbouring dioceses of Gazarta and Amadiya. The creation of the Zakho diocese likely came with the intention to limit the remaining influence of legitimist clergy opposed to the Chaldean project. The appointment of new bishops to a region or the formation of new dioceses was a traditional means to influence the local communities. In the period 1569–1596, for example, the legitimist line had at least two bishops appointed for Gazarta, as the Sulaqite patriarchs had established their own see of Gazarta in 1554 (Wilmshurst 2000, 102–3).

Gazarta had been an active see from at least the fourth century, only undergoing an apparently inactive era from the mid-fourteenth to the late fifteenth century from which time it was extant to 1918 (Wilmshurst 2000, 101). The credibility of clerical claims to hold influence with the civil power was to an extent reliant on a willingness to support structures which at least gave an appearance of communal strength. This was in part why Chaldean influence to Gazarta was present, at least ostensibly, from the formation of the Sulaqite Chaldean hierarchy (Wilmshurst 2000, 102). In the context of Ottoman administration, the need to affirm a reputation as the *true* East Syriac community was vital. However, Chaldean influence to the Gazarta region was undermined by the traditionalist patriarchal line which promoted a more active apostolate among its local clergy for much of the seventeenth and eighteenth centuries. Only the early nineteenth century resolution of Chaldean patriarchal leadership led to comprehensive efforts to induce conversions. This process was effected strongly and, by the immediate pre-First World War era, the remaining influence of the Church of the East (through the Sulaqite line) was nearly nil, with the newly established Chaldean dioceses and attendant missionary led education programmes proving attractive to many East Syriacs (Wilmshurst 2000, 102–6).

Following its initial Chaldean establishment, Zakho diocese was combined with those of Akra and Amadiya until the 1850s. Zakho again became an independent diocese from 1851, but a bishop, Basil Asmar, was only appointed from 1859 (Fiey OP 1993, 93). As with Amadiya in the aftermath of the massacres, the Diocese of Zakho held significance for bordering the new state of Turkey. It was in proximity to the former dioceses of Gazarta and Seert and became a point of entry into Iraq for East Syriac refugees. The diocese declined in ecclesial significance over the course of the twentieth century, with the movement of Chaldeans southwards or abroad. By way of comparison, the city of Zakho became politically and strategically significant in modern Iraq, as it was less than thirty kilometres from both the Syrian and Turkish borders. Diocesan life was greatly

162 *Ecclesiology and ecclesial organisation*

interrupted from the 1960s to the 2000s due to incidents of persecution from the Kurds, Iraqi republican governments and Baathist state.

Zakho was an occupied see from 1859 to 1987, with no gap in the episcopal succession longer than three years. However, at the death of Stephen Kajo, in 1987, Zakho did not receive another bishop until 2001. Given the proximity of Amadiya diocese and its bishop, Hanna Kello (1973–2001) it appears that he took on responsibility for both dioceses. This is supported by the fact that on his death, new bishops were appointed for both Zakho and Amadiya: Hanna Issa al-Harboli (2001–2010) and Rabban al-Qas (2001), respectively. Further ecclesial reform took place in July 2013 when the dioceses were again united, this time officially, and under al-Qas' leadership.

During the period 1987–2001, it is possible that the urbanisation of Iraqi life and Chaldean migration proved an inhibiting factor to the patriarch retaining developed consideration of those Chaldeans resident north of Mosul. It seems that only events from 2003 have ensured a reawakening of comprehensive concern for the northern dioceses. However, we should recall that the Chaldean leadership's response was difficult to formulate or implement given that Iraqi Kurdistan during Baathist rule was faced with intermittent conflict and the disruption of normal social interactions for months at a time. I suggest the northern dioceses, to an extent, became self-sufficient owing to this relative isolation.

Zakho's diocesan population has remained substantially larger than Amadiya's at least since the 1950s. Table 5.6, from *AP* figures, indicates the Amadiyan population has been four or more times smaller than that in Zakho. These figures provide some evidence of the dioceses' remarkably changing fortunes and the particularly strong effects of the Kurdish rebellion in its geographical remit. I suggest the sharp decline from 1970 to 1980 was expedited in the following decade as a result of migration post-Gulf War from 1991. These figures ought also to be

Table 5.6 Chaldean population in the dioceses of Zakho and Amadiya 1949–2010

Year	Zakho	Amadiya
1949	11,300	–
1959	–	6,783
1970	11,165	8,580
1980	7,400	2,500
1990	–	1,500
1998	6,548	2,452
2001	6,048	2,452
2002	12,000	2,000
2003	12,500	2,000
2004	12,700	–
2006	–	4,000
2009	26,000	3,800
2010	12,555	–

Source: *AP*

seen in the context of baptismal and marriage records for the Diocese of Amadiya gained during research in 2013. These data support the latter trend, in the *AP* figures, for a restoration of growth from 1996. The earlier years 1959–1970 saw a growth in population, according to the *AP*, whereas the lacuna in the figures gained in 2013 leaves little conclusion to draw other than that: it is possible that the 1960s saw overall population stability; although violent incidents occurred, they were not uniform to the area and the 1970s was a far more disruptive decade. The lacuna in the figures for 1963 to 1969 should not be overstated, for it could indicate merely the particular filing cabinet in which records were kept was in a fire or similar incident. However, that every other year has been collected even during times of political and social turmoil suggests more than one incident prohibited the collection of data.[19]

Zakho-Amadiya ecclesial organisation

As with Kirkuk-Sulaymaniya, the diocese of Zakho-Amadiya was formed as a merger in July 2013. Despite this reorganisation, a separate diocesan identity was still apparent in the two zones of ecclesial activity during research in October 2013. This was likely due to the clergy and communities of Zakho taking time to adjust to leadership from Amadiya. Such an identity perhaps related to the extended period of formal ecclesial self-sufficiency which the Chaldeans of Zakho diocese have experienced.

Zakho diocese centres on the city of the same name, whilst Amadiya has its administrative centre in the city of Duhok. This arrangement is retained under the Zakho-Amadiyan ecclesiastical structure. The diocesan population is spread across twenty-seven villages in this north-western region of Iraq, with 400 Chaldean families resident in Zakho (city) as of 2013 and c. 500 in the city of Duhok as of 2012.[20]

Table 5.7 Chaldean population of the Diocese of Zakho by settlement (Group A), 2012

Church, Settlement	Families	Persons
Mar Gewargis, Bir Sivi	295	1314
Sacred Heart, Beidar	74	283
Mar Gewargis, Shakfdale	20	88
Mar Keryakos, Sharanesh	42	180
Virgin Mary, Zakho	180	817
Mar Gewargis, Zakho	220	908
Mar Auraha, Livo	135	560
Virgin Mary, Dashta Takh	4	15
Mar Yusif, Badja	23	86
Mar Ithalaha, Duhok	c. 500	c. 4,000
Bakhoula	2	10
Al, Mansouri, Mansour	30	130
Mar Gewargis, Mangesh	300	1,200

Source: *Zakho Diocesan records*

164 *Ecclesiology and ecclesial organisation*

Table 5.8 Chaldean population of the Diocese of Zakho by settlement (Group B)

Church, Settlement	Families	Persons
Mar Yusif, Nefkendala	54	243
Mar Auraha, Merga Soor	26	109
Virgin Mary, Hezaywa	58	273
Mar Tishmooni, Berga	19	65
Virgin Mary, Feshkhabur	151	584
Mansour Depol, Avzerouk	32	166
Sacred Heart, Deir Abon	125	485
Virgin Mary, Qarayola	58	236
Church of the Martyrs, Suriya	9	35
Mar Gewargis, Sheuze	162	659
Mother of Mercy, Simele	54	251
Totals (Groups A & B)	2,573	12,697

Source: *2012 Zakho Diocesan records*

Map 5.2 Zakho, Duhok and surrounding region

The cities are far from Chaldean or Christian majority centres, with residents mostly Sunni Kurds.[21] Such a scenario is similar to the situation for the Chaldeans of Ankawa. However, the more explicitly Sunni cultural views of the local Kurds have seen cases of anti-Christian activity especially in Zakho. In 2011, following inflammatory sermons by local Muslim leaders, groups of young men attacked Christian businesses. The suggested basis of the attacks was the widespread sale of alcohol by Christian merchants. The riots lasted for four days, with attacks spreading throughout Iraqi Kurdistan. Whilst the KRG took a strong approach to restoring law and order and arrested the purported ring leaders, it seems that Islamic-inspired violence can be easily stoked when desired by unscrupulous leaders. This adds a dimension to Chaldean life which is far less commonly experienced in more secure settings such as Ankawa.

The current bishop of Zakho-Amadiya resides in Duhok which, as with Erbil, is a centre of Kurdish political and economic power with access to resources available to support the running of a modern diocese. Dohuk also offers an increased opportunity to impress the Chaldean presence into Iraqi-Kurdish society. This was evidenced in 2013 in the work of the contemporary bishop, Rabban al-Qas, whose primary and secondary school complex was highly regarded by the local Kurdish population and seen as a marker for what can be achieved by the Chaldeans if such efforts are conducted in an environment relatively open to public manifestations of Christian works. It was notable during research that such an atmosphere in Duhok ensured that the city was affirmed, along with Ankawa, as a preferred place of residence in Iraqi Kurdistan by Chaldeans. Such a level of Christian culture was further evidenced by the presence of a Syriac publishing house which supported the maintenance of Christian culture.

A senior cleric in the diocese characterised the working relationship with local administrators as 'they always respond positively' when a request is made for assistance (Conversation, Duhok, October 2013). Indeed, this was exemplified during a visit to one of the local Chaldean schools which displayed KRG symbols and posters throughout its buildings. The support of and from the KRG is a practical concession and entirely in keeping with the historical experience of the East Syriac tradition in making accommodation in *practical* matters in order to be able to sustain their community in its *religious* life.

KRG support of the Chaldean population in the diocese in direct terms is limited with between ID40,000–60,000 (about £30) given to each Christian family per month. This is only a fraction of what is realistically required for the sustenance of the communities, but is understandable in the Kurdish context, where the government has had to attempt to accommodate the migrant and existing populations. Nevertheless, the responsibility of the KRG to the Chaldean migrants should technically be as comprehensive as any other group given that they are also Iraqi citizens.

Chaldean villages and towns in the Diocese of Zakho-Amadiya

Due to time constraints in 2013, research visits could not be conducted to all twenty-seven settlements with a Chaldean presence in the diocese, and only limited access was gained to archival material. However, population data and baptismal records were collected in several instances, permitting some assessment of the situation: population figures as of 2012 for every town and village in Zakho diocese, baptismal records for Amadiya diocese as a whole for 1950 to2014 and baptismal records for the parish of Mar Gewargis church, Zakho.

The village of Araden is situated in the Sapna valley, an area long associated with East Syriac Christianity. Even into the early seventeenth century, religious life was still active in the village despite two preceding centuries of relative decline among the East Syriac communities. Perhaps part of this resilience was due to its connections with the wider East Syriac network throughout the Middle East. Wilmshurst, for example, notes a local monk donating a manuscript to the

166 *Ecclesiology and ecclesial organisation*

East Syriac community in Jerusalem in 1605 (Wilmshurst 2000, 69). As with the rest of the Amadiyan area, ecclesial affairs were largely directed by the legitimist patriarchal line and, such was their strength, that it was only in the 1830s that the Chaldean influence began to be extended into Araden. Joseph Audo obtained the village's allegiance, and the latter half of the nineteenth century saw the community grow strongly from fifty Chaldeans in 1850 to 650 by 1913 (Wilmshurst 2000, 131, 134). It further grew into the twentieth century, and by the 1950s, over 300 families (c. 1,200 people) were resident (Interview with parish priest, Araden, October 2013). The status of Araden increased such that it was used as an alternate residence by the Chaldean bishop of Amadiya.

It is unfortunate that data are not available for Araden's particular population or baptisms, which would serve to indicate the rate of change in the twentieth century. Nevertheless, from the overall baptismal and marriage records for the entire diocese of Amadiya, we can see a rapid drop from the high of seventy-four baptisms in 1955 down to five in 1961. The local area was a point of rapid dissolution of political power for the Iraqi central government, which struggled to contain the growing Kurdish rebellion with a coherent counter-insurgency strategy. Local residents in 2013 ascribed Chaldean migration from the town during that period as a result of this violence and, in particular, the overthrow of the monarchy and not to urbanisation. It appears in the years preceding the Kurdish risings the Chaldean population was, in fact, growing in Amadiya contrary to the general trend for the movement of Chaldeans to urban areas.

That the violence of the conflict was intense is further emphasised in baptismal and marriage records in the archive, which records that the data for 1963 to1969 were 'lost due to events in the north'. The data suggests that a return of stability came from 1975 onward. The spike in baptisms in 1974 seems likely to have been caused by residents returning after the area's gradual pacification and the desire for parents to have their children baptised in their parishes of origin.[22] In Araden's case, the Church, with the acquiescence of the state, attempted to restore the Chaldeans' position, with houses constructed through the intervention of the contemporary bishop, Hanna Kello, to support the return of some migrants in 1992 to 1993. This is not reflected in the diocesan baptismal figures, with the numbers declining year on year for 1991 to 1996. It is perhaps the case that a return of a more normal life could occur only a few years after resettlement in the Amadiyan region, and this is seen from 1997. Nevertheless, it proved difficult to return Araden to its former status or size and, as of 2013, only forty-six families were resident, a decline of about eighty percent from the 1950s.

A similar situation to that of Araden can be found in the village of Inishke, a village which also used to be associated with a substantial East Syriac monastic presence. The village's East Syriac community enjoyed particular strength in the tenth century, with the *Life of Rabban Joseph Busnaya* providing an account of this (Wilmshurst 2000, 132).

It is possible the textual sources for the later history of Inishke as presented by Wilmshurst (2000) may be at odds with the version of historical events which was stated in interview with the parish priest. The priest asserted that a Chaldean

Ecclesiology and ecclesial organisation 167

foundation in the village dated from 1785 and was related to the entry of members of the Nwyia family into the local area.[23] By 1880, the village had grown in size to over forty families, based around the church of Mar Shimon and Sons.

Wilmshurst asserts, following Badger, that the village initially entered into union with the Holy See in the 1850s, but was not secured as a Chaldean centre until the 1870s (Badger 1852, I:198–200, 283). From the mid-eighteenth century, the Amadiyan region was a focus of Latin and Chaldean missionary activity among the East Syriac communities. This apostolate was co-ordinated by Dominicans who resided in the area. The consummation of local East Syriac commitment to the Chaldean community, I suggest, likely came some time after these missionary endeavours. For the period 1800–1840, Latin orders were inconsistently present to Mesopotamia, which led to a slowdown in the advancement of the Chaldean project.[24] These circumstances may explain why the East Syriac communities wavered between ecclesial affiliations. Given that Amadiya and Mangesh had Chaldean communities from 1783 and 1791, respectively, it is possible that Inishke had a pro-Chaldean faction from around that time (cf. Wilmshurst 2000, 134).

As I outlined in Chapter 3, Inishke's fate was closely tied to the proximity of Kurdish rebel and Iraqi army engagements particularly from the 1960s, as well as its appeal as a vacation destination. The restoration of stability in the region was related to the particularly authoritarian attempts at restoring central Iraqi government control. These efforts saw an improvement of security in Inishke with direct support from Saddam Hussein for the reconstruction of homes and encouragement to rebuild the local tourist industry. This period of peace was interrupted again by the wars of 1991 and 2003 and their consequences: the former particularly complicating the lives of the Chaldeans as they gradually exchanged Sunni Arab rulers for the Kurds. Fortunately, Inishke was at least far removed from the main areas of operations during these conflicts. The town proved an attractive place for refugees and returning migrants, who more than doubled the pre-2003 war population of fifty families to 113 as of October 2013.

The increased population has seen the construction of a new school, and the local residents are keen for their children to attain as high a social status as possible. In this instance, unrealistic expectations have arisen relative to the local situation. Aspirations to train in the professions or to start a business are to be welcomed but do not necessarily fit to the requirements or traditional agricultural vocations with which the area's geography is suited. If such a situation continues, this could lead to the denuding of rural areas once considered Chaldean due to the willingness of Kurds to utilise the land more productively. The situation is further complicated by the competition with which all farmers in northern Iraq are faced from Iranian and Turkish producers. It appears, in general, the clergy encourage Chaldeans to return to traditional vocations, with an overarching concern for retaining territorial influence in northern Iraq through a widespread network of personal claims to working the land. Resentment towards this attitude was not noted *per se* but seen as another instance of the Church not being sufficiently aware or willing to accept the realities of life in 'the world'. It is, however, a wider

168 *Ecclesiology and ecclesial organisation*

issue of attempting to reconcile aspirations for material improvement with the ability to satisfy those desires in a way which can be accommodated in the social order. For Chaldeans in rural Iraq, this appears to necessitate migration to or direct involvement in urban life.

Prior to the twentieth century, Zakho itself had a small Chaldean population, with approximately ten to fifteen families resident from 1837 to 1913 (Wilmshurst 2000, 115). The community, as of 2012, stood at 400 families (1,725 people). Without population data for the intervening period (1913–2012), I can only infer from anecdotes, baptismal numbers and the *Annuario Pontificio* that this figure was likely much higher at times, especially during the 1920s–1970s. The population likely moved southwards or emigrated from Iraq during periods of conflict.

Data available for Zakho comes from one of the two parishes in the city – Mar Gewargis. From 1989 to 2013, a broad decline in communal life appears to have taken place. This is evidenced in the decreasing number of baptisms for the period (Graph 5.4). The years 2006–2008 are the only years which indicate a slight revival in the parish. This may be accounted for by the Sunni-Shia civil war in central and southern Iraq and the movement of Chaldeans to a more stable and secure environment in Iraqi Kurdistan.

In 2012, the parish population was 908 people (220 families). The number of baptisms per year was between 10 and 20 which is suggestive that it could maintain its population at c. 1,000 people in the short to medium term.[25]

The Zakho bishopric retains its *de facto* use as the focus of ecclesial administration in the local area, with pastoral work reliant largely on the efforts of three priests who are responsible for twelve of the surrounding Chaldean communities, with one serving six parishes. Such a state of affairs is not unusual in the Chaldean context, where the relatively small size of villages and their remoteness precludes the permanent residence of a priest.

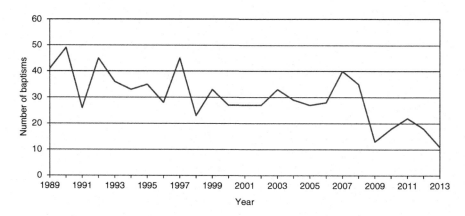

Graph 5.4 Baptisms at Mar Gewargis parish, Zakho 1989–2013
Source: *Zakho Diocesan records*

Aside from Zakho itself, research visits also took place to the villages of Deir Abon and Feshkhabur which are both located close to the Turkish and Syrian borders. Feshkhabur is separated from Syria only by the river Tigris, with a shrine to Our Lady Protector of Crops built into a cliff at the river's edge.

An East Syriac presence to Feshkhabur likely dates from at least the seventh century, and it appears the local region – the Khabur valley – became more densely populated by East Syriac communities in the sixteenth century. Extant manuscripts mention settlements in the area from this time onward including Deir Abon in 1671 (Wilmshurst 2000, 120–1). Feshkhabur was notable as a site of substantial Chaldean population growth in the late nineteenth and early twentieth centuries. In 1850, it was then part of the Diocese of Gazarta and sixty people were resident but by 1913 had 1,300 Chaldean residents (Wilmshurst 2000, 107). This increase can perhaps be put down to the attraction of the village as a centre of agricultural production but also from the efforts of Latin and Chaldean missionaries to gain the affiliation of members of the Church of the East in the region. This series of events would fit with the pattern of general Chaldean expansion in this era through the work of Joseph VI Audo. As of 2012, the village retained a population of 584, which was one of the larger Chaldean settlements in the diocese.

During the visits to the villages, it was stated that relative socio-economic stability had been experienced from the foundation of modern Iraq until the mid-1970s. Given the region's proximity to Turkey and Syria, it is possible the Iraqi army sought to avoid any internal conflicts spilling over to cause disputes with neighbouring states and viewed a peaceful locale as an absolute necessity to maintain stable borders. This was particularly important, as the Turkish government had historically viewed the region as within its purview. From the mid-1970s, the Kurdish wars impacted more heavily on Chaldean socio-economic life. This led to the start of a process of relocation and abandonment of villages which segued with Kurdish occupation of settlements. It is unclear as to whether this had specifically religious and/or national political justification. That the villages were Christian was perhaps of little account to Kurdish farmers who perceived fertile agricultural land was going to waste.

Although the KRG and Kurdish political élites have emphasised a secular and co-operative vision with other residents of northern Iraq, the historical memory of Kurdish persecution is still strong. Kurdish Islamist antagonism towards Christianity and non-Kurdish residents still exists. Therefore, even if Kurdish occupation of villages was not perceived as specifically anti-Christian by the Kurds it holds a very particular concern for Christians who see it as a return to persecution and the de-legitimisation of their presence to northern Iraq. From 2003, perhaps in recognition of Christian fears, the rebuilding of long-abandoned Chaldean villages was undertaken with the KRG's support. During the research visits to the Zakho area, the co-operative nature of the KRG was emphasised when attempting to resolve issues such as property disputes with local Kurdish residents. Accommodating Chaldean interests has little material cost to the KRG given the relative size of the Chaldean population, but whether KRG élites truly wish for equanimity for the Chaldeans is unclear. Chaldeans are cognisant of all the advantages – political and

170 *Ecclesiology and ecclesial organisation*

economic – which the Kurds hold, and are aware of the broader historical context of Christian-Kurdish relations: at times, relatively amicable but often violent.

Note on Amadiyan diocesan records[26]

Amadiyan diocesan baptismal and wedding records are entirely blank for 1964 to 1969, perhaps reflecting difficulties faced during the Kurdish rebellion's intensification, including the destruction of the Amadiyan bishopric in 1961 (Wilmshurst 2000, 12). It seems likely to have been difficult to restore Amadiya to its former status when the then bishop, Raphael Bidawid, was transferred in 1966 to Lebanon. His replacement Curiacos Moussess died in 1973 at the age of only fifty-one. To what extent his death was brought about by the stress of his time in office in a very difficult situation is unclear.

Conclusion: Dioceses of Zakho-Amadiya and Akra

The creation of the dioceses in the nineteenth century was a key point in the formation of what was to become the normative Chaldean ecclesiastical structure in northern Iraq for most of the twentieth century. With the destruction of the Chaldean dioceses of Mardin, Seert, Amid and Gazarta in Asia Minor during the 1915–1923 massacres, Zakho-Amadiya and Akra became home to refugees and migrants. The dioceses also became the chief representation of Chaldean presence to this region of Iraq. As ecclesiastical institutions, the dioceses were integral to re-emphasising the East Syriac tradition to a region which had once been so heavily associated with the Church of the East, monasticism and an active Christian presence.

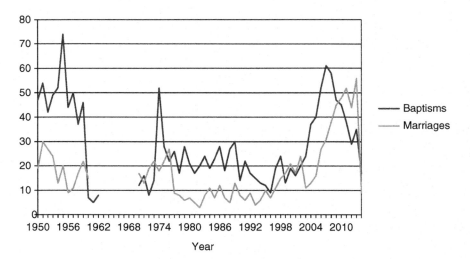

Graph 5.5 Number of baptisms and weddings in Amadiya Diocese 1950–2013

Source: *Amadiya Diocesan records*

Ecclesiology and ecclesial organisation 171

Through conversations and observations during research visits, it was very clear as to the sense of loss which was still felt by Chaldeans after the massacres. I suggest, for those in proximity to the Turkish border, there was also an understanding that the border was not only a geographic expression but a dividing point in communal memory. A perception appears to exist between a sense of completeness of the Chaldean Church and the gap in the Chaldean community for what might have been had the community retained a more diverse population through incarnating its presence in the Turkish state and *being a difference* in that *milieu* as well as Iraq, Syria and Iran from 1918.

Diocese of Alqosh

Alqosh and the Nineveh plain region has been a traditional focus of East Syriac life since the third century and a focus of Semitic religious activity for at least 3,000 years.[27] The town of Alqosh perhaps dates to as early as 750 BC and may have been named after the Assyrian deity El-Qushtu.

It is challenging to assert a comprehensive account of East Syriac history in Alqosh itself prior to the sixteenth century. However, it appears that the only period of limited ecclesial activity, and a qualitative deterioration in East Syriac life, came during the mid-fourteenth to mid-fifteenth centuries.

As of the mid-sixth century, the Mosul-Nineveh plain region was East Syriac in its religious character and formed part of the dioceses of Bet Nuhadra and Nineveh. Although members of the West Syriac community directed concerted and often successful efforts to gain the adherence of Christian settlements in the Nineveh region, Alqosh remained an East Syriac stronghold (Wilmshurst 2000, 188–9). Alqosh seems to have been a site of active Christian life at the latest by the start of the seventh century. The monastery of Rabban Hormizd had its earliest foundation from that time (Scher 1906, 479). The thirteenth to fourteenth centuries saw a general decline of Christian presence, with East Syriac settlements altering their religious allegiance. The social benefits of converting to Islam or a desire to reside in a more secure location were likely prominent reasons for this change (Wilmshurst 2000, 189).

The sixteenth to early seventeenth centuries largely saw the crystallisation of the East Syriac Christian geography of the region to the present. The main exception was the decline of the monastic presence. In 1610, there were five active sites. Only one, as of 2013 (and this effectively a new foundation in 1859). continued this tradition of East Syriac monasticism (Wilmshurst 2000).

Alqosh (and its immediate surrounds), as a specific site for monastic activity, dates from the early seventh century establishment of the monastery of Rabban Hormizd (see Budge 1902). What marked out Rabban Hormizd during the formative years of the Chaldean community was its position as the patriarchal headquarters of the traditionalist patriarchal line for the period c. 1600–1800 *and* its status and that of Alqosh as a centre for manuscript production (Wilmshurst 2000, 241–3, 248).

From the 1720s onward, interest among local East Syriacs in the Chaldean project increased the Latin presence to Mosul. The diocese and Rabban Hormizd

172 *Ecclesiology and ecclesial organisation*

became targets of the Latin-Chaldean factions. Both Alqosh and Rabban Hormzid's significance from the eighteenth century were not as great in the era of the seventh to fourteenth centuries, when both sites formed a part of the wider network of East Syriac ecclesiastical organisation and monasticism which were diffused throughout Asia. Nonetheless, by the sixteenth century, much importance can be ascribed to Rabban Hormizd and the Mosul region as centres of the greatest extant concentrations of East Syriac activity in the Ottoman Empire. Northern Mesopotamia was the area in which the East Syriac tradition was maintained in its strongest form, and where the heritage of its 'golden era' was manifested. However, association with Rabban Hormizd as a means for justifying legitimacy to the patriarchal office gradually disappeared, with the establishment of the 'lower monastery' of Notre Dame de Semences (at the foot of the mountain on which Rabban Hormizd is sited).

Quite apart from Rabban Hormizd's significance in the twenty-first century as a cultural heritage site, it offers some evidence as to the ecclesiological identity which the legitimist line advanced in the sixteenth to early nineteenth centuries in response to the development of the Chaldean presence. The monastery served as the burial site for the majority of the legitimist patriarchs between 1497 and 1804. Harrak has offered the most recent English translation of the funerary inscriptions of the entombed patriarchs, and has begun to develop an historical analysis of the inscriptions which are written in the first person and detail the patriarchs' Christological beliefs (2003).

The ecclesiology of the patriarchs develops with emphasis on those who were buried there from 1497 to 1558 (Shemon IV Basidi, Shemon VI Denha and Shemon VII Ishoyab), noting their status as the Catholicos-Patriarch but otherwise only outlining their Christology. In 1591, with the burial of Elias VII, the patriarch notes his desire to see ' "amen" said throughout 'the entire church' (Harrak 2003, 297). Elias VII entered office in 1558, three years after Sulaqa's death and six after the start of the first Chaldean patriarchal line. I suggest this desire for 'amen' was an indication of a hope for unity in the East Syriac community which had become factionalised, but without the connotations, as yet, of Christological or theological distinction between the communities. From Elias IX (d. 1660) onward, the patriarchs preface their description of the 'church' with 'orthodox' (Harrak 2003, 298f.). This change presumably came from a desire to clearly mark out their position as apart from the Chaldean faction, owing to increased awareness of the distinctiveness of the Tridentine Christological views and ecclesiastical boundaries which Latin missionaries pursued and encouraged. The inscriptions are thus notable for being a point from when the revivification of East Syriac Christological awareness began. This Christology, which for some time prior to this, perhaps since the Mesopotamian Christian revival in the twelfth to fourteenth centuries, had not been broadly reflected upon within the community. Moreover, East Syriac Christology or ecclesiology had not perceived the Church of the East as set apart from the Latin ecclesial community. The engagement with the Latins in a post-Tridentine environment created opportunity for the annunciation of a more well-defined ecclesiological and Christological position, and one which the

Ecclesiology and ecclesial organisation 173

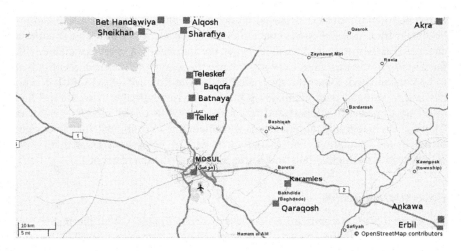

Map 5.3 Mosul and surrounding region

legitimist patriarchs perceived as necessary to defend. 'Orthodox' also implied that outside of this frame of reference and community there was something lacking in the heterodox community. Such a notion was framed and annunciated by the patriarch and the hierarchy, but would be diffused among the community to ensure the retention of members of the Church of the East in the face of attempts by the Chaldeans to draw East Syriac Christians into their own community.[28]

Although the monastery is, as of 2017, unoccupied except for a caretaker, it casts a metaphorical shadow over the running of Alqosh diocese and is linked to the perceived necessity to retain a strong Chaldean presence regardless of events. As the spiritual and previously temporal home of the East Syriac tradition in Mesopotamia, and a remnant of the great network of monastic centres throughout Central and West Asia, it is a tangible reminder of past glories. As of early 2017, Rabban Hormizd, like the Syrian Orthodox monastery of Mar Mattai near Mosul, stands virtually on the front line of the war between Iraqi and Kurdish forces against Da'esh. The monasteries act as a living rebuke to the terrorists, and in Mar Mattai's case, as a spiritual anchor in the unseen warfare which the remaining monks conduct through their prayers (cf. Ephesians 6:10–18).

Until 1960, and the overall growth of population in the Mosul archdiocese, the Chaldean hierarchy did not perceive a need for further administrative declension in the region. Alqosh up to that time was within the archdiocese's jurisdiction. I suggest that the leadership of Abdul-Ahad Sana, as bishop of Alqosh from the diocese's foundation until December 2001, left a particular identity upon the community. Given that Sana had been consecrated in 1961 with the purpose of his leading the diocese, we can wonder at the influence which he had in implementing ecclesiological changes after the Second Vatican Council. The Council

174 *Ecclesiology and ecclesial organisation*

segued with Iraq's rapid economic development as a result of the consolidation of the petroleum industry. Ecclesial modernism's influence upon Eastern Catholic life in Iraq was, therefore, concomitant with modern political and economic changes. Furthermore, as Alqosh had been predominantly a town associated with the Church of the East until the early nineteenth century, a Chaldean identity had to be consolidated. Sana was succeeded by Mikha Polo Maqdassi (2001–), who has had to contend with maintaining the East Syriac heritage. Also, he has had to create a means to support and retain the character of the modern Chaldean Church. The geographical territory is a challenging environment for the current bishop as the population, whilst largely Chaldean, is heterogeneous with numerical minorities of Sunni Arabs and Kurds as well as Yazidis resident.

Ecclesial Organisation

The diocese's main communities consist of Alqosh itself, where the bishop has his residence, and the towns of Teleskef, Baqofa, Batnaya and Sheikhan.(Cf Tables 5.9 and 5.10)[29]

In 2013, residents of Alqosh strongly affirmed that continued residence in the town was preferred to migration. Although Alqosh has been a point of departure for many, it retains a proportion of population who will likely never leave. This is evidenced by the return of a few families from the US who had attempted to settle there – the cultural and social barriers were too great to overcome. The strength of feeling about the local identity is such that Alqoshis are renowned locally for refusing to sell their properties to non-Alqoshis.

The extent of patronage which the Kurdish governors provided to the bishop was not clear. However, Alqosh, as a strategic location close to Mosul and under KRG control, presumably led to the cultivation of a strong working relationship.

Table 5.9 Total Chaldean population in the Diocese of Alqosh, 1970–2012

Year	Number of persons
1970	13,000
1980	13,000
1990	13,500
1999	16,190
2000	16,500
2001	17,000
2002	15,000
2003	17,947
2004	17,487
2006	20,820
2009	32,070
2012	22,300

Source: *AP*

Table 5.10 Chaldean population in the Diocese of
Alqosh, October 2013 by settlement

Town	Number of families
Alqosh	1,240
Teleskef	1,450
Baqofa	115
Batnaya	900
Sheikhan	140
Jambur	56
Sharifiya	27
Bet Handawiya	35
Naseriya	'a few families'
Total	c. 3,963 (c. 18,000 people)

Source: *Bishop Maqdassi of Alqosh*

Furthermore, the bishop for his part was attempting to advance social bridges with
the local non-Christian communities with the construction of a new school which
Yazidis and Kurds had indicated they would be pleased to attend on completion.
Although Alqosh has a mixed community, it was evident from observing the day-
to-day life in the town that the Christian presence was the strongest. Local Chaldean youths had erected a large cross on the side of the most prominent hill in the
north of the town which is illuminated every night. It is unlikely this would have
been permitted without at least tacit permission of the local authorities.[30]

Teleskef

The date of the first East Syriac presence to Teleskef is not certain. A Christian
presence of some kind possibly dates to around the late sixth or early seventh centuries given the settlement's position between Alqosh and Mosul, whose own East
Syriac communities were certainly present from at least that era. Nonetheless, and
perhaps more likely, Teleskef could have been of later foundation. A confirmed
textual reference for an East Syriac community is found only in the thirteenth century (Wilmshurst 2000, 202, 234). The community was of sufficient – if unknown –
size and status by the late fifteenth century to warrant two churches: Mar Giwargis
and Mar Yacob the Recluse (Wilmshurst 2000, 234).

With the trend for the patriarch to reside outside of Baghdad at times of persecution or conflict – especially during the initial phases of the Mongol occupation of
Mesopotamia – it is also realistic to suggest a trend for East Syriac communal movement to areas perceived to be likely safer or more remote such as the Mosul-Nineveh
plain and Erbil regions.[31] This would correlate to the consolidation of the East Syriac
presence between Alqosh and Mosul in the period twelfth to fifteenth centuries and
as to why Teleskef and other nearby villages emerge in the written record.

The town gained prominence as one of the Christian settlements sacked during the raids of the Turkish leader Bar Yak in 1508 – Teleskef along with Alqosh,

176 *Ecclesiology and ecclesial organisation*

Rabban Hormizd and Telkef were all affected. Scribal activity later became notable from the end of the seventeenth century. Interest in the religious life also appears to have been evident among the inhabitants with vocations to the monastic life sent to Rabban Hormizd during Gabriel Dambo's tenure, of whom one, Thomas Choa, became Chaldean Archbishop of Kirkuk in 1853 (Wilmshurst 2000, 235–6). As of 1867, approximately 1,800 Chaldeans were resident; in 1913, the population had risen to c. 3,500 which increased further to 5,705 in 1965 (Fiey OP 1965b, II:381; Wilmshurst 2000, 199). It seems very likely Teleskef was a beneficiary of the migrants and refugees who wished to settle in Iraq after the First World War. The town was an attractive site for those who sought to continue their work in agriculture – as refugees were largely previously living agrarian lifestyles – and benefited from the proximity to Mosul. The less substantial increase in total population size between 1913 and 1965 compared with 1867 and 1913 can be accounted for in Chaldean migration to central and southern Iraqi cities from the 1930s.

Bishop Maqdassi's 2013 figure of 1,450 families in Teleskef equates to c. 6,525 people – at an average family size of 4.5 persons. The retention of population, despite its proximity to conflict in Iraq proper and the challenging economic situation compared with the population in 1965, is notable. As with other towns in northern Iraq it is frustrating not to be able to form a more comprehensive estimate and determine causes of population change for intervening years from 1965 to 2013, when we are aware numerous events of economic, political and social significance took place. As will be seen in Graph 5.6, we can draw some conclusions from available data on baptisms and weddings.

For those who looked to depart Teleskef in 2013, the greatest evidence of the desire to leave comes via the collection of baptismal and marriage certificates

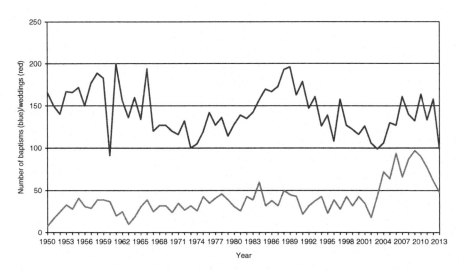

Graph 5.6 Number of baptisms and weddings in Teleskef 1950–October 2013
Source: *Alqosh Diocesan records*

Ecclesiology and ecclesial organisation 177

which act as the onward ecclesial passport for entry into the next diocese or parish location. Whilst the parish priest did not specify the total numbers to have departed since 2003, he indicated very large numbers had left. This, however, was balanced by his assertion that those who depart are replaced by migrants from southern and central Iraq.[32] This is indicative overall of the decline of the Chaldean population, and with the concurrent drop in the number of baptisms, points to a long-term inability to replace those who make the final decision to leave Iraq.

The rate of Chaldean departure from Teleskef, as of October 2013, was stated as one or two families per week or an average of seventy-eight families per year. Whilst, as of 2013 such a rate was not yet terminal, such a consistent pattern of decline, if it continued, meant that, without other families to settle as replacements, by 2018 twenty to thirty percent of the population will have left. A thirty percent population reduction has a wide impact insofar as the community's bonds and its social cohesion are fundamentally weakened. It is also of concern due to the loss of skills which the local economy requires to survive. Despite the town centre being dominated by shops and tradesmen, the majority work in agriculture. Such a transfer out of the population is likely to result in a concomitant decline which is largely irreplaceable in the short term, as an array of skills are lost which are required to maintain farming. Such a scenario adds further strain on the community which few external bodies are able to comprehend or assist in resolving.

The community is strained also because of the general insecurity of their situation. This is an issue which was reinforced during 2005 and 2007 when there were bomb attacks in the town and, as a result, a rise in departures. However, this appears to have been only temporary when looking at baptismal and marriage numbers for those years, as can be noted in Graph 5.6: 130/64 and 161/66, respectively. These figures at a consistent level and in keeping with numbers in years both before 2005 and after 2007. The Chaldeans remain resilient despite persecution and socio-economic decline, with the majority of the population choosing in the short term to return after displacement given the transitory nature of so much of the violence in the years prior to 2014 and the emergence of Da'esh.

Available records from Teleskef consisted of baptismal and marriage data from 1950 to October 2013. Graph 5.6 indicates that the relative strength of Teleskef as a place of Chaldean life was maintained throughout political events in modern Iraqi history. Perhaps most notable is the drop in baptisms in 1960 to nearly half of its level in the previous year. This may be an anomaly or could be related to the intensity of conflict of the Kurdish rebellion that year. Given that the number of marriages did not decline at a similar rate in the following years, I am inclined to see this as an effect of the Kurdish war, as there is a general drop in baptisms until 1973 from which time the population again grew. This in part was likely due to the migration of population during the Iran-Iraq War to northern towns and the gradual cessation of violence after the Kurdish rebellions. In comparison, the marriage numbers have remained far more consistent. It may be the case that for women, when pregnant, it is desirable to reside in an area more amenable to the challenges associated with such life-events. In contrast, weddings continue regardless, because they are events of short duration and traditionally conducted

178 *Ecclesiology and ecclesial organisation*

in the home parish of the bride. Overall, however, if we follow the lines of the graph, we can see the wedding figures largely mirror baptismal figures by a gap of c. one to two years, as might be expected.

Conclusion: Diocese of Alqosh

I have noted the importance of Alqosh and the towns within the diocese to the modern Chaldean Church. Da'esh's June 2014 advance into the Nineveh plain has seen the destruction of Christian life in their area of occupation. Of all the principal Chaldean centres of residence in the area between Mosul and Erbil, only Alqosh has remained free from Da'esh's occupation. These events pose a severe threat to the Chaldean community's viability at the regional level, but also to Chaldean identity internationally. With the removal of the Chaldean presence to the Nineveh region, the incarnation of the East Syriac Christian tradition, its communities and ecclesiastical structures has to begin again elsewhere and take into account new social, cultural and religious paradigms. The physical destruction of people, as well as material culture, is a set of circumstances which point to the removal of the Chaldeans from the historical and living record. What is also severely detrimental to the Chaldeans, however, is the loss of resilience and capability to remain in the area – something which, even despite persecution since 2003, has not previously been encountered. The level of purposeful and systematic removal of non-Sunni culture by Da'esh's forces, sees a brutality and criminality matched only by the massacres of the First World War.

A psychological shift has occurred among the Chaldeans. Even in Alqosh they are alienated from the land in which they have incarnated their Christianity. In combination with the ambivalence of non-Christian Iraqis to their situation, and the ineffectiveness of Coalition, Iraqi and Kurdish military responses, it is very doubtful that the Nineveh plain is a place where even those who previously expressed sentiments of being willing to stay or die in their lands can remain. When a flourishing life can be found abroad, why should residents choose a life in Iraq? For a community whose preceding generations have contended with persecution under a variety of rulers from Sasanian to Baathist and survived, the intervention of Da'esh has an air of complete finality about its ability to alter the social make-up of northern Iraq. Were Alqosh and Rabban Hormizd to be lost, it could be compared to the loss of Kosovo for the Serbs in terms of the spiritual, religious and cultural heritage which the two regions have, respectively, for the Chaldean and Serbian churches.

Archdiocese of Basra

I turn now to outline the dioceses in Iraq which were beyond the reach of direct research visits. Apart from two parishes in the Diocese of Mosul, I was unable to travel to the rest of the diocese or the Archdioceses of Baghdad and Basra. As such, the following assessment is grounded in a somewhat less nuanced perspective than that which I was able to gain in regions where direct research was conducted and where I was able to draw on more detailed information.

Ecclesiology and ecclesial organisation 179

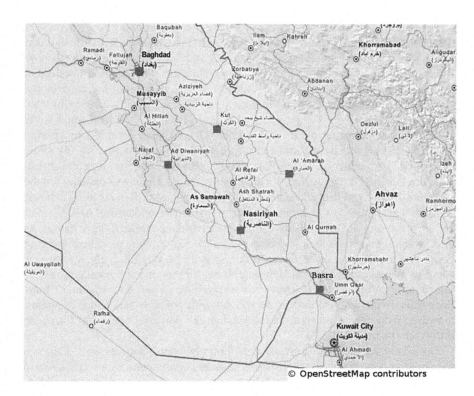

Map 5.4 Central and southern Iraq

The Basra region is one of the oldest, and was one of the most prestigious, centres of East Syriac life in Mesopotamia-Iraq. A bishop was likely present to the area from the late third century (Hansman 2011). In 410, at the Synod of Issac, the region was designated as the metropolitan province of Perat d'Maysan, having been named after the local Sasanian administrative district (Fiey OP 1968, III:263–4). Substantial ecclesial activity took place between the fourth and sixth centuries and, notwithstanding periodic Sasanian persecution, a secure East Syriac foundation was attained in southern Mesopotamia.

With the Arab invasion of 637–638 to southern Mesopotamia, the city of Maysan fell into disuse. A local army encampment was developed into the permanent settlement of Basra, on the site of the Persian town of Vaheshtabad Ardashir. The prominence of the burgeoning city was derived from its position on the route to Persia and further Muslim invasions of West and Central Asia. From an ecclesial perspective, it was key as a maritime point of departure to dioceses in the Gulf: Bet Qatraye (Qatar), Rev Ardashir (Bushehr), Bet Mazunaye (Oman) and further afield to the East Syriac communities in India and China.

The East Syriac community of Basra faced the destruction of their churches twice during the rule of the Abbasid Caliphs in the first and fourth decades of

180 *Ecclesiology and ecclesial organisation*

the ninth century. Abbasid antagonism towards the Church of the East varied, however, as in the intervening period the churches were rebuilt (Fiey OP 1968, III:269). The weakening of centralised rule over Basra brought with it instability. The city was sacked by the Karmatians in 923 and the Mongols in 1258 (Donner 1988). Basra sustained some form of active Christian presence and intellectual life into the thirteenth century, as is evidenced in the collation of literature by the then metropolitan of Perat d'Maysan, Shlemon of Akhlat, in his work on Christian history *The Book of the Bee* (c. 1222) (Budge 1886, I, pt. 2:iii). Shlemon is the last known named metropolitan, and it appears the province entered into a period of substantial decline by the mid-fourteenth century at the latest (Fiey OP 1968, III:265–6). The reduction of the East Syriac presence in terms of ecclesiastical structure ties in with the overall disruption of ecclesial life in Mesopotamia in the era 1300–1400, as well as with a northward geographical shift in ecclesial activity.

Basra's proximity to the Persian border, status as Mesopotamia's only sea port and position on the Gulf all saw it maintain continued strategic importance. As the Ottomans expanded their jurisdiction into the region, they were keen to bring Basra into their sphere of influence, doing so in 1534. It is likely the East Syriac community was largely sustained through Basra's economic significance as a continued point of mercantile interest eastward to India, south-east Asia and China. Encounters with Western traders, as well as with political and religious agents, increased from the seventeenth century, when the port was opened to European traffic (Hartmann 1913, 673).

The Chaldean ecclesial presence was formally established in 1860. This was chiefly to provide pastoral care for the Chaldean communities who were involved with the river transport businesses, which grew in significance as Ottoman administrative control was consolidated in Mesopotamia. Wilmshurst notes Basra was created as a diocese, but refers to it, as of 1913, as a patriarchal vicariate. This was practically what it was, given there were only c. 500 believers resident in its jurisdiction at that time (Wilmshurst 2000, 361). The pastoral oversight of the community varied: patriarchal vicars were named for only fourteen years of the period 1860–1953 until a bishop was installed (Fiey OP 1993, 60). I suggest the parochial clergy had responsibility for the community without direct episcopal oversight during the gaps. Moreover, due to the relative security of Basra during the aforementioned era, it was unnecessary to provide any further pastoral guidance.

From 1867, when baptismal records become available, we can see, in Graph 5.7, the Chaldean population appearing to have generally increased until the start of the Iran-Iraq War in 1980. Nonetheless, population growth, especially from 1914 to1970, was likely unsteady, as is indicated by the spikes and subsequent rapid declines in the number of baptisms. It is possible some fluctuations might be ascribed to natural trends or as anomalies. It appears the population was particularly badly affected during the mid-1930s with Mar Toma, Mart Mariam and the church in Amara all seeing substantial drops in baptisms. This is particularly surprising in the context of wider events. Basra had experienced a period in the 1920s of hope for independence inspired by a Shia regional political identity, as well as sympathy towards the British Empire as a patron of such a new arrangement.

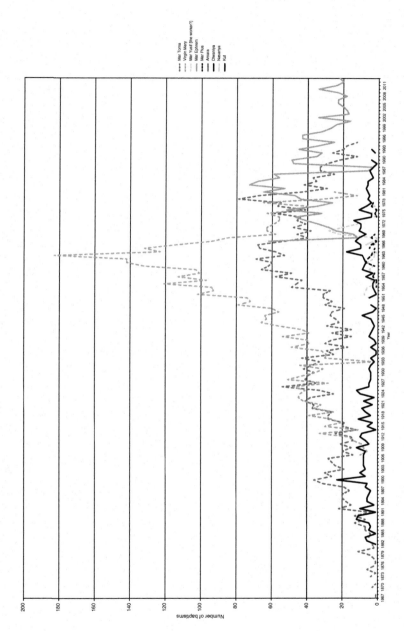

Graph 5.7 Baptisms in the Archdiocese of Basra 1867–2012

Source: *Basra Archdiocesan records*

182 *Ecclesiology and ecclesial organisation*

Relations were to be secured through Imperial access to southern Mesopotamia's oilfields. Such a scenario did not come to fruition but Basra was, during the 1930s, incorporated socially, economically and politically into Iraqi national life. It is possible that Chaldeans in the 1930s–1940s saw Baghdad as a better place for economic opportunity and migrated. Alternatively, as Chaldeans had concentrated in Basra during the First World War era to avoid the effects of conflict and persecution, so they now departed but even this does not seem to explain the average forty to fifty percent drop in baptisms during the 1930s by comparison with the preceding decade (cf. Visser 2005, 138–42ff.).

Aside from this era, the growth and decline of the Archdiocese was tied to the vicissitudes of the Iraqi state in general. The large drop in the late 1960s was linked with the knock-on effects of the economy due to political instability prior to the assumption of the Baath party to power. However, migration to Baghdad to take advantage of the increase in opportunities in the city likely played a key role in the substantial change in population in Basra. The cultural, social and economic attraction which Baghdad had for Chaldeans cannot be underestimated. To be Chaldean and to live a Christian life in Baghdad was eased by the concentration of population. It was far more challenging to do so in a strongly Shia cultural environment in southern Iraq, in which the numerical size of the Chaldean population was proportionately smaller than which developed in Baghdad in the second half of the twentieth century. Migration from Basra was also expedited by the onset of the Iran-Iraq War (1980–1988) and the desire to find relative safety in the capital, which was beyond the reach of the vast majority of military operations during the conflict. Nevertheless, Basra's strategic value and position placed it firmly as a target for Iranian attacks and Iraqi defensive actions.

Chaldean life was further disrupted in 1990–1991 and 2003, as Basra was a main invasion corridor of the Coalition forces in these years. However, this has had the benefit of seeing the rapid re-development of Basra because it is so vital to the stabilisation of Iraq's economy overall. As of 2013, the Archdiocese had one of the largest geographical territories in Iraq, with the towns and cities of Kut, Amara, Diwaniyah and Nasariya all included within its boundaries.

The main churches serving the Chaldeans of Basra were Mar Toma, Mart Mariam and, from the mid-1960s, Mar Ephrem. We can note a very substantial Chaldean presence in Basra in the 1960s, with baptismal figures peaking in Mar Toma at sixty-nine in 1962 and 183 in Mart Mariam in 1963. This was a rapid growth considering average annual baptisms in the 1950s had stood at 42.6 and ninety-seven, respectively, for these churches. The latter years of the 1960s, however, saw a decline in baptisms and population size. We should also note that between 1959 and 1969, the total population within the archdiocesan geographical territory – including all the non-Catholic populations – increased from 1,338,225 to 2,124,931 according to the *AP*. The Chaldean population thus decreased as a proportion of the population from 6.1 to 0.4 percent and, as can be seen in Table 5.11, also decreased in real terms to roughly ten percent of its former size.

This change in size – if the *AP* figures are correct – was likely due to the consolidation of the Shia presence and identity in southern Iraq and the weakening of

Table 5.11 Chaldean population in the Archdiocese of Basra 1959–2012

Year	Population
1959	82,000
1969	9,285
1980	6,700
1990	2,600
2000	2,500
2001	2,500
2002	2,500
2003	2,500
2004	2,500
2006	2,600
2007	1,000
2012	850

Source: *AP*

Chaldean socio-cultural affiliation with the region. Chaldean population change was perhaps also affected by the departure of the Jewish population in the 1940s and 1950s, which led to a lessening of the plurality of the country as a whole. Through migrating to Baghdad, where the concentration of Chaldeans was that much greater, it was easier to retain one's cultural identity and to live in a less sectarian *milieu* than existed in other areas where the boundaries between communities were more readily apparent.

Following its change of status from a diocese in 1953, the first Archbishop of Basra was Joseph Gogué (1954–1971). He had been born in Seert in 1886 and had seen the full spectrum of ecclesiological, political and economic changes with which the Chaldeans had had to contend following the end of the Ottoman hegemony. His life experience appeared to suit him well for his new role. Gogué's time in office saw the consolidation of ecclesiastical structures, but an overall numerical decline of the Chaldeans in the Archdiocese.

Ecclesial organisation – churches in Basra city

Normal conduct of ecclesial affairs was challenging during the Iran-Iraq War. As we can note from the data for the Chaldean cathedral (Mart Mariam), records ended abruptly in 1980. This lacuna is unsurprising when we consider the city was a particular focus of Iranian military engagements during the battles of Operation Ramadan (1982) and Operation Karbala 5 (1987). The latter was the biggest military operation of the war, which involved up to a million soldiers and led to substantial population displacement in the region.

The 2003 invasion of Iraq again interrupted the conduct of regular religious and social life. Generally, the level of *religious* persecution has been little evidenced by comparison with those Chaldeans resident in central or northern Iraq.

184 *Ecclesiology and ecclesial organisation*

Nevertheless, the Chaldean presence faced some level of opposition with the then apostolic administrator, Mgr Iman al-Banar, requesting that his communities celebrate Christmas in 2009 in an un-ostentatious manner. Al-Banar cited the need to show 'respect for Muslims, especially Shi'as, on the occasion of Muharram' which, that year, coincided with Christmas Day (Gisick 2009).

Various figures have been communicated during the course of research related to the total population of Basra archdiocese, which appear to vary in accuracy especially from year to year. One estimate states 5,000 in 2009, and another states 1,000 in the same year. Through direct contact with Chaldean community members, however, an estimate of 400 people was given as of 2013. Assuming this to be accurate, the loss of population, from even the lower end of 1,000 in 2009, is fatal to the continued Chaldean presence and their ability to maintain sufficient communal cohesion for a presence to remain. It is possible this figure may have risen since May 2014 given Basra's relative security in the context of the rise of Da'esh in western and northern Iraq.

Conclusion: Archdiocese of Basra

As we will see, whilst the Chaldeans of Baghdad faced very intense levels of persecution, the community was able to retain a degree of cohesion because of the mass concentration of Chaldeans in the city from the 1930s. Conversely, Basra is sufficiently tied to a local regionalist identity that separation from the majority of the Chaldean population is to be expected. Subsequent to this loss of communal attachment, however, has been the return of Basrawis to the north. For example: many Chaldeans from Teleskef settled in Basra, which demonstrates that the northern towns retain the loyalty of the East Syriac population at heart.

Archdiocese of Baghdad

Baghdad was the chief see and residence of the East Syriac patriarchs for much of the eighth to thirteenth centuries. The city was founded in 762 by the Abbasid Caliph al-Mansur as the dynasty's capital and is where the majority of his successors resided until the Mongol invasion in the thirteenth century. The city's construction marked the Abbasid's attempted assumption of authority over the Muslim community from the Ummayads (661–750), who had centred the caliphate's administration in Syria.

Contemporary views of the East Syriac patriarchal office and its status in Baghdad relate to perceptions of Louis Raphael I Sako's quite minor status in the city, with limited influence in political affairs and Iraqi life generally. However, until the late fourteenth century, the rôle of the East Syriac patriarch in Mesopotamian society was of one among many religious leaders under Sasanid, Ummayad, Abbasid and Mongol rule with whom the shah, caliph or khan was obliged to productively engage. Iraqi society's trend towards the denial of religious plurality only developed from the late twentieth century.[33]

The patriarch's relationship with the state in the Late Antique and Medieval periods was far from without problems, as the persecutions of various eras attest.

Ecclesiology and ecclesial organisation 185

Nevertheless, the relationship was reliable enough to show the patriarch's entanglement with the civil power was in order to gain position and influence for himself, his patronage network and the Church. The onset of *dhimmi* status from the Ummayad period set the relationship as one of qualitative disadvantage for the Christians. However, by virtue of their size, the wider plurality of south-west Asia, their involvement in civil administration and their commitment to scholarship, they were ensured to retain a significance to the civil power. East Syriac status altered substantially as the Church became a numerically minor community, with the lay élite no longer obliged to acknowledge their significance. Instead, they became a group who had a reduced importance to the conduct of rule and state administration. From the Ottoman era, they were outside of the concerns of the state's general administration because of the self-governance by communal laws and customs which the millet system encouraged.

Prior to Baghdad's foundation, East Syriac patriarchs had resided in Veh Ardashir (Seleucia), a suburb of the Sasanid capital Ctesiphon. Following the move to Baghdad, Veh Ardashir was retained as the traditional site for patriarchal enthronements. It is from there the title associated with the patriarch 'of Seleucia-Ctesiphon' is derived. Given that Ctesiphon was also the site of Sasanid coronations, the patriarch likely sought to emulate and associate himself with themes of sacred kingship. These were personified by the Shah, and ensured that his manifestation of Christian authority and jurisdiction aligned with that of the temporal power (cf. Kröger 2011).

A noted period of especially high status for the Church of the East in the city, which was accompanied by favourful recognition from the Muslim communities, came during the life of patriarch Timothy I, who was known for his theological engagements with caliph Al-Mahdi (775–785) (Fiey OP 1980, 38–9).

The Mongol invasion of western Asia saw a new dynamic of church-state relations set for the Church of the East. These varied over time and by locality in Mesopotamia. In Baghdad, at least, the initial Mongol occupation of the city in 1258 saw no adverse effects upon the East Syriac residents or Christians more widely. The intervention of Mongol élites well disposed to their new Christian subjects or of Christian belief themselves saw the Baghdadi Christian population spared from the widespread massacres and looting in the city, with tens of thousands of people estimated to have been killed (Fiey OP 1975, 22). During the 1260s, Muslim ire was raised against the Christians. They were temporarily in the ascendant, and through Mongol patronage were perceived to be a threat to the maintenance of Muslim dominance. The East Syriac position became so difficult that the then patriarch, Denha I (1265–1281), left the city for Erbil. Denha returned later in his reign and died in Baghdad in 1281 (Fiey OP 1975, 35; Wilmshurst 2000, 184).

Further Christian persecution took place in 1295 in Mesopotamia and Persia, following the conversion to Islam of the Il-Khanate Mongol ruler Gazan Khan, who was initially zealous in advancing his new religion through active persecution of his Jewish, Buddhist and Christian subjects – Shamanism as the traditional Mongol religion was for pragmatic reasons not directly attacked.[34] Despite Patriarch Yahballah III's previously close relationship with some Mongol rulers and extensive knowledge of their culture, he departed from his residence in Baghdad,

186 *Ecclesiology and ecclesial organisation*

following the confiscation of church property and appears not to have returned to the city. At his death in 1317, he was buried in the Il-Khanate capital of Maragha in north-western Persia (Wilmshurst 2000, 184). Yahballah's successor, Timothy II, was consecrated in Baghdad in 1318 and moved to reside near Erbil. His successor Denha II (c. 1336–1380) had limited connections with the city, and it is not known if he was enthroned in Baghdad (Wilmshurst 2000, 185).

The Christian emir Haggi Togai had some influence in preserving what East Syriac community remained in Baghdad in the 1330s. For example, he ensured that previously occupied churches were returned to East Syriac ownership (Wilmshurst 2000, 184). However, the East Syriac presence, other than as a token community, likely did not continue beyond 1401 following the widespread destruction which Tamerlane caused in Baghdad (Wilmshurst 2000, 185).

The accession of Mongol dominance in West Asia presented a challenge to how church-state relations should proceed. The relief which Mongol protection offered was an indication of the possibilities which the East Syriac patriarch and hierarchy could pursue at societal level, and to increase their influence in Mesopotamian society. However, Christians did not take into account the resilience of Islam and how strongly it was embraced by Gazan Khan and wider Mongol society in the 1290s. I suggest this marked a turning point which saw Islam set, for the indefinite future, as the religion of choice for the temporal rulers of societies in which the Church of the East was present. The Mongols appeared as the final potential hope for the elevation of East Syriac Christianity to the level of at least *a* if not *the* state religion. With their turn towards Islam, the Church of the East resigned itself to *dhimmi* status indefinitely. This was also ecclesiologically significant for dislodging the patriarch's position to Baghdad, as well as a situation which increased difficulties in cultivating a client-patron relationship with the ruling power.

The status of the Church at the macro level was reliant on forging some form of relationship which enabled the legitimisation of the East Syriac community in Mesopotamia. Since its foundation, the *state* had been a presence to the conduct of ecclesiastical affairs, and from the 410 Synod of Isaac, which was held in Seleucia-Ctesiphon, the *capital* had been linked with the headship of the Church of the East and the contemporary ruling power. Therefore, how should the patriarch navigate being disconnected from a link with the temporal élite and the loss of legitimation in Mesopotamian society which this entailed? In the longer term, this led to the geographical retreat to northern Mesopotamia and disintegration of the East Syriac presence south of Mosul. In the shorter term, this weakened the ability of church leaders to present a broader vision of scope for the East Syriac community's involvement and a *de facto* renunciation of their position in the ostensibly plural societies of West Asia. The loss of Christian presence to Baghdad was perhaps not necessarily viewed as, or leading to, the likely end of the East Syriac relationship with the state in this era. However, it was an inhibiting factor to the continued status of the Christians viewed as an essential part of Mesopotamian society, and lowered the confidence of the community in its leadership.

Outside of the level of societal stability and security which the temporal power could provide, the community was largely reliant on the protection offered by

Ecclesiology and ecclesial organisation 187

the ecclesiastical organisation and its patronage networks. If these networks were disrupted or suspended, self-reliance on a communal wide scale became of key significance for the functioning of ordinary life. With the Church of the East largely unable to call on the support of the coercive or restricting power of the state following the end of the Mongol empires from the 1330s and until the establishment of Ottoman hegemony, their position was precarious. The movement of the patriarchs away from Baghdad was, perhaps, also a policy of following their communities into an exile from the temporal order. Without a sustainable and active participation at the elite level of the state, there was less need or benefit in retaining their presence to the city. This also signalled a loss of a cosmopolitanism to the Church of the East and, for the future, was a challenge to the reintegration and re-creation of intra-societal networks: day-to-day interactions and successful engagements with the authorities taking time to reform.

The establishment of a Latin diocese for Baghdad in 1632 probably aided the East Syriac restoration to the city and from contemporary observers it appears there was an East Syriac community of about 500 people in the early seventeenth century (Wilmshurst 2000, 185–6). An East Syriac group sympathetic to union with the Holy See seems likely to have appeared by the late seventeenth century. We can note, for example, that the Amidite line patriarch Joseph III (b. ? d. 1757) was from Baghdad (Wilmshurst 2000, 186).

The Archdiocese of Baghdad is of great heritage in the Chaldean ecclesial structure. It appears the archdiocese was founded in conjunction with Yohannan Sulaqa's consecration to the patriarchate in 1553. At that time, it was the titular see 'of Babylon'. The formation of the Archdiocese of Baghdad took place simultaneously, and was united with the patriarch's jurisdiction despite his residence in the Mosul region. This is suggestive of the continued memory of Baghdad's former status as one of the centres of East Syriac religious life and a nexus of church-state relations. Nonetheless, the see of Baghdad only began to be permanently and physically occupied when it was given over to an auxiliary bishop in 1938, Souleyman Kutchouck Ousta (1938–1939), from which time one or more auxiliaries have been associated with the city.

From the 1950s onward, there was a substantial increase in the number of churches to cope with the growing community. Until the First World War, there were only two churches in the city for c. 7,000 Chaldeans but, by the end of the twentieth century, there were twenty-one parishes serving a population of possibly as many as 300,000 Chaldeans (Khayyath 1896, 433; Wilmshurst 2000, 186; Roberson CSP 2010, 4). This movement of population was tied into the twentieth-century urbanisation of Iraq and the broad Chaldean shift to cities. This was a significant change when we recall for most of the period c. 1550–1915 Chaldean ecclesiology and organisation had, notwithstanding the communities in Kirkuk and Mosul, been built around rural village and small town life in northern Iraq.

With the reconstruction of churches on a large scale, for the first time in nearly 1,000 years the Chaldeans came particularly to coagulate around the area of Dora. There were also churches spread across the centre of the city. Combined with St Peter's Seminary, various religious foundations, schools and St Raphael's

188 *Ecclesiology and ecclesial organisation*

Hospital, the Chaldeans were integrated in all levels of Baghdadi cultural and social life, and were by far the strongest in terms of influence on city life among the non-Muslim populations especially following the departure of Iraqi Jews in the 1940s.

The work of the clergy in this context was aided by Chaldean cultural engagement throughout Baghdadi society, which led to a very strong sense of attachment to the city and the expansion of publications in literature, poetry, ecclesial magazines and journals with much of this led by the laity. Thus, when the Chaldean situation began to decline from the mid-1980s, the sense of loss was significant to the ecclesiological identity of the whole church which had come to rely on the success or failure of the Chaldean presence in Baghdad to produce, lead and maintain the Church throughout the world. At the time when Chaldean cultural and social influence in Iraq was reaching its highest level since the Abbasid era, the population in Iraq began to dissipate, becoming, for the first time since the fourteenth century, an international presence beyond West Asia.

Despite the intensity of fighting during the Iran-Iraq War, the capital was little directly affected even during the so-called War of the Cities aerial bombing campaign. Nonetheless, the era was one in which the intensification of identity also took place, along with a popular fear of the implications of the Islamic Revolutionary government, upon the non-Muslim population were it to win the war. Despite the departure of some Chaldeans from Baghdad during the 1980s to avoid conscription or the effects of the war, the overwhelming majority remained. The final decline of the Baghdadi population began only as a result of sanctions post-1991. The clergy of the Archdiocese had limited practical means with which to strengthen the Chaldean population beyond their attachment to Iraq and the gradual growth of hope for a better future. However, it was only from 2003 that churches began to close in the face of violence. In the context of the persecution, which swiftly followed the invasion of March 2003, we can note the population's dissipation and the inability, due to violence and loss of economic opportunity, to remain in the city. This is most strikingly brought to light in the decline of the number of baptisms, as can be seen in Graphs 5.8 and 5.9.[35]

As of 2013, the level of decline appeared to have plateaued at least for a time. Those who remained were the poor, the disabled or the very determined. In speaking with clergy in 2014, who were previously resident in Baghdad, the sense of attachment to the city remained extremely strong, despite their difficult situation. This stemmed from Chaldean association with the city in the twentieth century, and awareness of an East Syriac presence to Baghdad from its foundation under the Abbasids.

Furthermore, there is a sense of injustice extending to the contributions which Iraqi Christians have made to the development of Baghdad and their subsequent rejection by the wider population. A sense pervades that Chaldeans should have earned their right to live in the capital and have fulfilled a debt to society and/or completed obligations which even the most biased of Islamists should see as granting them leave to remain in the city.

In terms of comparative examples for the twenty-first century situation in Baghdad, we might look back to Tamerlane's invasion of 1401 to see similar levels

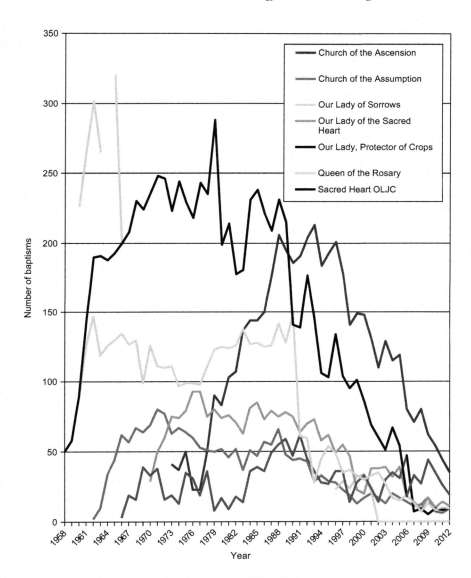

Graph 5.8 Baptisms Baghdad parish group A 1958–2012
Source: *Baghdad Archdiocesan records*

of destruction. If in the twenty-first century this is not affected in such a directly destructive manner, more recent events still have had the same long-term impact upon East Syriac Christians: departure. Possibly a better comparison is the situation for the East Syriac communities in China from the eleventh century, where under

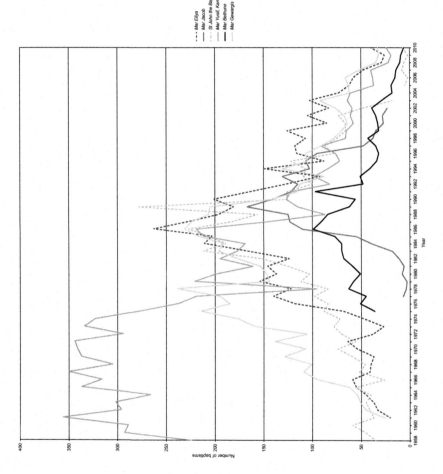

Graph 5.9 Baptisms Baghdad parish group B 1958–2012

Source: *Baghdad Archdiocesan records*

Ecclesiology and ecclesial organisation 191

the Song, Yuan and Ming dynasties, anti-Christian campaigns of some violence along with legal repression and the ambivalence of the population at large contributed to the gradual decline of the East Syriac community (Yuanyan 2013, 292).

Ecclesial organisation in Baghdad

As of October 2013, the vast majority of parishes remained open in Baghdad, with only the church of St Joseph the Worker having closed. The parish baptismal records largely follow the wider trends of Chaldean life and, as the northern dioceses declined in population, so Baghdad expanded particularly from the 1950s to 1970s.

Table 5.12 and Graphs 5.8 and 5.9 indicate that the patriarchal cathedral of Our Lady of Sorrows enjoyed pre-eminence in the city prior to the 1960s. From this time, there was a gradual movement to other parishes as they were established, and the population dispersed to those churches nearest their homes. Nevertheless, Mar Yusif, in the Karrada area, retained a substantial level of support and, even as of 2013, a large proportion of baptisms still took place in the Cathedral.

If we compare information from those churches in use prior to 1958, in Table 5.12, we see that although Our Lady of Sorrows exceeded all other churches by far, Mar Yusif, Karrada saw an increase in baptisms at a proportionately greater rate in the 1950s.[36] Such a change of population focus to Mar Yusif is likely due to the influx of Chaldeans in this era: new church construction permitted community members to choose a parish based on their preferences in priest, liturgical expression or parochial social and cultural activities.

As might be expected, the pattern of baptisms largely follows events in Iraqi society: there was a trend for significant growth at least from 1958 with an equally significant decline from the 1990s. Subsequently, the decline of parish life, especially from 2003, was strongly indicative of Chaldean migration. (Cf Table 5.13)

Baghdad and East Syriac ecclesiology

The consolidation of the patriarchal see in Baghdad in the eighth century, along with the foundation of the new Abbasid capital, was an attempt by patriarch

Table 5.12 Baptisms in Chaldean parishes in use prior to 1958 – Archdiocese of Baghdad

Year	Our Lady of Sorrows	Our Lady of the Rosary	Mar Yusif (Karrada)
1900–1910	2,172	0	8
1911–1920	1,190	0	26
1921–1930	3,673	51	85
1931–1940	4,112	103	282
1941–1950	5,973	Not possible to read figure	282
1951–1960	9,558	303	1,720
Totals	27,398	>469	2,306

Source: *Baghdad Archdiocesan records*

192 *Ecclesiology and ecclesial organisation*

Table 5.13 Chaldean population, Archdiocese
of Baghdad, 1980–2012

Year	Number of persons
1980	250,000
1990	481,000
1999	151,000
2000	151,000
2001	155,000
2002	145,000
2003	140,000
2004	130,000
2006	145,000
2007	135,000
2012	150,000

Source: *AP*

Timothy I to deliberately link the two institutions – Caliph and Patriarch – and to emphasise a paradigm of the normative nature of an East Syriac presence to the centre of temporal power.[37] Through the knowledge of the former 'golden' era of the East Syriac presence to Baghdad under Timothy's direction, it seems likely that this model of proximity to the temporal élite was present in the mind of Joseph VII Ghanima when he confirmed the transfer of the Chaldean patriarchate from Mosul to Baghdad in 1950.

In both instances, the patriarch's moving to the centre of political power demonstrated awareness of his status as the leader of a community which was integral to the development of Mesopotamia-Iraq. To most effectively represent its interests necessitated a substantial official presence to the city. In having lost, or been uncertain of, a place in new societies – whether Umayyad, Abbasid, Mongol or under the Iraqi monarchy – residence in the centre of political power permitted opportunities to redevelop patronage networks and engage with the ruling elites.

Through engaging with the elites, the patriarch and, by extension, the hierarchy, were in a better position to consolidate control over the East Syriac community. This was of greater importance in the post-Sasanian era. As the East Syriac community formed a large proportion of Mesopotamian society, it was necessary to re-legitimate the patriarch's ecclesial authority through the Abbasid caliphs as the Shah ratified ecclesiastical decisions during Sasanian rule (cf. Wood 2013, 226–7). This type of relationship likely still played a role in the Iraqi monarchist era because the Chaldean patriarch emerged as the *de facto* leader of all Iraqi Christians. This status was consolidated by the departure of the Church of the East's patriarch, Mar Shimun XXIII, in 1933. Through cultivating a relationship with the monarchy, an amelioration of the Christians' situation was possible. Under Patriarch Yusif VII Ghanima, the church building programme was developed with the monarchy's approval.

Moving the patriarchate also facilitated the patriarch's attempts to shape the contemporary East Syriac ecclesiological model through his proximity to a large proportion of his community. This was significant for influencing how the East Syriac community over six decades (1950s–2010s) and six hundred years (eighth to fourteenth centuries) would view the significance of Baghdad, and as to why East Syriac communities chose to remain in the city even throughout persecution.

To conclude, I can further suggest that the entry into Baghdad for Ghanima was an attempt at a deliberate break with a pre-existing vision of Chaldean ecclesiology chiefly formed through residence in northern Iraq. Through situating the church geographically in central Iraq, Ghanima was reacting to the political changes in the state and wider Middle East which necessitated that Christians become increasingly urbanised and in proximity to the political power of the day to ensure the welfare of the community. Were there any doubts to the wisdom of such a policy, Ghanima was in a position to defer to the precedent which Timothy I had established and was practically supported by the majority of Chaldeans in Iraq becoming resident to Baghdad.

Conclusion: Archdiocese of Baghdad

The displacement of the Chaldeans from Baghdad since 2003 has historical precedent in the East Syriac context. However, on more than one occasion, the community has been revivified to the centre of temporal power in Mesopotamia-Iraq. Therefore, events since 2003 should not necessarily imply that a long-term recovery of the community to the city is impossible. Nevertheless, that the recovery previously took nearly 600 years indicates a contemporary recovery would appear as only a hope at this time. How the break between the main body of the community, dispersed internationally, and the patriarch still resident in Baghdad can be reconciled could follow the precedent for the substantial distance from those who were resident in China during the Middle Ages. Yet, with the near destruction of the community to Baghdad and the persistent undermining of those who remain, what can be done? Ecclesiological imperatives to retain the Baghdadi Chaldean presence may seem of little import when the safety of the community as a whole people is threatened by violence. Nonetheless, the physical environment, in which a church incarnates its presence, community and culture does matter. The East Syriac community has been substantially linked with the sites of Seleucia-Cteisphon and Baghdad since the fifth century. The core of Chaldean ecclesiological identity would seem to be unsustainable if it loses its presence to the city. Without a sufficient critical mass of community members to represent the church, the Chaldeans are no longer able to act as *the* Christian difference in Baghdad and the *de facto* national church of Iraq, whereas, for the period 1921–2013, proximity to the leadership of the Iraqi state permitted the development and maintenance of patronage relationships with the political élite and popular representation of the Chaldean community to Baghdadi society.

The decline of a Baghdadi Chaldean presence from 2003 and the ethnic cleansing of the community in Mosul in 2014 has denuded the Chaldeans of essential aspects of their identity. These events have also caused a necessary readjustment of expectation to what the church means to Iraqi society and as to how the

194 *Ecclesiology and ecclesial organisation*

Chaldean patriarch can, though still resident in Baghdad, administer the community and retain its ecclesial unity in an international and globalised context. By way of comparison: for Timothy I, his leadership of the East Syriac community was at least over contiguous territories – one could theoretically walk from Baghdad to Khan Balik – and this entailed also a varied if contiguous spread of shared ecclesial culture.

For Louis I Raphael Sako, the geographical spread of the contemporary Chaldean community and its socio-economic diversity inhibit annunciating a unified and easily shared ecclesial culture. Sako is obliged to maintain a Chaldean ecclesiology which meets the distinctive needs and expectations of Chaldeans from San Diego to Aleppo, whilst also sustaining an East Syriac ecclesial identity which draws on its origins and continued incarnation in the Mesopotamian-Iraqi environment.

Archdiocese of Mosul

The significance of Mosul and the Nineveh plain region to the East Syriac community can hardly be overstated. For much of the period 1553–1950, the Nineveh plain was the principal focus of Chaldean life and, even following the patriarchate's transferral to Baghdad in 1950, it retained its place as a heartland of religious activity. The position of the Archbishop of Mosul was the second most important in Iraq after the patriarch, and the city was host to the Chaldean seminary of St Peter and the joint Chaldean-Syrian Catholic seminary of St John. Nonetheless, Mosul was not always a site of fixed allegiance to the East Syriac tradition, with the West Syriac community also having a strong presence into the modern era.

Mosul is situated close to the Tigris, and the surrounding region's suitability for agriculture have made it a popular area for settlement since at least the first millennium BC.[38] The Arab armies occupied the city in the 640s, and Islam emerged as the politically and socially dominant paradigm. Societal plurality was present to Mosul, but the prominence of the Arab Sunni community in culture and political life was challenging for Christians and a significant minority of Jewish residents. From the Medieval era until the rise of Da'esh, Christians have formed the largest non-Muslim community in the city. They have been proportionately influential in often high-ranking positions in civil services and private business.

This relative influence has also seen them, at times, become a particular target of Muslim governors and strongly impacted day-to-day Christian life. For example: an Islamisation of the city and surrounding area were heavily imposed in the 1170s during the governance of Nur al-Din, prince of the Zankid dynasty, which then ruled much of Syria and northern Mesopotamia (Tabbaa 2002, 340–2). Such events inhibited the sustainment of Christian identity especially when Christian properties were confiscated and given over to use by Muslims.

Another layer complicating Christian-Muslim communal relations were the extended periods of semi-autonomous rule which Mosul experienced apart from the contemporary governing powers in Mesopotamia. For most of the period of the sixteenth to early nineteenth centuries, prominent local families were responsible for the city's administration and not Ottoman leaders. I suggest, without the integration of Mosul into wider Ottoman society and the benefits which an overarching government offered, the Christian population may have struggled to solidly ground themselves in this environment or sustain a flourishing ecclesial life. It may only be coincidental, but it is interesting to note that the consolidation of the Chaldean patriarchal lineage took place contemporaneously with the extension of centralised Ottoman governance to Mosul in 1834. The stabilisation of governance in the civil realm offered an environment conducive to stabilisation in the ecclesial realm.

Christianity was present to the city by the start of the second century, and by the sixth century Mosul appears to have become a centre for monastic activity (Honigmann, Bosworth, and Sluglett 1991). Its significance as a site for monastic life was reinforced in the middle of the seventh century, when the noted theologian and spiritual writer Isaac was appointed bishop of Nineveh.[39]

It appears the diocese continued in to the ninth century, with Mosul itself gaining importance as the residence of the metropolitans of the ecclesiastical province of Adiabene from the ninth to twelfth centuries (Wilmshurst 2000, 191). Since the twelfth century, only Da'esh's invasion has seen the end of an uninterrupted East Syriac episcopal presence in some form. However, the presence of East Syriac bishops to the city cannot be directly confirmed in the fourteenth and fifteenth centuries, but given surrounding activity, such as Patriarch Denha II's residence in Karamles in the mid-fourteenth century and known scribal activity in manuscript production, it seems likely a bishop was present to the city (Wilmshurst 2000, 207–8).

With regards to the nomenclature of ecclesiastical structures in and around Mosul, it is possible that the Church of the East's 'diocese of Mosul' was never formally created. Instead, with the loss in size of the Church's jurisdiction and population, the diocese of 'Nineveh' changed in status and name to that of 'Mosul' which reflected the new reality and the relative extent of jurisdictional claims of the church in the region. In the context of the decline of Mesopotamian East Syriac ecclesiastical organisation in the fourteenth century, we may understand why such *de facto* changes were incorporated into diocesan structures.

Mosul's ecclesiastical structures became a focus of competition from the mid-fifteenth century. The diocese became the responsibility of the *Natar Kursya* and, as such, was closely linked to the patriarchal office (cf. Wilmshurst 2000, 193–6). The office of bishop of Mosul became of even greater significance during the three centuries between the formation of the Chaldean East Syriac faction under Yohannan Sulaqa in the 1550s and the unification of East Syriac factions around Yohannan Hormizd as Chaldean patriarch in the 1830s. Occupation of the see and the affiliation of its inhabitants were markers of the legitimate patriarchal successor's status in the East Syriac community. Latin missionaries also regarded Mosul as highly significant with the diocese the chief 'prize' in East Syriac ecclesiastical organisation.

Even from the presence of Latin missionaries to the city from the 1630s, it took some time before the city itself was brought entirely into affiliation with the Chaldean East Syriac faction. The start of the Chaldean movement in Mosul came via the interest of one 'Heder, son of Maqdassi Hormizd'. He had likely encountered Capuchin missionaries, who had a mission station in the city from 1636–1724 (Fiey OP 1959, 56).

196 *Ecclesiology and ecclesial organisation*

The local East Syriac communities around the city were all in union with the Holy See by the end of the eighteenth century. However, it was only with the resolution of the competition for patriarchal leadership between the legitimist and Josephite factions in the nineteenth century that the Chaldeans began to make inroads among the East Syriacs of Mosul itself (Wilmshurst 2000, 190). In a move which aimed at the consolidation of the Chaldean presence in central Mesopotamia, Baghdad's ecclesial structures were absorbed into those of Mosul diocese from 1863 (Wilmshurst 2000, 199). However, on a day-to-day basis, the two zones within the 'patriarchal archdiocese' were administered separately. Given the relatively small size of the Baghdadi Chaldean community at that time, this was a pragmatic change. It brought Chaldeans in Baghdad into a more normal ecclesial arrangement than which had existed previously whereby they did not have formal oversight from an auxiliary bishop. Instead, those in Baghdad were reliant on priests acting as patriarchal administrators.

In the broader Mesopotamian context, Mosul lost its status as a site of economic importance when the Suez Canal opened in 1869 and as Basra was developed into a modern maritime hub (Honigmann, Bosworth, and Sluglett 1991). Previously, Mosul had been a key stop on the trade routes across Syria and Mesopotamia. However, the city retained its strategic significance to the Ottomans due to its position on the Tigris.

For the Chaldeans, ecclesial activity was greatly advanced in the latter half of the nineteenth century, during which time resident Dominican missionaries built substantial momentum in Christian education, Syriac and Arabic publishing and vocational formation. The importance of the Dominican Press at Mosul should not be underestimated (Coakley and Taylor 2009, 1). Printing was undertaken from 1856 and supported the incarnation of Eastern Catholic identity and ecclesiology, and assisted in the revivification of the Syriac language. In this context. it may have been the case that the Dominicans were cognisant of the wider experience of Christians in the Middle East, particularly the Levant and their role in the development of modern Arabic literary revival and, in a local context, the work of Lazarist missionaries among the Syriac Christians of Persia (Coakley 2013).

The Dominicans' efforts ensured that the Christian communities gained an enviable position in local society. The Dominican presence also helped prevent the emergence of a formal schism between the Holy See and Joseph VI Audo in the 1870s. We can note then the modern Chaldean identity was facilitated at this nexus of Ottoman civil governance, the Chaldean patriarchal headquarters and Dominican ecclesiological direction.

In the first half of the twentieth century, Christian life in Mosul was challenged by the often less than hospitable nature of local Sunni administrators, and the controversy as to the lawful governing power: whether the Republic of Turkey or the Kingdom of Iraq after the First World War (Honigmann, Bosworth, and Sluglett 1991). After the overthrow of the monarchy in 1958, Chaldean communal life appeared initially uncertain. The patriarchate having been moved to Baghdad in 1950 perhaps caused some degree of questioning of identity and potential for maintaining the Chaldean community in the longer term. Modern Chaldean identity and connections to Mosul, whilst crucial even after 1950, were gradually weakened with the movement of the patriarchate to Baghdad. The élite factions of the modern state of Iraq and the Chaldean Church came to fruition in general through their presence in the capital, with Mosul missing out on the flourishing of Chaldean life which was so strongly developed in Baghdad.

The Chaldean situation was compounded in the early 1960s, when Mosul appeared to be emerging as a centre of activity for Islamist organisations such as the Muslim Brotherhood and Iraqi Islamic Party (Frantzmann 2016, 12). The establishment of Baathist rule saw such groups' influence inhibited with the emphasis on the lay-state paradigm. It is suggested by some authors that the period c. 1960–1990 was an era of relatively relaxed attitudes towards social interaction and communal relations (Al Aqeedi 2016, 3). This was perhaps related to the economic development of the city during the oil boom and a decline in interest in Islamism. From 1993, this outlook shifted strongly with the introduction of Saddam Hussein's 'Faith Campaign', which sought to revivify traditionalist Islamic identity and what were perceived as Islamic virtues in educational institutions and wider society (Al Aqeedi 2016, 3). It appears that the pressure of operating in a lay-state environment and the emergence of a revivified Islamist paradigm may have taken its toll from even earlier than 1993: the joint Syrian-Chaldean Catholic seminary of St John was closed in 1985 (cf. Richard OP 2001, 245).

Such a set of circumstances was further complicated by the strength of the Kurds, the Iraqi army campaigns in opposition to their presence and, from the 1990s, by the Kurdish capability to project influence over the territory in and around Mosul. The parishes of the contemporary diocese are no stranger to this. The churches in Telkef and Karamles are under KRG authority, for example, whereas the other parishes remained under ICG control.

Ecclesial organisation in Mosul Archdiocese

Since 2003, the archdiocese has epitomised the Iraqi Christian decline. (See Table 5.14) To June 2014, the situation in Mosul itself was particularly challenging,

Table 5.14 Chaldean population, Diocese of Mosul, 1969–2013

Year	Population
1969	17,000
1980	18,500
1990	19,850
1999	20,000
2000	20,000
2001	20,500
2002	21,105
2003	50,000
2004	20,600
2009	16,815
2013	14,100

Source: *AP*

198 *Ecclesiology and ecclesial organisation*

with Christian life conducted in the context of rigorous expressions of Sunni law and culture. The resilience of the Chaldeans to remain was deliberately weakened through violent persecution of a type not found in any other city of Iraq, apart from Baghdad. Between 2003 and 2014, this was evidenced most strongly in the martyrdom of Archbishop Paulos Faraj Raho and Fr Ragheed Ganni and his sub-deacons. From 2014, the entire character of Mosul has changed following Da'esh's occupation, and the city has effectively become the terrorist group's chief city in Iraq. At the time of writing, in early 2017, ongoing efforts are being made to liberate Mosul. However, even if this is successful, it is no guarantee that Christians would be inclined to return. Trust in the Iraqi state or KRG to protect Christians, along with alterations in culture and identity, all impede a desire to return, as do the physical and psychological traumas which ethnic cleansing has caused among the Christian population.

As a result of the consistently difficult situation, it is fortunate to have any research data from Mosul. The earliest baptismal figures for the Archdiocese come from 1870 in the town of Telkef, which has held a pre-eminent position in Chaldean life. The lack of data from Mosul city owes to the relative youth of some of the parishes – as Chaldean institutions – due to the long-term dominance of the Church of the East until the nineteenth century.

Mosul (city)

As of 1959, the following Chaldean churches were in use in the city:
Mar Isha'ya
Mar Shemon as-Safa (St Peter the Apostle)
Mar Gewargis
Mar Meskinta the Martyr (Chaldean cathedral and patriarchal seat to 1950)
Mar Pethyon
Mar Yusif
Umm al Ma'una (Our Lady of Perpetual Succour)
The convent church associated with the Dominican religious.[40]

As of 2013:
Mar Ishya
Mar Meskinta the Martyr
Umm al Ma'una
Al-Tahira
Cathedral of Mar Polos
Mar Ephrem (closed and severely damaged)
Holy Ghost (closed)
Mart Mariam (closed).[41]

As is suggested by the number of baptisms portrayed in Graph 5.10, the parishes in Mosul appear to have had generally stable populations until the invasion of 2003, from which time they trailed off to a subsistence level. It is notable that even

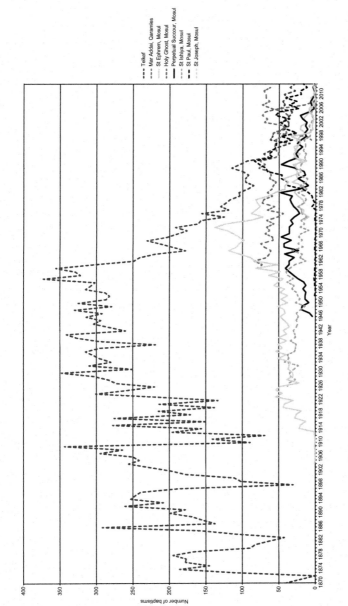

Graph 5.10 Baptisms – Archdiocese of Mosul, 1870–October 2013

Source: *Mosul Diocesan records*

200 *Ecclesiology and ecclesial organisation*

at times when population expansion might have been expected, it was not uniform across the city with, for example, Mar Ephrem, Mar Yusif and Mar Ishiya's baptismal rates declining after the Gulf War and those of Perpetual Succour and Mar Polos increasing. This is a state of affairs for which an explanation is not readily forthcoming as direct research could not be carried out to the city. It is possible, as Perpetual Succour was a very well-known centre of Chaldean activity and Mar Polos is the archdiocesan cathedral, that available resources were especially concentrated in these parishes.

Holy Ghost parish

The growth and decline of Holy Ghost parish from 1997 to 2008 was, largely, due to the leadership of some of the clergy including Fr Ragheed Ganni. His martyrdom in 2008 marked the end of the use of the church and, it appears in the following years, the departure from Mosul by a substantial proportion of the then remaining Chaldean population. As available information about Fr Ragheed and his parish are more well developed than any other, his experience and the church of the Holy Ghost will be used as a case study for the Chaldean community in Mosul.

The first indication of a violent change in circumstances for the native Christians of Mosul was in August and December 2004, when the cathedral of Mar Polos and the bishop's residence were attacked.[42] The wider context for Moslawi Chaldeans was the city's rise to prominence as the main hub for the organisation of Baathist and Islamist anti-Coalition forces following the March 2003 invasion. Mosul's Sunni Arab character coalesced with these two groupings and one fed off the other, creating an environment in which the Islamists could be relied on as the 'muscle' and the Baathist element as the 'brains'. That both were willing to work together was indicative of the loss of secularist mentality among the Baathists during Hussein's final years in power. This was a context in which party stalwarts such as Tariq Aziz could not comfortably have mixed.

The pressure on the Christian communities of Mosul became increasingly intense. The campaign against Fr Ragheed and his parish was pursued in a consistently combative manner, suggesting that his leadership qualities and charisma were acknowledged as a threat and obstacle to advancing an Islamist paradigm. Yet even in a context where the payment of *jizya* was established, there continued efforts to see the violent diminution of the Christians and the increasing ambivalence of the Sunni population to the Christians' fate. Facing persecution from a section of the population – even violent attacks – is in some respects incomparable with the withdrawal of normal social interaction by neighbours and the demonisation of your community on an ideological basis. Such circumstances weaken social bonds to the point where violence against you is regarded as a normative means for conducting social relations and the resolution of difference.

In August 2004, the church of the Holy Ghost was seriously damaged by terrorists to the extent that it had to be closed. It was hoped that it would be possible to repair the church and return it to full use. However, at the time at which parish activity was returning to a more normal state in 2006, it faced four attacks during September and October, with Mass being celebrated in the basement under police protection. After an attack in September 2006, one community member stated: 'Our faith is a challenge to violence. The militias fear us because our faith is stronger than their bullets' (*Asianews.It* 2006a). Such a response was characteristic of a redemptive approach to the suffering which they experienced. The Chaldeans were in a position to offer their spiritual action with a Faith that could overcome the world (1 John 5:4–5). Moreover, they exhibited, in a very strong way, the characterisation of martyrs. They witnessed to their Faith – and bravery – to those who sought their removal.

October 2006 also saw a particularly distressing incident, which brought into focus the difficulties facing priests: Fr Polos Eskander of the Syriac Orthodox Church was kidnapped and beheaded in Mosul. The manner of his death became an increasingly popular method of murder used by the Islamist forces. It was a brutal manifestation of the policy which the Islamists would use to destroy the community's leaders in highly publicised incidents. This ensured that any feelings of security were entirely destroyed among the Christian population. Another method was to weaken the institutions which supported the churches in their contributions to Moslawi society, and to deny the Christians opportunity for presenting the significance of their presence to wider society. The Catholic charity 'Caritas Mosul' was forced to close in November 2006 following demands for the payment of protection money with the implication that refusal would result in violence. Despite the dedication of ninety percent of the charity's work to Muslims in poverty, Caritas faced little alternative option but to suspend its work indefinitely (*Asianews.It* 2006b).

The situation continued to be tense into the next year. On Palm Sunday 2007, a police station near to Holy Ghost church was attacked and shots could be heard by those inside the church. Fr Ragheed described the situation: 'At this point we felt like Jesus when he entered Jerusalem knowing that the Cross would be the consequence of His love for man . . . So we offered our own suffering as a token of love for Jesus' (*Asianews.It* 2007). Meeting persecution in this way was one of the few means by which the Chaldeans could still positively respond to their situation. Entering into the Passion of Christ and sharing in this was a mentality which could strengthen the Chaldeans spiritually, if not lead to a temporal resolution of their situation. Union with Christ was that element of their lives which the faithful could not be denied by their attackers and permitted them to enter into the suffering of Christ in a very particular and real manner.

The perceived necessity to expedite Mosul's transformation into a Sunni enclave through territorial expansion and the expulsion of supposedly alien persons also underpinned efforts to weaken the Christian presence. As the lay and religious elements of being a Chaldean are closely linked, it was not the case that simply by hiding their religious activities or closing all the churches the Chaldeans could maintain their livelihoods in the city. The option with which they were being presented was to leave, or remain and suffer until Islamists effaced the Christian ethos, culture, people and material heritage of the city.[43]

202 *Ecclesiology and ecclesial organisation*

Conclusion: Mosul (city)

In the aftermath of the deaths of Fr Ragheed and Archbishop Raho, attacks on churches and harassment, assaults, kidnappings and murders of community members increased in number. The deterioration in the quality of life led only the very resilient to remain. If your culture and presence is being effaced and less than fifty miles away is relative security in the Kurdish administered provinces, where a Chaldean ecclesial culture in which you can take a full part is being developed, what will you do? What is to keep you in Mosul other than a very strong ideological belief in the necessity of staying and heroic fortitude?

Such types of persecution of Christians are far from without precedent in Sunni contexts. Muslim violence against Christians, with the purpose of eradicating their presence, was a feature of Tamerlane's campaigns, the rule of some Abbasid and Mongol leaders and was exemplified in the 1915–1918 massacres. This suggests that violent methods for expansion in territory and the alteration of culture to a Sunni paradigm are effective – the loss of an East Syriac presence in eastern Asia Minor is the clearest testimony. Whether Mosul's Islamists in 2003 were fully cognisant of these precedents and their significance to the Chaldeans is not known, but the manifestation of violence to rub away an irritation to the sacred space in which Sunni culture could be enforced was the practical outcome of their actions and in accord with these historical attempts to deny a Christian difference in Mesopotamian-Iraqi societies.

The deaths of Raho and Ganni should have been more concerning to external and interested powers to Iraq. The lack of response or ambivalence to their fates seemingly made their deaths a justifiable aspect of the new Iraq. Murdering Chaldean leaders brutalised the Church as a whole and denigrated the ecclesial offices, archdiocese and parish which the two men represented.

Telkef

Telkef may be a relatively young East Syriac community to the Nineveh plain. The town's foundation perhaps took place only in the late fourteenth or early fifteenth century. Its establishment was likely derived from the trend of patriarchs from Yahballah III onward to reside in northern Mesopotamia and the consolidation of the East Syriac communities in the region (cf. Wilmshurst 2000, 205). In a Chaldean context, the town had its status inflated to that of a diocese by Sulaqite patriarch Abdisho IV in 1562. He compiled a list of East Syriac sees supposedly loyal to him in an attempt to impress the Holy See of the vitality of his ecclesial organisation (Fiey OP 1965b, II:359). It seems unlikely Telkef held Chaldean diocesan status at that time in actual fact, but perhaps Abdisho named a cleric as titular bishop of the town. Chaldean sympathies seem to have stuck. Telkef became the first Chaldean majority East Syriac community in the Nineveh region, with several Chaldean patriarchs subsequently originating from the town. Joseph II of the Amidite line, for example, was born there in 1667, and a Chaldean inclined group of clergy signed a document there which rejected their

Ecclesiology and ecclesial organisation 203

supposed 'Nestorian' errors in 1719, presumably with the intention of impressing local Latin missionaries of their desire for recognition in the Chaldean community (Wilmshurst 2000, 224–5; cf. Fiey OP 1965b, II:360.) Certainly, we can recognise Telkef's significance to the Chaldeans in the nineteenth century, with many of its young men entering the monastic life or training as priests (Wilmshurst 2000, 223, 226). The town's position between Mosul and Rabban Hormizd was a convenient 'halfway point' between two centres of ecclesial life and became a centre of Chaldean development.

The significance of the town to the Chaldeans in the early twentieth century was seen when major reconstruction work started on the church of Mar Kyriakos. When completed, in 1931, it was one of the largest churches in Iraq at that time (Fiey OP 1965b, II:367). The necessity for expanding church facilities came from a desire to reinforce Chaldean identity, to further incarnate the Chaldean presence in Telkef and to meet the needs of the population which was steadily expanding.

A striking feature of the baptismal data from Telkef is the inconsistency of the number of baptisms for much of the era 1870–1940, even if the growth of the community is clear in general terms with it peaking by the 1950s. This is partly tied to the violence which marred life during the era: direct persecution, wars and their knock-on effects. It seems Telkef was also affected by the agricultural economy around which so much of life in Mesopotamia-Iraq revolved prior to modern urbanisation. We do well to recall the significance of the conduct of day-to-day life when affected by the success or failure of crops each year, with subsequent knock-on effects on the number of children born. That being said, the Chaldeans, of all the Christians in Iraq, were in the most stable position with regards to ecclesial structures during the early twentieth century. This suggests why Telkef was expanding at such a rate in the years prior to the First World War. This then may be a cause for the relatively rapid restoration of the level of population, even during the difficult years of Iraqi *risorgiomento* which the new state underwent in the 1920s and 1930s. By contrast, the decline of the Telkef parish has been far less volatile, with the 1960s signalling a rapid change with only the Iran-Iraq War era indicating something of a revival and this only transitory. In 1957, there were 7,307 inhabitants, of which the majority were Chaldean. Fiey noted that there were 900 Chaldean families (c. 3,600 people) in the town in 1961 (Fiey OP 1965b, II:355 n. 1). This was, however, a decline from the population size at the end of the Ottoman era (8,000 Chaldeans in 1913), reflecting migration to Mosul and further afield (Wilmshurst 2000, 199). A demographic change in this instance was driven by the free choice of the community to seek economic opportunities and not a reactionary policy driven by conflict or persecution. Telkef's baptismal rate began to rapidly decline from the start of the community-wide transfer of population to central and southern Iraqi cities in the 1960s.

Karamles[44]

Data is not available for Karamles prior to the 1960s, so it is difficult to determine if its population size was affected in the same way as Telkef. However,

204 *Ecclesiology and ecclesial organisation*

given it retained a relatively stable baptismal rate to the 1990s, I suggest the population of Karamles had less of a tradition of migration among its community. Telkef was known locally for the entrepreneurial nature of its community and propensity for migration. For example: the substantial control of riverboat transport services in central and southern Iraq by former residents of the town since the nineteenth century.

Established at least by 562, Karamles is of some significance as one of the earliest known East Syriac communities in the Nineveh plain (Fiey OP 1965b, II:401). The town was brought to prominence during the leadership of Patriarch Denha II (1336–1381), who moved the patriarchal see there from Baghdad. It is possible that Denha was himself consecrated patriarch in the town (cf. Wilmshurst 2000, 184). Whatever position Karamles may have held in the East Syriac ecclesiastical order in the fourteenth century, its relegation from extant ecclesial records until the 1560s is suggestive of a loss of significance. It also reflects the East Syriac community's general decline in the fifteenth century. The community re-emerged in the written record from the 1720s, when manuscripts were produced for the Chaldean community (Wilmshurst 2000, 219).

The mid-eighteenth century onward saw a consolidation of the Latin and Chaldean presence to the town. A Dominican missionary, P. Lanza OP, arrived in Karamles in 1765 and the first possibly explicitly 'Catholic' church in Mesopotamia – St Barbara's – dates from that time (Fiey OP 1965b, II:405). As of 2013, the church of St Barbara was no longer used except as a shrine, where local people hold a strong devotion to the martyr. The chief Chaldean church is that of St Addai, which was built in 1963. Notwithstanding its desecration by Da'esh from 2014 to 2016, the church still stands.[45]

As of 2013, Karamles was a recognisably Chaldean-dominated settlement, and from 2003 did not face overt difficulties in sustaining a Chaldean culture. Departing migrants have been replaced by new arrivals, with the town, in fact, growing in size over the ten-year period from approximately 500 families (c. 2,500 people) to 820 families (c. 4,000 people).[46] Karamles' political status was related to its geographical position on the border of KRG and ICG spheres of influence. To June 2014, the town's budget was granted by the ICG governor of Mosul, but allowances were also received from the KRG. The efforts by the Kurds to gain further influence among the Christians came through permitting Syriac to be taught in local schools but also including Kurdish in the curriculum. There was no especial opposition to Kurdish language instruction, and it is entirely pragmatic to take on the language of the dominating temporal power, which is something the East Syriac communities have always done. However, in so doing, the Chaldeans were unsettled because their ultimate political allegiance was theoretically still to the Mosul governorate. This had an Arab Sunni ethos strongly opposed to alternative foci of linguistic, cultural or religious expression.

Without a lasting resolution in political control over the town, Chaldean identity remained in flux – inhibited in adhering to an official allegiance to either the ICG or KRG. This was, and is, a situation far from uncommon in the Chaldean communities across the borders of the Kurdish and Iraqi administered provinces. The situation is similar to that of the East Syriacs, who were resident on the border of empires during periods of Roman-Sasanian conflict and diplomatic intrigue – both empires holding points of attraction for the Christians who could identify with both through culture, religion and language. The Chaldeans of Karamles in 2013, for example, looked to Mosul and Baghdad as historical centres of their religious tradition and yet were separated from them. This separation was similar to Christians who fled theological disagreements in the Roman world and entered the Sasanian Empire. They looked back to Antioch or Nicaea as once great bastions of their religious culture and beliefs, yet found a degree of security for their Christology under the Sasanians in the same way that Christians under KRG administration and influence have gained physical security.

Conclusion: Archdiocese of Mosul

In not having had the opportunity to visit Mosul itself, the portrayal of the Archdiocese is far from complete. However, I have begun to illuminate the reality of East Syriac life for the period 2003–2013. The cleaving of the Christian presence in Mosul was completed by Da'esh's expansion from June 2014. This is an expansion which ended the region's continuous Christian presence for the first time since at least the sixth century.

For the period 2003–2013, the Mosul-Nineveh region was transformed into a society which was incapable of meeting the challenge of incorporating religious difference. Such a set of circumstances reflected both the resilience and weakness of the East Syriac communities: resilience insofar as it took nearly 1,400 years for the East Syriac communal presence to be extinguished and weakness in the realisation that Sunni Islamist ideology, without some acquiescence to difference or sense of restraint, can become a vehicle for violent transformation of society – something which the Chaldeans are unable to oppose. When the assumption of Sunni superiority became actualised through the implementation of *sharia* and encouragement to *jihad* by Da'esh, the Chaldeans of Mosul discovered the Muslim population's ambivalence to their situation was transformed quickly into acceptance of their removal and the re-ordering of the social order.

It will be challenging to recover the Chaldean ecclesial identity which was created and developed in Mosul in its fullness. The city used to be looked to for leadership and vibrant East Syriac culture, now it represents a material Chaldean defeat and withdrawal from Iraqi society. A comprehensive resurrection of Chaldean life to the Nineveh region will be impossible until the defeat of Da'esh. However, this does not mean the community's historical contributions will be extinguished from East Syriac life and ecclesiology. Intangible metaphysical notions of what it means to *be* a Chaldean of Mosul cannot be so easily excised from history as church buildings. St Athanasius of Alexandria, whilst writing during the Arian crisis, referred to the true victory which the faithful could expect over those who had materially occupied ecclesial property:

> May God comfort you. I know moreover that not only this thing saddens you, but also the fact that while others have obtained the churches by violence, you are meanwhile cast out from your places. For they hold the places, but

206 *Ecclesiology and ecclesial organisation*

you the Apostolic Faith. They are, it is true, in the places, but outside of the true Faith; while you are outside the places indeed, but the Faith, within you. Let us consider whether is the greater, the place or the Faith. Clearly the true Faith. Who then has lost more, or who possesses more? He who holds the place, or he who holds the Faith? Good indeed is the place, when the Apostolic Faith is preached there, holy is it if the Holy One dwell there.

(1891, 550–1)

Is such a scenario so alien to those Chaldeans now forced into exile and pushed to the borders of Iraqi society because of their Christianity?

Notes

1 An example has been research conducted on the Carpatho-Rusyn (Ruthenian) migrations from eastern Europe and Ukraine to the US and the affects on their ecclesiology. See, for example, Simon (1993) and Marti (2009).
2 There was also the question of the reliability and provenance of data which I have utilised from the *Annuario Pontifico (AP)* to supplement my own data. As will be seen, I have used the *AP*'s data to provide an indication of population size. This is not without caveats, and these will be discussed. These data were gained from the online database *Catholic Hierarchy* <www.catholic-hierarchy.org/rite/ch.html> and Ronald G. Roberson CSP, 'The Eastern Catholic Churches 2014'. <www.cnewa.org/source-images/Roberson-eastcath-statistics/eastcatholic-stat14.pdf
3 It should be noted that this never occurred during fieldwork in Iraq or Jordan and only in one discussion with a Chaldean community member in London was it evident that the conversation should be ended due to the painful memories and emotional response to which a question gave rise.
4 Adiabene was the fourth province in seniority of the five named 'Mesopotamian provinces' of the Church of the East affirmed at the 410 Synod of Isaac. The others in order of seniority were Bet Huzaye, Nisibis, Perat d'Maisan and Bet Garmai (Wilmshurst 2011, 19–20). Metropolitan rank recognised the holder as the senior bishop within the province. He held oversight of the auxiliary (suffragan) bishops themselves responsible for the province's dioceses.
5 As with Shaqlawa, the village had an East Syriac presence in the fourteenth century and was brought within the Chaldean purview under Yohannan Hormizd in 1779 (Wilmshurst 2000, 168).
6 I am unable to provide greater and more detailed context to the village, as parish records of baptisms and weddings were unavailable for years prior to 1938.
7 I have not been able to gain a clear awareness of the Chaldean population size for that time. Anecdotal suggestions have put the total figure as c. 10,000 Chaldeans in and around Sulaymaniya in 1968. However, *AP* figures are much lower – in the hundreds – as can be seen in Table 5.4.
8 Fr Emmanuel Haddad (1976–1982), Abbot Yousif Ibrahim OAOC (1999–2006) and Archimandrite Denha Hanna Toma OAOC (2006–2013).
9 Three hundred families migrated/moved from Mosul and Baghdad; only 150 remained.
10 We do well to note the third 'ethnic' presence to Kirkuk – the Turcoman population which ensured that until at least the mid-twentieth century Turkish dialects were common in the city.
11 That Kirkuk and not Erbil had been named the chief city of the Archdiocese was due to historical precedent in ecclesial organisation but also likely due to the Ottoman administrative organisation in north-eastern Mesopotamia in which Kirkuk was the

Ecclesiology and ecclesial organisation 207

administrative centre of the ayalet of Sulaymaniya and because at the time of its establishment the Chaldean population of Erbil was relatively small (Kramers and Bois 1986).

12 These figures and from the preceding paragraph come from information provided by Chaldean migrants from Kirkuk who, as of October 2013, were resident in Ankawa.

13 Sako was born in Zakho in 1948, trained for the priesthood at the seminary of St John in Mosul and was ordained priest for Mosul Archdiocese in 1974. Prior to his appointment to Kirkuk, he had been Rector of St Peter's Seminary, Baghdad, for five years.

14 Mellus was resident in India for the period 1874–1882.

15 See also <www.catholic-hierarchy.org/diocese/daqra.html>

16 The other bishops were André Sana (1957–1977) and Abdul-Ahad Rabban OAOC (1980–1998).

17 The Amadiyan region in ecclesiastical terms also included the diocese of Marga which largely covers the area of the contemporary Chaldean diocese of Akra.

18 Yohannan as Metropolitan of Mosul consecrated one of his own nephews as bishop of Amadiya in 1790 as a rival to Hnanisho, who was then still also the legitimist bishop of Amadiya. It seems Yohannan's nephew was in a far more influential position than that of Hnanisho with the support of the Latin missionaries a decisive factor in his favour and led to his gaining the affiliation of the East Syriacs in the Sapna valley and Zibar district (eastern Amadiya) (Wilmshurst 2000, 128).

19 I do query the collection process of the *AP* figures which appear to suggest often estimations as opposed to an attempt at a census. Indeed, the appearance of just under 6,000 people between 2001 and2002 and the disappearance of c. 13,000 between 2009 and2010 is questionable as to exactitude. Nonetheless, the figures do reflect the trend for very large population movements which Chaldean residents of northern Iraq have faced during the twentieth century and the proportional size of diocesan populations.

20 See Tables 5.7 and 5.8. Wherever possible, I have localised these villages in Map 5.2. Other settlements now under the jurisdiction of the Diocese of Zakho-Amadiya and principally from the Amadiyan area of ecclesial influence include Komane (320 people), Araden (c. 240 people), Inishke (c. 450 people), Amadiya, Romta, Korrabin, War, Adna, Dawoodia, Tinna, Martabiya, Hamzikh, Sorka and Beydano. Without estimates for these settlements in the Amadiyan area, I cannot provide a complete estimate derived from fieldwork for the Chaldean populations of northern Iraq as of October 2013. That being said, through utilising *AP* figures for that period and preceding years an approximation can be made and which is outlined in Appendix B. As we have seen, however, *AP* figures are not always to be relied upon for complete accuracy. It is my impression that the overall quality of accounting for population by those responsible among the community for providing population data has improved since 2003 with the intention to realise a more comprehensive picture of the Chaldeans and to document their situation.

21 Duhok's population is 300,000 and Zakho's is 350,000.

22 One reason why baptismal figures should not necessarily be taken to represent the birth rate.

23 Whose descendants included the notable Chaldean scholar Fr Paul Nwiya SJ (b. 1925 d. 1980) (Nwyia 1970).

24 The Dominicans were absent from Mosul 1815 to 1841; the Capuchins from Amid (Diyarbakir) from 1803 only to re-establish in Mardin in 1841 whilst the Carmelites in Baghdad departed in 1825 (Bello OAOC 1939, 25).

25 The number of births are lower, however, than the national Iraqi birth rate which was 26.85 births per 1,000 population in 2014 ('Iraq' 2014).

26 See Graph 5.5.

27 As of 2017, one of the few remaining extant synagogues in Iraq is situated in the town and which contains the supposed tomb of the Prophet Nahum.

28 It is interesting that such a definite ecclesiological position should evolve after the irruption of Latin directed efforts to the region. Given the proximity of the West Syriac

208 *Ecclesiology and ecclesial organisation*

communities in Mesopotamia and eastern Asia Minor, one wonders as to why self-definition of orthodoxy was not perceived as necessary. It is perhaps most likely the case that differences were less fresh and *real* at that time with the disputes last having been affirmed some generations previously.

29 See Table 5.10. N.B. the town of Naseriya should not be confused with the town of Nasiriya in southern Iraq.

30 The level of security at checkpoints into and out of the town appeared also to be more substantial than other locations visited. This partly relates to Alqosh's relative isolation from surrounding settlements but also its aforementioned strategic location in any potential conflict scenario.

31 Denha I (1265–1281), Yahballah III (1281–1317), Timothy II (1318–1336) and Denha II (1336–1380) for whole or parts of their time in office resided in northern Mesopotamia or north-western Persia.

32 The return of Chaldeans of Teleskefi origin from Basra, Baghdad and Mosul has totalled 250 families (c. 1,200 people) after 2003. Such estimates are welcome as a guide to the *status quo*, but this type of record keeping completed to varying degrees of formality and often not in writing, with the 'knowledge' of the local priest often being the basis for accounting for statistics in his parish.

33 For example, up to a third of Baghdad's population was Jewish until the First World War.

34 Islam had become increasingly popular among the non-Muslim lower classes under Mongol rule (both Mongols and natives) in the second half of the thirteenth century, although a substantial minority of the élites retained their Christian, Buddhist or Shamanist religious affiliation (Fiey OP 1975, 54, 63–5).

35 I was informed the vast majority of the twenty-three Baghdadi Chaldean churches remained open as of late 2013. However, I was able to access baptismal data only from thirteen parishes.

36 N.B. data were not available in this instance on a per year basis. That data for the most part are unavailable prior to 1958 is not especially concerning given the population was largely based around the three aforementioned parishes. The only church for which I do not have data prior to 1958 and which was in use was St John the Baptist.

37 Patriarch Henanisho II (773–780) transferred the see to Baghdad in 775 and along with this movement it is quite possible that Timothy assumed the credit for some other aspects of Henanisho's work such as the codification of East Syriac canon law and missionary efforts in central Asia and China (Wilmshurst 2011, 115).

38 Its proximity to ancient Nineveh probably the reason why Mosul was not so intensively developed prior to the Late Antique era.

39 Latterly known as Isaac 'of Nineveh''. For further biographical detail, see the introductory chapter in Brock (2014).

40 For an in-depth historical and architectural account of all the churches, see Fiey (1959, passim).

41 Source: clergy of the Diocese of Mosul. N.B. following Da'esh's occupation, all churches were closed.

42 A group of protestant missionaries had earlier been murdered in 2003.

43 To my knowledge, the majority of Moslawi churches – of all denominations – were attacked at least once from March 2003 to June 2014.

44 Both Telkef and Karamles were occupied by Da'esh in August 2014 and liberated by Iraqi forces in January 2017.

45 Other extant, if little used, churches include Mart Mariam and Mar Gewargis. The churches of Mar Yonan, Mar Youkana and the Church of the Forty Martyrs were destroyed by the Persian ruler Nadir Shah in 1743.

46 Chaldeans are not the only religious community, with about thirty-five Shabak families also resident. A community which largely describe themselves as following a type of Shiism.

Ecclesiology and ecclesial organisation 209

Bibliography

Agenzia Fides. 2012. 'Father Dall'Oglio Welcomed in the Monastic Community Which Began in Sulaymanya, in Iraqi Kurdistan', December 10. www.fides.org/en/news/32844-ASIA_IRAQ_Father-Dall_Oglio_welcomed_in_the_monastic_community_which_began_in_Sulaymanya_in_Iraqi_Kurdistan#.UdvMf75wacw.

Al Aqeedi, Rasha. 2016. 'Hisba in Mosul: Systematic Oppression in the Name of Virtue'. Occasional Paper, Program on Extremism, George Washington University, Washington, DC. www.academia.edu/24513587/Hisba_in_Mosul.

Al Arabiya News. 2011. 'Iraq's First New Church Since 2003 US Invasion Opens', July 10. http://english.alarabiya.net/articles/2011/07/10/156972.html.

Anderson, Liam, and Gareth Stansfield. 2009. *Crisis in Kirkuk: The Ethnopolitics of Conflict and Compromise*. National and Ethnic Conflict in the 21st Century. Philadelphia, PA: University of Pennsylvania Press.

Asianews.It. 2006a. 'Radical Muslims Against Pope: Two Churches Attacked in Mosul and Baghdad', September 25. www.asianews.it/news-en/Radical-Muslims-against-pope:-two-churches-attacked-in-Mosul-and-Baghdad-7303.html.

———. 2006b. 'Threats and Extortion Force Caritas Mosul to Shut Down', November 22. www.asianews.it/news-en/Threats-and-extortion-force-Caritas-Mosul-to-shut-down-7815.html.

———. 2007. 'Mosul: Despite Bombs and Gunfire Near Churches the Faithful Have Not Forsaken Holy Week', April 4. www.asianews.it/news-en/Mosul:-despite-bombs-and-gunfire-near-churches-the-faithful-have-not-forsaken-Holy-Week-8917.html.

———. 2009. 'Archbishop of Kirkuk: For 1600 Years, Iraq Has Been a "Country of Martyrs"', October 13. www.asianews.it/index.php?l=en&art=16576&theme=5.

Badger, George Percy. 1852. *The Nestorians and Their Rituals: With the Narrative of a Mission to Mesopotamia and Coordistan in 1842–1844, and of a Late Visit to Those Countries in 1850: Also, Researches Into the Present Condition of the Syrian Jacobites, Papal Syrians, and Chaldeans, and an Inquiry Into the Religious Tenets of the Yezeedees*. Edited by John Mason Neale. Vol. I. 2 vols. London: Joseph Masters. https://archive.org/details/nestorianstheirr01badg.

Behn, Wolfgang. 2011. 'Bābān'. In *Encyclopaedia Iranica*. New York: Encyclopædia Iranica Foundation. www.iranicaonline.org/articles/baban-2.

Bello OAOC, Stéphane. 1939. *La Congrégation de S. Hormisdas et l'Église chaldéenne dans la première moitié du XIXe siècle*. Orientalia Christiana analecta 122. Rome: Pont. Institutum Orientalium Studiorum.

Ben-Yaacob, Abraham. 2007. 'Suleimaniya'. In *Encyclopaedia Judaica*, edited by Michael Berenbaum and Fred Skolnik. Detroit, MI: Macmillan Reference USA. Gale Virtual Reference Library. http://go.galegroup.com/ps/i.do?id=GALE%7CCX2587519346&v=2.1&u=imcpl1111&it=r&p=GVRL&sw=w&asid=ab149cb70826b441eb5a9ee8857749e0.

Ben-Yaacob, Abraham, Hayyim J. Cohen, Nissim Kazzaz, Asher Goren, and Amnon Shiloah. 2007. 'Iraq'. In *Encyclopaedia Judaica*, edited by Michael Berenbaum and Fred Skolnik. Detroit, MI: Macmillan Reference USA. Gale Virtual Reference Library. http://go.galegroup.com/ps/i.do?id=GALE%7CCX2587509571&v=2.1&u=imcpl1111&it=r&p=GVRL&sw=w&asid=6d4d8bdd959f3cae09bb28574ea77302.

Brock, Sebastian, trans. 2014. *The Wisdom of Saint Isaac the Syrian*. Sixth Impression. Oxford: SLG Press.

Budge, E. A. Wallis, ed. 1886. *The Book of the Bee*. Vol. I, pt. 2. Anecdota Oxoniensia Semitic Series. Oxford: Clarendon Press. https://archive.org/details/Budge1886TheBookOfTheBee TheSyriacText . . .

210 Ecclesiology and ecclesial organisation

———, ed. 1893. *The Book of Governors: The Historia Monastica of Thomas, Bishop of Marga A. D. 840*. Vol. II. 2 vols. London: Kegan Paul, Trench, Trübner & Co., Ltd. https://archive.org/details/bookgovernorshi01thomgoog.

———, ed. 1902. *The Histories of Rabban Hôrmîzd the Persian and Rabban Bar-'Idtâ*. Translated by Ernest Alfred. Wallis Budge. Vol. II, pt. 1. London: Luzac and Co. https://archive.org/details/historiesrabban00budggoog.

Chaumont, Marie-Louise. 1988. *La christianisation de l'Empire iranien: des origines aux grandes persécutions du IVe siècle*. Corpus Scriptorum Christianorum Orientalium, v. 499; t. 80. Lovanii: E. Peeters.

Chevalier, Michel. 1985. *Les montagnards chrétiens du Hakkâri et du Kurdistan septentrional*. Publications du Département de géographie de l'Université de Paris-Sorbonne 13. Paris: Dép. de géographie de l'Université de Paris-Sorbonne.

Coakley, J. F. 2013. 'The Vincentian Mission Press in Urmia, Persia: A Preliminary Bibliography'. *Orientalia Christiana Periodica* 79 (1): 209–26.

Coakley, J. F., and David G. K. Taylor. 2009. *Syriac Books Printed at the Dominican Press, Mosul*. Gorgias Handbooks 14. Piscataway, NJ: Gorgias Press LLC.

Donner, Fred McGraw. 1988. 'Basra'. In *Encyclopædia Iranica*. New York: Encyclopædia Iranica Foundation. www.iranicaonline.org/articles/basra-ar.

Fiey OP, Jean Maurice. 1959. *Mossoul Chrétienne: Essai Sur l'histoire, l'archéologie et l'état Actuel Des Monuments Chrétiens de La Ville de Mossoul*. Recherches Publiées Sous La Direction de l'Institut de Lettres Orientales de Beyrouth 12. Beirut: Imprimerie Catholique.

———. 1965a. *Assyrie Chrétienne – Contribution a l'Étude de l'Histoire et de la Géographie Ecclésiastiques et Monastiques du Nord de l'Iraq*. Vol. I. 3 vols. Recherches publiées sous la direction de l'Institut de Lettres Orientales de Beyrouth, XXII. Beirut: Imprimerie Catholique.

———. 1965b. *Assyrie Chrétienne – Contribution a l'Étude de l'Histoire et de la Géographie Ecclésiastiques et Monastiques du Nord de l'Iraq*. Vol. II. 3 vols. Recherches publiées sous la direction de l'Institut de Lettres Orientales de Beyrouth – Série III: Orient Chrétien, XXIII. Beirut: Imprimerie Catholique.

———. 1968. *Assyrie Chrétienne – Bét Garmaï, Bét Aramāyé et Maišān Nestoriens*. Vol. III. 3 vols. Recherches publiées sous la direction de l'Institut de Lettres Orientales de Beyrouth – Série III: Orient Chrétien, XLII. Beirut: Imprimerie Catholique.

———. 1975. *Chrétiens syriaques sous les Mongols (Il-Khanat de Perse, XIIIe-XIVe s.)*. Corpus Scriptorum Christianorum Orientalium, v. 362; t. 44. Louvain: Secrétariat du CorpusSCO.

———. 1980. *Chrétiens syriaques sous les Abbassides, surtout à Bagdad (749–1258)*. Corpus Scriptorum Christianorum Orientalium, 420; Subsidia t. 59. Louvain: Secrétariat du CorpusSCO.

———. 1993. *Pour un oriens christianus novus: répertoire des diocèses syriaques orientaux et occidentaux*. Beiruter Texte und Studien 49. Beirut: Franz Steiner Verlag.

Flannery, John. 2008. 'The Syrian Catholic Church: Martyrdom, Mission, Identity and Ecumenism in Modern History'. In *Christianity in the Middle East: Studies in Modern History, Theology and Politics*, edited by Anthony O'Mahony. London: Melisende.

Frantzmann, Seth J. 2016. 'Mosul: The Origins and Future of Competing Agendas Over Retaking the City From ISIS'. *Middle East Review of International Affairs* 20 (2): 10–19.

Gisick, Michael. 2009. 'Christians in Basra Subdued for Holiday'. *Stars and Stripes*, December 15. www.stripes.com/news/christians-in-basra-subdued-for-holiday-1.97279.

Ecclesiology and ecclesial organisation 211

Hansman, John. 2011. 'Characene and Charax'. In *Encyclopædia Iranica*. New York: Encyclopædia Iranica Foundation. www.iranicaonline.org/articles/characene-and-charax-spasinou-in-pre-islamic-times.

Harrak, Amir. 2002. 'Trade Routes and the Christianization of the Near East'. *Journal of the Canadian Society for Syriac Studies* 2: 46–61.

———. 2003. 'Patriarchal Funerary Inscriptions in the Monastery of Rabban Hormizd: Types Literary Origins, and Purpose'. *Hugoye: Journal of Syriac Studies* 6 (2): 293–309.

Hartmann, R. 1913. 'Al- Baṣra'. In *Encyclopaedia of Islam*, edited by Martijn Theodoor Houtsma, T. W. Arnold, R. Basset, and R. Hartmann. Leiden: Brill.

Honigmann, E., Clifford Edmund Bosworth, and Peter Sluglett. 1991. 'Al-Mawṣil'. In *Encyclopaedia of Islam, Two*, edited by Clifford Edmund Bosworth, E. van Donzel, W. P. Heinrichs, and Charles Pellat. Leiden: E. J. Brill.

'Iraq'. 2014. In *CIA World Factbook*. Washington, DC: Central Intelligence Agency. www.cia.gov/library/publications/the-world-factbook/geos/iz.html.

Khayyath, Georges Ebed-Jesus V. 1896. 'Etat Religieux des dioceses formant le Patriarcat Chaldeen de Babylone au 1er janvier 1896'. Edited by Jean-Baptiste Chabot. *Revue de l'Orient chrétien*, Series 1, 1 (4): 433–53.

Kramers, Johannes Hendrik., and T. Bois. 1986. 'Kirkūk'. *Encyclopaedia of Islam, Two*. Leiden: Brill.

Kröger, Jens. 2011. 'Ctesiphon'. In *Encyclopaedia Iranica*. New York: Encyclopædia Iranica Foundation. www.iranicaonline.org/articles/ctesiphon.

Marti, Federico. 2009. *I Rutheni negli Stati Uniti: Santa Sede e mobilità tra Ottocento e Novecento*. Pontifical University of the Holy Cross – Monografie Giuridiche 36. Milan: Giuffrè.

Medlycott, Adolphus. 1912. 'St. Thomas Christians'. In *The Catholic Encyclopedia*. New York: Robert Appleton Company. www.newadvent.org/cathen/14678a.htm.

Morony, Michael G. 1989. 'Bēṯ Selōḵ'. In *Encyclopaedia Iranica*. New York: Encyclopædia Iranica Foundation. www.iranicaonline.org/articles/bet-selok.

'Msgr Yousif Mirkis, OP Speaks on the Chaldean Church'. 2014. January 20. www.op.org/en/content/msgr-yousif-mirkis-op-speaks-chaldean-church.

Nwyia, Paul. 1970. *Exégèse Coranique et Langage Mystique: Nouvel Essai Sur Le Lexique Technique Des Mystiques Musulmans*. Recherches Publiées Sous La Direction de l'Institut de Lettres Orientales de Beyrouth 49. Beirut: Dar el-Machreq.

O'Mahony, Anthony. 2008. ' "Between Rome and Constantinople": The Italian-Albanian Church: A Study in Eastern Catholic History and Ecclesiology'. *International Journal for the Study of the Christian Church* 8 (3): 232–51. doi:10.1080/14742250802256367.

Pétridès, Sophrone. 1907. 'Amadia and Akra'. In *The Catholic Encyclopedia*. New York: Robert Appleton Company. https://archive.org/details/07470918.1.emory.edu.

Richard OP, Jean. 2001. 'Le Seminaire de Saint-Jean de Mossoul'. In *Les Dominicains at les mondes musulmans*, edited by Claude Gilliot OP and Sophie Hasquenoph. Mémoire dominicaine: Histoire – Documents – Vie dominicaine 15. Paris: Cerf.

Roberson CSP, Ronald G. 2010. 'The Eastern Catholic Churches 2010'. www.cnewa.org/source-images/Roberson-eastcath-statistics/eastcatholic-stat10.pdf.

Sako, Louis. 2014. 'The Church: Unity and Communion'. Chaldean Patriarchate. www.chaldeaneurope.org/2014/01/28/a-pastoral-letter-of-patriarch-louis-raphael-sako/.

Scher, Addai. 1906. 'Notice sur les manuscrits syriaques conservés dans la bibliothèque du couvent des Chaldéens de Notre-Dame-des-Semences'. *Journal Asiatique*, X, 7: 479–512.

Sellwood, David. 2011. 'Adiabene'. In *Encyclopædia Iranica*. New York: Encyclopædia Iranica Foundation. www.iranicaonline.org/articles/adiabene.

212 *Ecclesiology and ecclesial organisation*

Simon, Constantine. 1993. 'In Europe and America: The Ruthenians Between Catholicism and Orthodoxy: On the Eve of Emigration'. *Orientalia Christiana Periodica* 59 (1): 169–210.

St Athanasius of Alexandria. 1891. 'From Letter XXIX (for 357.)'. In *Nicene and Post-Nicene Fathers*, edited by Archibald Robertson. Vol. IV, Athanasius: Select Works and Letters. II. Edinburgh: T & T Clark. www.tertullian.org/fathers2/NPNF2-04/Npnf2-04-92.htm#P9679_3470755.

Streck, M. 1913. '' Amādīya'. In *Encyclopaedia of Islam*, edited by Martijn Theodoor Houtsma, T. W. Arnold, R. Basset, and R. Hartmann. Leiden: Brill.

Tabbaa, Yasser. 2002. 'The Mosque of Nur Al-Din in Mosul, 1170–1172'. *Annales Islamologiques* 36: 339–60.

Tfinkdji, Joseph. 1913. *L'Église Chaldéenne Catholique Autrefois et Aujourd'hui*. Paris: Bureaux des études ecclésiastiques.

Tisserant, Eugène. 1931. 'L'Église Nestorienne'. In *Dictionnaire de Theologie Catholique*. Edited by Alfred Vacant, Eugène Mangenot, and Emile Amann. Paris: Letouzey et Ané.

Visser, Reidar. 2005. *Basra, the Failed Gulf State: Separatism and Nationalism in Southern Iraq*. Politik, Forschung Und Wissenschaft 22. Münster: Lit Verlag.

Whooley, John. 2004. 'The Armenian Catholic Church: A Study in History and Ecclesiology'. *The Heythrop Journal* 45 (4): 416–34. doi:10.1111/j.1468-2265.2004.00264.x.

Wilmshurst, David. 2000. *The Ecclesiastical Organisation of the Church of the East 1318–1913*. Corpus Scriptorum Christianorum Orientalium ; Subsidia, vol. 582. tomus 104. Lovanii: Peeters.

———. 2011. *The Martyred Church: A History of the Church of the East*. Sawbridgeworth, Hertfordshire: East and West.

Wood, Philip. 2013. *The Chronicle of Seert: Christian Historical Imagination in Late Antique Iraq*. Oxford Early Christian Studies. Oxford: Oxford University Press. http://fdslive.oup.com/www.oup.com/academic/pdf/openaccess/9780199670673.pdf.

Yuanyan, Wang. 2013. 'Doubt on the Viewpoint of the Extinction of Jingjiao in China After the Tang Dynasty'. In *From the Oxus River to the Chinese Shores: Studies on East Syriac Christianity in China and Central Asia*, edited by Li Tang and Dietmar Winkler, Paperback, 279–96. Orientalia – Patristica – Oecumenica 5. Zürich: Lit Verlag.

6 The Chaldean community in Jordan

Chaldean population movement on a large scale has been a constant factor in the community's history in the twentieth and twenty-first centuries. Consideration will now be given to migration external to Iraq to the Hashemite Kingdom of Jordan.

Iraqi Christian migration to Jordan has been mentioned in studies by Sassoon (2009) and Chatelard (2002) but without consideration of the particular Jordanian context and its importance to the Eastern and Latin Catholic communities, nor the ecclesiological significance of the Chaldean presence to Jordan. Estimates have been given to as many as 30,000 Chaldeans migrating through or residing in Jordan since 2003, but no study has considered the importance of Jordan to the Chaldeans. This lack of study is reflected in the lack of attention the Chaldeans of Jordan have been afforded by their own hierarchy, with only one Chaldean chaplain resident in the country at any one time.

Studies on the effects of Iraqi Christian migration to North America and continental Europe have been completed, and it seems an optimal time to provide an opening for studies of Eastern Catholic migrants to Jordan, to introduce a widening of the scope of studies undertaken by Atto (2011), Hanoosh (2008) and Sengstock (1974) and to place migration into the context of church history rather than allowing it to remain largely considered from an anthropological or sociological perspective.

A sense of ecclesiological self-awareness is nourished through the built and natural environment in which one resides. To be removed from this and to traverse significant distances geographically and culturally leads to an alteration in the sense of self and attachment to religious identity. In instances where Chaldeans migrate to North America and Australasia, and to a lesser extent Europe, this displacement appears not to entail as extensive separation from the community or Chaldean religious identity. The overall size of the Chaldean presence and its incarnation in the American environment is very strong, for example, in Detroit and San Diego. California is also home to the only Chaldean seminary outside of Iraq (Mar Abba in El Cajon).

In Jordan, the population is faced with the challenge of retaining its cohesion as a Chaldean ecclesial group when several more easily accessible communities are available for religious activities. The situation is compounded by the lack of a diocesan structure and proximity of trauma to the conduct of day-to-day life in

214 *The Chaldean community in Jordan*

refugee camps. This is further reinforced through the humiliation of being obliged to accept low paying jobs despite formerly higher socio-economic status in Iraq. The lack of structure in the immediate term, and having been faced with relocation, weakens the ability to maintain an expression of identity in an often alien environment. When the reason for leaving Iraq is primarily due to religious identity to find a lack of structure with which to uphold religious identity in the diaspora inhibits the continuance of or desire to remain part of the Church and express a Chaldean identity.

Jordan has historically served as a transfer point for Christian migrants. In the aftermath of the 2003 Iraq War, an increased trend began for families to travel there either directly from Iraq, or via Syria, prior to onward travel to the West. Overshadowing the Chaldean presence in Jordan is the sense, however unjustified, that the community is foreign to Jordanian life and history. This is an issue exacerbated by the complicated relationship which has existed between Iraqi and Jordanian governments since the foundation of each state after the First World War. Both countries have been ruled by members of the Hashemite family but Jordan, unlike Iraq, has retained its monarchy to the present. Despite the sometimes fractious relationship between the two countries, a substantial minority of Iraqis have resided in the Kingdom. Jordan became a prominent home for Iraqi political exiles during the rule of Saddam Hussein. The geographical proximity and Western-influenced culture of Jordan, with less strongly enforced paradigms of Arab nationalism, meant it was perceived as a more liberal option than Iraq for those whose views and personal ties clashed with that of Hussein and the IBP.

Shared by Jordan and Iraq was a broadly sympathetic attitude towards the maintenance of their Christian populations among the political élites. This attitude has been seen, for example, in the affection which the present monarch, King Abdullah II (1999–present), continues to hold the work of the churches. Christians form about five percent of the total population but contribute strongly to Jordanian cultural, economic and educational life.

Notwithstanding the state of Israel's occupation of East Jerusalem, there is also an awareness that the Jordanian monarchy is one of the guardians of the Holy Land and its various shrines. The monarchy takes this rôle very seriously and widens the King's interest in the Jordanian Christian constituency. The stake which the Jordanians have in this rôle is bound up with maintaining the Christian population of Jordan and another reason for resolving to defend a type of religious pluralism in the Kingdom.

Chaldean origins to Jordan

Prior to the late nineteenth century, no Chaldean presence to the Transjordan region is recorded and an East Syriac presence to the Holy Land, particularly to Jerusalem, appears to have lost an ecclesiastical presence by the early eighteenth century (Brock 2006, 189). However, it seems unlikely that the lack of an East Syriac hostel or chapel would have dissuaded East Syriac pilgrims from travelling to the Holy Places.

The first arrival of Chaldeans appears to have been from the late nineteenth century and was consolidated with the establishment of a Patriarchal Exarchate in 1908 by Patriarch Emmanuel II Thomas. It is possible an increase in the Chaldean population took place at the end of the First World War. The opportunity for a complete break with the tragic events in northern Mesopotamia and eastern Asia Minor during the War, likely encouraged some to migrate to Transjordan. The familiarity with British Imperial influence and administration to and in Mesopotamia also perhaps was a cause of increased interest in migrating to the Holy Land.

Whether the Chaldean patriarchal vicar of Jerusalem would have responsibility also for the Chaldeans in Transjordan is unclear. Following the loss of East Jerusalem to the state of Israel, it seems plausible he would have split his duties as required.[1] Until 2002, there was no formal Chaldean ecclesial structure in Jordan, with those resident either attending Latin or other Eastern Catholic communities. It is unclear when the regular celebration of the Chaldean liturgy began, but I presume at least from the 1990–1991 Gulf War that a priest would visit to minister to the community.

April 2002 saw the establishment of the Chaldean Patriarchal Vicariate for Jordan under the leadership of Fr Raymond Moussali, who has remained as the incumbent priest to the present. The community is focused on the parish of the Sacred Heart in Jebel al-Weibdeh, Amman, out of which is operated the usual liturgical services, Sunday school and more regular informal educational classes. The parish also serves as a point of contact for Chaldeans resident in Amman.[2]

The status of the Chaldean community in the Jordanian Christian context

The situation for Chaldeans in Jordan is difficult. Their continued presence relies on the hospitality of the monarchy and the support of Jordanian Christians. The Chaldeans' situation is ameliorated by the tradition of Jordan acting as a point of refuge for large numbers of displaced persons in the Levant, especially Palestinians. That being said, a wider concern is to the physical capability of Jordanian society to retain its cohesion through introducing any more people. There is a fear of repeating problems which occurred with Palestinian population movement to the Kingdom in 1948 and 1967, and with the growth of stateless groups within Jordan's borders, over which the Jordanian state has *de facto* responsibility.

The general culture of Jordan is towards permitting the presence of migrants on a substantial scale. In practice, and when faced by the competing influences in the region of surrounding governments and the demands of different refugee groups, the social and geographical space which the Kingdom has to offer can appear to be close to being overwhelmed. The situation of the state in holding together Jordanian society and its response to the refugees is alleviated to some degree by the preponderance of related NGOs to Jordan and through the assistance of the churches in pastoral and material needs.

To ensure a Jordanian identity to the nation, disincentives for migrants to arrive and/or incentives for migrants to become Jordanian must be employed. Inhibiting

216 *The Chaldean community in Jordan*

a narrative which portrays Jordanian society as *the* home for migrants in general in the Levant is key. Nevertheless, it seems likely that Jordanian society – by its openness to Christianity and recognition of the anti-sectarian nature of most Christian migrants – would be capable to hold all those Christian Iraqis who wish to reside there.

The Jordanian situation, in general, is not hopeful for the Chaldeans in the long term if they are unable to depart for another location. In the short term, Jordan is a safe haven for Iraqi Christian refugees. However, if they remain beyond a year their opportunities decrease and a loss of momentum to move onward is engendered. Legal residence to Jordan after a six-month period requires payment of a fine on a daily basis to remain. The economic opportunities, even for those who could strongly contribute to Jordan, are limited, with an atmosphere of killing time underwritten by a sense of hopelessness to their situation. To rejuvenate their presence in Jordan is not practically a solution, given the lack of a pre-existing community on such a scale or diocesan structure on which to build. This is a cause of Chaldean submergence into other churches in the Kingdom.

Insofar as the Kingdom is a generous host, the ability or interest in grasping the differences of need for Iraqis, and in turn for Iraqi Christians, is limited. Indeed, what more could be expected of the Kingdom given all which it has already given? The situation would appear to require sufficient funds to support those displaced, but the basic material requirements even were they accomplished, do not provide a solution to the societal issues which the migrant presence creates. A Jordanian attempt to retain the coherence of its population is to not give the legal classification of 'refugee' to forced migrants. This insures the Jordanian population against losing their own sense of identity.

The status of 'refugee' would also imply the Jordanian state has a duty of care for the populations which 'migrant' does not necessarily imply. This division is enforced through limits on employment and higher than normal fees for medical treatment. These are pragmatic policies adopted by the Jordanians, if not popular ones among refugees. The physical restrictions of Jordanian geography and the limited material resources such as water, which is an issue of increasing concern, regulate, in a very clear manner, how Jordan can meet the needs of its refugee-migrant populations.

The rapidity of change is also something with which the Chaldeans in Jordan and Jordanian society have been ill equipped to deal. The Chaldean ecclesiastical presence, in never having had to contend with such a large community, has, on balance, not been able to incarnate a Chaldean ethos and distinctive contribution to the Kingdom at a high level.

As of 2013, the Chaldean community was supported largely through the efforts of the Latin Patriarchate of Jerusalem in Jordan. On the other hand, the Chaldean ecclesial presence is sustained through the office of the Chaldean patriarchal vicar. The distinction is important, for it notes the theoretical and practical aspects which can lead to the inflating of ecclesiastical appointments with power and influence they do not possess. It is also suggestive of the crisis which the Chaldean diaspora in Europe will face if efforts are not made to regularise their situation through the creation of a clearer ecclesiastical organisation, which provides a basis around which identity – communal, cultural and ecclesiological – can be founded. For the organisational situation to continue as it is invites stagnation and a reactionary approach to events instead of grasping the initiative to secure a future for Chaldean ecclesial identity.

Latin and other churches' involvement in support for Iraqi Christian migrants has become necessary due to the lack of distinction made by secular NGOs of the particular difficulties with which Christians are faced. In collating the number of migrants entering Jordan, the United Nations High Commissioner for Refugees (UNHCR), for example, makes no record of each person's religion. Without an awareness of the causes of migration and forced displacement, NGO responses focus on alleviating the material conditions in what might be thought of as a neutral manner. Yet given the disproportionate numbers of Iraqi migrants who are Christians, the lack of specific understanding of at least their broad narrative is to the detriment of a long-term resolution of their status in Jordan.

Jordan's Christian environment, from the Catholic perspective, is an anomaly in the Middle East. Surrounding countries' Catholic populations largely form part of one of the Eastern Catholic churches, whereas most Jordanian Catholics are Latin. The balance of population has altered with the arrival of refugees, but the Latin ecclesial structures and associated charities remain very strong contributors to addressing the needs of Christian refugees beyond the purely basic needs of housing and food.[3] The NGOs involved vary in size and in the apostolates which they pursue. The more well-established organisations include Caritas and the Jesuit Refugee Service, but more personal initiatives have been established such as the *Messengers of Peace* (MoP) led by Fr Khalil Jaar, a priest of the Latin Patriarchate of Jerusalem. MoP was formed in early 2007 to alleviate the particular circumstances of the Iraqi refugees in Jordan. At that time, the situation in Iraq – civil war – determined the Iraqi presence to Jordan was in the first place of concern. It was also a time before the start of the rebellions in Syria, which would later lead to a shift in regional and international focus to the displaced Syrian populations.

Reliance on the initiative of individuals or small groups to relieve the Chaldean situation is partly as a result of the weak ecclesial presence, which the predominantly Iraqi churches have in Jordan. The Syrian Catholic population in Jordan, according to *AP* figures, jumped from 960 in 1990 to 10,298 in 2000 before dropping again in 2013 to 1,506. For the Chaldeans, robust ecclesial intervention to support the community appears to have been lacking even despite their change of population to Jordan being at least as great. Estimates collected during research from May to June 2013 were 20,000 (2002–2006); 40,000 (2007); 5,000–7,000 (2008–2012) and 5,000 (2013). The rapid change in population size from 2008 accounted for by resettlement outside of the Middle East.[4]

The MoP role, acknowledged by secular NGOs, is to alleviate physical need, but also to attempt to ensure the issue of persecution of Christians is not forgotten, and further, to also ensure Iraqis are equipped to navigate the UNHCR and Jordanian state bureaucracies. Engagement with the UNHCR is a cornerstone for those

218 *The Chaldean community in Jordan*

wishing to move outside of Jordan and seek asylum in the West. Other charitable work also includes summer and holiday programmes for young people to provide some type of normal life and alleviate the trauma which many have experienced. This is combined with services to alleviate psychological difficulties with which young people have been affected and which have led to developmental and speech disorders and/or arisen due to missing out on a more normal educational pattern and experience of social relations.

The immediate needs once MoP began operating in April 2007 were the provision of extra food, heaters and blankets for six months to 1,600 Iraqi families. This number increased to 2,000 families by February 2008. Of those who approach the charity, seventy-five percent are Christian who have not found succour from Muslim-led NGOs or awareness of the particularities of their situation from the UNHCR. Some effort has been made by UNHCR representatives to better comprehend the Christian scenario through meeting with refugees and Christian charities, but this does not appear to have impacted their day-to-day operational practices. Through refusal to record the religion of the displaced, the UNHCR continues to restrict the narrative of forced displacement to universal causes of movement such as war or economic hardship, as opposed to the reality of a layered narrative determined by a variety of factors including anti-Christian persecution. As average resettlement time (i.e. onward migration from Jordan) can be up to two years, the intervening period requires support of charities, such as MoP, to ensure the survival of refugees until they are able to secure asylum. The length of time to reach resettlement is dependent on the willingness to accept refugees and the capability of UNHCR to expedite the administrative process. It is possible, that as the seriousness of the Syrian crisis became apparent from 2011, the needs of displaced Iraqis became deprecated just at the time when their situation was beginning to be better understood. Nonetheless, suggestions of deliberate delay in this process by UNHCR were variously raised to me during research and were indicated as being an issue even prior to the start of the Syrian crisis.[5]

Conclusion: Chaldean presence to Jordan

Attempting to write a basic historical outline of the Chaldean Church in Jordan can be a tangential process whereby discussion of population displacement overrides what earlier aspects of this study have focused on: ecclesiastical organisation, dioceses and bishops and more definitive numerical outlines. The ethos of the Church, for Chaldeans in Jordan, is diffused throughout the community because the Chaldean ecclesial presence to Jordan is weak. Nonetheless, it is important to avoid portraying the community as weak as a result of not having a hierarchy, because the survival of Chaldean religious identity is reliant on community adherence to the essential aspects of the Church such as liturgy, language and cultural life. However, a hierarchy provides a definitive outline to the community and a clear point of recognition and establishes a place for the Chaldeans in Jordanian society.

Political considerations may be a leading cause to prevent this, as the creation of an Iraqi-led Christian community in Jordan would be concerning to the Jordanian state which, if open to the Christian presence, is still desirous of managing this presence on their own terms. Outside of this issue there seems little necessary cause for not elevating the vicariate to diocesan status given its size by population equals or far exceeds other dioceses in Iraq: Basra, once one of the five major ecclesiastical provinces of the East Syriac church in Mesopotamia, is as of 2013, reduced to a few hundred people. The relative ease of establishing a Chaldean diocese in Australia or Canada, by way of comparison, comes due to the lack of religious literacy which Western states have and the limited awareness of the significance of the Eastern Christian communities in their borders.

The Chaldean Church, however, in administering its community in the Kingdom, is seemingly at a loss as to the most effective means to respond. This also forms part of the context in which the Jordanian and Iraqi states have acted through avoiding acknowledging in public the scale of the changes in their respective populations. In under-acknowledging population movements, the Iraqi state reveals its failure to retain a plural culture and instead demonstrates that it is driven by a sectarian mentality with limited interest in effecting real change to support non-Muslims to remain.

Notes

1 There were four patriarchal vicars for the period 1908–2011. Bishop Ishaq Khoudabash initially, followed by Fr Boutros Sha'ya (1955–1978). His successors were not Chaldean: Fr Henri Gouillon (1980–1990) and Fr Paul Collin (1990–2011). Please note that owing to the extremely limited information on this subject area, I have been unable to confirm the dates of Bishop Ishaq's time as patriarchal vicar other than some period of 1908–1955. Even the usually comprehensive directory maintained by the Latin community from where some information was gained is not clear on this matter (*Directory of the Catholic Church in the Holy Land* 2012, 110).
2 It was notable that there were no members of the Church of the East encountered during research. In discussion with NGO workers it was stated that, at least in Amman, they did not have a presence. This is possible, but with the size of the Chaldean population, I would suggest it is more likely there was a limited awareness of ecclesial difference than that the Church of the East is absent entirely. The Christian culture of Jordan can be perceived as very Latin/ 'Catholic' in atmosphere, so this is possibly a reason why members of the Church of the East would prefer to travel to Syria or Lebanon in the first instances where a greater plurality of Christian culture exists or if travelling to Jordan to swiftly migrate onward (if possible) to the diaspora hubs in North America, Europe and Australasia.
3 Material support for non-Christians is also provided to those who approach Christian-led charities.
4 In this instance, I suggest *AP* figures for the Chaldean Patriarchal Vicariate in Jordan are indicative and not definitive, with the population rising from nought to 7,000 between 2000 and 2010. It may simply have been a case of the *AP*s' figures taking some time to be collated prior to establishing a more accurate record (Roberson CSP 2014).
5 Waiting time for some has been up to seven years.

Bibliography

Atto, Naures. 2011. *Hostages in the Homeland, Orphans in the Diaspora: Identity Discourses Among the Assyrian/Syriac Diaspora*. Amsterdam: Leiden University Press.
Brock, Sebastian. 2006. 'East Syriac Pilgrims to Jerusalem in the Early Ottoman Period'. *Aram Periodical* 18: 189–201. doi:10.2143/ARAM.18.0.2020728.

220 *The Chaldean community in Jordan*

Chatelard, Geraldine. 2002. 'Jordan as a Transit Country: Semi-Protectionist Immigration Policies and Their Effects on Iraqi Forced Migrants'. Working Paper 61, New Issues in Refugee Research, United Nations High Commissioner for Refugees, Florence, Italy. www.unhcr.org/refworld/docid/4ff3fcbe2.html.

Directory of the Catholic Church in the Holy Land. 2012. Jerusalem: Assembly of the Catholic Ordinaries of the Holy Land.

Hanoosh, Yasmeen S. 2008. 'The Politics of Minority Chaldeans Between Iraq and America'. Ph. D. thesis, University of Michigan. http://hdl.handle.net/2027.42/61663.

Roberson CSP, Ronald G. 2014. 'The Eastern Catholic Churches 2014'. Annuario Pontifico. www.cnewa.org/source-images/Roberson-eastcath-statistics/eastcatholic-stat14.pdf.

Sassoon, Joseph. 2009. *The Iraqi Refugees: The New Crisis in the Middle East.* International Library of Migration Studies 3. London and New York: I.B. Tauris.

Sengstock, Mary C. 1974. 'Traditional and Nationalist Identity in a Christian Arab Community'. *Sociological Analysis* 35 (3): 201–10.

Conclusion

This study has been a wide-ranging survey of the Chaldean Catholic Church, highlighting, in particular, its historical development and ecclesiological identity. Through outlining the Church's ecclesiastical organisation in Mesopotamia-Iraq, I have reflected on the incarnation of Chaldean ecclesiology in that environment. I have also considered the significance of Chaldean ecclesial structures to the realisation of a Chaldean *difference* within the plural societies of West Asia to the second decade of the twenty-first century.

In researching Chaldean ecclesiastical history, it has been challenging to build on the few foundations for this area of scholarship. I am aware also of the study's limits and, even despite presenting an overview of Chaldean ecclesiology and ecclesiastical organisation, much work remains to be done. This includes a far more comprehensive historical study of Chaldean communities in the Diocese of Zakho-Amadiya and the Archdioceses of Baghdad, Basra, Kirkuk-Sulaymaniya and Mosul. However, such a study is, as of early 2017, practically impossible for the indefinite future. Nevertheless, in noting these limits, it is especially important, given the circumstances since June 2014 and the advance of Da'esh, to represent the Chaldeans in academic research. One has to start making observations from some vantage point at some time. The material destruction which has been experienced perhaps, even if only in a limited manner, may be ameliorated by documenting the community and realising more widely the historical strength of Chaldean culture and the East Syriac Christian tradition in and to Mesopotamia-Iraq.

Mesopotamia-Iraq and the patriarchal office's influence on Chaldean identity formation

The Mesopotamian environment has been fundamental to the formation of Chaldean identity. The influence of local languages, cultures, places and peoples are integral to the Chaldean sense of being and the manifestation of Chaldean ecclesiological thought. For example: would the Chaldean Church be the same without having been present to Baghdad and Mosul and at the centre of the transformation of civilisations in West Asia from Late Antiquity to the Modern era? The East Syriac tradition and the patriarchal office, in particular, has been fortunate to have had a seat at the window of history affording a view of societal change and, often,

222 *Conclusion*

the opportunity to influence and be a part of implementing change. If the patriarch had not been present to Baghdad and engaged with Sasanian, Abbasid, Mongol, Ottoman and Baathist élites, Christian influence would have been severely curtailed. By way of comparison, we can consider the negligible political status of the Yazidis or Turkmen into the twenty-first century, despite both groups having populations roughly equal to or larger than the East Syriacs.

Running through Chaldean history, the use of Syriac has also bound together the community and its identity even to the present, and maintained a boundary around Chaldeans apart from the surrounding population. This boundary has been necessary to defend and uphold their community but also to consolidate the Church's status as a bearer of some of the most ancient liturgical traditions of the apostolic churches.

Nonetheless, it was not always apparent what features made the Chaldean community distinctive within the East Syriac tradition, at least for the first 150 years of its existence. It is perhaps easier to circumscribe the Chaldeans from the post-First World War era because 'to be a Chaldean' became more clearly delimited: it was to be largely Arab linguistically, Catholic in a broad sense, increasingly urban and acquiescent to the contemporary government. During the Chaldeans' formative period in the sixteenth to eighteenth centuries, there was no definitive point of coagulation around which the community formed beyond the figure of the Chaldean patriarch and a notion of being in union with the successor of St Peter in Rome. Once a clearer particular sense of *Chaldean-ness* developed, through the direction of the Josephite patriarchs and latterly figures such as Joseph VI Audo, a *Chaldean* identity emerged as a distinct aspect of the East Syriac tradition. This is not to say that distinctive communal formation and the separation of Chaldean and Church of the East factions in the East Syriac community did not exist. These did form to some extent and, as I have suggested from the evidence of the patriarchal funerary inscriptions at Rabban Hormizd, an awareness of Christological difference was present following the establishment of the Sulaqite patriarchal line. This, however, was distinct from the creation of an explicitly Chaldean identity and a Chaldean ecclesiological model.

I have largely avoided the use of the term *Catholic* with reference to the Chaldean process of ecclesiology and identity formation, in the study. It is a difficult term to apply to communities who, I suggest, likely never viewed themselves as set apart from communion with the Latin West or juridically broken away from the See of Peter. This is why I would characterise Sulaqa's intentions and those of many of the East Syriac patriarchal claimants to the late seventeenth century, as more focused on revivifying their relationship with the Pope as Patriarch of the West rather than perceiving the need to form an Eastern Catholic rite. It was only with the establishment of the Josephite line and sustained Latin missionary efforts, inspired by the Council of Trent, that East Syriac communities become fully recognizant that *to be Chaldean* was to recognise the contemporary pope as their chief source of ecclesiastical authority.

Furthermore, as I have indicated, it was Joseph VI Audo that first grasped and held to an awareness of the notion of the Chaldeans as an Eastern Catholic

Conclusion 223

community in union with the Holy See. Audo was also the first Chaldean patriarch to defend the notion of the Chaldeans as an ecclesial body, with the rights and prerogatives of the successor to the Church of the East. Moreover, his patriarchal office represented the contemporary successor of the Catholicos-Patriarch of Seleucia-Ctesiphon. Nevertheless, the legitimacy of such an ecclesiology, also a key aspect of Chaldean identity, was only fully manifested once it was widely held by the community and assumed as part of their heritage. In order for the Church to function, ecclesiology also had to have a basis from the bottom up, even if the ideals which Audo pursued were encouraged from the top down.

In these efforts, in creating a Chaldean ecclesiology inclusive of the East Syriac tradition, the Chaldeans became the chief maintainers of this ecclesial culture to Iraq. Suggestive of this status was the Chaldean assumption of the dioceses of the legitimist patriarchate from the early nineteenth century and the chief institutions of the community such as Rabban Hormizd monastery. Through doing so, the Chaldeans absorbed the resources of the Church of the East, and through gaining the legitimist patriarchal lineage, became the inheritor of the successor to the see of the Catholicos-Patriarch of Seleucia-Ctesiphon.

A further aspect indicative of the assumption of East Syriac heritage was, and is, the celebration of the plural cultural heritage which predates the Chaldean emergence in the 1550s. The Chaldeans have embraced a variety of ideals, sub-ecclesial identities and cultures within the community as derived from the East Syriac tradition's spread across Asia and its incarnation in local contexts. This emphasises the heterogenous nature of the Church, and avoids the advancement of ethnic identity as the principal factor in determining membership. This permits the incorporation of other nations and cultures into the incarnation of East Syriac life: one does not have to advance an Assyrian ethnic identity to be a Chaldean.[1]

We can also recognise that the Chaldean patriarchs have followed the precedent for a model of church-state relations in existence since the Sasanian era. They have acknowledged the importance of engaging with the established political order and not a withdrawal from it: from 1921, patriarchs have been members of the Iraqi legislature (to 1958) or resident in Baghdad in the centre of political power.

Zones of Chaldean ecclesial influence in Iraq

I turn now to conclusions regarding the Chaldean situation in Iraq and especially the northern dioceses in 2003–2013. I have opened up discussion of the notion of zones of Chaldean ecclesial influence in Iraq as a result of the 2003 invasion. From 2003 to 2013, all the bishops of the northern dioceses saw the expansion of their pastoral remits, none more so than Bashar Warda of Erbil. Through a combination of political and social factors, I suggest his rôle became the second most influential office in the Chaldean hierarchy in Iraq. This is not an entirely unprecedented situation in the East Syriac tradition when we consider the city was home to metropolitans of the ecclesial province of Adiabene from the fifth century. However, the proximity of Alqosh and Mosul limiting Erbil's ecclesial influence *is* novel in the Chaldean community from its foundation in 1968 until

224 *Conclusion*

2003. The enmeshing of the city as the Kurdish capital has raised its importance in the economic and political order to the same status as Baghdad is to the ICG. As a parallel context, the Erbil and Baghdad Archdioceses reflect the separation of the KRG and ICG's paradigms generally.

Whilst it is difficult to ascertain an exact figure for those Chaldeans remaining resident in Baghdad, the largest proportion of Chaldeans now resides outside Iraq or in the northern dioceses. Ecclesial influence, to a large extent, followed the population out of Baghdad. Aside from the status which is attached to the patriarchal office, Baghdad, as an archdiocese, has a weakened status in the Chaldean ecclesiastical organisation aside from remaining church property and religious institutes. The transfer of population, and hence material resources to the north along with St Peter's seminary, reduces reliance on the patriarch's oversight and the attendant influence which the patriarchal office holds.

The north, as of early 2017, is the chief zone of Chaldean ecclesial influence. Nevertheless, through his presence in Baghdad, the patriarch still retains access to the centre of political power and the ecclesiological significance of the link to the See of Seleucia-Ctesiphon. Moreover, the patriarch is still *the patriarch*, with key links to the resources of the Holy See and the wider Syriac communities which his office affords. Since the expansion of Da'esh from 2014, the challenge has been to maintain the significance of the office in the face of violence and to formulate a response to the removal of the Christian presence from the area of Iraq north of Baghdad to just south of Alqosh.

The distance, whether geographical, or from the patriarch's jurisdictional influence, is an issue which is not unusual to the East Syriac tradition. In many circumstances, the devolution of decision-making powers to the local bishop was obligatory when immediate methods of communication were impossible. This concept of ecclesial subsidiarity was historically as important to East Syriac communities in Akra as to Khan Balik in their day-to-day management. In the modern Iraqi Chaldean context, it also became more apparent during the final years of Bidawid and Delly's leadership which saw a substantial loss of patriarchal oversight. Sako, as patriarch, appears to want to reaffirm a stronger rôle for his office, but this is a difficult trend to alter as, since the Gulf War (1990–1991), the northern bishops have been obliged to act to an extent on their own initiative in the resolution of ecclesial affairs.

There is no active attempt within the clergy in Iraq to instigate a schism but, owing to force of circumstances, northern Iraq has emerged as an enclave in which the majority of Iraqi Christians now resides. This is very challenging to Sako's participation in the direction of Chaldean life. He is not able, for example, to advance as strong a working relationship with the state as many of his predecessors, such as Emmanuel II Thomas, because the community is spread to two zones of political influence of the Iraqi Central Government and the Kurdistan Regional Government.

A key aspect of effective East Syriac church governance in the majority Muslim context has also been access to patronage via the state or an external supporter. Without an 'in' to the civil power, East Syriac patriarchs struggled to maintain their communities. For example: the qualitative decline of the Sulaqite patriarchate and community by the early nineteenth century and its relative revival with British and Russian imperial and ecclesial support. With the decline of the Chaldean population size and thus influence, less can be requested by the patriarch from the state, whilst expectations by the state for Chaldeans to contribute to Iraqi society are also lessened. Different circumstances have emerged for those under KRG administration, with the appropriation of some of the patron-client relations by Christian political parties previously within the church hierarchy's domain. I suggest that the development of Kurdish autonomy from the early 1990s saw a preference for engaging with other explicitly political bodies similar in organisation and background such as the Assyrian Democratic Movement. To engage with a Christian ecclesial body as the chief representative group of the community may have been something by which Kurdish officials were challenged. Such an approach, altered over time through recognition that Chaldean ecclesiastical institutions more effectively sustain the community on a day-to-day basis than Christian political parties. This likely led to a reassessment of how the KRG was to engage with non-Muslim communal organisations.

The Holy See, the Chaldeans and the Church of the East

I have indicated that, since the Second Vatican Council, the Holy See has largely withdrawn its interventionist rôle in Chaldean affairs, which characterised the two ecclesial bodies' relations to the end of the nineteenth century. We can note how the Chaldeans have turned to the Holy See for pastoral oversight during the difficulties of electing Patriarch Bidawid's successor and looked to the contemporary pope as a figure to highlight their situation especially since 2003 among Western Christian communities.

This withdrawal of direct action in Chaldean affairs is in accord with the ecclesiology of a Catholic communion of *sui juris* churches focused upon the institution of the Holy See as the visible head of the communion and arbiter in ecclesial affairs. This new ecclesiological model is distinct from the Tridentine paradigm which had proposed a Catholic Church of rites with the pope as leader of this church. Popes John Paul II and Benedict XVI demonstrated awareness of the importance of retaining a close fraternal relationship with Chaldeans. It is not yet fully apparent how Francis I views his responsibilities to the Eastern Catholic churches, having made few specific statements. However, he seems to have a general awareness of the significance of engaging with Eastern Christians as exemplified by his meeting with Patriarch Kiril of the Russian Orthodox Church in February 2016. Also, during Francis' visit to Georgia in September 2016, he met with the local Chaldean community and Patriarch Sako. This speaks to a cognisance of the particular situation of the Chaldeans as a diaspora-oriented community and consolidated in locations often culturally or geographically removed from their traditional places of origin.[2] This suggests some hope for a pontificate willing to consider the majority Latin Catholic identity as well as that of the diverse character of the Eastern Catholic churches.

226   *Conclusion*

I suggest that, despite their *sui juris* status, the Chaldeans are somewhat uncomfortable with the lack of more resolute direction from the Holy See on the particular issues with which they are faced. There is awareness of the formerly very close relationship between the community, Latin missionaries and the papacy. The Chaldeans could, perhaps, be considered as a prototype Tridentine Eastern Catholic community at their foundation with, over time, increasingly direct Latin guidance as to their ecclesiology and identity. With the advent of the Second Vatican Council and a more 'hands-off' approach by the Holy See and Latin institutions, the Chaldeans have struggled to regain a clear working relationship. It is unclear as to the limits of the remit of the Chaldean patriarch in ecclesial affairs and how much reliance should be placed upon the pope for guidance and decision making. On a day-to-day basis, the patriarch leads the church, but with any intentions to radically alter the relationship between the East Syriac communities perhaps reliant on the acquiescence of the Holy See. We can note, for example, Louis Sako's suggestion in June 2015 for a united East Syriac patriarchate of the Church of the East and Chaldean Church, going so far as to state his willingness to resign his own position to make way for a preferred unity candidate were it to engender the security of the East Syriac Christian communities and support their long-term survival to the Middle East (Valente 2015).

Sako's proposal came in the context of the devastating situation for East Syriac Christians in Iraq, following Da'esh's invasion of the Nineveh plain and the death of the Church of the East's patriarch Mar Dhinka IV in March 2015.[3]

Sako's five-point plan was as follows:

1   The current Patriarchs: Louis Raphael Sako, Patriarch of the Chaldean Catholic Church, and Mar Addai II, Patriarch of the Ancient Church of the East, would submit their resignations without any conditions, but their desire for unity.
2   The Bishops of the three churches would meet to choose a new Patriarch.
3   The elected Patriarch should have assistants from each branch to enhance the "weft" (the permanent Synod).
4   The Patriarch and the Synod would leave national interests to the laity, because the church should be open to everyone and concerned with the best interests of all.
5   The Patriarch and the Synod would prepare for a General Synod to develop a new road-map for The One Church of the East.

(Sako 2015)

Sako's suggestions raise numerous issues, not least of which is whether the Holy See would perceive there to be no remaining theological or ecclesiological difference between the Church of the East and the Chaldeans and therefore assent to a new arrangement. Furthermore, how would the Holy See form a clear relationship with a *sui juris* church with which it is in communion if the chief source of communion – the patriarch – alters the existing model of church governance? Does an Eastern Catholic patriarch have the canonical right to resign his office with the intention of ecclesially uniting with another community of the same ecclesial tradition? Is the situation in Iraq so acute for East Syriac Christians that this is acceptable from the perspective of the Holy See?

What is perhaps most notable about Sako's proposal is not necessarily the implication that the churches share the same ecclesiology but the willingness to deprecate his own position in time of crisis and restore the structures of the Church of the East under one patriarch. The overall proposal and its implications require an extended academic assessment which cannot be offered in the conclusion to this study. Nevertheless, we are fortunate that Mar Awa Royel, the Church of the East's bishop of California, offered an extensive and erudite response to Sako's proposal and its connotations for East Syriac ecclesiology.

Royel began to explore whether such a union of the churches is practically possible given their respective views on East Syriac ecclesiastical organisation (Royel 2015). Royel, whilst open to discussing a possible resolution, concludes that Sako's parameters are not yet acceptable to the Church of the East in its contemporary form and that his proposal cannot fully fit with what he perceives as traditional East Syriac ecclesiology. This is primarily due to Sako's view of the necessity for any future united East Syriac church to be in full communion of unity and faith with the Holy See (Royel 2015, 1, 6).

We are presented with two differing versions of East Syriac ecclesiological thought: (1) Sako perceives the Chaldeans to be an heir to the East Syriac tradition and in no way outside of it. He also understands that formal union with the Holy See does not contradict in any way Chaldean or East Syriac eccleisal independence. Indeed, the ecclesial link with the Holy See is normative and not a novelty. (2) Royel regards his community as effectively the chief true maintainer of the East Syriac traditions, with the Chaldeans having detracted from this through union with the Holy See and their willingness to submit to the jurisdiction of the papacy. Royel is evidently keen to maintain and sustain the identity and character of the East Syriac tradition in the Church of the East and, as he perceives it, to secure it from errors which an authoritative rôle for the contemporary pope and ability to intervene in East Syriac affairs may present (Royel 2015, 2–3).

Certainly, Royel provides sustained and well-reasoned argument for his position, and that of the Church of the East, throughout his article. He highlights, for example, the fractious relationship between Patriarch Joseph VI Audo and Pope Pius IX. For him, this relationship is indicative of the real difficulties in ensuring that the offices of Patriarch and Pope, along with their respective powers, can be reconciled. For Royel, the Patriarch of the Church of the East should not be considered in any way below the pope in ecclesial dignity or rank. Nonetheless, and despite Royel's long-standing involvement in modern ecumenical discourse on behalf of the Church of the East, he does not appear to suppose that the authoritarian rule which the papacy may once have asserted over Eastern Catholic communities has been in considerable decline since the Second Vatican Council. Further, the *primus inter pares* papal rôle he perceives as acceptable for any formal Holy See-Church of the East relationship, and in accord with East Syriac ecclesiology, is at least, in theory, already in existence (Royel 2015, 5–6).

228   *Conclusion*

However, we should consider that Royel perceives that he has a duty to defend and uphold the traditions he regards as essential to East Syriac identity and ecclesiology – full ecclesial independence for the community, as led by the Patriarch and integral to all its actions and its very existence. Nonetheless, it is possible that, in fact, Royel is perhaps far more aware of the potential advantages which a relationship with the Holy See could bring to a united East Syriac patriarchate. Although he titled the article as a personal reflection, he was also obliged to defend the formal ecclesiological position of the Church of the East regardless of his own perceptions as to a suitable resolution. Indeed, his article made evident a strong belief in the independent missionary activity of the Church of the East throughout Asia as divine in origin, and that he is looking to defend and uphold the Church from good intentions and a well-formed intellect and conscience. Royel was not retaining traditional ecclesiology for its own sake. It will be crucial to the future of the East Syriac community as a whole – Chaldean or Church of the East – to see whether the new patriarch of the Church of the East, Mar Gewargis III (2015–present) will choose to advance ecclesial reconciliation or develop a response to Sako's proposal in light of Royel's critique. As Royel noted, at that time, without a patriarch he was not in a position to determine and speak on behalf of his community in a definitive manner. Any final decision would perhaps take far longer to be reached than may have been possible in earlier eras when the community was far more geographically concentrated in Mesopotamia (Royel 2015, 6). With the diaspora growing ever stronger and more diverse, with a plurality of opinion as to the proper future course of the Church of the East and with the political and economic difficulties in Iraq itself, the contemporary reconciliation of the churches of the East Syriac tradition may face a far longer and more challenging journey towards unity than was possible in the 1820s.

As of early 2017, it appears the proposal has been neither formally rejected by the Church of the East nor withdrawn by Sako. As such, it remains a potential means by which the East Syriac churches could establish a united ecclesial community. If the proposal is to be advanced in the future, it would seem likely to require East Syriac leaders willing to transcend loyalties to existing ecclesial institutions and ideologies and foster a shared will and vision to drive through changes in their respective organisations. From a historical perspective, this is not seemingly impossible, as change in ecclesiological models has occurred throughout East Syriac history. As has been demonstrated in this study, changing types of relationships with the Holy See, Anglican Communion, Russian Orthodox Church and between East Syriac churches have been major features of the history of the Church of the East.

To suggest that the autocephaly of the Church of the East, which emerged from the fifth century and came to be a key marker of its identity, may be impinged upon as a result of union with the Holy See, in a future united East Syriac church, is a sensitive issue. The Church of the East, as it exists in the present, perceives that doing so would inhibit its traditions and identity at a time when the Church is facing a crisis of existential proportions. Although at one level, Sako's proposal is very relevant, at another, it may be perceived, in the Church of the East, as a

Conclusion 229

potential danger for further weakening it, precisely because of the circumstances the Church is already facing.

It is notable that during the period between Dhinka's death in March 2015 and Gewargis' election in September 2015, the Synod of Bishops of the Church of the East did, briefly, comment on attempts to conclude ecclesiastical union ('Statement of the Council of Hierarchs of the Assyrian Church of the East' 2015). However, their statement only referenced engagements between the Assyrian and Ancient Churches of the East – no mention was made of Sako's proposal.[4] This is suggestive of the ecclesial difference which is perceived to still exist between the Church of the East and the Chaldeans. However, it might be the case that the Assyrian Church of the East envisions a union with the Ancient Church of the East prior to the more substantial negotiations which would be required to bridge the perceived gap between the Chaldeans and the Church of the East.

Mar Gewargis altered church organisation when he moved the Church of the East's patriarchate back to Iraq in September 2015. The relocation of the Church of the East's patriarch to Iraq speaks to a determination, on the part of its leadership, to strongly engage with its resident communities and attempt to revivify the Church's place in Iraqi society – through the office of the patriarch – on a substantial scale for the first time since 1933.[5]

The move also suggests that regardless of the larger proportion of the Church's population resident in North America, the patriarch needs to be near the site of the crisis faced by the community in Iraq if the Church is to retain its cultural heritage and ecclesial identity. If one prediction may be made, it is that Da'esh will likely be defeated in the medium to long term. After this, it will be essential, in whatever altered political form the Iraqi state and Kurdish region assume, for Christian leaders to be present and annunciate how they are to contribute to and remain part of Iraqi and Kurdish society.

Gewargis appears to be an excellent choice to propel the Church of the East into a new and more dynamic era. Having grown up in Iraq and having served as Metropolitan of Baghdad during some of the most trying years of the modern Iraqi state (1981–2015), he is fully cognisant of the challenges which the Church of the East faces.

As someone working from the Iraqi context, he has made substantial effort to build up the Church of the East in the Middle East, chiefly through encouraging educational initiatives and the establishment of a printing house in Baghdad. He also appears to understand the varied international character of the East Syriac diaspora in the US and more broadly. As Metropolitan, he facilitated the foundation of the parish of St Mary in Moscow to support the East Syriac communities in the Russian Federation ('Biography of His Holiness Mar Gewargis III, Catholicos-Patriarch of the Assyrian Church of the East' 2015).

In many respects, he could be compared to Louis Sako in the Chaldean context for his willingness to try to develop the East Syriac tradition, communities and culture in Iraq and internationally, even despite trying circumstances. It is to be hoped that co-operation between the two leaders can help lay the foundations for a more secure future for East Syriac Christianity.

230   *Conclusion*

The Chaldean presence to Iraq in the context
of the rise of Da'esh

The Chaldean situation since June 2014 has been perilous in the extreme. The events which have led to the extinction of the Christian presence in Mosul and much of the surrounding Nineveh plain, and the truly brutal and horrifying physical persecution, reveal the worst excesses of man's fallen nature. Formulating an effective response to Da'esh, aside from physical military engagement, is seemingly impossible. At a fundamental level, how ought you constructively engage with a group who seeks to kill you, with society at large broadly ambivalent or opposed to your continued presence?

The events for Christians of the East Syriac tradition are one among many persecutions of a similar type, insofar as a non-Christian power has aimed at the denigration of their position and violent removal of their community from society. Events are, however, also different as, since 2014, one entity has aimed at a coerced transformation of society from one paradigm – with a relative openness to societal plurality – to another with the loss of or inclination to resolve 'difference' in any way but through violence. For the Chaldeans, their position is compounded by the widespread ambivalence of the Muslim population, both Sunni and Shia, to their situation; the instability which the community experienced prior to these events (Iraq has been at war or under economic sanctions since 1980) and the lack of an external power with the will or capability to intercede on their behalf.

A comparative context was the removal of the Chaldeans from Asia Minor in 1915–1918 and the coerced delocalisation of the church. The response to this was broadly similar to the outcomes so far in the expansion of Da'esh. It appears the see of Mosul is becoming a titular diocese *in partibus infidelium*, much like those of Mardin, Gazarta and Seert. The making and un-making of the existing Middle Eastern political order since the Arab Spring is beginning to appear on the same scale and level of impact as the loss of the Ottoman order after the First World War. If this is such an epoch-shattering set of circumstances, the subtleties and niceties of social relations are easily lost. Those such as the Chaldeans, who offered a distinctive and often subtle *difference* to cultural, educational and societal development in Mesopotamia-Iraq, are unable to extend a response which secures their community through force and instead are reliant on the goodwill and co-operation of those who can accommodate them such as the KRG.

The Chaldeans were fortunate, under the Iraqi monarchy, to find leaders willing to involve them in the creation of the new state. From the start of republican rule in 1958 this was gradually lost, with a loss of awareness to the particular qualities which they contributed as a Christian body to Iraq. The lack of a reliable ally within Iraqi society, and the factionalisation of Iraq into a society of conflict instead of stability, was fundamental in weakening their ability to respond. The Chaldean openness to being diverse, vertically integrated members of society is something which sectarian cliques could not cope with nor comprehend. From 2003, they possessed a communal willingness to live within a predominantly Islamicised and political unstable environment. They accepted the restraints which this placed on them, but still offered their contributions and qualities in a process of communal and individual self-sacrifice.

Conclusion 231

Notes

1 Patriarch Bidawid responded to a question regarding ethnicity in the East Syriac community with the following: 'I personally feel once you lock a church into a single ethnicity, you end that church. My church and the church of the Assyrians are one church. If I come today and state that this is an Assyrian church or a Chaldean church, I am in effect terminating this church. In our history, our church did not stop among Assyrians, but spread Christianity in Turkey, Afghanistan, China, Southern Asia, Tibet, among others, and had millions of followers. So a person, who is a Christian and is a member of our church cannot be necessarily called an Assyrian, but they can all be called sons of the Church of the East. We have to separate what is ethnicity and what is religion. This is very important' (Quoted in Petrosian 2006, 116–17).
2 There has been an East Syriac presence to Georgia since the mid-nineteenth century and was at its greatest extent, as a place of refuge, during and after the 1915–1918 massacres (Chikhladze and Chikhladze 2003).
3 Sako's proposal was not an unprecedented attempt to unite the East Syriac communities following the death of a patriarch. We may compare the unification of the legitimist and Josephite patriarchal lineages in the 1820s under the leadership of Yohannan Hormizd in the aftermath of the death of the Josephite patriarch.
4 The concluding statement of the Church of the East's November 2016 Synod noted the 'importance of dialogue between the Assyrian Church of the East and other apostolic Churches'. However, it does not specifically refer to Sako's plan for unification ('Final Communique of the Second Holy Synod during the Patriarchate of His Holiness Mar Gewargis III Sliwa' 2016).
5 It should not be thought that the twentieth century was consistently a difficult period for the Church of the East (Coakley 1996, 187–91). The community developed a consolidated population albeit largely in the diaspora (c. sixty to seventy percent of the 500,000 members of the Church of the East live outside Iraq) and a strong sense of ecclesial identity. The affirmation of a particular Assyrian ethnic identity is not universally assumed by its members but provides a means to bind together those who are in Iraq and abroad. For those members who are of South Asian descent, the Assyrian heritage may not easily fit into their broader ecclesial identity (c. 30,000 people).

Bibliography

'Biography of His Holiness Mar Gewargis III, Catholicos-Patriarch of the Assyrian Church of the East'. 2015. Holy Synod of the Assyrian Church of the East. http://news.assyrian church.org/biography-of-hh-mar-gewargis-iii/.

Chikhladze, Iraklii, and Giga Chikhladze. 2003. 'The Yezidi Kurds and Assyrians of Georgia: The Problem of Diasporas and Integration Into Contemporary Society'. *Central Asia and the Caucasus* 21 (3). www.ca-c.org/journal/2003/journal_eng/cac-03/23. chieng.shtml.

Coakley, J. F. 1996. 'The Church of the East Since 1914'. *Bulletin of the John Rylands University Library of Manchester* 78 (3): 179–98.

'Final Communique of the Second Holy Synod During the Patriarchate of His Holiness Mar Gewargis III Sliwa'. 2016. Assyrian Church of the East. http://news.assyrianchurch.org/ wp-content/plugins/google-document-embedder/load.php?d=http%3A%2F%2Fnews. assyrianchurch.org%2Fwp-content%2Fuploads%2F2016%2F12%2FFINAL-COM MUNIQUE-OF-THE-SECOND-HOLY-SYNOD-OF-THE-PATRIARCHATE-OF-HIS-HOLINESS-MAR-GEWARGIS-III-SLIWA.pdf.

Petrosian, Vahram. 2006. 'Assyrians in Iraq'. *Iran & the Caucasus* 10 (1): 113–47. doi:10.1163/157338406777979322.

Royel, Mar Awa. 2015. 'Authenticity in Unity: A Personal Reflection on Present-Day Questions Concerning the Unity of the Church of the East'. *Assyrian Church News*.

232 *Conclusion*

http://news.assyrianchurch.org/2015/07/10/authenticity-in-unity-a-personal-reflection-on-present-day-questions-concerning-the-unity-of-the-church-of-the-east/12378.

Sako, Louis. 2015. 'The Unity of the Church of the East'. Chaldean Catholic Patriarchate, Baghdad. http://saint-adday.com/permalink/7572.html.

'Statement of the Council of Hierarchs of the Assyrian Church of the East'. 2015. Assyrian Church of the East. http://news.assyrianchurch.org/wp-content/plugins/google-docu ment-embedder/load.php?d=http%3A%2F%2Fnews.assyrianchurch.org%2Fwp-conten t%2Fuploads%2F2015%2F06%2FCOMMUNIQUE-IN-ENGLISH.pdf.

Valente, Gianni. 2015. 'Chaldean Patriarch Gambles on Re-Establishing "Church of the East"'. *Vatican Insider*, June 25. http://vaticaninsider.lastampa.it/en/world-news/detail/articolo/sako-41976/.

Appendix A
Overview of the Iraqi political system post-2003

Iraq is in principle a 'federal parliamentary representative democratic republic' with an elected head of state (the President) with an executive consisting of the Prime Minister and a Council of Ministers. The legislature which elects the President and Prime Minister is formed of two parts in the Iraqi Parliament:

The Council of Representatives (i.e. the lower house)
The Federation Council (i.e. senate/upper house)

The Council of Representatives initially had 275 members from 2006 to 2010 but from the 2010 Parliamentary elections was expanded to 325 MPs.

The majority of MPs is elected via the greatest percentage of votes received with additional compensatory seats for those who may otherwise not be represented due to insufficient votes. For example, numerical minorities such as the Christians or Yazidis.

Iraq has over forty active political parties, but not all are represented in parliament. The main political blocs in the Iraqi parliament, as of 2014, were as follows:

- State of Law Coalition (Islamic Dawa Party)
- Al-Muwatin (Shia Islamist)
- al-Wataniya (Secularist)
- al-Ahrar (Shia Islamist – following the religio-political direction of Muqtada al-Sadr)
- KDP (Kurdish nationalist)
- PUK (Kurdish socialist nationalist)
- Gorran – Movement for Change (Kurdish liberal secularist)
- Muttahidoon (Sunni conservative)
- al-Arabiya (Sunni conservative).

Within the Iraqi parliament, the political blocs often (but not always) represent a coalition of parties with shared interests. For example, in the parliamentary election of 2010, the State of Law Coalition included al-Maliki's party the Islamic Dawa Party as well as smaller ones such as the Islamic Union of Iraqi Turkomen.

On the ballot paper, each person votes for parties in their order of preference within the bloc. Parliamentary seats are then assigned in proportion to their

234 *Appendix A*

ranking as per the electors' ballot papers – a so-called open list electoral system. This may seem a somewhat complicated system by comparison with the 'first past the post' system used in Britain, for example, but it is perceived to grant voters more chance to influence election outcomes and a fairer representative spread of the parties in parliament.

Below parliamentary level, political power is further devolved upon the nineteen provinces of Iraq, each of which has its own elected representative council and which are further split into the 120 districts of Iraq. Three of the provinces are officially under the control of the Kurdistan Regional Government (KRG) and also – until June 2014 – large parts of Kirkuk, Sulaymaniya and Nineveh provinces.

Another layer of political representation in Iraqi Kurdistan is the Kurdish Parliament which has 111 members and in which Christian political activity is particularly closely engaged. As of 2014, the Kurdish President was Massoud Barzani (also leader of the KDP) and the Prime Minister was Nechirvan Barzani (a senior member of the KDP).

In the 2013 Kurdish parliamentary elections, the KDP, PUK and Gorran gained the largest share of the seats (80/111), with the Assyrians having five reserved seats and the Armenians one. This compares, for example, to the Turkomen who between them are reserved five seats.

- Assyrian Democratic Movement: 2 MPs
- Chaldean Syriac Assyrian Popular Council: 2 MPs
- Sons of Mesopotamia: 1 MP
- Armenian independent candidate, Berunt Nissan Markos: 1 MP.

Appendix B

Chaldean population estimate in northern Iraq, 2013

Total number of families/persons by diocese (October 2013)

- Alqosh: c. 3,913/17,069
- Akra: 165/743
- Erbil: 8,610/38,745
- Mosul: 3,539/15,926
- Zakho: 2,721/12,245 (in 2012)
- Sulaymaniya: 195/878
- Amadiya: c. 850/3,800 (estimates from *AP* figures).

Total from figures obtained **19,143** Chaldean families. Assuming average family size as 4.5 persons[1] = total Chaldean population c. 89,500 in northern Iraq. If we consider total population (not families), figures from Roberson in the *AP* (2010) for the years 1990, 2000, 2010 and our own data from 2013, we can estimate the following approximated comparisons in Table BM1.1:[2]

Table BM1.1 Number of Chaldeans in northern Iraqi dioceses 1990–2013

Diocese	1990	2000	2010	2013
Alqosh	13,500	16,190	32,070	17,069
Akra	230	176	1,051	743
Erbil	12,314	12,000	20,000	38,745
Mosul	19,800	20,000	16,815	15,926
Zakho	7,000	6,548	26,000	12,246
Amadiya	2,000	2,452	4,000	3,800
Sulaymaniya	500	400	440	878
Total	55,344	57,766	100,486	89,407

Notes

1 A figure given by several priests during my visit to northern Iraq.
2 Roberson can be accessed here: <www.cnewa.org/source-images/Roberson-eastcath-statistics/eastcatholic-stat13.pdf>

Appendix C

The Church of the East in the twentieth century: a brief overview[*]

For the Church of the East, the early twentieth century was a trying period. The ethnic cleansing and genocide of 1915–1923, the rapid succession of two young patriarchs in 1920 and Mar Shemon XXI/XXIII's expulsion from Iraq in 1933 meant the Church was in some peril. Its leadership was geographically detached from its community, and community members were deeply affected by the psychological and physical traumas of the genocide.

Nonetheless, the era 1933–1968 was a period of relative consolidation and during which time the community grew substantially in the diaspora in North America from a few thousand to c. 100,000 people. In general, a clearer and more cohesive ecclesial identity also emerged. The recognition of the importance of the Syriac language and the grounding of the East Syriac traditions in the diaspora along with the acceptance of an Assyrian ethnic heritage all aspects of this emergent identity. The situation for members of the Church of the East in Iraq was more challenging and, as has been related in the main body of the text, related to the perceived and, often, actual political separatism which Assyrians pursued from 1933.

The period 1968–1975 saw substantial upset in ecclesial and communal life and set back the consolidation which the Church of the East had undergone in the preceding thirty-five years.

In 1968, a schism emerged as a result of disputes surrounding the introduction of the Gregorian calendar and the use of the Latin date for Easter. Those members of the Church opposed to these changes formed around the figure of Mar Thoma Darmo, Metropolitan of the Church of the East in India (1952–1968). The new community settled on the name 'Ancient Church of the East', and Darmo was the first patriarch (1968–1969); his successor Mar Addai II remains in office to the present.

Initially, the Ancient Church held the support of the Iraqi government, but by 1970, the state gave its patronage to the Church of the East instead and permitted Mar Shemon XXI/XXIII to visit Iraq in 1970 and 1971, the first visit of the Church of the East's patriarch since the expulsion in 1933. It might have been thought that this offered the potential for the transferral of the patriarchate to Iraq from its then location in Chicago. However, it appears the Iraqi government was concerned with the possibility of the patriarchate becoming a focus for Assyrian

Appendix C   237

political separatism. The Church of the East also was aware of the influence and pull of the diaspora on ecclesial life.

The issue was indefinitely put on hold following Mar Shemon's resignation from the patriarchate, marriage and subsequent reinstatement as patriarch from 1973 to 1975. It appears Shemon was desirous of retiring and living a more conventional life than his patriarchal status would permit. It might also have been the case that he was seeking some way to introduce the possibility of a married episcopate. Whatever his intentions, his life was brought to a tragic close when he was murdered in San Jose, CA. on 6 November 1975.

The attacker was a member of the Church of the East and it was suggested at his trial that motivation derived from Assyrian nationalism: insofar as Shemon was regarded as being insufficiently active in advancing Assyrian political interests in Iraq.

Shemon's successor was Mar Dinkha IV (1976–2015). who pursued a more conciliatory approach to church leadership than Shemon had in his final years. Dinkha was notable for encouraging his clergy to focus on attaining higher degrees in theology and starting to rebuild the great tradition of East Syriac intellectual life. He also supported ecumenism with the Holy See and the Chaldeans and formally ended the practice of hereditary succession to the patriarchate and synod of bishops.

With the onset of Iraq's involvement in successive wars from 1980, Dinkha was faced with similar circumstances as that experienced by the Chaldean patriarchs. He was further disadvantaged, however, through his geographical separation from the centre of Iraqi political life in Baghdad. This was especially concerning during the lead up to and immediate aftermath of the 2003 invasion when it was very challenging to consistently advance the Church of the East's position and place in Iraqi society and where responsibilities were devolved on a day-to-day basis to the local clergy.

Note

* For detailed and extended accounts of the Church's recent history and from where much of the information for this overview is derived, please refer to Baum and Winkler (2003), Baumer (2006), Coakley (1996), Joseph (2000), Mooken (2003) and Wilmshurst (2011). It is to be hoped that a further monograph on the Church of the East's history in the twentieth and twenty-first centuries will be written to follow on from Mooken's work in light of the conflicts and political changes in Iraq since its publication in 2003.

Bibliography

Baum, Wilhelm, and Dietmar W. Winkler. 2003. *The Church of the East: A Concise History*. Translated by Miranda G. Henry. London: RoutledgeCurzon.

Baumer, Christoph. 2006. *The Church of the East: An Illustrated History of Assyrian Christianity*. London: Tauris.

Coakley, J. F. 1996. 'The Church of the East since 1914'. *Bulletin of the John Rylands University Library of Manchester* 78 (3): 179–98.

238 *Appendix C*

Joseph, John. 2000. *The Modern Assyrians of the Middle East: Encounters With Western Christian Missions, Archaeologists, and Colonial Power.* Studies in Christian Mission 26. Leiden: Brill.

Mooken, Aprem. 2003. *The History of the Assyrian Church of the East in the Twentieth Century.* Mōran 'Eth'ō 18. Kottayam, Kerala: St. Ephrem Ecumenical Research Institute. www.worldcat.org/oclc/52443629.

Wilmshurst, David. 2011. *The Martyred Church: A History of the Church of the East.* Sawbridgeworth, Hertfordshire: East and West.

Index

Page numbers in bold indicate a table on the corresponding page.

Abbasid dynasty 4
Abdisho IV 25, 202
Abdisho of Nisibis 14, 47
Abdullah 68
Abdullah II 214
Abdulmecid I, Sultan 49
Abouna, Albert 19
Abulyonan, Elias XII Peter 34, 53–4
Aflaq, Michel 83, 85
Akra, Diocese of 157–9
al-Din, Nur 194
Alexander VII, Pope 26
al-Harboli, Hanna Issa 162
Ali, Mohammed 46
Ali, Rashid 78
al-Mahdi, Caliph 78, 128
al-Maliki, Nouri 127, 128–9
al-Mansur, Abbasid Caliph 184
al-Mutawakkil, Abbasid caliph 151
al-Qas, Rabban 142, 162
Alqosh **140**; Diocese of 171–8; ecclesial
    organisation 174–5
Amid, Josephite patriarchal line in 30–4
Anglican Church 54
Ankawa 142–7
Annuario Pontificio 155
Antiochene school 6
Arab nationalism 50
Arab Revolt, 1920 70
Arif, Abdul Salam 82
Armenians 49, 56, 59
Armota 147–9
Asmar, Basil 161
Assyrian Democratic Movement (ADM)
    87, 115–16, 129–30
Assyrians 61, 68, 71–3, 86, 236
Atto 213

Audo, Israel 66, 67
Audo, Joseph VI 166, 169, 196,
    222–3, 227
Audo SJ, Antoine 114
Aziz, Tariq 69, 88, 89–90

Babaca, Stéphane 141
Baghdad, Archdiocese of 184–94, 196;
    and East Syriac ecclesiology 191–3;
    ecclesial organisation of 191
Baghdad Pact, 1955 79
Baram, Amatzia 86
Barazani, Mustapha 90
Bar Yak 175–6
Basra, Archdiocese of 178–84; ecclesial
    organisation of 183–4
Baum, Wilhelm 1
Baumer, Christoph 1, 25
Benedict XI, Pope 11, 22
Benedict XV, Pope 59
Benedict XVI, Pope 69, 122, 125, 132, 225
Bet Dasen 159–60
Bet Nuhadra 159–60
Bet Selok 151, 156
Beulay, Robert 102
Bidawid, Raphael I 90, 94–7, 123, 225;
    death of 114; final years of 100–1
Bocco, Riccardo 68
Book of the Bee, The 180
Book of the Magnet 32
Book of the Pearl 14
Book of the Polished Mirror 32
Borrut, Antoine 67
Bosworth, Clifford Edmund 117
Bouvet, Béatrice 69
Brock, Sebastian 69
Buddhism 7, 185

240 Index

Budge, E. A. 19–20
Bush, George H. W. 95
Buti, Rafael 76
Butti, Rafael 89

Capuchins 31, 32, 195
Caritas Iraq 96
Casmoussa, Georges 90
Cathedral of the Sacred Heart 155
Catholic Church *see* Holy See, the
Catholic Herald, The 125
Centre for Christian Affairs 125
Chabot, Jean-Baptiste 56
Chaldean Church and community 1–2;
    approach in studying 4–5; Dembo and
    Yohannan as opposition figures in 38–9;
    ecclesiology (*see* ecclesiology and
    ecclesial organisation, Chaldean); effect
    of 2006–2007 civil war on 121–4;
    effect of 2003 invasion on 114–15;
    emergence from the Church of the East
    12; first hierarchy in union with the
    Holy See 14–22; First Vatican Council
    and 51–5; identity, post-invasion, 2003
    112–13; identity development in the
    sixteenth century 24, 221–3; identity in
    post-war Iraq 130–1; in international
    Christian tradition 4–5; involvement
    and new constitutional order 119–21;
    Iran-Iraq War, 1980–1988, and 88–9;
    in Jordan 213–19; Josephite patriarchial
    line in Amid 30–4; Latin presence in
    Mesopotamia and 27–8; legitimist line
    of patriarchs, 1591–1700 28–9; meeting
    the varied needs of, in Iraq 99–100;
    migration, 1991–2003 97–9; missions
    to the Church of the East 55–6; modern
    ecumenism and 101–2; narrative in Iraq,
    situating the 131–2; nomenclature of
    2–3; origins 10–11, 214–15; Ottoman
    massacre, 1915–1918, and 56–61, 67;
    population estimate in northern Iraq,
    2013 235; PTSD among 118–19, 144;
    reasons for emergence of 34–6; regional
    effects of the war and response by
    125–7; representation in the new Iraqi
    government 129–30; responses to new
    Iraqi society 128; rise of Da'esh and
    230; speaking with one voice 115–16;
    Sulaqa's legacy and early community
    of 22–4; zones of ecclesial influence in
    Iraq 223–5; *see also* Church of the East;
    Iraq, modern, 1918–1947; Iraq, new,
    2003–2013
Chaldean identity 1–2

Charbonnier, Raymond 102
Chatelard, Geraldine 213
Cheikho, Paul II 80–1, 86–7, 140, 158–9
Cherubini, Roberto 101
Choa, Thomas 176
Christology 6, 47, 172, 222
Church of England 54
Church of the East 1–2, 225–9; Chaldean
    missions to 55–6; ecclesiological
    discourse and developments 46–9; first
    union 11–12; heritage of the undivided
    48–9; Latin presence in Mesopotamia
    and 27–8; Mongol empire and 185–7;
    nomenclature of 2–3; origins and
    status to the late Medieval Period 6–7;
    significance of church-state relations and
    3–4; status in 1450 and development of
    hereditary succession to the patriarchate
    12–14; in the twentieth century 236–7
Coalition Provisional Authority (CPA)
    113–15
Cobb, Paul M. 67
consolidation, Eastern Catholic 51–5
Conway, Agnes 74
Coptic Catholic community 35
Corbon, Jean 97
Council of Ephesus 6, 13
Council of Trent 12, 16, 17, 25, 222;
    Josephite patriarchial line in Amid
    and 31

Da'esh/ISIL 5, 139, 150, 157, 205, 224;
    Chaldean presence to Iraq in the context
    of the rise of 230; emergence of 126;
    Mosul region and 195, 198
Dall'Oglio SJ, Paolo 156
da Novana, Tommaso 28
Daoud, Basman Yousef 123
Delly, Emmanuel III 114, 115, 116, 123,
    125, 131
delocalisation 97
Dembo, Gabriel 38–9, 46, 160, 176
Denaud, Patrick 69
Denha II 186, 204
dhimma concept 30, 185
Dickens, Mark 4
Discalced Carmelites 33
Dominicans 33
Duhok 163, 165

East Syriac tradition: approach in
    studying 4–5; churches in 1–3; Eastern
    Catholic consolidation between the
    Chaldeans and the First Vatican Council
    51–5; ecclesiological discourse and

Index 241

developments in 46–9; ecclesiology and Baghdad 191–3; and Latin ecclesiological perspectives on the proto-Chaldean community 15–17; Latin presence in Mesopotamia and 27–8; nomenclature 3; origins and status of the Church of the East to the late Medieval Period in 6–7; Ottoman massacres of 56–61, 67; patriarchs and origins of the Chaldean community 10–11; perspectives on the Petrine See 19–22; significance of church-state relations in 3–4

Ecclesia in Medio Oriente 132

Ecclesiastical Organisation of the Church of the East 1318–1913, The 47

ecclesiology and ecclesial organisation, Chaldean: Amadiyan diocesan records and 170; ancient discourse and developments 46–9; Archdiocese of Baghdad 184–94; Archdiocese of Basra 178–84; Archdiocese of Erbil 139–40, **140**, 141–50, 152; Archdiocese of Kirkuk 154–7; Archdiocese of Kirkuk-Sulaymaniya 139, **140**, 148, 150–3; Archdiocese of Mosul 194–206; Chaldean ecclesiastical life in Ankawa 142–7; Chaldean *status quo* in northern Iraq, 2003–2013 137–8; Chaldean villages and towns in the Diocese of Zakho-Amadiya 165–70; Diocesan study overview 138–41; Diocese of Akra 157–9; Diocese of Alqosh 171–8; in Sulaymaniya 152–3; Teleskef 175–8; what is, and how has it been altered 136–7; Zakho-Amadiya ecclesial history 159–63; Zakho-Amadiya ecclesial organisation 163–5

Edessa tradition 6

Egypt 79–80

Elias IX 28–9

Elias VIII 28, 172

Elias X 29, 31

Elias XIII 160

Eliya *(Natar Kursya)* 14

Erbil, Archdiocese of 139–40, **140**, 141–50, 152; Chaldean ecclesiastical life in Ankawa 142–7; parishes outside of Erbil 147–50

Eskander, Polos 201

Eugene IV, Pope 12

Feisel I, King 67, 69–70

Feisel II, King 70, 80

Fiey, Jean Maurice 5, 69, 136, 154, 203

Fikr al-Masihi 66

First Vatican Council 51–5

First World War 56–61, 75, 90–1, 144, 159, 160, 182

Flannery, John 136

Galadza, Peter 80–1

Ghanima, Joseph VII 77–8, 79, 80, 86, 140

Ghanima, Yusif 76

Ghazi, King 70

Gogue, Joseph 82

Grant, Asahel 47, 48

Gregory XVI, Pope 49

Gulf War, 1990–1991 93, 95, 152, 215, 224; Iraq after 95–7

Habbi, Yusif 18

Hani Abd al-Ahad 124

Hanna, Wadid 123

Hanoosh, Yasmeen S. 213

Hatti Humayun 50

Hatti Serif 50

hereditary succession to the patriarchate, development of 12–14

Hindi, Augustine 47–8, 160

Hnanisho 14, 160

Holy Ghost parish, Mosul 200–1

Holy See, the 7, 10–11, 196, 225–9; Chaldean narrative in the new Iraq and 131–2; Church of the East first union with 11–12; first Chaldean hierarchy in union with 14–22; First Vatican Council and 51–5; historical context of Sulaqa's engagement with 17–19; Josephite patriarchal line in Amid and 30–4; legacy of Sulaqa and 22–4; Saddam Hussein and 101; Second Vatican Council and 80–1, 101, 136–7, 172–3; successors of Sulaqa and 24–7

Hormizd, Maqdassi 195

Hormizd, Yohannan VIII 151, 157, 160, 195

Hunter, Erica C. D. 68

Husry, Khaldun S. 75

Hussein, Saddam 69, 80, 83–4, 86–9, 95, 103, 113; after the Gulf War 95–7; Archdiocese of Kirkuk and 154; Faith Campaign 197; final years of 100–1; Kurdish rebellions and 92; Tariz Aziz and 89–90

India 51, 180, 236

Innocent IV, Pope 10

Innocent X, Pope 26

242 *Index*

Iran-Iraq War, 1980–1988 80, 88–9, 180, 182

Iraq, modern, 1918–1947 66–7; Baath party in 69, 83–4, 85; building on current scholarship on Christians in 67–9; Chaldean involvement in political activity of 75–7; Chaldean migration, 1991–2003, and 97–9; Chaldean state and inter-communal relations with 70–1; Cheikho, the Baath and Saddam Hussein in 86–7; Christian involvement with revolutionary movements in 81–3; Emmanuel II Thomas and 73–5; finals years of Hussein and Bidawid in 100–1; Gulf War, 1990–1991, and 93, 95; invasion of 2003 into 2, 102–3; Iran-Iraq War, 1980–1988 80, 88–9, 180, 182; Joseph VII Ghanima and 77–8; Kurdish rebellions and Christian involvement in 90–4; military elite and Assyrians 71–3; modern ecumenism and Chaldean involvement in 101–2; new political order in 69–70; Paul II Cheikho, new Catholic ecclesiology of the Second Vatican Council, and 80–1; political change impacts on Chaldeans in 84–6; post-Gulf war 95–7; Raphael I Bidawid and 94–5; 1958 rebellion against the monarchy of 78–80; Tariq Aziz in 69, 88, 89–90

Iraq, new, 2003–2013 112; Chaldean identity in post-war 130–1; Chaldean identity post-invasion and 112–13; Chaldean responses to new society of 128; Chaldean *status quo* in northern 137–8; Christian political representation in 129–30; electoral process and government formation, 2003–2013 128–9; historical overview, 2003–2008 113–19; historical overview, 2008–2013 127–32; Iraqi civil war, 2006–2007 121–4; new constitutional order *and* Chaldean involvement 119–21; political system overview 233–4; regional effects of the war and the Chaldean response 125–7; rise of violence against Christians in 116–17; situating the Chaldean narrative in 131–2; zones of Chaldean ecclesial influence in 223–5

Iraq Baath Party (IBP) 69, 83–4, 85, 113; social and psychological affects after end of rule by 117–19

Iraqi civil war, 2006–2007 121–4

Iraqi Communist Party (ICP) 82

Iraqi Governing Council (ICG) 115, 126, 130, 204

Iraqi Islamic Party 197

Iraq War, 2003 2, 102–3

Israel 83, 215

Issayi, Youhannan 88

Jaar, Khalil 217

Jews 74–5, 79, 185; Kingdom of Adiabene 151

John Paul II, Pope 69, 101, 225

Jonas, Mar 58

Jordan 99–100, 147, 213–14; Chaldean origins to 214–15; status of the Chaldean community in Jordanian Christian context and 215–18

Joseph I 31, 33

Joseph II 32, 202

Joseph III 32–4

Josephites 30–4, 196

Joseph IV 33–4

Joseph V 39, 160

Joseph VI Audo 39, 46, 51–4, 97

Julius III 21

Kajo, Stephen 162

Karamles 203–5

Karrada 191

Kello, Hanna 166

Khan, Gazan 186

Khan, Ghengis 13

Khayat, Hanna 89

Khayyath, Georges Ebedjesu V 19, 54–5, 56, 136

Khoury, Dina Rizk 36

kidnapping 124

Kirkuk, Archdiocese of 154–7

Kirkuk-Sulaymanya, Archdiocese of 139, **140**, 148, 150–3

Kurdish Democratic Party (PDK) 84

Kurdistan Regional Government (KRG) 113, 126, 130, 164–5, 169, 204, 224–5, 234

Kurds 30, 46, 56–7, 67, 72, 75, 76, 82; infighting in Erbil 146; in the Mosul region 174–5; new Iraqi society and 128; rebellions and Christian involvement 90–4

Kuwait 95

Labourt, Jérôme 25

Lampart, Albert 32

Lanza OP, P. 204

Latin church *see* Holy See, the
League of Nations 69, 77
Lebanon 147
L'Eglise Chaldéenne 55
Leo XII, Pope 39
Life of Rabban Joseph Busnaya 166

Maddenhaye 3
Mahmud II, Sultan 46
Malabarese community 51–2
Mansfield, Peter 84
Mar Dhinka 229, 237
Mar Ephrem 200
Mar Gewargis 168, 228, 229
Mar Ishiya 200
Mar Polos 200
Mar Shemon XXI/XXIII 236
Mar Shimon and Sons church 167
Mar Shimun XXIII 72, 73, 192
Mar Thoma Darmo 236
Martin, Jean Pierre Paulin 56
Mart Mariam church 152–3, 180, 182
Mar Toma 180, 182
Mar Yusif 191, 200
massacres of Chaldeans, 1915–1918
   56–61, 67
Mattai, Bishop 159
Mecca 70
Mehmed V, Sultan 59
Melkite Catholic community 35
Mellus, Yohannan Elias 158
Mesopotamia: Archdiocese of Basra and
   178–80; ethnic and religious plurality
   50; Latin presence in 27–8, 36–8;
   migration of displaced persons to 161;
   Mosul and 196; Ottoman massacre,
   1915–1918 56–61; Ottoman rule of 46,
   50; and patriarchal office's influence on
   Chaldean identity formation 221–3
Mesopotamian identity in modern
   Iraq 86
Messengers of Peace (MoP) 217
Middle East Council of Churches
   (MECC) 102
Mirkis OP, Yousif Thoma 157
Mohammad (Islamic prophet) 70
Mongol empires 13, 185–7
Mosul, Archdiocese of 194–206; ecclesial
   organisation of 197–200; Holy Ghost
   parish 200–1
Mosul-Nineveh region **140**, 171–8;
   Karamles 203–5; Teleskef 175–8;
   Telkef 202–3
Moussali, Raymond 215

Murre-van den Berg, Heleen L. 1, 4, 20,
   21, 35
Muslim Brotherhood 197
Muslims 7, 50, 56–7, 69, 184; relations
   with Christians in the Mosul-Ninevah
   region 194–5
Mylroie, Laurie A. 94

Naayem, Joseph 60
Nasser, Gamal Abdal 79–80
Natar Kursya 195
natio, context of 24
Nestorianism 2–3, 47, 53, 203
Nestorius 2, 28, 58
Nicholas IV, Pope 19–22
Nicholas I Zaya 49, 51
Ninevah *see* Mosul, Archdiocese of;
   Mosul-Nineveh region
Nisibis tradition 6

O'Mahony, Anthony 67, 136
Operation Desert Fox 96
origins, Chaldean 10–11
Ottoman Empire 28; administrative
   influence on Church of the East
   29–30; Arab Revolt, 1920, and 70;
   massacres by, 1915–1918 56–61, 67;
   nineteenth-century changes among
   49–50; rule of Mesopotamia 46, 50
Our Lady of Sorrows 191
Oussani, Gabriel 56, 60
Ousta, Souleyman Kutchouck 187

Padroado 51
papal infallibility 53
Pasha, Daud 46
Perez, Timoteo 28
Petrine See 19–22
Petros, Agha 59–60
Pius IX, Pope 52, 53, 227
Post-Traumatic Stress Disorder (PTSD)
   118–19, 144

Qasim, Abd al-Karim 82, 83
Qusenjaq 147, 149

Rabban Hormizd 14, 33, 35, 38, 39, 46,
   55, 222–3; Mosul-Nineveh region
   and 171–2, 178, 203; Nicholas I Zaya
   and 49
Ragheed Aziz Ganni 123–4, 198,
   200–1, 202
Rahema, Layla Yousif 124
Raho, Polos Faraj 128, 198, 202

244   Index

Raphael I Bidawid 94–5
Rassam, Suha 1, 67
Ratel, A. 55
Roman Catholic Church *see* Holy See, the
Royel, Mar Awa 227, 228
Russian empire 58–60, 71
Russian Orthodox Church 225

Sabrisho V ibn al-Masihi 10
Sa'igh, Najib 77
Sako, Louis 131, 156, 194, 225, 228
Sana, Abdul-Ahad 172
Sassoon, Joseph 213
Sawma, Rabban 11, 19–22
Scher, Addai 59
Second Vatican Council 80–1, 101, 136–7, 172–3
Second World War 102
Sefaro, Eliya 158
Seleucid Empire 151
Sengstock, Mary C. 85, 213
Shaqlawa 147
Shemon IV Basidi 14
Shemon IX 25
Shemon VII 14, 23
Shemon X 25
Shemon XI 25, 26
Shemon XII 26
Shemon XIX Benjamin 58
Shemon XVIII Rubil 54, 58
Shia Muslims 70–1, 72, 74, 75, 82; revolutionary movements and 82–3
Shimun XIII Denha 30, 31
Shlemon of Akhlat 180
Simele massacre 72–3
Sixth and Seventh Crusades 10
Sleiman, Jean 117
St. Athanasius of Alexandria 205–6
Suez Canal 196
Sulaqa, Yohannan 14, 15–17, 51, 151, 195; early Chaldean Catholic community and legacy of 22–4; engagement with the Holy See 17–19; successors of 24–7
Sulaymaniya 152–3; *see also* Kirkuk-Sulaymanya, Archdiocese of
Sunni Muslims 69, 70–1, 74, 75, 78, 82, 164, 174, 205
Synod of Dadisho 48
Synod of Isaac 186
Syriac Corporation 66
Syrian Catholic community 35

Tamerlane 7, 13, 29, 202
Tanzimat 49
Taoism 7

Tejel, Jordi 68
Teleskef 175–8
Telkef 202–3
Teule, Herman 1, 68
Tfinkdji, Joseph 55, 136
Theocritos 151
Theodore of Mopsuestia 6
Thomas, Emmanuel II 67, 71, 73–5, 76, 86, 215, 224
Three Creatures God never created – Persians, Jews and flies 88–9
Timothy I 4, 78, 194
Tisserant, Eugène 136
Togai, Haggi 186
Treaty of Sèvres 69
Tridentine Christology 26–7, 32, 172, 226
Tripp, Charles 92
Turco-Persian Wars 25

Ummayad dynasty 4
United Nations High Commissioner for Refugees (UNHCR) 122, 217–18
United States, Chaldean migration to the 98

Valognes, Jean-Pierre 67
violence against Christians 116–17, 123–4

Warda CSsR, Bashar 142, 223
West Syriac church 7
Whooley, John 136
Wilmshurst, David 1, 25, 47, 67, 136; on the Ottoman massacres, 1915–1918 59–61; study of East Syriac ecclesiastical organisation 139, 165–6, 166–7
Winkler, Dietmar W. 1
World Council of Churches 102

Yacoub, Joseph 67
Yahballaha III 10–11
Yahballah III 159, 185–6, 202
Yahballah IV 25
Yazdgard I, Shah 30
Yazidis 72, 91, 93, 114, 175
Yohannan, Mikhael 89
Yohannan VII 24–5, 38–9
Yohannan VIII 39, 46, 49
Young, Wilkie 56–7
Yusuf, Yusuf Salman 82

Zakho-Amadiya **140**; Chaldean villages and towns in Diocese of 165–70; ecclesial history 159–63; ecclesial organisation 163–5
Zoroastrianism 4, 156